Ge   Anderson
Tir
Je

Sams **Teach Yourself**

SAP

in **24** **Hours**

SAMS   800 East 96th Street, Indianapolis, Indiana 46240 USA

ISBN-13: 978-0-137-14284-2
ISBN-10: 0-137-14284-6

Library of Congress Cataloging-in-Publication Data

Anderson, George W.
  Sams teach yourself SAP in 24 hours / George W. Anderson, Tim Rhodes, Jeff Davis.
    p. cm.
  Includes index.
  ISBN 0-13-714284-6 (pbk. : alk. paper)
  1. SAP ERP. 2. Integrated software 3. Client/server computing. I. Rhodes, Tim. II. Davis, Jeff. III. Title.
  QA76.76.I57.A63 2008
  004'.36–dc22

                        2008031734

Printed in the United States of America
Second Printing September 2008

Trademarks

All terms mentioned in this book that are known to be trademarks or service marks have been appropriately capitalized. Sams Publishing cannot attest to the accuracy of this information. Use of a term in this book should not be regarded as affecting the validity of any trademark or service mark.

Warning and Disclaimer

Every effort has been made to make this book as complete and as accurate as possible, but no warranty or fitness is implied. The information provided is on an "as is" basis. The authors and the publisher shall have neither liability nor responsibility to any person or entity with respect to any loss or damages arising from the information contained in this book.

Bulk Sales

Sams Publishing offers excellent discounts on this book when ordered in quantity for bulk purchases or special sales. For more information, please contact

  U.S. Corporate and Government Sales
  1-800-382-3419
  corpsales@pearsontechgroup.com

For sales outside of the U.S., please contact

  International Sales
  international@pearson.com

Editor-in-Chief
Mark Taub

Signing Editor
Trina MacDonald

Development Editor
Songlin Qiu

Managing Editor
Kristy Hart

Project Editor
Anne Goebel

Copy Editor
Bart Reed

Indexer
Lisa Stumpf

Proofreader
Leslie Joseph

Technical Editor
A.J. Whalen

Publishing Coordinator
Olivia Basegio

Cover Designer
Gary Adair

Composition
Nonie Ratcliff

Contents at a Glance

Part V: Using SAP

Part VI: Developing a Career in SAP

Appendix

Table of Contents

Contents

About the Authors

George W. Anderson, Chief Technologist for HP's SAP and Enterprise Applications consulting practices, currently resides in Cypress, Texas, with his wife and three children. An SAP consultant for 11 years and IT professional for more than 20, he has had the privilege of working on countless implementations, upgrades, migrations, technical infrastructure refreshes, and other enterprise consulting engagements. George is a certified SAP Technical Consultant, PMI PMP, and MBA, and has authored a number of other books and magazine articles. He is also one of several technical editors for the *SAP Professional Journal*. When not spending time with his wife and kids, friends, and extended church family, he looks forward to reading your thoughts and insights; reach him at george.anderson@hp.com.

Tim Rhodes is a Senior Technical Consultant in HP's SAP and Enterprise Applications consulting practice. He resides in Houston, Texas, with his wife and three children, and is a 7-year-veteran of many SAP implementations, tuning engagements, migrations, and other consulting projects. He has been working in the Information Technology field for more than 15 years. Tim is an SAP Certified Technical Consultant, Oracle Certified Professional, Microsoft MCSE, HP Master ASE, and recently received his MBA. You can reach him at tim.rhodes@hp.com.

Jeff Davis, an SAP NetWeaver Consultant, lives in Houston, Texas, with his wife and son but works across the Americas. With 13 years in Information Technology and over 8 years specializing in SAP, Jeff has served in senior Basis, Project Management, and NetWeaver Architect roles on large SAP implementations, including international and public sector projects. Although SAP consulting is his career, Jeff will tell you that his real passions are knowing Christ more and enjoying time with his family. You can reach Jeff at jeff.davis2@hp.com.

John Dobbins leads one of several SAP consulting teams for HP Services' SAP Applications consulting practice. Residing in Houston, Texas, John is a certified SAP Technical Consultant, SAP OS/DB Migration Consultant, and MCSE. With 8 years of SAP experience, John brings a wealth of knowledge in SAP infrastructure, high availability, upgrades, and migrations. Outside of work John spends most of his time with his family and serving others through several ministries based in his local church.

Andreas Jenzer is a Principal Consultant with 10 years of SAP experience. Andreas has enjoyed the privilege of contributing his consulting services to the whole SAP project life-cycle, from developing and executing sales programs to conducting business development, functioning as a project manager, and performing hands-on technical consulting work. He currently focuses on Business Technology Optimization solutions for SAP environments. Andreas is a graduate engineer in Information Technology and holds a masters degree in service management. He currently resides in Boulder, Colorado, and can be reached at andreas.jenzer@hp.com.

Dedication

George: *To my wife and best friend, thank you for always supporting and loving me (and all my projects!). This book is dedicated to you, Michelle.*

Tim: *To my wife and family, thank you for your patience, love, and support.*

Jeff: *To my late father, Raymond Davis, who always wanted me to write. He didn't care what; he just wanted me to write. I dedicate this to you. I miss you, Dad.*

John: *To my wife and family, who put up with my hectic travel schedule and still manage to love me unconditionally.*

Andreas: *To my wife, family, and friends, Thomas and Michel.*

Acknowledgments

From George: To my Jesus, my family, my friends, my colleagues, and my readers, I simply say thank you. As I write this, I can't help but think of how blessed I've been in the last several years. The Lord has surrounded me with family and friends like I never would have imagined. He has replaced things I thought were great with things even greater, and has given me opportunities and purpose beyond what I ever dreamed. And remarkably, He still has an amazing plan for my life—and yours as well. May we pursue you, Lord, as aggressively as you pursue us. Thank you for every good thing in our lives.

From Tim: I would like to thank my friends, colleagues, and customers for supporting and challenging me over the years. I would like to think you have improved me both personally and professionally. A special thanks to George Anderson for helping me become an author and for his mentorship over the years. Finally, I would like to thank my family for their patience while I took time from them to work on this and other projects.

Acknowledgments

From Jeff: To George, my family, and my friends—thank you for your encouragement to write this book. To my wife Mandi and "Daddy's Favorite Guy" Ealon—you are my joy and are with me in everything I do. Most of all, thanks to God. I am forever humbled by Your grace and mercy. All that I am and all that I have is because of You!

From John: First and foremost, I acknowledge my Lord and Savior Jesus Christ, who gives me the strength, ability, and guidance to succeed in everything. By you Lord, all things are possible. To my family and friends, thank you for supporting me; your love means more than you know.

From Andreas: George Anderson, thank you for the great opportunity to be a coauthor of this manuscript. I am looking forward to contributing to our next book. Readers, stay tuned....

We Want to Hear from You!

As the reader of this book, *you* are our most important critic and commentator. We value your opinion and want to know what we're doing right, what we could do better, what areas you'd like to see us publish in, and any other words of wisdom you're willing to pass our way.

You can email or write me directly to let me know what you did or didn't like about this book—as well as what we can do to make our books stronger.

Please note that I cannot help you with technical problems related to the topic of this book, and that due to the high volume of mail I receive, I might not be able to reply to every message.

When you write, please be sure to include this book's title and author as well as your name and phone or email address. I will carefully review your comments and share them with the author and editors who worked on the book.

Email: mark.taub@pearson.com

Mail: Mark Taub
            Editor-In-Chief
            1330 Avenue of the Americas
            New York, NY 10019

Reader Services

Visit our website and register this book at www.informit.com/title/9780137142842 for convenient access to any updates, downloads, or errata that might be available for this book.

Introduction

Welcome, and thank you for picking up this latest edition of *Sams Teach Yourself SAP in 24 Hours*. Inside these pages you will find six newly renovated SAP parts and 24 hours of instruction refocused to better teach the SAP newcomer. My colleagues and I have spent a considerable amount of time aligning the content with what a person new to SAP needs to know up front, and we've done this from several different perspectives—the information technologist, the end user, the project manager, the wannabe SAP developer or programmer, and the business professional.

We have organized each hour (or chapter) around one of several common themes, beginning naturally with introductory materials useful in helping most anyone understand the underlying technology, business basics, and various SAP implementation roadmaps. Next, we cover SAP's products and components in detail, laying the groundwork for the next part of the book, which covers implementing SAP. By addressing SAP deployment from project management, business, and technology perspectives, we have strived to give our readers enough real-world breadth and depth to make the book a truly useful guide. Additional SAP technical considerations round out this breadth and depth, followed by a section focused on end users: how to log in, use the various SAP interfaces, customize the interface, and execute common business functions such as reports and queries. The final part of the book concludes with materials designed to help our readers land a job in SAP, including pointers to readily available Internet-based and other resources.

Though necessarily broad, our new approach accomplishes two things. First, it gives the new reader an opportunity to understand all that SAP comprises, particularly with regard to the many changes we've witnessed in the world of SAP since 2005. Second, the third edition makes for less jumping around from hour to hour, and is therefore an easier read. If your company has just announced it is deploying SAP, or you have just joined a company using SAP, you'll find it easy to navigate the book and quickly come up to speed. For example, end users may want to first read Parts I and IV before focusing their attention more fully on Part V, whereas technologists might prefer to focus their attention fully on Parts II and IV. Meanwhile, decision makers and project managers might find Parts II and III most useful, and SAP hopefuls might turn immediately to Part VI for advice aimed at breaking into the SAP workforce.

For you, our reader, picking up this book represents an assertive step forward. You are going with the market leader, the model of endurance, and the preeminent technology front-runner and enterprise solution enabler. As a result, after about 24 hours of reading, you will possess a solid foundation upon which to build greater capabilities or even a career in SAP. Your knowledge foundation will be broad, certainly, and in need of further bolstering before you're an expert in any sense of the word. But the great thing about your decision is simply that you'll know what you know and have a handle on what you still need to learn. You'll know where you want to go, and be smart enough about it to navigate a roadmap and career of your own choosing. That good sense alone will be enough to get you on the road toward making something new happen in your career, maybe even your life. And in the meantime, your 24 hours of investment may serve you well in your current employment position, too. Armed with insight, skills, understanding, and a broad sense of the big picture facing most every company in business today, you will no longer look at business applications and the technology solutions underpinning those applications in the same way again. You'll be wiser and more able to contribute to a greater extent than previously possible from several different perspectives, ranging from business and application expertise to technology, end-user, and project management insight. You'll be a "SAPling" in the broadest sense of the word.

SAP's Journey

SAP has come a long way since this first edition of this book was published in the heyday of R/3. In the last several years alone, we've witnessed an explosion in both technology and business applications, the frontlines of which SAP has arguably pushed harder than any other software company. Certainly, SAP's competitors and partners have provided great incentive to the developers and executives over in Walldorf, Germany. But with a revamped suite of core offerings surrounded by new products and new enabling technologies, SAP's stable of contemporary business solutions is unparalleled. And the company remains a model of both evolution and revolution. SAP may be found in 46,000 different firms around the world, ranging from multinational corporations to government entities, small/medium businesses, and everything in between. SAP has successfully engaged what is often termed the "mid market." That is, SAP is no longer only the best solution provider for big companies; it's also the best solution for the rest of the industry. Armed with state-of-the-art development tools, a focus on really delivering on the promises of Service-Oriented Architecture (SOA), and the willingness to reinvent how business does business in our new world, SAP is making it easier and easier to, well, do SAP.

What's New, and Who Should Read This Book?

Like its predecessors, this book is divided into 24 chapters, or "hours," that can each be completed in about an hour. This book covers everything you need to become well acquainted with the core SAP products and components that are often collectively referred to simply as SAP. The book is organized to provide visibility into key facets of SAP terminology, usage, configuration, deployment, administration, and more. As such, it is necessarily general at times rather than exceedingly detailed, although a certain amount of depth in much of the subject matter is purposely provided where deemed critical to further your understanding. The book serves as several intertwined roadmaps as well. In this structure may be found the book's true value—the content herein is broad enough to paint a picture most anyone can understand, yet deep enough to provide more than an introduction to the subject matter along several different paths or routes. And the flow of material moves along the same lines, from general to specific, from SAP products and components to post-implementation support and use, and from project management planning and preparation to project realization.

Sams Teach Yourself SAP in 24 Hours begins with the basics and terminology surrounding SAP, SAP NetWeaver, and what an SAP project looks like, and from there begins the process of carefully building on your newfound knowledge to piece together the complex world of SAP. The pace of the book is designed to provide a solid foundation such that you may grasp the more advanced topics covered later in the book. In this way, the novice may quickly realize what it means to plan for, deploy, and use SAP, in the process unleashing the power that comes with understanding how all the pieces of the puzzle come together to solve business problems. With this understanding also comes an appreciation of the role that SAP's various partners play with regard to an implementation project—how executive leadership, project management, business applications, technical deployment, and system end users all come together to create and use SAP end-to-end.

Organization of This Book

From the basics surrounding what SAP comprises and the technologies underneath it, to understanding and developing business and technology roadmaps, Part I, "Introduction to SAP," gives you a foundation. Part II, "SAP Products and Components," revolves around SAP's products and components, from the groundwork provided by SAP NetWeaver to SAP's core ERP product, its Small/Medium Business (SMB) offerings, and finally SAP's full-featured SAP Business Suite. Part III, "Implementing SAP," then turns to implementation matters, providing project management, business, and technical roadmaps after setting the stage with SAP's development tools and methodologies and how SAP leverages SOA in the real world. The technical concentration in Part IV, "SAP Technical Considerations," brings together what we've been told over and over again by new technologists looking for an introductory SAP book—how to install SAP, how to integrate it with Microsoft's ubiquitous Office offerings, how to manage and maintain the system, and finally what it means to upgrade or enhance SAP once it's in production. Part V, "Using SAP," brings us to the world of using SAP, from logging in, to customizing SAP's display, printing, creating reports, and executing queries. Finally, Part VI, "Developing a Career in SAP," concludes as stated earlier with what it takes to develop a career in SAP.

All told, this latest edition of *Sams Teach Yourself SAP in 24 Hours* serves as an excellent launchpad for using and managing SAP in the real world of business and IT. To test and reinforce your knowledge, each hour concludes with a case study and related questions. The questions provide you an opportunity to put your newfound hours' knowledge and understanding to the test as well as into practice. And with the answers to the questions found in Appendix A, "Case Study Answers," it will be an easy matter to verify your newfound knowledge.

From all of us at Sams, we hope you enjoy and get a lot out of the third edition of *Sams Teach Yourself SAP in 24 Hours*!

Conventions Used in This Book

Each hour starts with "What You'll Learn in This Hour," which includes a brief list of bulleted points highlighting the hour's contents. A summary concluding each hour provides similar though more detailed insight reflecting what you as the reader should be walking away with. In each hour, any text that you type will appear as **bold monospace**, whereas text that appears on your screen is presented in monospace type.

```
It will look like this to mimic the way text looks on your screen.
```

Finally, the following icons are used to introduce other pertinent information used in this book.

By the Way presents interesting pieces of information related to the surrounding discussion.	

Did You Know? offers advice or teaches an easier way to do something.	**Did you** *Know?*

Watch Out! advises you about potential problems and helps you steer clear of disaster.	**Watch** *Out!*

Each hour concludes with a case study germane to the hour's materials. By providing an hour-specific situation involving a fictional company called MNC Global Inc., the questions (and follow-on answers found in Appendix A) provide the reader with real-world reinforcement.

PART I

Introduction to SAP

HOUR 1

What Is SAP?

What You'll Learn in This Hour:

▶ An introduction to SAP's history and legacy

▶ A review of common SAP business applications

▶ An overview of SAP's technical architecture

Welcome to Hour 1 of the updated and greatly augmented third edition of *Sams Teach Yourself SAP in 24 Hours*. This first hour provides an introduction to SAP so that we can all talk the same language. Thus, a combination of history, business, and technology is covered. Don't be alarmed at this breadth of coverage, though. We're going to ease into this thing together to ensure we leave no readers behind. If you are a self-described expert in SAP, you may want to jump ahead. Welcome aboard.

Overview of SAP

A look into the current state of affairs along with a brief history lesson is warranted before we go further. SAP (pronounced *S-A-P*, not *sap*) is based in Walldorf, Germany, and is among the world's largest software companies. Though SAP and its primary competitors Oracle and Microsoft are all distinctly different from one another, they are markedly similar as well. Each provides enterprise-class business software, solutions for small and medium-sized businesses, platforms for web and application development, integration solutions enabling disparate systems to be tied to one another, and more. Each fundamentally supports and helps sustain the others, too; SAP counts Oracle as its largest database vendor, for example, whereas Microsoft Windows is SAP's most popular underlying operating system in both the data center and in terms of client desktop and laptop user environments.

Those of us who work with SAP tend to refer to the company and its products inter-changeably; the term *SAP* is used to describe both the company and its software. SAP was founded in 1972 in Mannheim, Germany, by a group of ex-IBM engineers who had a great idea: to develop a software package that integrated and combined a company's myriad business functions together in a manner that reflected business or industry best practices. In this way, a company could replace 10 different business systems of record—such as financials, warehousing, production planning, and so on—with a single system of record, and in the process gain the synergies and com-munication benefits inherent to maintaining a single version of the truth. Their idea grew into what soon became Systems, Applications, and Products in Data Processing (SAP), or in German *Systemanalyse und Programmentwicklung*.

SAP's goal from day one was to change the world, or at least the way business was conducted around the world. The five original ex-IBM engineers delivered on a vision to create a multilingual and multinational platform capable of easily chang-ing internally (to enable flexible business processes) as well as from an information technology perspective. That is, SAP purposefully chose to break away from the monolithic technology architecture model that defined mainframes and their busi-ness applications of the day, instead modeling its software solutions to run on a variety of standard or de facto hardware, operating systems, and database systems. Through this flexibility and openness, SAP in turn gave its customers flexibility and choice. Such a revolutionary departure from the norm created a tipping point in enterprise business software development and delivery that helped propel SAP into the forefront of IT and business alike by the early 1990s. Today, SAP supports more than 40 languages, 50 currencies, nearly 30 industry solutions, and more than 20 different combinations of popular hardware platforms, operating systems, and database releases.

Less than 20 years after its inception, SAP was not only Germany's top software ven-dor but was giving IBM and others a serious challenge in the enterprise market-place; new large entrants to the enterprise software field emerged during this time, including Baan, Oracle Corporation, PeopleSoft, and JD Edwards. Soon afterward, smaller players began gaining ground as well, including Great Plains and Navision. Though still widespread, mainframes had simply grown too cumbersome and expensive for the majority of firms and other large organizations to deploy and operate. Instead, IT organizations found that smaller UNIX-based hardware plat-forms represented better value, while databases from vendors such as Oracle and Informix offered nice alternatives to the old mainframe database offerings. By the mid-1990s, when SAP began supporting Microsoft Windows and SQL Server, and soon afterward Linux, SAP's place in the enterprise software market was firmly planted—the company's founders had truly delivered on their vision of a multi-national, multilingual business solution capable of running on diverse platforms operated and maintained by equally diverse IT organizations. SAP had succeeded in changing the world.

SAP Business Applications or Components

From a business applications perspective, SAP can be all things to nearly all businesses that operate today. SAP's application software foundation is built on the concepts of specialization and integration. That is, each component or product within the SAP family of products and services meets a particular need, such as providing web-based access to other SAP systems (SAP NetWeaver Portal), facilitating day-to-day financial and resource management (SAP ERP, or Enterprise Resource Planning), addressing product lifecycle planning requirements (SAP PLM), supporting internal company procurement (SAP Supplier Relationship Management), interconnecting different systems to ease integration headaches (SAP NetWeaver Process Integration), and so on. Divided by SAP into the SAP Business Suite (comprising all the business applications) and SAP NetWeaver (components of which essentially enable the SAP Business Suite), all of these products and more are explained in subsequent hours of this book; suffice it to say here that there are many components, many products, and therefore many potential SAP solutions.

Looking at it from another perspective, individual SAP modules combine to form an SAP component, application, or product. It is within a particular module or component that a company's business processes are configured (such as the order-to-cash process, which comprises the various steps involved in taking sales orders into the system, managing purchase requisitions and purchase orders, "picking" inventory to be sold, creating a delivery, and invoicing). SAP is well known for reflecting industry's best practices for the different business processes necessary to run a company. By adopting such best practices, companies grow more efficient serving their customers, constituents, and other stakeholders. This is a big reason SAP has been so successful—SAP stays on top of many different industries, making it easy for such companies to adopt SAP's software. Its industry solutions are currently divided into three core industry areas: Manufacturing, Service Industries, and Financial/Public Services. These, in turn, include such industries as Aerospace & Defense, Automotive, Banking, Chemicals, Consumer Products, Engineering & Construction, Healthcare, High Tech, Insurance, Media, Oil & Gas, Pharmaceuticals, Public Sector, Retail, Telecommunications, Utilities, and more (see Figure 1.1). The nice thing about these industry solutions is that they are simply "installed" atop SAP's core products such as ERP; a pharmaceutical company, for example, may deploy vanilla ERP to design and customize its own business processes, or it can deploy the SAP Pharmaceutical industry solution atop SAP ERP and gain the advantage of built-in best practices.

FIGURE 1.1
SAP provides a wide range of industry-specific solutions.

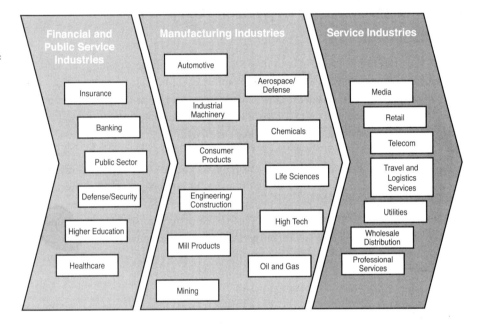

Another benefit of SAP is that the solutions can be combined to create broad platforms for conducting business. In this way, SAP allows companies to obtain greater visibility into their sales and manufacturing trends, or to allow new methods of entering or tracking such trends (and thus to maximize revenue and profit) by extending business processes in several different directions. A good example is order-to-cash, which is traditionally seen as a back office accounting process. By combining multiple SAP applications, a company can create what is called a *cross-application* or *extended* business process. These so-called cross-application business processes might be initiated through SAP's Enterprise Portal, which allows a broad base of a company's users or even its partners and suppliers to access the company's SAP system. Once in, a user might "punch through" to SAP ERP to actually place an order. Through the business logic enabled at the business process level, control might be passed to SAP's Customer Relationship Management (CRM) application to determine a particular customer's buying preferences or history. CRM's business logic might then essentially direct or influence the business process in a particular way, seeking to ultimately increase order size or gross margin. Next, SAP's Supply Chain Management (SCM) system might be accessed to revise a supply chain planning process for a set of potential orders, looking to optimize profitability as the system seeks to balance the needs of many different customers with the organization's access to materials, people, and other resources. Finally, the SAP NetWeaver BI offering might be queried to pull historical data relevant to a customer's credit history, financial terms, and sales patterns within a particular geography or during a particular season. After these details are analyzed, control can be turned back over to SAP ERP or SAP NetWeaver Portal to track warehousing, drive the pick-list process, track and manage the order-shipping process, and conclude with the accounts receivables portion of the overall business process.

SAP Modules and Business Transactions

As you may have already guessed, applications or components such as SAP ERP can be broken down into many different modules—we've already touched on several of these. Modules are portions of business functionality within a component such as ERP that are more discrete in nature, geared toward addressing a specific business function (which in turn is composed of even more specific business transactions). By way of example, SAP ERP is composed of modules such as Financials, Sales & Distribution, various Logistics functions, Human Capital Management, and more. Individually, each of these modules effectively serves to manage a business area or functional area for which a particular company department often is responsible. Prior to extending a line of credit, for instance, a company's Accounts Receivables group may run a business transaction within the Financials module of SAP ERP to check a customer's credit and on-time payment history. Likewise, the Shipping department will regularly run a business transaction to check inventories at a particular warehouse. Other departments may be responsible for managing payables, real estate, sales estimates, budgeting, and so on. Together, all the various departments in the company work together to do the business of the company, using SAP across the board to enable a great amount of consistency and linkages between departments while giving the company's management the high-level visibility it needs to make the necessary strategic decisions keeping everyone employed.

Do you see a common thread? SAP's products are used to satisfy the needs of enterprises, big and small, enabling the enterprise to tend to the business of running the business. Unlike specific user-based productivity tools such as Microsoft Excel and Adobe Acrobat, SAP's software products are generally all about the "big picture"— about conducting business by connecting people, resources, and processes around the globe. After all, every enterprise needs to manage its inventories, generate and track sales, deliver services, maximize revenue, optimize its supply chains, and so on. SAP and its enterprise application competitors—Oracle and Microsoft, along with several much smaller niche players—enable this capability on a grand scale, integrating many otherwise discrete functions under a single umbrella.

Though its major competitors are stronger than ever, SAP continues to reign as the Enterprise Applications software market leader. Listed on the New York Stock Exchange (NYSE) under the symbol SAP, the company employs 43,000 people and keeps a base of over 2000 SAP implementation and support partners busy as well. SAP does business in more than 50 countries. It has such manpower and reach that it literally touches *most* of the business world we know—comprising more than a million users across 100,000+ installations (reflecting 46,000 different customers—companies and other organizations that have deployed at least one SAP system). How this breadth was accomplished is due in large part to the technical platform SAP's engineers developed over the years, which is outlined next.

SAP Technical Architecture and WebAS

SAP's latest products are built on a very powerful and highly standardized platform called Web Application Server, or *WebAS*. WebAS may be installed on a variety of popular hardware platforms and database releases, giving a company's IT department great flexibility in terms of what SAP is installed on. WebAS is also flexible relative to its development capabilities; all the most popular computer programming languages and protocols are supported, including Web Services, XML, classic HTML, SAP's traditional ABAP/4 programming language, and the industry-standard Java language as well.

As you can imagine, with the flexibility and power inherent to WebAS, you can navigate a number of very different implementation paths. Some might choose to deploy SAP in a manner that emulates how the company does business today, for example, rather than adopting new best practices. Such a company could then evolve its business model over time rather than doing so immediately. This approach, although not generally preferred, makes it possible to avoid a prolonged implementation to introduce SAP inside an organization.

Most companies seek to transform how they do business and thus adopt SAP's ERP solution and best practices for their particular industry, likely deploying the industry solution and its industry-specific business processes and content in the process.

Other companies might introduce a specific SAP component such as Supply Chain Management to address a strategic need within its own business computing environment. This might not only fill in the gap but also help extend the company's band of suppliers and vendors, or enable improved reporting, or even allow business to be conducted over the Internet.

Still other companies might introduce one of SAP's access or integration solutions rather than its business applications. For instance, a company might enable broader customer access by deploying SAP NetWeaver Portal to those who demand communications with the company over XML, HTML, or Web Services. Another company might introduce SAP NetWeaver Process Integration and Master Data Management (MDM) solutions into its business environment to gain control of these respective areas.

Technical Architecture Overview

At a high level, an SAP business application such as ERP is traditionally architected (think "designed") in a very straightforward manner. Front-end client access devices such as individual PCs, laptops, workstations, mobile devices, and so on, run a piece of software used to "talk" to the SAP application back in the company's data center. These front-end clients are also called *presentation servers*, because they present the SAP interface to its end users. The software running on these presentation servers or clients might consist of a special installation of one of SAP's graphical user interfaces (atop Microsoft Windows, Apple's Mac OS, or various Linux-based desktop operating systems, for example), or it might simply comprise Microsoft's ubiquitous Internet Explorer. Whatever the case, the front-end software interfaces with one or more back-end *SAP application servers* (computers running your SAP application) via some kind of network connection. The Internet might provide the connection, or it might be provided via a company-specific intranet, local area network, dial-up line, or other similar network connection. In this way, end users can run business transactions from virtually anywhere on the globe—it all depends on the company's investment in these front-end and network resources.

Three-Tiered Architecture

Business transactions require data such as customer records, inventory status, financial information, and so on, to actually run. Thus, the SAP application servers mentioned previously are in turn connected to a database server where these kinds of records are maintained. SAP purposely designed this three-tiered arrangement so that the presentation or client layer, application logic, and data management layers of its solutions were all logically separate as well as potentially physically separate from one another. In this way, a flexible system could be architected (see Figure 1.2), where additional headroom could easily be added where needed. For instance, if the SAP application started to run slowly over time, IT could provide additional application

FIGURE 1.2
The SAP classic three-tiered architecture requires a database server, one or more application servers, and any number of front-end clients.

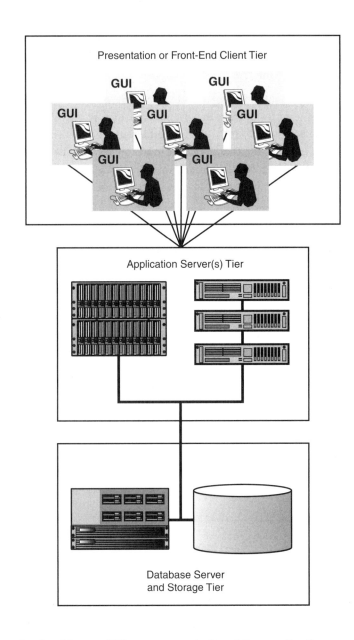

Presentation or Front-End Client Tier

Application Server(s) Tier

Database Server
and Storage Tier

servers or simply add more CPUs or memory to its existing application servers—all without having to make changes to the front-end clients or back-end database system. And if the relational database management system (RDBMS) used to maintain all the SAP data similarly got bogged down, it could be upgraded as well without having to touch the servers running SAP's business logic. As should be evident, then, the resulting three-tiered architecture essentially subdivides SAP into three architectural layers based on function:

- ▶ The user interface layer ("front-end" client or presentation server)

- ▶ The business logic layer (the "application" tier upon which SAP's programs actually execute)

- ▶ The database layer (the "back-end" RDBMS that houses all the SAP data)

Three-tiered architectures allow the most basic and otherwise unavoidable issues down the road to be easily resolved. Such issues include performance, scalability (a lack of it, actually), network connectivity, the need to easily upgrade business application logic, and the desire for technical flexibility. To this last point, the engineers at SAP wanted to abstract the operating system and database layers of an SAP system so that many different technology combinations could be supported without having to go back and rewrite existing programs.

SAP and Service-Oriented Architecture

To easily "extend" SAP's business processes to other business applications or sources of data, SAP has ensured its latest round of applications support yet another industry architecture called Service-Oriented Architecture (SOA), often pronounced *so-uh*. SOA is important enough and complex enough to warrant its own hour in this book (Hour 14, "SAP and Enterprise SOA"). Suffice it to say here, though, that SOA provides a more robust blueprint for designing an adaptable enterprise computing solution. Though it requires a "hub" of SAP's latest and greatest NetWeaver stack (see Hour 7, "Laying the Groundwork: SAP NetWeaver"), a SOA-compliant architecture can support older SAP business applications such as R/3 and everything in between. The idea is that applications are treated and thus connected to one another similar to how you might personally access an everyday service or utility. Electricity and gas services, our water and sewer systems, and even our cable and satellite televisions are utilities common to our everyday life—services that can be ubiquitously accessed with little thought as to the plumbing or wiring behind the scenes. At the end of the day, if an application can share data via industry-standard XML (eXtensible Markup Language, a standard "open" method of structuring and sharing data between different computers or systems via the Internet among other mechanisms), it can be connected to SAP and thus easily used and accessed like a shared reusable service. Such services might include pricing engines or web applets that manage orders or customer account information. The idea is for a company to eventually publish a list of all services available to its business (an applications services portfolio, if you will), making it even easier to change and flexibly grow the company's enterprise computing platform based on changing needs. SAP NetWeaver merely provides the vehicle for connecting such application services; it provides the platform. Figure 1.3 is a good example of how a typical three-tiered architecture can be "SOA enabled" to take advantage of this application services concept. Note the focus on applications rather than technologies—this is the crux of Service-Oriented Architecture. In this example, a centralized SAP system acts as a hub to multiple applications services available inside the company data center, or via third-party computer systems, or even from the Web via Web Services. Don't worry too much about all this now; beyond Hour 14, the various enabling technologies making all this possible are explored further in Hour 4, "Infrastructure Technology Basics: Hardware, Operating Systems, and Databases" and elsewhere.

FIGURE 1.3
SOA allows SAP to be easily extended to take advantage of readily available service-based applications and utilities.

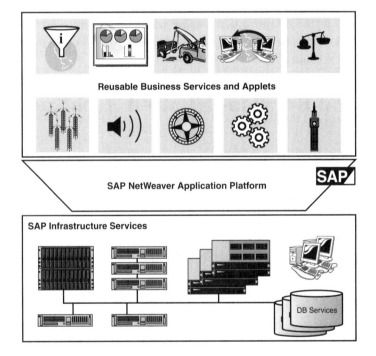

Reusable Business Services and Applets

SAP NetWeaver Application Platform   **SAP**

SAP Infrastructure Services

DB Services

Summary

This hour provided you with an introduction to the world of SAP. You gained an understanding of SAP's legacy and some of the specific business and technology considerations. You are now becoming more familiar with SAP's vernacular and many of the acronyms that surround its use as well, all of which are detailed in subsequent hours.

When all is said and done, remember that the real work of a computing system is not accomplished by technology but by business processes that have been specifically configured for a company. Business processes are industry-unique, and in many cases company-unique as well. Within these business processes, individual SAP business transactions are used to get the actual work done of running a business. We are now ready to turn our attention toward understanding what an SAP project or system looks like in Hour 2, "SAP Basics: What It's All About," further grounding you in the basics. But first, try your hand at the following case study.

Case Study: Hour 1

This case study winds its way through each hour, and is designed to help you review and synthesize what you have learned, as well as help you to think ahead as you seek to put your knowledge into practice. The "answers" posed in the questions related to this case study may be found in Appendix A, "Case Study Answers."

Situation

MNC Global, Inc., or simply MNC, is a large multinational mining company with manufacturing and distribution facilities in 20 countries around the world. Although MNC is a fictional amalgamation of many real-world companies that use SAP, the challenges it faces are very relevant to those faced by contemporary organizations today. Ongoing financial transparency issues, lack of supply chain visibility, and recent concerns with worldwide sales and lost market opportunities have reemphasized to the MNC executive board its need to adopt an integrated business application. The board is particularly concerned with the firm's requirement to address multiple languages and currencies; with 100,000 Microsoft Windows–based users spread out across 500 different offices and other locations, the board is also concerned with how it can possibly connect its diverse user community to a single system of record. Currently, MNC is running several different homegrown business applications along with several mainframe-based packages, none of which are tied together in real time. By walking the board through the following questions, your task is to help the MNC leadership team understand what SAP is and how the firm should proceed.

Questions

1. Outside of SAP, which enterprise software companies should MNC also consider investigating?

2. Which SAP components or products would the board be most interested in first learning about?

3. Is there an Industry Solution offered by SAP that would be especially useful to MNC?

4. Given the great number of employees (and therefore potential SAP end users) that MNC employs, what are some key technology infrastructure considerations the board should address early on?

5. Will language and currency support issues be a problem for SAP?

HOUR 2

SAP Basics: What It's All About

What You'll Learn in This Hour:

▶ What it means to run SAP

▶ SAP new project basics

▶ SAP system basics

▶ How to access an SAP system

Even with Hour 1 behind you, if you are new to SAP, you may still find yourself unclear as to what SAP is beyond simply a German software company or a set of integrated business applications. This hour touches on more of the basics, from describing an SAP system to investigating what it means to run and use SAP. Let's get started.

Running SAP

How many times have you run into someone who told you, "My company runs SAP" or "We're getting ready to bring in SAP"? Or maybe you're like literally a million other people out there and work for a company that already runs, deploys, or in some way supports SAP. What does this mean?

Historically, it meant that SAP R/3 was either installed or going to be installed. For years SAP R/3 was synonymous with SAP: They were one and the same, and to say you ran SAP was the same thing as saying you ran R/3. R/3 was SAP's first true client/server–based online transaction processing (OLTP) system—a system that by its very nature satisfied day-to-day transactional needs of typically many users. Like its mainframe predecessor R/2, within R/3 was a number of business modules, such as Finance, Logistics, Human Resource Management, Warehouse Management, and more.

In the late 1990s, SAP introduced several more applications to complement SAP R/3. SAP's first data warehouse was released at this time, as was the company's first stab at a business-to-business integration solution and a supply chain management system called Advanced Planner and Optimizer (APO). Together, these were lumped into an umbrella of offerings that SAP termed "New Dimension" products. Other products such as Internet Transaction Server made it possible for SAP's end users to access SAP R/3 via a browser. Additional applications soon followed. SAP introduced an early portal solution called SAP Workplace in 1999, for example, and broadened its business integration solutions with a business-to-consumer product, among others. Like many of its competitors, SAP adopted a "dot-com" strategy and renamed its product suite mySAP.com. The company brought out several new solutions, too, including SAP Customer Relationship Management (CRM) and a broader internal procurement suite called Supplier Relationship Management (SRM). A useful management cockpit for SAP's Business Warehouse called Strategic Enterprise Management (SEM) was introduced as well. And then came the dot-com crash, and SAP responded by slowing things down a bit.

By stepping back in the wake of dot-com, SAP had the opportunity to rationalize and revamp its business software. It introduced the NetWeaver suite, a set of products intended to make SAP more accessible, more easily integrated, and more open to competing technology standards such as Microsoft's .NET and Sun's Java development environments. Even more importantly, during this time SAP's adoption of Service-Oriented Architecture (SOA) changed how the company's software solutions were designed and the ease with which new solutions could be built. Within a few years, SAP R/3 morphed into R/3 Enterprise and then into ERP Central Component (ECC). This was in response to several inherent client/server architecture limitations; SAP's venerable R/3 offering was never intended or designed to support Web Services or a Service-Oriented Architecture. Most recently, SAP ECC was renamed to simply SAP ERP.

In a nutshell, then, SAP ERP represents the natural evolution of R/3 toward a more open and accessible architecture based on Web Services, which is discussed in detail in Hour 14, "SAP and Enterprise SOA." So today, when you hear people say they are running SAP, be sure to ask them what that really means in their specific case—with so many different products and solutions out there bearing the SAP label, it's no longer safe to assume they're running R/3!

SAP Project Basics

Like with companies that run SAP, if someone mentions his company is busy deploying SAP, be sure to ask what that entails. What exactly is the company deploying? Remember from Hour 1 that companies around the world are still busy introducing SAP ERP to their employees, but by the same token other companies are "merely" adding capabilities to their existing SAP landscape or perhaps extending their business processes to augment Customer Relationship Management capabilities or extend reporting functions via SAP's Business Intelligence offerings.

Though the products and their purpose differ, a new SAP implementation project reflects several common themes, among them business requirements, SAP application functionality, underlying or enabling technologies, and implementation project management concepts. These can be viewed in terms of roadmaps—for every new SAP project, key decisions and factors are related to how business, functionality, technology, and overall project management requirements are weaved together and addressed. Like traffic in a busy city, the most important and immediate matter is "simply" getting everyone moving in the same direction (see Figure 2.1).

The business...

SAP functionality

IT Department

Project Management

FIGURE 2.1
An SAP project requires everyone moving in the same direction.

Thus, from an SAP project perspective, four primary "views" or dimensions must be addressed:

- ▶ Business view

- ▶ Functional (application) view

- ▶ Technical view

- ▶ Implementation (project management and oversight) view

Each view requires attention in terms of vision, stakeholder buy-in, staffing and other resource requirements, time lines, and much more. Although much of the book is dedicated to expanding these views, respective views are covered in much detail in Hour 3, "Business Basics: Developing a Roadmap for Deploying SAP," Hour 5, "Developing a Technical Roadmap for Deploying SAP," and Hour 10, "Implementation Overview: A Project Management Perspective."

SAP System Basics

After all the work of designing, configuring, testing, and deploying SAP business processes atop an SAP infrastructure platform has been completed, an SAP end user is trained and finally given the go-ahead to actually *use* the system in his daily routine—moving and tracking inventory, reporting on financials, supporting the sales team by helping to manage order status, and so on. Although this might sound straightforward, a number of matters still need to be addressed before using the system. The remaining sections in this hour cover these basics, while more detailed matters are covered thoroughly in Hour 20, "SAP GUI Screen and Printing Basics," Hour 21, "Customizing Your SAP Display," and Hour 22, "Reporting and Query Basics."

SAP GUI Basics

To use SAP's applications requires a method of accessing the SAP system. This is accomplished by installing an SAP-specific user interface that is then subsequently executed by a user whenever he wishes to run an SAP business transaction. The SAP GUI (pronounced *goo-ee*) for Microsoft Windows is the most popular user interface available for SAP systems today. Also called the "WinGUI" or the "fat client," the Windows interface requires a good amount of disk space and memory to run well. Similarly, the Java GUI for SAP is also a fat client; it enables SAP access by non-Microsoft-based front-end clients. See Hours 19 through 21 for much more detail.

For access to SAP from front-end clients with less power, little disk space, or simply to avoid having to maintain a GUI interface on perhaps thousands of individual desktops and laptops, SAP may be accessed via Internet Explorer (IE). In terms of network bandwidth, IE is not as efficient as its fat-client counterparts. However, it's ubiquitous and therefore easily called upon. Another method—Citrix's Presentation Server—offers an alternative to locally installed user interfaces. With its best-in-class network and processing bandwidth (very small and, therefore, quite fast!), it's the leanest and most easily managed approach available for SAP access.

Regardless of user interface, a number of matters are universal. These include system access methods and the concepts of sessions and clients, which are outlined next.

System Access

Regardless of the particular SAP product, SAP solutions are designed as "end-user" or client systems. That is, most of these systems are geared toward satisfying business-oriented requests. This means you have the freedom to operate the system from any computer that has the SAP GUI (SAP's user interface, also called *presentation software* by the folks at SAP AG) or Internet Explorer (in most cases). This user interface connects to the SAP *central instance* (the SAP "executables"), which in turn talks to the back-end database holding all the programs, data, and so on. The key here is that you are not required to be at your particular desk working from a special desktop or client machine to complete your daily tasks. Instead, if you happen to be visiting your warehouse and realize that you forgot to perform a task back at your office, you can perform it from this site (assuming the computer is connected to SAP via the company network or intranet). SAP recognizes who you are and what activities you are allowed to perform through your SAP user ID.

All SAP users are assigned a user name (although it is not uncommon to see infrequent factory, distribution site, and warehouse workers sharing a single SAP user ID). In most cases, it is your own name or initials, similar to the PC logon name you're accustomed to using. When you connect to SAP using your initial password, you are forced to change it immediately upon logging in, thus securing your user ID even from system administrators and others tasked with maintaining security.

The SAP Client Concept

In the world of SAP, clients are essentially self-contained business entities or units within each SAP system; using one of SAP's user interfaces, you log in to a client to actually access and use the system. Each system—SAP ERP, CRM, SCM, and so on—has a unique system-specific client you'll log in to. Contemporary organizations thus have multiple production clients, as well as other clients used by the IT group to develop and test the business functionality that will one day be handed over to the company's end users.

A client retains its own separate master records and own set of tables. The best way to think of this is in the form of a company—within a large multinational organization, for example, you might have five or six companies. Each client within SAP represents a different company; the company might structure its clients around discrete business groups or functions, or by geography. In this way, you might log in to a particular client or company and do your work while others in the company might log in to a different client on the same SAP system. In the end, the results can be easily rolled up so that the multinational organization as a whole can easily report on its cross-company financials, inventory levels, and so on.

In the same way, an SAP system also tends to maintain different clients strictly for convenience, or to segregate critical data from perhaps less critical data. Here is a general example: When you are first installing SAP and configuring the system, you will likely have a set of systems that you can log in to. Most SAP customer sites maintain a development system, QA or test system, and a production system. Within each of these systems you can choose the specific client you want to log in to. For instance, within the development system you might maintain a "business sandbox" or "crash and burn" client along with your workhorse development client and later a copy of this workhorse client, called a "Golden Master" by many. These very distinct client environments within each system enable you to segregate your critical data (important golden development or production client data, for instance) from your test and what-if configuration data.

You might have *many* clients configured within a particular system. For example, the technical team might implement a new client in your development environment for special developer training purposes, to be used to teach developers how to use the system without actually making any changes to the important development data. This same client configuration is often established in your other systems, too— from production down to the QA and test systems, and so on.

Regardless of the number of clients, each one is assigned a unique three-digit number, which you are required to know and type at login time. This makes it easy to distinguish between clients. A developer might log in to client 100 to do training, client 200 to review and approve new business logic, and client 500 to conduct actual development activities for the company. In the same way, an end user might log in to client 300 in the production system to do his day-to-day work, and occasionally client 900 in the QA or test system to check on the status of new functionality being developed for production.

Within the SAP world, the term *client* is used to describe something distinctly different from what the Information Technology (IT) world in general uses the term for. In IT, a client represents an individual PC or workstation. For our purposes here, though, we will use client in the manner used by SAP—to describe a logically discrete or separate business entity within an SAP system.

Session Basics

Each time you connect to SAP via the SAP GUI user interface, you begin a user session. An *SAP session* simply means you have started the SAP GUI (the SAP graphical user interface) and established a connection with a particular SAP system—you're connected, so to speak. You can have multiple sessions open with multiple SAP components—such as SAP ERP, CRM, and so on—or you can open one or more sessions with a single system. The number of the current session is displayed in the status bar, which you will see in a few minutes.

One of the benefits of this multiple session option is that you can multitask. Assume that you are processing a new customer order and your boss asks you to generate a report. There is no need to stop processing the order. You can leave that session (screen) open on your computer and begin a new session. With this new session, you can request and generate your boss's report. By default, you can open up to six sessions at the same time, although the default can be increased by a system administrator knowledgeable in maintaining SAP from a technical perspective. With six sessions, think about how much more work you can do! Multitasking is indeed alive and well in the world of SAP.

Summary

Hour 2 walked you through what it means to run SAP, including some of the basic matters surrounding an SAP project. We also explored SAP system, user interface, and session basics. These fundamentals set the stage for the remaining hours in this book.

Case Study: Hour 2

Consider the following case study and questions, the answers to which may be found in Appendix A, "Case Study Answers."

Situation

You and your good friend are the latest additions to the staff at MNC Global, a large multinational mining company. You have been appointed to the position of ERP IT Project Director, whereas your friend has been tasked with managing the company's largest Inventory Warehouse team. Both of you are well aware that the executive management team has decided to implement SAP ERP, SCM, and SAP NetWeaver Portal, the sum of which will impact everyone companywide.

Questions

1. What should be your response upon being asked by your new team what it means when the CEO tells everyone, "We're going to be running SAP!"?

2. Several of your team members have worked at other companies where SAP was implemented, and they are curious if MNC is putting in SAP R/3. Explain how R/3 has evolved over time into SAP ERP.

3. Your CIO wants your high-level thoughts on what you believe is the most important and most immediate matter on the horizon relative to getting this new SAP implementation right. What might you tell the CIO?

4. Your friend asks you how his Warehouse team will one day use SAP. He's specifically interested in the interface the team will actually use to access the system. What is the most popular user interface for SAP?

5. Your friend understands the SAP GUI concept, but is unclear as to what an SAP "client" is, as opposed to the term "front-end" client he often reads about. Explain the difference.

Business Basics: Developing a Roadmap for Deploying SAP

What You'll Learn in This Hour:

▶ What constitutes a business roadmap
▶ Business blueprinting
▶ Mapping business needs to SAP technologies
▶ How SAP technologies support business needs

Though the company provides quite a breadth of technical offerings intended to enable business needs, SAP is by no means the only game in town; when it comes to a business roadmap, products are second to what the business needs to compete in the marketplace. Also, implementing and providing ongoing support for SAP equate to more than a technical process or project methodology. Indeed, before SAP can be properly deployed, an organization needs to invest the time to develop a business roadmap, which in turn connects people, business applications, and technologies.

The SAP Business Roadmap

What exactly is a business roadmap? In simplest terms, it is the path or process by which an organization's vision and business requirements are translated into a set of fundamental business processes, which in turn are married to SAP (and other) applications, products, and components. The business roadmap is essential to "getting it right the first time." Like building a highway without plans, a poorly conceptualized business roadmap will likely fail in helping an organization achieve its present-day mission, let alone its strategic long-term goals.

The concept of a business roadmap may also be explained in terms of what it is not:

▶ It has nothing to do with technology, at least not directly.

▶ It is not predicated on a particular implementation process or methodology, although SAP offers its tried-and-true ASAP methodology and Solution Manager product to enable such implementation.

▶ It has nothing to do with enterprise architecture despite the fact that a good business roadmap is enabled by such a framework.

Instead, the business roadmap provides the highest level of business abstraction surrounding the implementation effort. And in doing so, the fundamental principles of business administration and operations are made possible. Thus, the business roadmap ultimately, though in a roundabout way, makes technology relevant to business operations; it synthesizes the two into what we eventually call a "business solution." Technologies, and the applications atop the technologies, are simply tools used to navigate and fulfill the roadmap's purpose.

Traditional Business Concerns

Businesses exist to provide a service in a manner that either creates profit for the company (the usual goal) or acts as a cost-recovery model underpinning a presumably greater purpose (charities and other not-for-profit firms). If a business is unable to recoup its costs, it will fail. It therefore makes sense to view the business in terms of a set of concentric circles, the center of which is the business's service or primary purpose. Auto companies sell cars, oil companies sell oil, and services companies sell services. How *well* a company performs this service is another matter entirely, though. Many different dimensions come into play, from financial aspects to matters of sales, marketing, supply chain/logistics, product lifecycle management, and so on. The firm's people and material invoices must be paid, processes must be managed, and goods delivered.

But at the heart of the matter is the service being delivered, how consistently profitable that service may be provided, and how that service might be refined or optimized to meet changing business needs, respond to changing market conditions, and in the process maximize profits over a particular period of time. To survive in a market economy, firms focus on the following:

▶ Increasing sales and therefore top-line revenue

▶ Decreasing costs so as to increase profitability (for example, the cost of goods sold or the cost of expenses incurred through labor, materials, and everything else brought to bear to deliver the service)

These two tenets of business are explored next.

Increasing Sales, Decreasing Costs

Business is admittedly more complicated than increasing sales and decreasing costs. However, there's merit in taking this simplistic approach to running a business. For example, a closer look at how to increase sales yields the following steps an organization may take:

▶ Identify new customer markets (take a broader sales tact).

▶ Innovate in terms of products and services to fill new niches or provide new value-added services (a breadth and depth play).

▶ Augment the firm's relationship with its existing customers so as to sell more goods per customer (that is, establish a deeper sales relationship).

In the same way, costs may be reduced through several methods:

▶ Manage current business operations to maximize efficiency; better balance both fixed and variable costs to maximize asset productivity and minimize unproductive time, reduce operational and other process costs, and so on.

▶ Reduce the firm's cost of raw materials through vertical consolidation, for example, or by simply negotiating better rates on people, materials, and so on.

▶ Improve how the firm services the various steps in the service delivery process (from better managing manufacturing processes to reengineering supply chain and customer relationship processes, for instance); focus on core competencies and outsource the rest.

▶ Reduce the "cost of change" by proactively managing it across the organization's breadth of stakeholders.

▶ Innovate not from a products and services perspective but rather from a process control, operations, or management perspective; continuously strive to shrink costs.

▶ Enhance how the company manages, delivers, optimizes, tracks, and improves on its products and services—or the processes used to drive the same—through the application of specific business applications and subsequent enabling technology.

Firms that can increase sales while reducing costs will realize greater business success than their industry counterparts. Of course, another factor comes into play—risk. Next, we discuss how to manage it.

Managing and Mitigating Risk

With every change introduced into the business or the IT organization responsible for supporting the business comes the opportunity to make minor missteps and major blunders. To counter the negative impact inherent to such errors (in judgment, leadership, product marketing, sales strategies, IT alliances, you name it), an organization needs to identify, manage, and mitigate risks. This applies to efforts aimed at increasing revenue *or* decreasing costs. From both business and IT perspectives, this will include the following:

▶ Assessing shifts in strategy

▶ Proactively managing how work and its subtasks change in response to changing strategies as well as changes in project scope

▶ Testing every conceivable case and exception to the rule

▶ Developing a communication plan

▶ Reviewing the project management process, resources, timelines, and the critical path

▶ Proactively developing a problem-escalation plan

▶ Developing contingency plans for each risk scenario

This final factor is especially important. An SAP implementation is so far-reaching and subsequently so complex that "Plan B" is simply unavoidable. Knowing and preparing for Plan B can make the difference between a successful (albeit less than ideal) business solution and a business solution that's never actually implemented. Successfully developing and executing against this kind of deployment mindset brings up another dimension of an SAP business roadmap—business agility, which is covered next.

Business Agility: A Growing Business Concern

Business agility has garnered a great amount of press lately. Agility speaks to a firm's ability to transform its products, services, supply chain, sales strategy, IT underpinnings, and so on, in such a way as to more nimbly meet customer demand. The agile organization enjoys a leg up on the competition. Agility is by no means an easy thing to accomplish, though. To change means to fight the inertia of the "way things have always been done." Fighting inertia also means adjusting how people work and processes flow, thereby affecting the status quo. As too many firms find out the hard way, maintaining the status quo is no way to run a business. Indeed, implementing SAP is often seen as a way of disrupting the status quo and reinventing how the work of running the business is optimized, divided, and addressed. Optimization is probably the key in all this; in the end, increasing business agility equates to reducing the delays related to decision-making, which in turn enables the following:

▶ Better and faster customer relationship management

▶ More effective and less expensive supply chain management

▶ Increased transparency and compliance relative to company—internal, government-mandated, and other regulations

▶ A better balance between cost and risk

▶ Measurable business-enabling IT return on investment (ROI)

> What does all this have to do with developing a business roadmap? Simply put, if the roadmap does not enable a firm to do business more efficiently, more quickly, more nimbly, or more effectively, the project will not only waste a huge amount of time and money, but will fail.

By the Way

Only a well-developed business-enabling roadmap has a chance of transforming the business through increased revenue or decreased costs. Sure, other factors will come into play that might derail how the roadmap is translated into an SAP implementation. The business roadmap provides the most fundamental if not most essential foundation; however, the actual development is described by SAP as "business blueprinting."

Business Blueprinting

Identified as Phase 2 in SAP's ASAP methodology, business blueprinting entails defining a firm's to-be business processes, identifying gaps between the current state and this to-be state, determining how well SAP's templates can be applied, identifying and prioritizing the need for customizations to these templates, and then locking down the scope of work necessary to make all this happen. There's also follow-on preparation and planning work that dovetails with Phase 1's project preparation-related tasks. In short, though, business blueprinting serves as a culmination of the initial roadmap development work.

We look at business blueprinting as one of four dimensions or views of an SAP implementation (refer to Figure 3.1), the others of which are functional, technical, and project implementation.

FIGURE 3.1
Viewing the business roadmap through one of four views or "lenses" helps maintain a complete and yet easy-to-understand SAP implementation perspective.

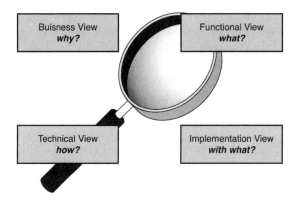

The Business View

As we have covered in this hour, developing a sound business view is a critical first step. The business view articulates *why* a particular problem needs to be solved or opportunity needs to be explored. Developing a firm's unique business view mandates addressing the following:

- ▶ The identification of business-relevant stakeholders

- ▶ Long-term strategy enablement

- ▶ Short-term business objectives

- ▶ Core competencies

- ▶ Competencies other than the core competencies (and thus opportunities for partnering, developing alliances, or contracting out specific services)

- ▶ Procurement and other sourcing strategies (and how those strategies and relationships might change over time)

- ▶ SAP globalization and localization realities (where the emphasis tends to shift back and forth between enabling global consistency and roll-up financial reporting, for example, along with addressing the currency and language requirements for local user communities)

The most relevant stakeholders at this level are those involved in strategically aligning and executing the actual business processes (sometimes called *workstreams*) necessary for survival. Thus, business executives and other officers of the board, along with functional managers and team leads, business analysts, and any other line-of-business leaders will have a need to be included in developing and communicating the business view.

How SAP Technologies Support Business Needs

With the business view nailed down, the next several tasks of business blueprinting may be addressed. Among other tasks, this includes developing the underlying architecture and designing the IT platform. In this way, the business roadmap has a much better chance of actually aligning to business goals predicated on responding in an agile manner to changing markets, new business needs, increased governance, and so on—all of which requires an agile technology platform. Technology basics are covered in Hour 4, "Infrastructure Technology Basics: Hardware, Operating Systems, and Databases," setting the stage for developing the technology roadmap in Hour 5, "Developing a Technical Roadmap for Deploying SAP."

Working with Stakeholders

Building a business roadmap is impossible without understanding the various stakeholders and their particular perspectives. Therefore, a quick look at stakeholders is warranted. In general, stakeholders are those who are most affected by the problems or concerns of an organization and therefore have significant interest in some aspects of a proposed solution. They can represent the entire company (such as the board of directors) or a just a few people within a particular team or specific function (such as IT, the finance group, or the sales and marketing team). By directly engaging stakeholders and extracting their priorities and concerns *initially as well as over the course of an implementation*, the SAP Project Sponsor along with the SAP Project Manager may together effectively plan and execute a successful project. In this way, because the right people are involved from the onset and given a "voice" throughout, the project will be more likely to actually solve the problems outlined in the first place.

There is no one best way to engage stakeholders. Common methods include kick-off and regularly scheduled follow-up meetings, function-specific workshops, and executive milestone or status meetings. Regular email updates reflecting changes in the project plan, scope, resources, and so on may be appropriate as well. Frequency of communication tends to be more important than the actual length of time spent providing updates.

> It's also important to give stakeholders access at some level to the repositories of data used to track and maintain all the business, functional, project management, and technical decisions made, problems resolved, contact information, and similar such details. By being completely transparent and ensuring stakeholders feel recognized and "in the know," a project team will have a much better chance of building and *maintaining* the critical buy-in necessary to successfully pursue and complete a complex implementation such as SAP.

Mapping Business Needs to SAP Technologies

Because stakeholders typically lack the breadth of experience necessary to grasp all the complexities of implementing SAP or a competing ERP solution, other views into the ultimate business solution can be helpful. A functional perspective followed by a more technical view and project implementation perspective allows business stakeholders to envision the solution in its entirety, for example. In the same way, for IT stakeholders a view into the business, functional requirements, and project perspectives help fill in their knowledge gaps as well. We have already outlined the business view in this hour; functional, technical, and project implementation views are covered next.

Functional View

The functional view is the easiest to grasp for individuals intimately familiar with how to run a business. It is the most difficult to grasp for non-functional experts, however. This view addresses the *what* surrounding a solution. Not how, or when, or with what, but simply what. What will a particular business process do? In this way, the functional view does the following:

▶ It describes or communicates the flow of work (workflow) in a stepwise fashion. (What steps are necessary to execute a business process and thereby achieve a particular end state?)

▶ It describes the properties or qualities to be exhibited by the business process. (What characteristics or properties should the business process encompass, and to what degree?)

▶ It addresses the preceding from a technology-independent and SAP-independent perspective.

As you can imagine, the key stakeholders for such a view are the end users who will ultimately execute the business process as part of their daily work. Business process designers, line-of-business leaders, and others involved with the functionality to be embodied by the solution are important stakeholders, too.

Technical View

The technical view addresses the *how* part of the solution equation. It gives legs to the functional view in that the technical view describes how the business solution will work. Important considerations include the following:

▶ Focusing on the key dimensions of the system; how the system will deliver the performance, availability, scalability, security, agility, systems manageability, and so on required by the business.

▶ Describing the solution's overall components in terms of business applications and other SAP components, data and relevant dependencies, interface requirements, underlying technical infrastructure, and all the intercomponent relationships and integration points necessary to enable the previously described functional view.

▶ Providing to the extent possible a technology-independent perspective as to how all this is accomplished.

Primary technical view stakeholders include solution developers and programmers, infrastructure and other technology specialists, and other technology-focused suppliers, vendors, and partners.

Project Implementation View

The project implementation view is probably the simplest to comprehend. It answers the question *with what* shall the solution be built, and over what time period leveraging what resources? The project implementation view, or more simply the implementation view, accomplishes the following:

▶ Describes and details the deployment plan, which in turn encompasses organizational and third-party resources, timelines, constraints (business, functional, technical, and other), and so on.

▶ Describes the SAP products and components to be used to fulfill the functional vision/view, and how they will be configured.

Common implementation view stakeholders are project managers and coordinators, technical specialists, developers/programmers, testers, business process owners, executives, business leaders, power users, and more.

To be sure, nearly anyone remotely involved with the deployment will be an implementation stakeholder in one form or another. But the degree of relative importance or influence will separate critical stakeholders from those less critical to implementing successfully.

Bringing the Four Views Together

The four views described this hour work together to completely describe a system's purpose (why), its functions (what), its technical underpinnings (how), and its implementation details (with what). By breaking a solution down into these four views, a firm may effectively communicate the breadth surrounding an SAP implementation. You probably noticed, however, that references to specific SAP products and components were lacking in this hour. There's good reason for this—a solid business roadmap should be developed well before a specific ERP solution is decided upon. Like putting the cart before the horse, planning a roadmap based on the business solutions offered by a particular software vendor (SAP included) makes no sense at all. Figure out what the business needs to accomplish first, and then determine how SAP and other vendors in the enterprise resource planning space might best address those needs.

Not to worry though—there's plenty of SAP-specific reading awaiting you. In the succeeding hours we will cover the SAP-specific details necessary to move from conceptual roadmaps to firm implementation plans, technology platforms, and functional business solutions.

There's often a strong temptation to align specific views with certain disciplines or areas of expertise. Perhaps most obviously, the business and functional views might be lumped into business concerns, whereas the technical view might be seen as an "IT" thing and the implementation view as a "project management" thing. Try to avoid creating these silos; instead, remember that a successful SAP implementation depends on a firm working well together. Break down the walls and encourage teams with different backgrounds and responsibilities to have a distinct voice in the overall implementation (keeping in mind, of course, that strong leadership will be required to ensure the project indeed moves forward). The results—a better business solution atop a more resilient technology platform—will be reward enough.

Summary

The concepts outlined in this hour have prepared you to develop a business roadmap. In this way, the company's business needs may be later married to SAP's underlying technologies, which in turn set the foundation for SAP's business solutions and components. This enables a firm's synthesis of technology and business. Before such a marriage is possible, though, the business's strategic and more immediate business needs must be identified, prioritized, and communicated. This includes methods of increasing revenue, decreasing costs, and managing the risk of change. We also discussed the importance of facilitating *business agility*, or the ability of a firm to nimbly transform and therefore respond to the changing business environment in which it finds itself operating. Finally, we investigated the four high-level views or dimensions by which a business problem or solution may be seen: business, functional, technical, and project implementation.

Case Study: Hour 3

Consider the following case study and questions related to developing a business roadmap for SAP, the answers to which may be found in Appendix A, "Case Study Answers."

Situation

In a benchmark of its competitors, MNC Global has found it seriously lags in several areas. MNC's customer base does less repeat buying, tends to exhibit less product loyalty, and costs more to service than similar customer-competitor relationships. Further, the business landscape is clearly evolving to one favoring a more direct sales model for MNC's commodity goods. Opportunities for growth capable of out-pacing the competition seem reasonable, if not likely, so MNC's board of directors is encouraged more than ever to pursue its tentative ERP implementation plans. To that end, you have been selected to join a task force to identify important startup concerns. Using the knowledge you gained this hour, answer the questions that follow.

Questions

1. Given the early and tentative nature of this ERP project, is it prudent to assume SAP will be selected?

2. Which primary tenet of business aligns best with MNC's problem surrounding a lack of repeat buyers?

3. What are the four views that need to be explored by the task force?

4. Which view addresses the "what" surrounding a business solution?

5. What does the technical view address?

Infrastructure Technology Basics: Hardware, Operating Systems, and Databases

---

What You'll Learn in This Hour:

▶ Hardware basics: server and disk subsystem infrastructure

▶ Partnering with your infrastructure providers

▶ Supported operating systems for SAP

▶ An introduction to database basics

With the business fundamentals covered in Hour 3, "Business Basics: Developing a Roadmap for Deploying SAP" behind us, it's now time to turn our attention to the infrastructure technologies that underpin SAP. In this hour, we take a closer look at the three broad infrastructure technologies that come into play when deploying SAP—hardware, operating systems, and databases. In later hours, we examine the SAP-specific application and integration technologies as well.

Why Is This Important?

Hardware, operating systems, and databases represent the underlying technologies that make up the lowest layers of an SAP business software solution. Called a *solution stack* or *technology stack*, these layers of enabling technology combine to create the basis of an SAP system. Similar to building a house or skyscraper, the underlying technology solution is like a foundation; it's the base layer of the building and arguably one of the most important aspects of an SAP system. An improperly built foundation weakens the ability of your

SAP system to weather storms, survive changing business needs, and meet the expectations of its occupants—your SAP end user community. Hour 4 covers the ins and outs of choosing these components wisely in order to build a firm, solid foundation, thus affording optimum system availability, longevity, and to some extent performance.

Hardware for SAP: An Introduction

Hardware, although often an afterthought in an SAP project, is an essential component of an SAP system. Hardware comprises the servers (think "data center computers"), disk storage systems, network gear (such as routers, network switches, and security firewalls), and tape backup units all working together to create the infrastructure or base layer of an SAP system. If any one piece is overlooked or skimped on, it creates a weak link or single point of failure that may cause something down the road as simple as a one-time nagging glitch or as major as a series of significant system outages, costing your company precious dollars. When hardware purchases are addressed late in an implementation, inevitable budget cuts (yes, implementing SAP tends to be more expensive than most companies estimate up front) often restrict purchasing what could have been a robust and highly available system. Advance planning will help you avoid this problem when designing the overall solution.

The major players in the SAP hardware marketplace sell systems that fit all types of solution needs, from small/medium user platforms reflecting commodity solutions and low cost, to larger and highly resilient platforms capable of scaling on the fly to meet the changing or growing needs of thousands of users. Choosing a partner simply based on name recognition is a good place to start, to be sure. However, take care to investigate and compare hardware solutions from competitors that are truly apples-to-apples solutions. A million-dollar commodity hardware solution might support the same workload as a high-end proprietary system costing twice as much, but do they offer the same levels of availability, scalability, and flexibility your business needs to survive month-end closing? By the same token, will saving a few dollars on hardware (or database software, for that matter) require the IT department to spend more money every year on systems management, maintenance activities, and downtime for upgrades and patches?

Server Hardware

We view server hardware as coming in three main initial acquisition "cost" classes or performance categories: small or low, medium, and high (see Figure 4.1). Costs per server can range from a few thousand dollars to several million. Performance can vary as well, depending on the number of CPUs, amount of RAM, internal server architecture factors, support for high-speed disk operations, and much more. Different hardware platforms are developed to support various operating systems and levels of system availability. They differ in terms of configuration flexibility and on-the-fly adaptability too.

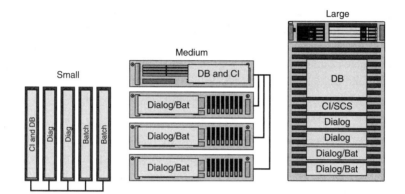

FIGURE 4.1
Servers for SAP come in a variety of sizes and configurations.

Interestingly, a single SAP solution may utilize servers from one, two, or all three categories. For instance, SAP solutions are commonly designed to leverage a high-end server for the database tier, a mid-tier server platform for the SAP central instance or applications servers, and perhaps very inexpensive servers to address web server needs, noncritical bolt-on solutions, and so on. Conversely, other SAP IT departments might choose to put all their SAP components on only a few high-end servers that can be carved up into partitions or virtual machines as necessary. And some small/medium businesses (SMBs) may choose to run SAP solely on low-cost servers (relying on SAP's built-in application server horizontal scalability to keep them out of trouble should their workload grow). In any case, overall system availability, a comprehensive total cost of ownership analysis (reflecting technology, people, and process costs over time as well as up front), and anticipated future business requirements should drive your hardware platform decision.

Several of the largest and certainly best-known hardware vendors use proprietary CPU chips in their servers and support a proprietary OS as well. IBM's PowerPC chip running AIX is a good example, as are HP's end-of-life PA-RISC and more contemporary Itanium2-based IA64 platforms running HP-UX. Be sure to investigate your platform's ability to host other operating systems as well; this can be beneficial down the road when you need to retire your SAP system and seek to redeploy it internally rather than toss it in the dumpster. HP's IA64 chips support Windows, Linux, and OpenVMS, for example, whereas Sun's latest offerings support Solaris, Windows, and Linux.

Clearly the trend of late is around deploying low-cost servers based on commodity CPU chips from Intel and AMD (often referred to generically as "x64" platforms). HP and Dell are the biggest players in this market, though Sun offers a bit of choice here as well. Interestingly, these platforms are growing more and more powerful each year, supplanting some of the bigger server platforms in the process. Commodity server form factors continue to expand and provide IT departments with choice—from dense blades to slim-line "pizza box" designs to more traditional big-box designs. Meanwhile, hardware vendors in this space continue to develop high-availability, virtualization, and other technologies and solutions that help put these servers on more of an equal footing with their proprietary counterparts. In all the excitement and hype surrounding these well-performing upstarts, though, take care not to overlook trade offs. Low cost up front doesn't always translate to low cost over a system's lifetime, for example.

When purchasing servers and associated hardware for SAP, consider investing in the high-availability features offered for the platform, even if an additional charge is involved. Most servers offer redundant power supplies, redundant memory, disk array (RAID) controllers capable of running even after a disk drive fails, and support for multiple network interfaces cards (NICs) to avoid failure of a network segment, network switch, or single card. Leveraging these technologies will certainly increase the overall uptime of your SAP solution, typically adding only incremental cost in the process.

Server networks should be configured in a redundant fashion as well. In many IT data centers, the network represents a major—and avoidable—single point of failure. Dual switches and the use of the aforementioned redundant NICs can eliminate or mitigate what otherwise could be a major outage. Of course, these NICs and switches must be properly and professionally installed, cabled, and configured to actually work well; attention to high availability is just as important after the purchase as beforehand.

Disk Subsystem Hardware

Most server hardware vendors also sell disk subsystems, which are essentially enclosures for multiple disk drives used by SAP and other applications to house the application's database, its installation binaries or executables, and so on.

The most robust and well-performing disk subsystems today are in the form of storage area networks (SANs) and to a lesser extent network-attached storage (NAS) systems. Similar to how servers are marketed, vendors sell low-tier, mid-tier, and high-end SANs and NAS devices. At a minimum, the storage chosen for SAP should support redundant connectivity between the storage and the servers connected to it, so as to avoid a single point of failure. RAID (Redundant Array of Inexpensive Disks) level 0, 1, 5, or 10 should be configured as well to protect against disk failures. As Table 4.1 suggests, different RAID levels provide various combinations of availability, cost, and performance.

TABLE 4.1 Disk Subsystem RAID Types, Advantages, and Disadvantages

RAID Level	Method of Availability	Advantages and Disadvantages
RAID 0	Disk striping	Spans multiple disks, all of which are available for storage. RAID 0 is great when maximum space is needed, and it provides excellent performance as well. However, no disk redundancy is afforded, and it's not viable for production systems.
RAID 1	Disk mirroring	Mirroring provides best-in-class performance and excellent redundancy, although it's costly (a 500GB database requires a terabyte of raw disk capacity at minimum).
RAID 5	Disk striping with parity	Stripes data with parity, making for wonderful disk read performance, though to some extent a disk write penalty; excellent redundancy balanced by best-in-class low cost.
RAID 10	Disk mirroring and striping	Data is both striped and mirrored; best performance and redundancy, although this is the most costly method of providing disk subsystem availability.

High-end SAN storage typically supports advanced replication technologies, too, which can be useful for disaster recovery purposes among other things. Be sure to look into such capabilities—the ability to copy data between remotely connected SANs or to create "snapshots" of SAP databases on the fly is useful in many different ways, from enabling rapid system backups, to allowing systems to be cloned for offline testing and training, to supporting disaster and business continuity requirements in the wake of a severe data center outage.

SAP-Supported Operating Systems

An operating system (OS) is software that allows applications to interface with a computer or server. The OS is the middleman, making a system's hardware accessible to an application sitting atop the OS while providing basic services to applications (such as file sharing, support for network connections, and so on) in the process. Operating systems such as Microsoft Windows Server, Red Hat and SUSE Linux, and the many popular UNIX variants (HP-UX, AIX, and Solaris) are common in today's SAP environments. Even the occasional IBM iSeries or AS/400 (running the OS400 operating system) or mainframe (running z/OS) can be found supporting SAP today as well.

Figuring out which is the best for your solution can be a daunting task, however. More and more, the OS playing field is being leveled. Robust 64-bit technology in the commodity server market has many SAP shops rethinking their strategy. When choosing an OS, it all comes down to relationship, confidence, supportability, and particularly your in-house IT skill sets and personal biases. To this end, always take care to factor in your current in-house skill sets, comfort levels, and ability to be "retooled." The cost and time of retraining or hiring additional resources can weigh significantly on an IT department. And as with your hardware decisions, look for a company that has a solid relationship with SAP and verifiable satisfied client references.

In 2007, SAP announced it would generally only support 64-bit operating environments for new installations going forward. As SAP software evolves and low-cost 64-bit hardware becomes more prevalent, the need to run 32-bit servers and therefore 32-bit operating systems is falling by the wayside. Don't waste your time on such environments. Unless the company is already running an older version of SAP or has some odd bolt-on software only supported in 32-bit environments, there is simply no need to run a 32-bit server and OS in an SAP environment anymore.

Basic OS Features

Some of the features to look for in an OS are memory management, crash recovery, patch management, security, and advanced features such as clustering capabilities. Other things to consider when choosing an OS are support for third-party management utilities or the presence of built-in ones. Take a look at how the management and monitoring solutions in your IT environment today might fit with your prospective SAP solutions and the possible OS choices you face. Utilities such as monitoring applications, virus-scanning utilities, and backup software need to be validated to make sure they will work with existing toolsets as well as with SAP. In some cases, new toolsets must be invested in, which may not be cost effective or consistent with your IT department's future vision.

SAP File Systems and the Role of the OS

SAP in relationship to an OS is a set of executables and libraries that allow users though various front ends to connect to application servers to submit and retrieve data to an SAP database. SAP starts multiple OS-level services and processes, thereby making efficient use of a server's available memory and CPU power. A UNIX or Linux OS containing an SAP instance has a directory named /usr/sap (or x:\usr\sap in the case of Windows) that contains several subdirectories with executables, log files, and profiles. In Windows, x:\usr\sap is shared as SAPMNT and is accessible as \\servername\sapmnt. On a Windows server with multiple instances of SAP and a single OS installation, all SAP instances must be installed to the same SAPMNT directory; there can be only one SAPMNT share. In UNIX, /sapmnt is mounted as an NFS (network file system) mount, whereas /usr/sap/<SID> is a local file system.

In both UNIX and Windows, the SAP system identified (SID) is at the next directory level. See Figures 4.2 and 4.3 for the SAP directory structures of a Windows and a UNIX system for SAP, respectively. In Windows, the service SAPOSCOL runs the OS collector and allows SAP to gather OS-related performance and other statistics such as CPU utilization, memory utilization, disk input/output (I/O) activity, and more. All SAP systems contain one instance of the OS collector, although this collector is not required for SAP system operation.

Another Windows service is SAPService<SID>, where <SID> is the system identifier of the SAP instance. One SAPService<SID> exists for each instance of SAP on a machine, and it is started using sapstartsrv.exe. The service is started by the SAP service account of the <SID>adm account, depending on SAP version. This service calls the SAP start profile, which tells the system how to start SAP and registers a number of environmental variables. Suffice it to say here that these matters can be fairly complex.

The term *SAP system* refers to a single system or collection of systems hosted by one database that uses one SID name (system identifier). For example, an SAP ERP production system named PRD may consist of one database (nearly always), one central instance, and perhaps two, eight, or sixty different application servers, depending on workload. This collection of multiple SAP instances and the database make up an SAP system. Thus, an SAP instance is synonymous with one installed component (or "installation") of SAP on a server (also called a "host"). One host can contain multiple SAP instances, too, which belong to different SAP systems.

FIGURE 4.2
SAP file systems installed on Windows SAP systems.

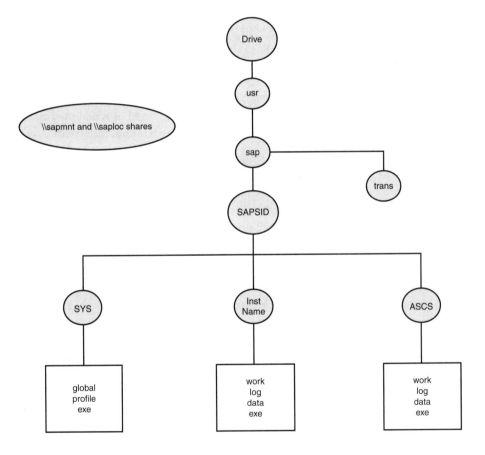

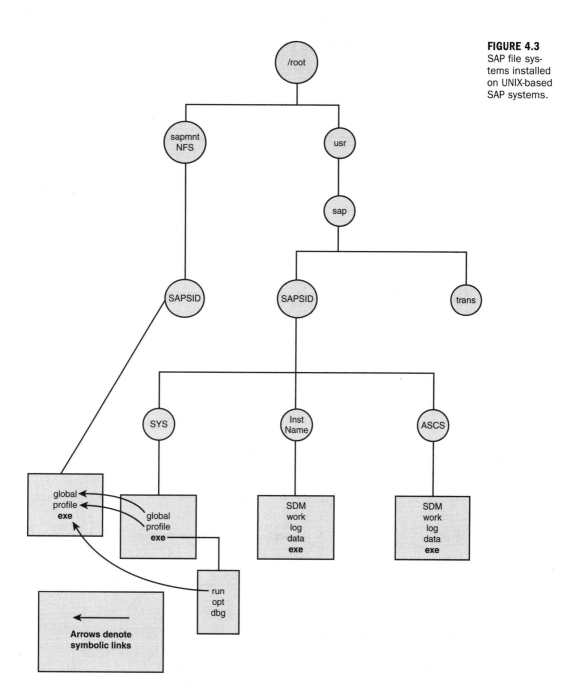

FIGURE 4.3
SAP file systems installed on UNIX-based SAP systems.

SAP OS-Level Work Processes

At an OS level, SAP has eight different work process types, as detailed in Table 4.2. Sometimes you will see them referenced as DVEBMSG. The *D* equates to dialog work processes, whereas the *V* references update work processes (differentiated by V1 and V2 priority types), *E* is enqueue, *B* is for background/batch jobs, *M* is the message service, *S* is used for print spooling, and *G* represents the SAP gateway. The instance profile of an SAP instance dictates how many of each type of process will start at system startup time. You can see which work processes your OS is running by running an applet or utility on the OS itself or using SAP's own transactions SM50 and SM66. Though we are getting ahead of ourselves, this ability to review the status of your SAP work processes is very important; beyond providing a view into the system's workload, it also reveals in real time the status of the system in terms of what each work process is performing on a particular SAP instance or group of instances. SM50 shows you only the work processes on the current application server you are logged in to, whereas SM66 gives you a global work process overview; SM66 is your window into what is happening with every active work process running across an entire SAP system.

TABLE 4.2   SAP Work Processes

Work Process Type	Description
Dialog	D: Processes real-time information in the foreground.
Background	B: Background processing for long-running processes, reports, and batch jobs.
Synchronous Update	V1: Processes immediate updates to the database.
Asynchronous Update	V2: Processes updates to the database on a lower priority than V1 (that is, when time permits).
Enqueue	E: Manages database locks.
Message	M: Manages communication between application servers.
Spool	S: Manages print jobs (the print spool).
Gateway	G: Communicates with other SAP and non-SAP systems.

SAP OS-Level Profiles

SAP contains three profiles: the default, start, and instance profiles. Profiles are essentially text files that, for the purposes of version control, are imported into and maintained by the SAP database. The default profile contains information common to all instances of SAP in an SAP system. For example, PRD may have a database, central instance, and three application servers; these would all use the same default profile. The start profile calls the executables to start SAP. Finally, the instance profile contains detailed information for each SAP instance in a system that makes up a common <SID>. This detailed information reflects specific memory configuration parameters, defines how buffers and work processes are defined and utilized, and a myriad of other information as well. Use SAP transaction RZ10 to change and maintain all these profiles, and to access a handy list of all available profile parameters.

Database Basics for SAP

With hardware and operating system details behind us, it is now time to turn our attention to the role of the database underneath an SAP business application. The same care that goes into choosing a hardware platform and OS should be used when choosing a database. Depending on your platform and SAP version, you may be restricted to only a few database choices (which underscores the importance of looking at your SAP infrastructure holistically). SAP tends to support most mainstream databases such as Microsoft SQL Server, IBM DB2, and Oracle's ubiquitous database offerings. SAP also supports its very own database called MaxDB, which has an interesting history of acquisitions and continues to grow in popularity. More common for SAP-on-Linux platforms, MaxDB is an interesting and low-cost alternative to the other primary SAP-supported database offerings. Indeed, it is serving to level the playing field in the same way that commodity hardware and OS solutions are leveling the hardware and operating system playing fields.

Most IT departments choose a database based on what their current database administrators (DBAs) are familiar with or know. In the past, it has been a daunting task to retrain DBAs for a new database platform, particularly one associated with mission critical applications such as SAP. Today, though, low-overhead database offerings from Microsoft and IBM are making this transition easier.

Relative to selecting a database platform for SAP, you need to base your decision in part on the advanced functionality of database software you may need to meet your business user's response-time and availability requirements. Microsoft SQL Server and Oracle both support log shipping and clustering technologies for increasing the availability of SAP systems. Log shipping allows you to maintain a secondary copy of your SAP (or any) database on another system to fail over to in case of a disaster situation. Sometimes log shipping is called "poor man's DR." Regardless, it is a robust and widely used technology for SAP as much as any other business application.

A Database Primer

Whichever database you choose, enterprise applications such as SAP are essentially made up of programs along with the data that is both used by and created by those programs. The data is organized in a meaningful way within a database, making it easy for the programs to access and find the data necessary to do something useful like run a financial report or create a sales order. In the case of an SAP component or product such as ERP, the programs and data reside together in the same database. Each component generally has its own database (although exceptions exist)— a production system landscape composed of SAP ERP, SAP NetWeaver Portal (EP), and SAP Customer Relationship Management (CRM) consists of three production databases, for example.

A database is essentially an electronic filing system that houses a collection of information organized in such a way that it allows a computer program to quickly find desired pieces of data. In the simplest form, a database is composed of tables, columns (called fields), and rows (called *records* or *data*). The basic structure of a database is quite similar to the well-known Microsoft Excel spreadsheet, where columns (fields) store row after row of records (data). The biggest difference between a database and a spreadsheet is simply that databases can contain multiple (and extremely large) tables that are connected to one another through relationships. Thus, a database can be thought of as a much more complex, and ultimately much more useful, spreadsheet. The database plays a key role in each SAP system because it houses all the data used by that particular SAP component or application.

Tables, Indexes, and Structure

The SAP database contains literally thousands of tables that store information. Some products, such as ERP, comprise greater than 30,000 tables, whereas less complex offerings such as SAP NetWeaver Process Integration (PI) might have fewer than 10,000. It is noteworthy to know that in most SAP systems, 10% of the tables house 90% of the data, so some tables can get quite large and be subject to constant change, whereas others tend to remain very small and relatively static. Regardless of the number, though, these various tables are all tied to each other through established relationships. It is precisely this series of connected multiple tables that creates what is known as a *relational database management system (RDBMS)*.

Databases are made up of indexes, too; whereas tables house the data, indexes are used to speed up the retrieval of data from those tables. An index might best be described as a copy of a database table reduced to only the key fields. The data in this reduced copy is sorted according to some predefined criteria, enabling rapid access to the data. Not all fields from the copied table exist in the index, and the index contains a pointer to the associated record of the actual table. You might be surprised to know that indexes make up approximately 50% of the overall size of an SAP database!

SAP uses another concept called *transparent tables*, which are SAP database tables that only contain data at runtime. A transparent table is automatically created in the database when a table is activated in the ABAP/4 Data Dictionary. This transparent table contains the same name as your database table in the ABAP/4 Dictionary. Each of its fields also contains the same names as their database counterparts, although the sequence of the fields might change. The varying field sequence makes it possible to insert new fields into the table without having to convert it, all of which allows for more rapid access to data during runtime.

Database structure is another technical term that you really do not need to concern yourself with too much, but it's important nonetheless. Simply remember that database structures are a group of internal fields that logically belong together. Structures are activated and defined in the ABAP/4 Data Dictionary and only contain data temporarily—during the execution of a program. Structures are differentiated from database tables based on the following three criteria:

▶ A structure does not contain or reflect an associated ABAP/4 Data Dictionary table.

▶ A structure does not contain a primary key.

▶ A structure does not have any technical properties such as class, size, category, or buffering specifications.

Partnering with Your Infrastructure Providers

As you have seen, there is much to consider when developing an infrastructure design or plan for SAP. Choosing an infrastructure provider or network of providers is therefore serious business. Do not just automatically choose a hardware, OS, or database vendor your company is already familiar with in the context of desktop PCs or laptop purchases. Look to your data center standards first, to get a sense of whom you might already be comfortable with. And then look at competitors. It is certainly a fine strategy to choose a hardware partner you know and trust, for example, but too much is at stake to not conduct a more thorough assessment.

Be sure to investigate any prospective infrastructure providers in light of their relationship with SAP. Do they have a long history of partnering with SAP? Are they "certified" for SAP, or do they hold SAP's Global Technology Partner status? Check with potential providers for SAP-specific customer references, and follow up by talking with these references over the phone or via an onsite visit if possible. After all, it is helpful to see and hear from other customers; their experiences with SAP and your other likely infrastructure partners can really shed some light on whether your proposed infrastructure solution will provide the foundation the company needs. References in a similar industry or reflecting SAP components and products hosting similar workloads or scope are even more valuable.

Attending an SAP tradeshow such as SAP TechEd, ASUG, or any number of SAP Insider conferences is a great place to meet other SAP customers as well as potential infrastructure providers. SAP is generally happy to make these introductions, but don't fear striking out on your own. This process is akin to peer support, similar to what is seen in the open-systems arena. Many SAP customers have peer contacts with other companies, sometimes even their own competitors, which can be leveraged to share various experiences and technical challenges as well as answer questions related to how well the provider supports and maintains its customers *after* money changes hands.

Bottom line: It is not advisable to bet your SAP environment's viability on a whim, on a relationship that has not been vetted over time or shown to be fruitful by others, or on a little-used technology. Save your cutting-edge IT decisions for something less critical and less essential to the company's financial well-being. Finally, do your homework, and do it early—before all the SAP project's budget money is spent on consultants!

Summary

In Hour 4, we covered the key components of SAP infrastructure: hardware, operating systems, and databases. And we looked at what it means to choose and partner with the vendors that will ultimately work together to create your infrastructure platform for SAP. A new SAP implementation requires a solid, well-thought-out foundation. Leverage the information presented here when researching the best alternatives for your company, keeping in mind the following:

▶ Does my current hardware provider have solutions for SAP?

▶ Does my current hardware provider have a relationship with SAP?

▶ What are the current in-house skill sets at my company that may be called upon to support the SAP solution?

Ask the same types of questions in relationship to your operating system and database providers, and then perform an apples-to-apples cost and capabilities analysis to really vet out the right fit for your company and its SAP environment.

Case Study: Hour 4

In light of your newfound hardware, operating system, and database knowledge, consider this hour's case study and answer the questions that follow. Answers may be found in Appendix A, "Case Study Answers."

Situation

MNC Global recently acquired a company in the process of upgrading to a new release of SAP ERP 6.0. Currently, the acquisition runs SAP R/3 4.6C hosted by IBM on older 32-bit hardware, running AIX 5.x and an older release of Oracle (8.1.7), all connected to a best-in-class third party storage system. The $6M annual price tag associated with hosting is greater than MNC wishes to spend in the future, though. Fortunately, the outsourcing contract is coming to a close in the next 12 months. Thus, the combined company has made a strategic decision to in-source its new SAP environment in an effort to provide greater flexibility to its business while hopefully cutting IT costs in the process. The current SAP R/3 database is 500GB in size and supports about 1000 users.

MNC has several options as they see it. First, they can buy new IBM AIX-supported equipment and move the database to MNC's local datacenter. In this way, they can stay on the same platform, making the technical transition fairly straightforward. Once the system is hosted in-house, the upcoming SAP technical upgrade could then be performed. Neither MNC nor the firm being acquired has IBM AIX expertise in house, but both are strong when it comes to Oracle administration and support.

Another option put forth by MNC's IT department is to buy less-expensive commodity hardware and move SAP to a new platform. MNC IT has grown comfortable with supporting Microsoft Windows and both Oracle and SQL Server over the last several years, and is anxious to apply their knowledge to SAP. Such a transition or "replatforming" to a Windows platform would cost $500K in consulting and migration services and another $2M annually in hardware, OS, and database licenses, acquisition, and ongoing maintenance costs. The technical upgrade could then be performed afterwards. While MNC Global has the skill-sets in the datacenter to host the new platform, the acquired company has very little SAP Basis knowledge and MNC has only begun to develop its own in-house SAP expertise.

Questions

1. For each hardware/OS/database platform choice outlined above, list several advantages.

2. What are the disadvantages or potential challenges for each platform?

3. In your estimation, is there a clear option or path that MNC Global should choose?

4. Is there another potentially good alternative that might need to be explored?

5. What new performance enhancing technology is available to MNC Global when the move is made to a new platform and upgrade is performed?

Developing a Technical Roadmap for Deploying SAP

What You'll Learn in This Hour:

▶ Key installation planning tasks

▶ Technical preparation tasks

▶ Basic technical considerations

▶ Technical team staffing considerations

With the business roadmap and IT basics behind us, it's time to turn our attention to planning for and developing a high-level technical roadmap for SAP. This is therefore a necessarily high-level hour of instruction; further information may be found in Hour 12, "Implementing SAP: A Technical Perspective," and Hour 15, "Technical Installation of SAP." Installing SAP may be broken down into three phases: planning, pre-installation, and installation. This hour focuses squarely on the first of these, whereas Hours 12 and 15 cover the next two areas, respectively.

From Business to Technical Implementation Planning

Once the business blueprinting and project management tasks are addressed, as outlined in previous hours, the next phase in planning for an SAP deployment involves outlining a technical roadmap. Central to this roadmap is identifying the technical infrastructure underpinning SAP's components and products, starting with selecting the actual components to be deployed (based on the business requirements outlined earlier). Blueprinting and design work then give way to questions of how to integrate the various SAP and third-party applications, the specific development and testing methodology to be put into place, and finally the evaluation and selection of the SAP infrastructure platform—a combination of hardware, one or more operating systems, and a database release.

Next, hardware sizing for each component must be completed in conjunction with identifying system landscape requirements, addressing server and disk configuration, performing network planning, reviewing various end-user access strategies, and beginning the process of addressing a myriad of other technically oriented operational issues. If you're beginning to get lost in the complexity of it all, a great place to start is with SAP's own installation guides, outlined next.

Master Installation Guides

Preparing for installing SAP—not to mention the actual installation process—can be confusing at first blush. One often overlooked key to successful SAP installations is reading (and following!) the excellent installation documentation provided by SAP, starting with the SAP component-specific Master Guide. The Master Guides are worth their weight in gold. Use them. For example, if you are tasked with installing SAP ERP 6.0, simply download the "SAP ERP 6.0 powered by SAP NetWeaver 7.0 Master Guide" to get a quick handle of what this particular installation entails. The Master Guide provides a wealth of valuable information, and it also points you to where to go for the actual electronic media required for your installation (assuming you don't have your SAP DVDs handy). The Master Guide also covers different installation scenarios, which essentially guide you through installing the different combinations of software components necessary to create a particular technical foundation for an SAP solution. For example, if your company has decided to implement SAP Employee Self-Services (ESS) and SAP Manager Self-Services (MSS), the Master Guide serves as your high-level roadmap, explaining the installation sequence for each particular implementation scenario. With all the details spelled out, it's difficult to go wrong.

Obtaining the SAP installation guides and associated installation-specific notes (SAP Notes) is not as confusing as it might appear. The installation guides are available from the SAP service marketplace under keyword *instguides* (http://service.sap.com/instguides), whereas the relevant notes may be searched for via http://service.sap.com/notes (the latter of which requires an SAP Service Marketplace user ID). For example, to install an Oracle-based SAP Web Application Server (WebAS) on the Linux operating system, the first step would be to download the following:

▶ Part I—Planning and Preparation

▶ Part II—Installation and Post-Installation

▶ Note 171356—SAP software on Linux: Essential Information

▶ Note 958253—SUSE LINUX Enterprise Server 10: Installation Notes

Before SAP is technically deployed, it only makes sense to outline exactly *what* is being deployed and under what circumstances and scenarios. An ABAP+Java implementation of SAP Enterprise Portal front-ending ERP, CRM, and SRM is a much different technical solution than a classic ABAP-derived SAP ERP implementation, after all. So again, take the time to read through the guides to determine if you're indeed ready to continue. Are you missing a particular piece of software? Do you have all the latest patches and updates recommended by the installation guides? Are your server and disk platform standards up to the task? These and other questions need to be addressed before you move on.

Setting the Stage: Landscape and System Sizing

A typical SAP environment consists of multiple SAP instances (or installations) in a landscape. A three-system landscape is still the most common approach and comprises the development system, quality assurance or test system, and production system. IT organizations interested in doing technical training or having a safe place to try new installations will add a sandbox system to this list. In the same way, instances for testing new components and functionality, dedicated business training systems, and production break/fix or "staging" systems are also common in many environments.

So, from a technical roadmap perspective, determine what your system landscape is going to look like before you actually start doing any installations. And just as importantly, take a critical look at how these various systems are architected, or "sized." This is discussed next.

Architecture and Hardware Sizings

Before an SAP installation is ever performed, someone must plan for, or "architect," the SAP environment. This design process is called *sizing*. Decisions have to be made as to which SAP components are going to be deployed, and how they will be deployed. For example, the number of application servers must be taken into consideration given the workload expected to be hosted by SAP. Also, the size of the database server—the most critical component of all, given that it hosts all the company's data—must be determined. Other metrics or sizing dimensions must be taken into account. How scalable does the system need to be? What kind of availability or disaster recoverability is necessary to meet the business's needs without breaking the IT bank? What kind of online response time performance is acceptable, particularly under changing workloads such as those associated with month-end financial closings?

To answer these questions, the customer IT department works with SAP, their prime integrator (Big 4), and their hardware partner. Combined, all these partners will lend their expertise and knowledge of real-world SAP deployments to help the customer design a system that truly meets the business's needs. Sizing is a balancing act between what the business thinks its new system needs to do and how it needs to perform. Sizing is also an art; there are literally hundreds of unique solutions capable of hosting a 1000-user SAP ERP workload, for example. Our recommendation is to start the sizing process early. Engage the business as quickly as possible. Listen to their business application, performance, and availability requirements, and then help the prime integrator and hardware partners translate these requirements into robust and properly architected SAP sizings.

ABAP and Java Architecture

Before sizing, it's necessary to determine the technical stack that will eventually be deployed. The SAP NetWeaver platform supports both ABAP and Java stacks, either alone or in conjunction with one another. Typically the decision as to which platform to use is dictated by the SAP components being deployed. For example, Employee Self-Service requires Java, whereas ERP 6.0 requires ABAP.

How do you find out which technology stack you need to install? Turn to your Master Guide. The SAP Master Guides outline the required components for a scenario as well as the underlying technology stack (ABAP or Java). The SAP enterprise architecture needs to specify the number and function of the underlying servers for each component, too, and whether they require Java or ABAP. Look to your functional team leadership to help determine which might be most appropriate when there's a choice.

Hardware Sizing

With the technology stack noted, it now falls to someone to take the list of all the required SAP components and products and convert this into a hardware-focused architecture. Beyond the list of software components (such as SAP ERP 6.0), the modules being deployed and the number of users for each module are important—the number and their "weight" (heavy, medium, or low) will help the hardware partners make the right choices in terms of memory and processing power required for each server.

All SAP-certified partners maintain an SAP Competency Center (if not several, perhaps based on geography or specialization). The output of these typically time-consuming and very detailed sizing efforts is a diagram and bill of materials reflecting the SAP software components and the associated servers (including number of CPUs and RAM required) for each landscape and component. The solution sizing also accounts for acceptable performance, availability, and scalability, as noted earlier; any required disaster recovery solutions or other technology components are detailed in the sizing, too.

The solution must also reflect whether the various SAP application servers are going to run Java, ABAP, or both. For example, you might very well choose to install WebAS ABAP+Java and run both ERP and ESS on the same server. For larger systems, or systems where the workload might be less understood, the architect might configure these systems to run on separate servers. In the end, most of these decisions can be revisited; it is recommended that you take a conservative approach at first, and then let your budget and data center constraints drive any final tuning and tweaking of your SAP sizings.

High Availability and Performance

Arguably, availability and performance are probably the two most important considerations in your SAP architecture. There are many high-availability options for SAP installations, each of which depends on the hardware platform, operating system, and integration requirements. Options such as hardware-based clustering and replicated SAP enqueue provide protection for the database and central instance against unplanned downtime. SAP applications servers are normally made highly available through a combination of redundancy in the form of multiple application servers and the use of SAP logon groups. Other high-availability offerings can prove useful as well; look to Microsoft SQL Server database mirroring and Oracle Real Application Clusters (RAC) for HA solutions that begin to approximate disaster recovery solutions, as covered next.

Disaster Recoverability

Once SAP is deployed, it is very likely the business will depend on the new system's availability for the firm's very existence. With all the firm's revenue flowing through the system, and all the books of record maintained in one place, it's simply not acceptable to just have some kind of plan in case of a disaster. In conjunction with business interruption or business continuity planning, a disaster recovery (DR) plan is necessary—it marries the business side of DR with technical requirements.

SAP and its hardware and software partners support many different disaster recovery solutions. Some of these are hardware specific and therefore demand attention during the sizing and architecture phases. Other "bolt-on" DR solutions can be addressed later in your technical roadmap. Here's a list of some of the more common disaster recovery solutions:

▶ Basic backup/restore from tape or disk (an essential part of any disaster recovery plan, which may or may not include the options that follow)

▶ Database log shipping (for example, via Oracle or SQL Server)

▶ Solutions involving storage replication technologies (for example, via your EMC, HP, or IBM storage systems, or software-based solutions)

Well before you ever think about purchasing a DR system, spend your time talking with colleagues or peers at other firms who have already implemented a similar solution.

You might be surprised at how complex DR solutions can become once all the business requirements and technology constraints are brought to bear. By the same token, leverage your hardware and OS partners for real-world lessons learned and other takeaways.

Back to the Basics: Addressing Technical Roadmap Gaps

Up to this point, much of our discussions have been focused on SAP rather than the technologies that enable SAP to run. Now it is time to turn our attention to these more foundational technical matters, from client access strategies, to network and storage considerations, to backup strategies and more. Our technical roadmap is nearing completion.

Client Access Strategy

A client access strategy answers the question of how an SAP application's end-user community will actually access the system. Will they use a common web browser and connect over the Internet? Will they dial up or connect via a Citrix account? Will they launch SAP's very own "fat client" SAP graphical user interface? Or will they perhaps perform a combination of these activities, depending on the application they're accessing or which office they are sitting in?

Each client access strategy has its own set of advantages and disadvantages. Regardless of method, each strategy requires some kind of network connection between the SAP user and the data center housing the SAP servers and data. Users at headquarters may leverage their fast access over the local area network (LAN), whereas remote office users might connect over slower wide area network (WAN) links. Meanwhile, home-based users might dial-in via a phone line to a Citrix server farm (and still enjoy excellent response time performance!), whereas a company's suppliers and vendors may be given ubiquitous access over the Internet. In some cases, companies (including SAP itself, as it seeks to help its clients manage their systems) find that deploying Terminal Services or Citrix is a key element of their access strategy. The key to determining the best access strategy falls back to balancing the level of functionality required by the user against what constitutes acceptable performance delivered in a secure manner.

Network Considerations

To install SAP, all that is seemingly needed from a network perspective is for the SAP servers to be available on the network and to have an IP address. But for the network team, matters aren't quite this simple—a network architecture has to be developed that encompasses access, security, provisioning, and a host of various network services. Fortunately, the bulk of IT organizations tasked with supporting an SAP implementation are well aware of these requirements simply because of all the other mission-critical applications they have likely already been supporting.

One of the major considerations in a network design for SAP is related to whether each environment (production, test, development, and so on) will have its own network segment.

> Within each system of an SAP system landscape, it is further possible—and often desired—to create separate network segments. Some of these might be dedicated to end-user access, whereas others might serve only the intense database-to-application server traffic, or traffic dedicated to network-based server backups. A fourth network segment might even be designated for systems management and monitoring traffic. In all these cases, the overwhelming need is based on preserving network speed or throughput without sacrificing network speed elsewhere, particularly speed needed by the SAP system's end users.

By the Way

The availability of SAP components through the Internet (if applicable) must also be addressed. The goal of all this is to provide a secure environment for the SAP servers without impacting the application's ultimate functionality. Depending on the specific situation, the network might need special firewalls or proxy servers or other such devices targeted to provide a more secure environment for SAP.

SAN and Other Disk Considerations

For capacity and performance reasons, SAP databases typically require SAN-based storage—high-performance, high-capacity storage systems that, like networks, have been designed to provide a service (in this case, data storage). For an SAP installation to proceed, the SAN/disk team needs to allocate storage space from the SAN, first for all the SAP application DVD images and other installation media, and next for the various file systems required by SAP. This normally includes space for the database housing SAP's master and transactional data, SAP's binaries or executables, space for the database's logs and other temporary needs, and more.

Most SAP implementations require a storage infrastructure designed for excellent performance and outstanding availability. There are many considerations for storage design (refer again to Hour 4, "Infrastructure Technology Basics: Hardware, Operating Systems, and Databases"). Suffice it to say here that designing and deploying a well-performing SAN is a project unto itself. From determining file system layouts and allocating LUNs to assigning these chucks of disk space to host servers and then running fiber cables between host servers, SAN infrastructure switches, and the database, this is essentially a complex and mission-critical architecture project similar to designing a well-performing and highly available network.

Backup Strategy

It is important to develop a backup/recovery strategy prior to Go-Live. The backup/recovery strategy doesn't affect the SAP installation process—it generally involves something such as loading a backup agent on the database server. You have probably heard it before, but testing the backup/recovery strategy is a vital step before Go-Live.

Technical Support Organization Staffing

A technical roadmap is incomplete without discussing the need to develop the technical organization responsible for deploying and managing SAP. One of the most valuable resources behind an SAP implementation, this group of technical resources affects in a variety of ways what will eventually become a mission-critical production system. This includes everything from installing the system to maintaining steady-state operations, minimizing downtime via smartly applied change management practices, calculating the impact of growing workloads down the road, spearheading to business-aligned IT projects, planning for and completing SAP functional migrations, and more. Such a team typically comprises the following:

▶ The management team, consisting initially of project resources and later a combination of project and steady-state/operational folks.

▶ A data center team tasked with deploying and managing the server and SAN infrastructure, the network infrastructure, and the racks, cooling equipment, and overall facilities making up an enterprise data center site.

▶ A server team tasked with racking and building out servers, loading operating systems, and generally preparing and maintaining the various database, application, Internet, and other servers for the specific roles they will play in the SAP landscape.

▶ A SAN/disk subsystem team responsible for SAN design, deployment, performance, and maintenance oversight. The SAN/disk team plays a critical role given that the lifeblood of the system—the data—sits squarely within its area of responsibility.

▶ A security team composed of both physical security specialists and SAP-specific security specialists; this team is responsible for ensuring the integrity and safety of the system across the board.

▶ A database team responsible for deployment and administration, working closely with the SAN/disk and SAP Basis teams.

▶ A computer operations team tasked with ensuring that backup and restore, systems monitoring, and basic availability tasks are regularly and proactively addressed.

▶ An SAP Basis team responsible for the planning, deployment, and ongoing technical management of the SAP applications themselves, including SAP administration and maintenance. Given its central role in the project, it's not surprising that the SAP Basis team works very closely with every other team listed.

Only a well-structured and completely staffed SAP IT organization can pull off a new implementation, much less maintain an SAP production system over many years. Although the list of teams provided here might seem extensive, this is only the beginning. Work with your prime integrator, hardware partners, SAP, and existing IT department to determine the best mix of teams and resources given your unique SAP system landscape and project constraints.

Did you Know?

At the end of the day, once all the technical implementation roadmap planning is out of the way, the people tasked with actually managing the project, installing SAP, and configuring the system will have a much better chance of implementation success. You'll certainly be clear as to the questions to ask and how the system must first be technically readied for your installation, too, and thus be ready to finally install, for example, an ERP 6.0 ABAP-only instance and database on a pair of clustered HP ProLiant DL585 servers configured with four CPUs and 32GB of RAM each, running a particular version of Microsoft Windows 2008 and Oracle 10*g* atop an HP EVA storage production-ready system configured with 80 disk spindles, armed with network and backup strategies, and staffed by a technical support organization. But hold on a minute! There's still much to cover before we actually explore the detailed preplanning and finally the technical installation of an SAP component. In the next several hours, we first take a look at the myriad of SAP components and products, followed by a closer look at implementing SAP from three different perspectives— project management, business/functional, and finally technical. So thanks in advance for being patient. We'll get to the actual technical installation of SAP in no time!

Summary

In this hour, we have addressed the fundamental technical roadmap planning necessary to mesh the business requirements with the various technologies and technical considerations underpinning an SAP implementation. From addressing which components to plan for, along with architecture and sizing, we have also noted basic network, storage, and client access matters that need to be addressed well before SAP is installed. A brief introduction to the development of the SAP-specific IT teams necessary to deploy and maintain SAP concluded this hour.

Case Study: Hour 5

Consider this technical roadmap-related case study and questions that follow, the answers to which may be found in Appendix A, "Case Study Answers."

Situation

As a new Senior Technical Lead for MNC Global's upcoming Human Capital Management implementation, you have been asked to review the current state of affairs and recommend a basic technical organization structure. In your review, you note that MNC has excellent computer operations, server, and database administration teams, but that there seems to be poor alignment between the company's current mainframe computing standards and the proposed SAP ERP HCM environment (which is being built atop a Linux/Oracle platform). The company is also used to supporting mission-critical computing applications with development, test, and pre-production staging environments, though surprisingly the company has no formal experience with disaster recovery. Answer the following questions.

Questions

1. Are there any current technical teams that might not require reinvention or new/incremental staffing?

2. Where will you point the team to begin preparing for installation planning?

3. Would you recommend MNC Global maintain its current system landscape strategy?

4. MNC Global's HCM implementation includes ESS. Does this equate to an ABAP, Java, or ABAP+Java installation?

5. From a disaster recovery perspective, MNC is quite familiar and comfortable with performing regular tape backups and restores. What are two other types of DR solutions you might look into, though?

PART II

SAP Products and Components

HOUR 6

SAP Overview: SMB and Enterprise Products

What You'll Learn in This Hour:

▶ Key requirements for small and midsize enterprise (SME) solutions

▶ Detailed descriptions of SAP's SME solutions

▶ How to pick the right solution for your small or medium business

As you know by now, SAP is the market share leader for large enterprises. Were you aware, though, that SAP also has over 28,000 small and medium business (SMB) customers? Indeed, SAP is the market leader in what they term the small and midsize enterprise (SME) segment, with a 37% share of the market. In this hour, we will investigate SAP's various SME solutions and make some distinctions between these solutions and SAP's venerable Business Suite.

SME Requirements

In what may come as a surprise to you, SAP is not just for large firms. Although the SAP Business Suite has firmly planted SAP as the market leader in the Enterprise Business Software space, it is not for everyone. Simply put, small and medium businesses are different from large enterprises and have different business software requirements and a smaller financial appetite for what still amounts to a substantial IT investment. For these reasons, SAP markets three different solutions for the SME market: SAP Business One, SAP Business ByDesign, and SAP Business All-in-One. SAP has publicly stated that the SME area is where it expects to achieve much of the growth in its customer base over the next few years. In fact, SAP has a goal of achieving 100,000 installations by 2010—the key to which is its continuing success in the SME space.

Small and medium enterprises (SMEs) choose not to implement the SAP Business Suite for multiple reasons:

▶ The cost and complexity of the SAP Business Suite are certainly among of the factors. The cost of procuring and implementing the SAP Business Suite is often cost prohibitive to many SMEs.

▶ Many SMEs may not have the information technology (IT) staff necessary to maintain a powerful, complex business software package such as SAP's Business Suite—and they may have no desire to move in that direction.

▶ Many SMEs are risk adverse and full-blown SAP Business Suite implementations are fraught with risk—big budgets, tight timelines, and the potential impact to the business are among the many risks associated with full-blown SAP implementations.

▶ SMEs require software that is easy to use. They may lack the time to invest in training their end users on a more comprehensive or feature-rich business solution. They need software that allows workers to do their job without a lot of training, and from a technical perspective they need software that is easy to maintain and configure.

Problems SMEs Typically Face

Keep the following problems in mind as you read along this hour—with its three business solutions, these are some of the key business issues SAP is trying to resolve for SMEs:

▶ **Business integration and collaboration**—In many SMEs, work is sometimes duplicated because departments are using different applications that do not interface with each other.

▶ **Visibility and decision making**—This may make it difficult to get a clear picture of how the business is performing, thus requiring reports from different applications/individuals.

▶ **Regulatory compliance**—Regulatory compliance affects many small and medium businesses. This has become especially prominent since the passage of Sarbanes-Oxley in the U.S., but a host of other regulations affect SMEs.

Beyond these problems, picking the best solution still remains a critical decision for small and medium businesses, as outlined next.

Selecting the "Best" Solution

The "best" solution depends on many factors, including cost, required functionality, features, preference for onsite vs. hosted solutions, size, and complexity of the business processes to be configured. SAP provides a breadth of products, each targeted a bit differently at addressing these factors, which are detailed next.

Cost

The cost of any business software is much more than the initial cost of the software licenses. Cost is normally a very important factor in the decision-making process, so it is important that the true cost be determined. The following should be accounted for when determining the true cost of an SME solution:

▶ Initial costs, including licenses, installation, and configuration (especially true of on-premise rather than hosted solutions), the cost of data migration (from the current systems, if necessary), the cost of customization, and the cost of integration (with other systems that will remain intact, as applicable)

▶ Ongoing "operational" costs, including support (both technical and functional in nature) and software maintenance (an annual fee paid to the software provider)

Despite the initial outlay of cash, it's actually the ongoing costs that add up to represent the greatest expense over the business solution's lifetime.

Functionality

The solutions offered by SAP and their competitors may differ significantly in regards to functionality. The key here is to find a solution that meets the business' requirements—for example, it doesn't make sense to pay for functionality you will never use.

Features

Many of the features involve making the application easier to use. If two competing solutions provide approximately the same functionality, the solution providing the feature set most applicable to your business is probably the best choice.

Hosted or On-Premises?

One of the primary considerations is whether a business wants to house the solution on its premises or have it hosted by SAP or a partner. Business ByDesign is a hosted solution, whereas Business One and Business All-in-One are normally housed at the customer's site. Keep in mind that it is possible to have a partner host the on-premises solutions—for a fee, of course.

Number of Employees

SAP has established guidelines concerning the size of a business appropriate for each solution. Business One is generally targeted at companies with fewer than 100 employees. Part of this probably has to do with the underlying technology—Business One is designed to run on a single server and is therefore limited to some extent by the underlying computing platform which is comprised of hardware, operating system, database, and any requisite middleware. Business ByDesign is targeted at companies with between 100 and 500 employees—SAP requires that at least 25 users be licensed. At the high end, Business All-in-One is suitable for companies with between 100 and 2,500 employees.

Complexity of Business Processes

Business process complexity has to do with how customizable the software in question is. SAP Business All-in-One is very customizable—it is based on SAP ERP 2005 and runs on the NetWeaver platform (for more on what NetWeaver entails, see Hour 7, "Laying the Groundwork: SAP NetWeaver"). On the other hand, Business One is designed for small companies with relatively straightforward business processes. It is important to keep in mind that SAP partners have built solutions for specific industries and verticals; therefore, a prepackaged solution might already exist for your specific industry or business.

SAP Business One

The idea behind Business One is to replace isolated, disparate applications with an integrated software system handling customer relationship management (CRM), manufacturing, and financial solution requirements—much of what a small business needs in a single system.

SAP Business One is designed for small firms—those with typically fewer than 100 employees across five branches or locations and independent subsidiaries. SAP positions Business One as the ideal solution for multinational company subsidiaries because the solution is easily linked with SAP's Business Suite solution back at corporate headquarters (which is often employed by such multinational companies). Business One is designed to be affordable and is delivered to the customer via SAP's worldwide network of qualified business partners. Another key selling point is the solution's relatively short implementation time. In fact, whereas Business Suite implementations are measured in months (if not years), Business One implementations are typically measured in weeks. With such a small timeframe, it's easier to develop a quick estimate of the implementation cost, and the disruption and impact to the business are minimized as well.

Functionality

Like its more capable counterpart, Business One supports the following key business processes:

- ▶ Financial Management
- ▶ Warehouse Management
- ▶ Purchasing
- ▶ Inventory
- ▶ Manufacturing
- ▶ Banking
- ▶ Customer Relationship Management (CRM)

Business One also provides web-based customer management. Further, it allows for the implementation of an e-commerce solution, which in turn enables the business to market and sell goods and services online while providing integration with financials, inventory, and shipping information.

Features

One of the key features of Business One is that it increases control by providing almost instant access to all the business information in one system. Because Business One is a complete, integrated system, there may be no need to integrate it with other systems (although this is certainly possible). This results in savings in both integration costs and the maintenance costs associated with maintaining multiple systems.

Business One is designed to be easy to use; it includes the Drag & Relate feature, which provides users with end-to-end visibility into operations and allows for the easy creation of reports. The solution is also integrated with Microsoft Outlook, which supports management by exception alerting and business process workflow. Finally, SAP has designed the application to be easily customized without the need for expensive and time-consuming technical training.

Implementation

Business One is designed to be implemented quickly and provides for country-specific localizations. Business One is implemented on a single server—there's no need for the traditional SAP three-system landscape as described in Hour 4, "Infrastructure Technology Basics: Hardware, Operating Systems, and Databases." Changes can be implemented almost immediately because there are no development or quality assurance systems to contend with.

Technically speaking, Business One is implemented on the Windows Server platform. This makes for a straightforward installation and enables IT organizations with only moderate experience running Windows-based applications to quickly hit the ground running. Leveraging either Microsoft SQL Server or IBM DB2 Universal Database Express edition, Business One is not only simple to administer from a database perspective, but its database licensing costs won't reflect a great financial burden either.

Development

Business One is not simply a scaled-down version of existing SAP software components; it was in fact developed as a completely separate product. As such, development is different from a traditional SAP ERP environment. Mentioned earlier, most Business One customizations may be implemented without technical training and nearly instantaneously. Business One has its own software development kit (SDK). The SDK contains three APIs: a User Interface API, a Data Interface API, and the Java Connector. In addition, SAP partners have developed over 430 industry-specific and other solutions handy in extending Business One's usefulness across a growing enterprise.

SAP Business ByDesign

The newest SME offering from SAP, Business ByDesign, is designed for midsized companies with between 100 and 500 employees supporting multiple locations and independent subsidiaries. Business ByDesign was known by its codename, A1S, prior to its official launch on September 19, 2007. SAP initially rolled out Business

ByDesign to a small group of customers in only four countries, but availability continues to expand rapidly.

You may encounter the term *Software as a Service (SaaS)* or *software on-demand* when discussing Business ByDesign. This essentially means that SAP itself hosts the application while the customer only needs to busy itself with providing web-based access to its users. Customers pay a $149 monthly fee to SAP for each user (with a minimum of 25 users, and lower pricing for self-service users). The idea is structured around a pay-as-you-go concept, and the system can easily add users in the future. It's similar to a telephone or electric service—it's ubiquitous. SAP takes care of everything on the back end, leaving the customer to merely log in and get to work. SAP Business ByDesign allows customers to focus on their business, leaving SAP to worry about maintaining hardware and software, running database backups, addressing performance and capacity planning, implementing updates and fixes, and so on. By providing a standardized solution, SAP reduces the complexity, cost, and risk normally associated with introducing business software in an organization.

Business ByDesign is marketed as a complete, integrated solution designed to provide a low total cost of ownership (TCO), especially when compared to compiling and integrating a collection of miscellaneous "point" solutions, which when cobbled together provide the same or similar functionality. SAP does not position ByDesign as a competitor to Business One or Business All-in-One. Rather, it is a solution intended to fill a market of customers seeking to avoid investing in business software and all the necessary infrastructure and support personnel associated with such an investment.

Implementation and Adaptability

One of the primary advantages to Business ByDesign is the ease of configuration. Again, SAP developed Business ByDesign from the ground up. It includes many of the latest innovations from SAP—some of which are not even available in its flagship SAP Business Suite (although you can expect to see many of these features eventually made available through SAP's product-specific Enhancement Packages). Without getting too technical, Business ByDesign is compelling in that nontechnical users can build business processes using visual modeling tools and web services.

The underlying technology includes the NetWeaver Composition Environment (CE), Enterprise Services Repository, and Enterprise SOA. The important thing to remember is that you do not require SAP partners or consultants to implement Business ByDesign—the software was designed for do-it-yourselfers using modeling environments and services built in to the tools. The same logic holds true for changing business processes in response to new business requirements after implementation: Even from a maintenance perspective, it's a do-it-yourself solution.

Functionality

If there is one drawback to this do-it-yourself approach, it's that the degree to which Business ByDesign can be customized is sacrificed; at best, the product supports only moderately complex business processes. The current functionality is most applicable to companies in the following industry sectors: discrete manufacturing, process industries, consumer products, life sciences, professional services, and wholesale distribution. If you have a need for deep, industry-specific functionality in a highly customizable solution, look elsewhere. Business ByDesign meets the needs of many small businesses, though, with its support for the following business processes:

- ▶ Financials
- ▶ Customer Relationship Management
- ▶ Human Resources Management
- ▶ Supply Chain Management
- ▶ Project Management
- ▶ Supplier Relationship Management
- ▶ Compliance Management
- ▶ Executive Management Support

In addition, Service and Support as well as Business Analytics are built in to the Business ByDesign solution.

Features

One of the common themes among SAP's SME offerings is providing a superior user experience. Business ByDesign includes features such built-in learning, help, and support, all designed to improve the user experience and increase adoption. Another idea taking place at SAP is the idea of communities. In addition to the SAP support center, you can tap into the knowledge and experience of experts and other users all over the world—at the end of the day we're all in the same boat, so we might as well help each other out.

Advantages of Software as a Service (SaaS)

SAP hosts your system in an enterprise class data center—your business-critical data is housed in an environment specifically designed to provide availability and reliability. In addition to providing the hardware and software, SAP maintains the solution. For example, SAP takes care of backups, including offsite media protection.

Business ByDesign provides automated support via automated health checks. You also receive automatic updates so your software is always up to date. The net of all these features is that you don't need any technical resources to maintain or configure Business ByDesign—remember, the advanced capabilities even enable business users to configure business processes. Plus, SAP is responsible for maintaining the availability and performance of the solution. Add to that predictable costs—you know how much it will cost you each month based on the number of users, and you don't have a large, upfront capital expense. It is easy to see why Business ByDesign is generating a lot of excitement.

Business ByDesign and SAP Partners

Although Business ByDesign undoubtedly has a lot going for it, a few obstacles stand in its way. First, it remains to be seen how well SAP's partners will promote this new solution for their joint customer base. Traditionally, SAP's partners have profited by adding value in the form of installation, integration, and customization, and support services; for Business ByDesign, such services are simply not necessary to the same degree. In the same way, Business ByDesign does not enjoy the same specialized solution development opportunities SAP's partners perform for Business One or Business All-in-One. With little opportunity to bring in extra income, SAP will have to find a way to convince partners to sell Business ByDesign to SMEs—a real paradigm shift for the vendors, and therefore an enormous challenge for SAP.

The next challenge is convincing customers to house their data and run their systems from SAP's own data centers. SAP needs to convince SMEs that their data is indeed at least as safe and secure as if the solution were housed on their own premises. SAP has a long and rich history of hosting and co-hosting its solutions, however, so this should present less of a problem than simply selling SAP's Business ByDesign.

SAP All-in-One

SAP All-in-One is designed to meet the needs of midsize companies with between 100 and 2,500 employees, supporting multiple locations/divisions and all types of subsidiaries. All-in-One is a complete business solution—an integrated suite of products designed to provide increased control via real-time information and to allow for more efficient workflows. SAP All-in-One is adaptable, built on the SAP NetWeaver platform, including Enterprise SOA. It is a proven business solution, too, based on ERP 6.0, with a custom CRM solution specifically designed and built in to the product to address midsize company needs. This means that medium-sized businesses receive the same benefits of SAP ERP that enterprise customers enjoy, plus the benefits of best practices, including quicker, more predictable and therefore less costly implementations. Finally, All-in-One provides a more intuitive user experience, based in large part on the use of the new SAP NetWeaver Business Client.

Functionality

If you turn back and review the goals of SME solutions presented at the beginning of this hour, it should be obvious how well All-in-One meets a small or medium business organization's requirements. The All-in-One solutions include the following core business processes:

- ▶ Analytics
- ▶ Planning
- ▶ Purchasing
- ▶ Inventory Management
- ▶ Production
- ▶ Sales
- ▶ Marketing (CRM)
- ▶ Financials and Controlling
- ▶ Human Resources
- ▶ Industry-specific business processes for discrete manufacturing, process manufacturing, professional services, wholesale/distribution, retail, and many other industries delivered via preconfigured best practices from SAP. Further extensibility is made possible via partner solutions—more on this later this hour.

Mentioned earlier, the CRM functions built in to All-in-One include the following:

- ▶ Account & Contact Management
- ▶ Activity Management
- ▶ Pipeline Performance Management
- ▶ Campaign Management
- ▶ Segmentation

All-in-One provides enhanced business visibility and reporting, too. Boasting tight integration with Microsoft Excel, SAP makes it possible to access custom analytical reports in Excel—where user's can manipulate, display, and analyze their data using Excel's familiar features and tools. This eliminates the need to pull reports from various systems, too, or to integrate disparate systems in order to obtain a complete picture of the entire business. And with All-in-One's support for regulatory compliance (including documentation and reporting by country and industry for select regulations, including Sarbanes Oxley in the U.S.), All-in-One's customers need not fear a lack of business transparency necessary in today's post-Enron world.

All-in-One Partners and Solution Centers

SAP All-in-One benefits from an ecosystem of over 1,000 partners supported by regional SAP-based Solution Centers. SAP Partners build and deliver solutions designed to cover highly specific industry needs (SAP refers to these as *micro-vertical solutions*). So far, more than 575 solutions have been developed by partners in 50+ countries. The SAP Solution Centers qualify partners. This makes it apparent which solutions deliver the functions and processes appropriate to your industry. You can find a complete listing of the qualified solutions in the SAP Software Solution Partner Catalog (http://preview.sap.com/catalog/index.jsp). Here's a sampling of the breadth of solutions available:

- ▶ **Automotive**—72 partner-developed solutions qualified

- ▶ **Chemicals**—58 partner-developed solutions qualified

- ▶ **Consumer products**—83 partner-developed solutions qualified

- ▶ **Professional services**—47 partner-developed solutions qualified

Check out the catalog—you just might find the perfect solution already tailored to meet your business needs. A couple of final notes are in order, though, relative to SAP's partners and the SAP Solution Centers. Partners play an important role in All-in-One. In addition to developing solutions, partners provide implementation and support as well as customizing expertise. The SAP Solution Centers aid partners by providing deployment tools and methodologies, as well as detailed documentation of business processes to help accelerate implementation.

Features

SAP had to make All-in-One easier to use, configure, and administer when compared to the SAP Business Suite in order to compete in the mid-market. To this end, SAP also provides a user-friendly interface (the new SAP NetWeaver Business Client software) based on predefined roles, making it easy for employees to accomplish their daily tasks. A related feature is Power Lists, which list activities related to the current business process. Role-based reporting is also included, plus the ability to use the SAP Business Explorer tool (smart plug-in for Excel). Put together, these features make it easier for a user to accomplish his or her job—and the roles can be customized if needed.

Predictable Cost of Ownership/Best Practices

An important feature of Business All-in-One is the ability to provide a predictable cost of ownership, which starts with a predictable implementation time and cost. This is realized by using SAP Best Practices during the implementation to simplify configuration of Business All-in-One, thereby making implementation time more predictable. This is because SAP Best Practices facilitates the creation of industry-specific business processes and operations. The advantage to Best Practices is that the business processes have been tested—you're not building business processes from the ground up.

SAP has built a Best Practices library based on over 35 years of customer implementations in more than 25 industries worldwide. You can take advantage of the lessons they have learned from this experience to implement documented, preconfigured business scenarios—in many cases specific to your industry. The documentation includes end-user training guides as well as configuration guides.

Adapting to Changing Needs/SAP NetWeaver

One of the selling points of Business All-in-One is the ability to adapt to changing business needs in a rapid fashion—a key requirement for midsize businesses. The primary enabler of this adaptability is the SAP NetWeaver platform. In addition, Business All-in-One is extensible via partner solutions, as you learned earlier this hour. Finally, remember that Business All-in-One is essentially SAP ERP 6.0 and can be customized in the same manner.

SAP Business All-in-One is built on the SAP NetWeaver platform, the same platform used by the SAP Business Suite. NetWeaver is based on industry-standard protocols, which can be used to integrate Business All-in-One with third-party products (it also provides the integration platform for SAP solutions). One of the major features of the NetWeaver 2004s platform is Enterprise Service-Oriented Architecture (Enterprise SOA), which you will learn much more about in Hour 14, "SAP and Enterprise SOA." The general idea behind Enterprise SOA is that business processes can be easily created and extended using the services, simplifying both implementation and subsequent ongoing development. In addition to supporting the development of Enterprise SOA–based applications, NetWeaver provides a Java development environment and supports applications developed in the Microsoft .NET and IBM WebSphere development environments.

Intuitive User Experience/SAP NetWeaver Business Client

Business All-in-One comes with the latest version of the SAP NetWeaver Business Client and is designed to provide a more intuitive user experience with an easy-to-use interface. SAP is trying to reduce the disruption inevitably caused by the introduction of new business software, which can potentially change existing business processes. SAP has improved usability through role-based navigation, which can be configured to meet your requirements. Examples of predefined roles include Financial Accountant, Sales Person, Purchaser, and Shop Floor Specialist.

As an example of how the focus on roles simplifies usability, a user's role determines the contents of the user's navigation list—the user only sees the tasks relevant to his or her role. The user's role also controls the Power Lists presented to him or her. Power Lists are links to navigation folders and links to business objects, such as all open sales orders—the activities relevant to completing tasks required by the user's role. Access to reports is also based on roles. The end result is that users have access to the business objects relevant to their role in the organization in an intuitive manner, while administration is made easier.

In order to improve productivity, SAP has also included guided procedures with embedded contextual help. The guided procedures walk the user through completing a task while providing help on the screen (this can be turned off when it is no longer needed). The idea behind all these improvements is to minimize the disruption of a new business application by creating an intuitive user experience.

Summary

Table 6.1 shows the similarities and differences among SAP's SME solutions. The most obvious difference is that Business ByDesign is a hosted solution, whereas the others are on-premises. In addition to the preference for a hosted or on-premises solution, the size of the business is also an important differentiator. SAP's 35 years of experience in the enterprise are reflected in each product—the most prevalent example being the best practices included with Business All-in-One. What's more, each of the solutions aims to increase control by providing a single, integrated view of the business operations. The products are all marketed as affordable solutions providing lower total cost of ownership than their competitors in this space. Finally, SAP's partners are an important component of the sales and support for these solutions—although exactly how this will play out with ByDesign remains to be seen.

TABLE 6.1   Summary of the Key Differentiators Among SAP's SME Solutions

SAP SME Solution	Business One	Business ByDesign	All-in-One
Marketing tag line	A single solution to manage the entire business	A complete, on-demand business solution that is affordable, predictable, and easy to adopt	A comprehensive, extensible, and customizable business solution with support for industry-specific requirements
Number of customer employees	< 100	100–500	100–2500
Implementation type or method	On-premises	Hosted	On-premises
Transaction volume	Low	Moderate	High
Nature of business processes	Relatively straightforward	Moderately complex	Deep micro-vertical and industry-specific

Case Study: Hour 6

Consider this SME case study and the questions that follow, the answers to which may be found in Appendix A, "Case Study Answers."

Situation

MNC Global has a number of subsidiaries loosely defined as small and medium enterprises. Although these subsidiaries report up through MNC Global, they have their own distinct requirements from a business software package perspective. MNC has just acquired a new company that will operate as a subsidiary. Poorly funded, this new subsidiary has several software packages that are neither integrated nor particularly well suited for interfacing with MNC Global's SAP ERP and other flagship systems. Your job is to assist the subsidiary with selecting the "right" solution from SAP's SME lineup.

Questions

1. Which is the best solution from SAP if the subsidiary has highly complex business processes?

2. What is the best solution from SAP if the subsidiary is small (less than 100 employees) and has fairly straightforward business processes?

3. The CEO of the new subsidiary has expressed a reluctance to implement a business solution because the company really does not have the appropriate infrastructure or personnel to maintain it. What solution from SAP might you suggest?

Laying the Groundwork: SAP NetWeaver

SAP NetWeaver provides the technology foundation for the entire SAP suite of products. In this way, it is much like the foundation of a building, supplying vertical and horizontal underpinnings on which to build other structures (or in this case, systems). In Hour 7, we discuss the building blocks of NetWeaver, including how they can be used individually or combined to design an SAP environment architecturally.

A Brief History of SAP NetWeaver

Prior to SAP NetWeaver, the SAP technology stack was simply referred to as the *Basis layer*. In fact, even today the term *Basis* describes administrators and technical consultants that architect, support, and monitor SAP systems. Common system administration tasks such as performance monitoring, tuning, and security have historically been supplied through the Basis layer, including internal and external systems connectivity, faxing capabilities, email broadcasting, and more. It also included the development repository of SAP's ABAP programming language and database objects. In this way, the Basis layer provided the necessary development, communication, and monitoring infrastructure necessary to meet the needs of the client/server era.

With the Internet boom of the 90s, the demand for applications to adapt to the Web was vital, and SAP was particularly keen to get a jump in this area. As a result, SAP Web Application Server (WebAS) was introduced to the market. It essentially extended the Basis technology stack to the Web. This also marked the beginning of the initiative to integrate the SAP Internet Transaction Server (ITS), formerly a separate product, into SAP's core technology stack. It further introduced SAP Java, which SAP chose strategically to provide a platform-independent model for web development (consistent with the company's vision to adopt open standards while providing a choice).

WebAS was SAP's initial move to offer a standalone technology product that could be installed independently from the SAP business modules as either a traditional ABAP technology stack, a Java technology stack, or both. The goal was to separate the technical layer from the business layer so that companies could perform more modular upgrades rather than being forced to upgrade the technical and application stacks at the same time—a process that is both time consuming and costly. This more componentized model paved the way for the release of SAP NetWeaver.

In 2004, SAP introduced SAP NetWeaver and broadened the technology stack concept into a complete integration platform (thereby simplifying how SAP connected with other systems). In addition to the WebAS ABAP and Java components, SAP aligned the former New Dimension and technology products, such as Business Warehouse, Enterprise Portals, and Exchange Infrastructure, and created a methodology around people, information, and processes. NetWeaver made it possible to install these components individually or combine them to form custom solutions. Later, NetWeaver helped create a consistent technical foundation for the SAP business suite applications, too, such as the SAP ERP Core Component (ECC), SAP Supplier Relationship Management (SRM), and more.

Strategic Benefits of NetWeaver

Given what we have already covered, it should be clear that SAP implementations based on NetWeaver provide benefits on several fronts:

▶ Decreased development costs.

▶ Easily enabled integration, thus speeding up the time necessary to deploy SAP as well as shrinking the time necessary to perform system upgrades and so on.

▶ Reduced total cost of ownership, primarily because maintenance and support costs are dramatically reduced in the wake of technical platform standardization (before NetWeaver, each SAP product was installed a little bit differently than its counterparts).

▶ Greater potential for innovation. Through NetWeaver, a company's IT organization needs to spend less time maintaining existing solutions and thus can spend more time meeting the changing needs of the business.

While the initial version of NetWeaver, termed *SAP NetWeaver 2004*, made huge strides toward a more flexible SAP technology platform, it represented only the beginning. Within a short period, SAP NetWeaver 2004s was released and the component model was replaced by a newer and bolder concept including broader support for SAP's most recent applications. In the next section, we discuss these changes.

> SAP NetWeaver 2004 was the first release of NetWeaver. Predicated loosely on the WebAS 6.20 platform, it was synonymous with mySAP ERP 2004. When SAP upgraded its Business Suite in 2005 and 2006, however, it needed to provide an updated NetWeaver stack along with support for WebAS 6.40. SAP provided this support via what was termed a "minor release" in the form of SAP NetWeaver 2004s, which incidentally also supported mySAP ERP 2005, a new release of BI, and several other new components and xApps. Later, SAP NetWeaver 2004s was renamed SAP NetWeaver 7.0.

By the Way

SAP NetWeaver 7.0

In early 2007, SAP NetWeaver 2004s was renamed to SAP NetWeaver 7.0. Certainly, these labels are still somewhat interchangeable. Make no mistake, though—SAP NetWeaver 7.0 sets the new standard SAP NetWeaver naming convention for the foreseeable future.

In Hour 5, "Developing a Technical Roadmap for Deploying SAP," we discussed the concept of IT Practices and IT Scenarios in relation to developing an SAP Technology Roadmap. SAP realized that although the NetWeaver component model was an improvement, it did not provide the flexibility and agility required of today's businesses. NetWeaver components such as Business Warehouse and Enterprise Portal provided core reporting and accessibility capabilities to SAP, for example, but these business solutions better needed to map back to specific business requirements to support SAP's customer needs. For this reason, SAP developed the concept of installable software units that today represent the system building blocks of SAP systems. These building blocks are installed as either mandatory or optional components based on the particular IT Scenario needed by the business. That is, a financial solution requires one set of building blocks, whereas a Human Capital Management solution requires a decidedly different set of blocks. These blocks or units may be further broken down into three primary areas: systems with usage types, standalone engines, and clients.

Systems with Usage Types

The systems with usage types listed in this section are part of the core group of what was previously known as the SAP NetWeaver 2004 technology components discussed in the last section, admittedly with a few additions and changes (now called SAP NetWeaver 7.0). The Development Infrastructure, known for a time as *Java Development Infrastructure* or *JDI*, is a change management system for Java development objects. SAP applied the same concepts used for years in the Central Transport System of the ABAP stack to the Java world. Additionally, a new BI usage type, BI Java, extends BI capabilities for features such as information broadcasting.

The SAP NetWeaver Portal is comprised of two usage types. The Enterprise Portal Core includes the base components formerly installed during the standard portal installation. The Enterprise Portal installation now bundles the former add-on components such as Collaboration, Knowledge Management, and others into one usage type.

Development Infrastructure (DI)	Business Intelligence Java (BI Java)
Enterprise Portal (EP)	Enterprise Portal Core (EPC)
Business Intelligence (BI, formerly BW)	Process Integration (PI, formerly XI)
Application Server Java (AS Java)	Application Server ABAP (AS ABAP)

Standalone Engines

Standalone engines are software or services that generally combine with usage types to enhance functionality or extend usability. For instance, the Search and Classification engine, TREX, works along with SAP NetWeaver Portal and SAP Business Intelligence applications to improve the performance of search and query functions. Likewise, the SAP Web Dispatcher provides load-balancing capabilities for WebAS ABAP and WebAS Java systems. The six engines install on a separate server or along with other system usage types on the same server:

Content Server	Gateway
SAP Job Scheduler by Redwood	liveCache
Search and Classification (TREX)	Web Dispatcher

Clients

The SAP Clients are a combination of front-end components and development tools provided to facilitate or customize the user experience. The traditional SAP GUI options for Windows, HTML, and Java are still available, as well as standard web browsers and the BI Business Explorer. The J2SE Adapter Engine provides an alternative for PI platforms that do not support the J2EE engine. The Developer Workplace (of which Developer Studio is a subset), the Mobile Infrastructure Client, and Adobe LiveCycle Designer offer rich development environments for Java applications, mobile devices, and SAP forms, respectively.

SAP GUI	Business Explorer (for BI)
Developer Workplace	Developer Studio
Adobe LiveCycle Designer	Web Browser
J2SE Adapter Engine (for PI)	Mobile Infrastructure Client (MI Client)

Bringing It All Together—Using the Building Blocks

So, now that we have covered the history of SAP NetWeaver and what it looks like today, we need to discuss how this applies to actual SAP implementations. Hour 2, "SAP Basics: What It's All About," presented what an SAP project looks like, and Hour 5 outlined the concepts of blueprinting and requirements gathering. As companies meet new business challenges and decide to use new SAP technology or extend current SAP technology, they must gather requirements to determine the type of solution needed. As discussed, SAP has organized a broad group of common business process criteria into IT Practices and IT Scenarios. This allows companies to match their business requirements to the appropriate IT Practice, narrow the focus to a particular IT Scenario, and ultimately define which SAP NetWeaver technologies are required for implementation.

SAP provides the SAP NetWeaver 7.0 Master Guide for system administrators and technology consultants to assist with the implementation of SAP NetWeaver systems. This guide is available at http://service.sap.com/instguidesNW70 (see Figure 7.1). Note that it is only available to those with a valid SAP Service Marketplace user ID.

The Master Guide provides a common reference for the entire SAP NetWeaver implementation cycle and is a valuable resource for those new to NetWeaver.

FIGURE 7.1
The SAP
NetWeaver 7.0
Master Guide is
available online
to SAP Service
Marketplace
users with a
valid user ID.

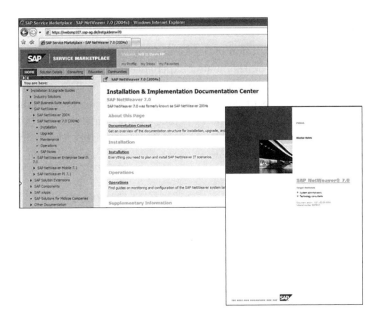

Now that you understand the basics of NetWeaver 7.0 and have the Master Guide reference materials by your side, consider the following example.

A company has decided to use SAP to build a new collaboration portal for its sales force. After gathering requirements, the company has determined that it is operating under the IT Scenario "Enabling User Collaboration," so it looks to its SAP technical team to help decide precisely what to implement. The SAP technical group references the SAP NetWeaver 7.0 Master Guide and finds that the following installable units need to be in place to provide the technical foundation for this collaboration portal:

▶ **Usage types**—BI (also requires AS ABAP) and BI Java (which requires AS Java, EP, and EPC)

▶ **Standalone engines**—Search and Classification Engine (TREX)

▶ **Clients**—SAP GUI and BI Business Explorer

The technical team can now take this information and begin to assemble an SAP landscape for the company's collaboration portal using the system-specific installation and configuration guides available from the SAP Service Marketplace. It is important to determine how the various SAP NetWeaver Portal's users will access and subsequently take advantage of the portal's functionality; usage types, client access methods, and the role of the standalone engine all need to be decided in advance (see Figure 7.2).

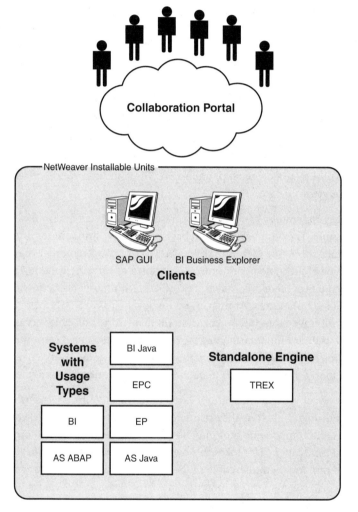

FIGURE 7.2
This figure depicts the SAP NetWeaver installable units as the foundation to build the company's collaboration portal for their end user community.

With this example, it is easy to see that SAP's new design with NetWeaver 7.0 greatly simplifies the process of mapping business requirements to technology capabilities. In addition, it provides more flexibility around implementation because you no longer have tightly coupled components that have to be installed together. In the next section, we shed additional light on SAP as it continues to introduce new technologies and new business-enabling capabilities with SAP NetWeaver 7.1.

What's Next for SAP NetWeaver?

With SAP NetWeaver 7.0, SAP established its latest architecture for innovation going forward. Now, it looks to extend this technical platform with additional services and a move toward Enterprise Service-Oriented Architecture (Enterprise SOA). In Hour 14, "SAP and Enterprise SOA," we discuss SAP and Enterprise SOA in detail. For now, we just discuss some of the concepts and outline what is on the horizon with SAP NetWeaver 7.1.

Web Services and Enterprise Services

As NetWeaver evolves in response to a changing world, SAP has bet the bank on a number of technologies and approaches intended to minimize integration headaches, total cost of ownership, and so on. These include Web Services and Enterprise Services.

Though not synonymous, Web Services represents the vehicle that makes Enterprise Services possible. They are beginning to become the new standard for interapplication communication. The idea is that Web Services are "open" rather than tied to a particular type of technology or hardware platform or software vendor. This platform independence, therefore, makes it possible to communicate between vastly different technology platforms. At the end of the day, by using NetWeaver 7.1 your developers will have more time to focus on implementing valuable services, rather than spending their time figuring out the intricacies of technical communications protocols. This makes Web Services a valuable attribute of any NetWeaver solution—particularly those that wish to get a jump start on new SOA-enabled solutions.

Enterprise Services, on the other hand, extend the use of Web Services by combining them into a usable context as they relate to a business process. In this way, they become reusable components that may be shared across partners and organizations to foster real innovation. SAP takes this a step further by packaging these Enterprise Services and making them available in the new Enterprise Services Repository (included in SAP NetWeaver 7.1) and the Enterprise Services Workplace out on SDN (the SAP Developer Network, accessible to registered developers and others at https://www.sdn.sap.com).

SAP NetWeaver 7.1

SAP NetWeaver 7.1 introduces a number of new capabilities geared around business process innovation and Enterprise SOA. Key components include:

▶ SAP Process Integration 7.1

▶ SAP NetWeaver Composition Environment (CE) 7.1

- ▶ SAP NetWeaver Mobile 7.1

- ▶ The Enterprise Services Repository (included with SAP PI 7.1 or SAP CE 7.1)

Although each of these are discussed in detail in Hour 14, they all serve the purpose of further integrating Enterprise SOA into the NetWeaver platform by leveraging the Enterprise Services Repository.

Summary

From its inception, SAP NetWeaver was established to reduce the amount of time necessary to integrate disparate applications, reduce deployment and development time associated with new implementations, and minimize ongoing support and maintenance associated with in-place solutions. As NetWeaver has evolved, these goals have remained consistent. SAP has added to this strategy to increase business agility across enterprises by building a technical platform with ultimate flexibility. Now that we have laid the groundwork with SAP NetWeaver, we discuss in Hour 8, "SAP ERP: SAP's Core Product," and Hour 9, "The SAP Business Suite," SAP ERP and the SAP Business Suite, respectively, as well as how SAP provides a robust business application layer atop the SAP NetWeaver technology stack.

Case Study: Hour 7

Consider this NetWeaver-centric case study and the questions that follow, the answers to which may be found in Appendix A, "Case Study Answers."

Situation

MNC Global has recently upgraded its SAP Business Warehouse system to the new SAP Business Intelligence application based on NetWeaver 7.0, and the company now wishes to take advantage of some of BI's new features. MNC Global has a number of financial and purchasing reports currently running in the enterprise that end users access via the Business Explorer (a special SAP user interface for BI). MNC's purchasing department wants these same reports to be available via email, using information broadcasting, and has asked the company's SAP technical team to answer the following questions to assist with the design and implementation of the required new BI functionality. For this case study, you are a member of the SAP technical team tasked with satisfying the purchasing department's request. Based on the discussion in this hour, answer the following questions.

Questions

1. What are some of the strategic benefits that MNC may realize by implementing this new NetWeaver functionality?

2. What sources or guides can be used to assist with the planning and implementation of information broadcasting on the new BI 7.0 system?

3. In regard to information broadcasting, with what is the IT Scenario category associated?

4. For each of the following, list the installable software units:

   a. Systems with usage types

   b. Standalone engines

   c. Clients

SAP ERP: SAP's Core Product

What You'll Learn in This Hour:

▶ The role of SAP ERP

▶ Differentiating between SAP ERP, ECC, and R/3

▶ A closer look at several SAP ERP solution offerings

▶ An overview of core modules underpinning SAP ERP's solution offerings

SAP ERP and its predecessors or components, ECC, R/3 Enterprise, and the original R/3, are online transaction processing (OLTP) systems—systems that by their very nature are employed by end users, day in and day out, in the course of doing their job. Within ERP or R/3 are a number of modules or subcomponents. At a high level, this includes finance, logistics, human resource management, customer service, and quite a few others we will look at this hour.

OLTP systems are nothing new; they're simply systems used in business that host lots of users who run lots of transactions. A transaction might include booking an order, creating a reservation, posting a change to a material or warehouse requisition, deleting an invalid accounting entry, or changing an employee record when someone leaves the company.

SAP ERP Versus ECC and R/3

SAP ERP is simply the evolution of SAP's original R/3 (which itself evolved from the mainframe-based SAP R/2). SAP ERP consists of SAP ECC; the two are synonymous. ECC stands for ERP Central Component, though you will probably see the terms *ERP Core*

Component and *Enterprise Core Component* incorrectly used across different websites, blogs, whitepapers, and other literature. SAP ERP supports open Internet and Web Services standards alongside Microsoft .NET and J2EE interoperability and is therefore more extensible and powerful than its older R/3 sibling. And it is much more nimble as well; by embracing a Services-Oriented Architecture and leveraging a web-based computing platform, SAP ERP is more adaptable and agile than R/3. You can change business processes on the fly, and as an SAP developer you can turn around updated business solutions and scenarios in days or weeks rather than months or years. Like R/3, SAP ERP itself supports several different business scenarios, as outlined next.

SAP ERP Business Scenarios

SAP R/3 and SAP ERP differ in terms of the business solutions and full-fledged business scenarios each can support. Within the SAP ERP umbrella, you can quickly deploy scenarios or SAP-customized solutions, each of which is geared toward supporting essential business functions such as the following:

▶ **SAP ERP Financials**—Provides built-in compliance for Sarbanes-Oxley and Basel II, which takes financial reporting and corporate governance to another level. Admittedly, you can configure R/3 to do the same, but at a much greater investment in time and cost.

▶ **SAP ERP Operations**—Composed of Procurement and Logistics Execution, Product Development and Manufacturing, and Sales and Service. These solutions take logistics to the next level, introducing sales, warehousing, procurement, transportation, and distribution into the realm of collaborative business solutions. By extending these core business processes to include customers and suppliers, and enabling employees with Portal and even mobile access, ECC is truly at the core of a solution that R/3 could never so easily or inexpensively support.

▶ **SAP ERP Human Capital Management (HCM)**—Transforms an HR department into an organization well equipped to manage and retain the core of any successful business—its people. HCM pushes HR business processes out to the Web, enabling long-time mainstays of HR organizations such as recruiting, e-learning, and employee self-services to change and evolve with much greater velocity and agility than its predecessors. In this, SAP ERP HCM maximizes workforce potential.

▶ **SAP ERP Corporate Services**—Wraps up a set of core services into a neat package. Processes ranging from Project and Portfolio Management to Environment, Health, and Safety (EH&S) Management, Real Estate Management, Travel Management, and Quality Management are unified and streamlined like never before possible.

▶ **SAP ERP Analytics**—A targeted and robust solution, marrying financial, operations, and workforce-based analytics and reporting.

The preceding list comprises SAP ERP's latest business solution offerings. The latest version of SAP ERP also includes numerous functional enhancements—more than 300 of them—for better addressing an organization's finance, HCM, operations, and vital corporate services functions. SAP ERP also provides its users with the ability to obtain these enhanced business capabilities more easily, because all new functional enhancements through at least the year 2013 will be available as SAP ERP extensions (optional enhancement packages) rather than gained through expensive and time-consuming business application upgrades. And by taking advantage of its Enterprise Service-Oriented Architecture (Enterprise SOA) underpinnings, SAP lets its customers change the way they do business by making it easy to extend features and functionality beyond SAP's core platform and its inbuilt capabilities.

It is interesting to note that the core business modules shared among R/3 and ECC are essentially the same; only the arrangement and specific configuration of each module helps differentiate R/3's somewhat vertically oriented deployment methodology over SAP ERP's more horizontally oriented and much-extended approach. See http://www.sap.com/erp/ for additional information about SAP ERP.

Core SAP Business Modules

As indicated previously this hour, SAP ERP and its OLTP brethren are composed of many modules, often referred to as *business modules*. By combining business modules (and perhaps other SAP technologies or components), SAP enables an organization to create the specific business solutions outlined earlier. With SAP's architecture, a company deploying SAP ERP need not completely develop each module within its implementation. For example, if you are bringing in SAP to take care of financial accounting, controlling, and perhaps treasury cash management, there might be no need to develop SAP's logistics offering, HCM capabilities, and so forth. You might already have another system that takes care of these other needs. In that case, SAP might simply be constructed to interface with (talk to) these preexisting systems.

Because SAP ERP is such a tightly integrated application, though, it is nearly impossible to maintain a singularly focused implementation of one SAP ERP module. Why? Because business processes still need occasional access to a certain amount of business rules, master data, and perhaps customer data outside of a single module, and you will find it easier to include that basic information within SAP ERP rather than building an interface to another system.

SAP ERP Financials

SAP touts its SAP ERP Financials package as enabling financial transformation. New general ledger capabilities streamline the financial reconciliation process, reduce the cost of administration and control, and minimize user error. This in turn frees up an organization to focus strategically—another area SAP ERP Financials enables. By offering more effective collaboration with its customers, vendors, and suppliers, SAP ERP Financials enables governance, helps manage risk and compliance, increases inventory turns, frees up cash and working capital, provides greater financial transparency, and simplifies other complex invoicing and payment processes. The ability to drill down into areas such as profitability analysis and take advantage of built-in analytic solutions empower end users as they make better decisions faster across many different financial domains and, therefore, address financial matters like the following:

▶ Governance, Risk, and Compliance (GRC)

▶ Financial and Managerial Accounting

▶ Controlling (financial controls and audit support)

▶ Enterprise Controlling

▶ Treasury Management

▶ Global Trade Services (GTS)

▶ Financial Supply Chain Management (FSCM)

Each of these is discussed in more detail next.

Governance, Risk, and Compliance (GRC)

SAP provides a solution for governance, risk, and compliance called SAP Governance, Risk, and Compliance (GRC). With its integrated SAP ERP back end, SAP is well positioned to provide the kind of visibility and transparency that organizations demand in response to various regulatory body and internal control requirements. SAP GRC enables a firm to effectively manage risk and increase corporate accountability, thereby improving the firm's ability to make faster, smarter decisions and protect its assets and people. By giving end users a tool to simply recognize critical risks and analyze risk-reward trade-offs, the time and expense required to implement SAP GRC is quickly recouped in cost savings. The solution also allows a firm to implement proactive, collaborative cross-company processes that let a firm evaluate new business opportunities against potential operational or legal risks and other trade-offs.

Ultimately, SAP GRC's business benefits include the following:

- Well-balanced portfolios boasting well-vetted risk/reward analyses. Through GRC's transparency, visibility, and companywide hooks, the solution can enable a firm's decision makers to make smart decisions—decisions based on risk and the probability of return.

- Improved stakeholder value, yielding preserved brand reputation, increased market value, reduced cost of capital, easier personnel recruiting, and higher employee retention.

- Reduced costs relative to governance, risk, and compliance. GRC is no longer an optional service a firm should provide on behalf of its stakeholders but rather a mandatory part of doing business in a global world tainted by less-than-ethical business practices. Effective GRC becomes a differentiator, then, in terms of reducing the time and effort necessary to manage a firm's compliance and manage risk.

- Enhanced business performance and financial predictability. SAP GRC provides executive teams the confidence they need in their numbers, along with the tools necessary to report on and proactively pursue remediation.

- Organizational sustainability despite the risks associated with poorly managed governance, risk, and compliance, particularly legal and market ramifications.

All of this amounts to increased business agility, competitive differentiation, and other brand-preserving and company-sustaining benefits.

Financial and Managerial Accounting

The Financial and Managerial Accounting module provides an end user the ability to enhance companywide strategic decision-making processes. It allows companies to centrally manage financial accounting data within an international framework of multiple companies, languages, currencies, and charts of accounts. The Financial and Managerial Accounting module complies with international accounting standards, such as GAAP and IAS, and helps fulfill the local legal requirements of many countries, reflecting fully the legal and accounting changes resulting from Sarbanes-Oxley legislation, European market and currency unification, and more. Financial and Managerial Accounting contains the following components:

▶ **General Ledger Accounting**—Provides a complete record of all your company's business transactions. It provides a place to record business transactions throughout all facets of your company's business to ensure that the accounting data being processed in your SAP system is both factual and complete.

▶ **Accounts Payable**—Records and administers accounting data for all vendors in your SAP system.

▶ **Accounts Receivable**—Financially manages your company's sales activities. It records and administers the accounting data of your customers through a number of tools specializing in the management of open items.

▶ **Asset Accounting**—Manages and helps you supervise your company's fixed assets. It also serves as a subsidiary ledger to the General Ledger, providing detailed information on transactions specifically involving fixed assets.

▶ **Funds Management**—Designed to support you in creating budgets by way of a toolset that replicates your budget structure for the purpose of planning, monitoring, and managing your company's funds. Three essential tasks include revenues and expenditures budgeting, funds movement monitoring, and insight into potential budget overruns.

▶ **Special Purpose Ledger**—Designed to provide summary information from multiple applications at a level of detail that you specify according to your business's needs. This function enables you to collect, combine, summarize, modify, and allocate actual and planned data that originates from SAP or other external systems.

Accounts Payable and Accounts Receivable sub-ledgers are integrated both with the General Ledger and with different components in the Sales and Distribution module. Accounts Payable and Accounts Receivable transactions are performed automatically when related processes are performed in other modules.

Controlling

Cost accounting is handled by the Controlling module, which provides the functions necessary for effective and accurate internal cost accounting management. Its complete integration allows for value and quantity real-time data flows between SAP Financials and SAP Logistics. The Controlling modules contain the following subcomponents:

▶ **Overhead Cost Controlling**—Focuses on the monitoring and allocation of your company's overhead costs and provides all the functions your company requires for planning and allocation. The functionality contained within the Controlling module supports multiple cost-controlling methods, giving you the freedom to decide which functions and methods are best applied to your individual areas.

▶ **Activity-Based Costing**—Enables you to charge organizational overhead to products, customers, sales channels, and other segments, and permits a more realistic profitability analysis of different products and customers because you are able to factor in the resources of overhead.

▶ **Product Cost Controlling**—Used to determine the costs arising from manufacturing a product or providing a service by evoking a real-time cost-control mechanism (capable of managing product, object, and actual costing schemes).

▶ **Profitability Analysis**—An effective tool useful in analyzing the profitability of a particular organization or segment of your market. In the latter case, these segments can be organized by products, customers, orders, or a combination thereof.

Another module, Enterprise Controlling, extends cost accounting to several corollary areas, as outlined next.

Enterprise Controlling

SAP's Enterprise Controlling module is divided into a number of components:

▶ **Business Planning and Budgeting**—Designed to assist in creating high-level enterprise plans that allow for the adaptable representation of customer-specific plans and their interrelationships. This also takes into consideration the connections between profit and loss, balance sheet, and cash flow strategies.

▶ **Consolidation**—Enables you to enter reported financial data online using data-entry formats and to create consolidated reports that meet your company's legal and management reporting mandates.

▶ **Profit Center Accounting**—Used to analyze the profitability of internal responsibility or *profit centers* (where a profit center is a management-oriented organizational unit used for internal controlling purposes).

▶ **Executive Information System (in R/3)**—Provides an up-to-the-minute overview of the critical information required in order for your company to effectively manage its resources. It collects and appraises information from various areas of your business, including financial information and information contained within your Human Resources Information System and the Logistics Information System.

Another important financial module is the Treasury Management module, outlined next.

Treasury Management

The Treasury Management module contributes the functionality that your company needs to control liquidity management, risk management and assessment, and position management. The Treasury Management module includes the following components:

▶ **Treasury Management**—Used to support the management of your company's financial transactions and positions through back-office processing to the Financial Accounting module. It also provides a versatile reporting platform that your company can use to examine its financial positions and transactions.

▶ **Cash Management**—Designed to facilitate an optimum amount of liquidity to satisfy required payments as they become timely and to supervise cash inflows and outflows.

▶ **Market Risk Management**—Quantifies the impact of potential financial market fluctuations against a firm's financial assets. The Cash Management package, in combination with the Treasury Management package, sets the foundation for your database for controlling market risks, and includes interest and currency exposure analysis, portfolio simulation, and market-to-market valuation.

▶ **Funds Management**—Designed to sustain your company's funds management processing from the planning stage clear through to the payments. Using this component, your company can create different budget versions, making it possible to work with rolling budget planning. SAP's latest Funds Management offering tightly integrates with Employee Self-Services' online travel booking function to track estimated and real costs.

Global Trade Services (GTS)

In reality, the component of SAP GRC known as SAP Global Trade Services (or GTS) is also an SAP ERP Financials solution that further qualifies as an SAP Corporate Services solution and global supply chain enabler. GTS makes it possible for international companies to connect and communicate with various government systems using a companywide trade process spanning SAP both internally and externally. In this way, SAP GRC Global Trade Services lets a business do the following:

▶ Ensure it meets international regulatory requirements

▶ Manage global trade by integrating companywide trade compliance across financial, supply chain, and HCM business processes

▶ Facilitate and expedite the import/export process for goods traveling through different country customs organizations

▶ Facilitate increased supply chain transparency by sharing cross-border trade-related information with partners (from insurance entities to freight handlers, banking institutions, and regulatory bodies)

SAP GRC GTS thus enables a firm to mitigate the financial and other risks associated with doing business around the globe. By ensuring compliance with international trade agreements, SAP GRC GTS customers can optimize their supply chain, reduce production downtime, and eliminate errors that otherwise yield expensive penalties. In a nutshell, SAP GRC GTS makes it possible for firms to do business across country borders, and to do so more consistently and profitably.

Financial Supply Chain Management (FSCM)

With all the attention today on driving inefficiencies out of an organization's supply chain, there's little wonder why SAP created or enhanced existing functionality to streamline supply chains from a financial perspective. Financial Supply Chain Management (FSCM) gives an organization the following functionalities:

- ▶ Credit Limit Management and Control

- ▶ Credit Rules Automation

- ▶ Credit Decision Support

- ▶ Collections Management

- ▶ In-House Cash Management

- ▶ Dispute Management

- ▶ Electronic Bill Presentment and Payment

- ▶ Treasury and Risk Management

As you've probably noticed by now, there is quite a bit of overlap between particular solutions and modules. While it can be confusing, this flexibility is one of SAP's greatest strengths—the ability to customize a business solution makes it possible to create innovative business processes capable of meeting the needs of most any organization's finance team.

SAP ERP Human Capital Management

In the 1990s, SAP made the strategic decision to incorporate human resource management, or what it has termed *Human Capital Management (HCM)*, into its core OLTP system. A dramatic departure from SAP's roots in manufacturing and financial support systems, HCM really completed SAP's R/3 and subsequent systems. Why? People are an organization's greatest asset, making a company's human resources management system one of the most critical systems deployed by the firm. In HCM, SAP has pulled together a robust collection of integrated and self-described "talent management" capabilities. HCM improves organizational insight into the talents of the firm, provides hiring and ongoing training support. And because the system reflects the languages, currencies, and regulatory requirements of more than 30 different countries, HCM can be deployed by global firms seeking to adopt both a comprehensive and a consistent method of managing its people.

SAP HCM also facilitates an HR shared services center augmented by reporting and analytics capabilities. In this way, HCM marries what the organization needs to measure internally (related to how well its own HR teams are performing against targets and other metrics such as hiring goals, for example) with the organization's services to its customers—the firm's employees, long-term contractors, and others. This self-service functionality includes or supports a number of roles and company needs, including the following:

- A centralized employee interaction mechanism, which is nothing more than a central point of contact for employees that acts as a single source of company, HR, and other related information. As the primary venue for interacting with the employer, this tool becomes a ubiquitous source of "the answers" companywide. Meanwhile, the company's HR team uses the tool to access and help manage the information needed behind the scenes.

- Employee Self-Service (ESS), which is perhaps best known as a tool used to maintain personal data, book travel, and conduct other administrative activities that lend themselves to an "online" support environment. Questions such as "How many dependents am I claiming?" and "Who is named as the beneficiary of my life insurance policy?" used to take up way too much time to address. In response to this problem, SAP developed ESS, an effective means of providing real-time access and data upkeep capabilities to employees.

With SAP Employee Self-Service, employees can be responsible for the preservation of their own employee data and can get access to their information, on their own time, without requiring a PC connected to SAP, and without any SAP training. This saves time for the employees because they no longer need to stop working and visit the Human Resources department, and it saves time for the Human Resources professionals who otherwise need to stop their other important work to assist the employees.

By the Way

- Workforce process management, or the bundling of common country-specific employee self-services. This might include time entry, payroll, employee benefits, legal reporting, and organizational reporting—all of which are brought together and standardized to meet local regulations or country codes (in this regard, 47 countries are currently supported worldwide).

- Manager Self-Service (MSS), a cockpit of data used by leadership to identify, retain, and reward the firm's top performers; manage budgets, compensation planning, and profit/loss statements; sort and conduct keyword searches of employees' records; conduct the annual employee review process; and address other administrative matters quickly and from a centralized location.

SAP's Manager Self-Service is a manager's equivalent to Employee Self-Services. It enables a manager to do his or her job well, and successfully manage a team—to grow it, care for and feed it, use it in the smartest way possible given any number of business or personal constraints and other factors, and retain the members of the team.

▶ Workforce deployment, which is for project teams rather than individuals per se. Teams are created based on projects, and individual team member competencies and availabilities may then be tracked along with time, tasks, and so on.

Several of these HCM services actually fall into two broad focus areas that SAP still tends to use as labels—Personnel Administration (PA) and Personnel Planning and Development (PD). Each addresses different aspects of a company's Human Resource functions; the integration of the two creates a well-oiled Human Resources machine that, when integrated with a firm's other business processes, creates a competitive advantage for the business.

SAP Talent Management: More Than Personnel Administration

The Personnel Administration module of HCM manages company procedures, including payroll, employee benefits enrollment, and compensation. This module's focus serves all the required Human Resource functions that most companies use. Benefits Administration provides the functionality required to offer and enroll your employees into benefit plans, for example. This includes the functionality to manage eligibility requirements, evidence of insurability, cost tracking and management, Flexible Spending Account (FSA) claims processing, benefit terminations, and COBRA.

Beyond personnel administration, SAP's Talent Management, the hottest addition to SAP ERP HCM, enables recruiters, managers, and other company leadership visibility into the various phases of employment, from employment advertising and recruitment through onboarding, employee development/training, and specific retention activities. This tool also provides a companywide profile of the firm's human capital (people!), making it possible to seek out and manage the careers of people holding particular skills, jobs, or roles. Talent management encompasses a number of solutions in its own right, from Enterprise Compensation Management to E-Recruiting, Succession Management, Performance Management, and others, several of which are outlined here:

▶ Enterprise Compensation Management is used to implement your company's pay, promotion, salary adjustments, and bonus plan policies. Functions managed by this solution include salary administration, job evaluations, salary reviews, salary survey results, compensation budget planning and administration, and compensation policy administration. In addition, Compensation Management gives an organization the capability to create pay grades and salary structures necessary to describe the internal value of the jobs and positions available within. More compelling, Enterprise Compensation Management gives managers and payroll administrators the ability to produce compensation adjustment justifications—the kind of proactive process necessary to retain top talent. SAP accomplishes this by marrying performance ratings with compensation standards, industry trends, performance-based pay standards, bonus payouts, and more, which not only helps create bulletproof justifications but reduces the time, the effort, and therefore the risk otherwise germane to such time-sensitive matters.

▶ E-Recruiting 6.0 enables you to manage the process of employee recruitment. Recruitment initiates from the creation of a position vacancy through the advertisement and applicant tracking of potentials, concluding with the notification of successful and unsuccessful applicants and the hiring of the best candidate. E-Recruiting has come a long way in the last several years, though, and encompasses much more than the applicant-tracking functionality for which Talent Management was initially known. E-Recruiting ties attracting, acquiring, educating, and developing talent, along with identifying and developing future leaders, to a single system of record. And with custom browser interfaces tailored to management, recruiting, and applicant roles reflecting country or company-specific tenets, E-Recruiting provides the kind of efficient and personalized access to data necessary to identify and retain a talented workforce.

▶ Time Management provides a flexible methodology for recording and evaluating employee work time and absence management. Time Management is also integrated to other SAP ERP components that can make use of this data. A key benefit of the Time Management component is that it enables you to represent the time structures in your company in accordance with your actual conditions, using the calendar as a basis. Use it to address time models (such as flextime, shift work, and normal work schedules) to plan work and break schedules, to manage exceptions such as substitutions or business trips, and to meet regulatory requirements relative to absences, breaks, and holidays.

▶ Payroll efficiently and accurately calculates remuneration for work performed by your employees, regardless of their working schedule, working calendar, language, or currency. Payroll also handles fluctuating reporting needs as well as the constantly changing compliance requirements of federal, state, and local agencies.

In contrast to these solutions, SAP provides tools to better manage people and traditional HR functions, including organizational management and workforce planning. Some of these include the following:

▶ **Organizational Management**—Designed to assist in the strategizing and planning of the comprehensive Human Resource structure. Through the development of proposed scenarios using the flexible tools provided, you can manipulate your company's structure in the present, past, and future. Using the basic organization objects in SAP, units, jobs, positions, tasks, and work centers are all structured as the basic building blocks of your organization.

▶ **SAP Enterprise Learning**—Another hot solution within SAP ERP HCM that encompasses SAP's legacy Talent and Event Management (TEM) solution and adds much more functionality. SAP Enterprise Learning helps a company coordinate and administer companywide training and similar events, and also contains functionality to plan for, execute, confirm, and manage cost allocations and billing for your company's events. SAP Enterprise Learning gives employees the training they need to develop skills necessary for the future. By creating an efficient and personalized learning process and environment, SAP Enterprise Learning takes into account an employee's job, job tasks, qualifications, and objectives to create a custom training regimen that aligns with preestablished career development goals.

▶ **SAP Learning Solution**—A component of SAP Enterprise Learning that also falls under the Talent Management umbrella (discussed previously), the SAP Learning Solution links employee learning to a firm's business strategy and objectives. To pull this off, the SAP Learning Solution brings together SAP ERP HCM with knowledge management and collaboration solutions and provides this in an innovative Learning Portal. Intuitive in form and function, the Learning Portal encompasses not only specialized learning management software, but also tools to author tests, manage content through a customizable taxonomy, and collaborate across an enterprise.

Why SAP ERP HCM?

As is evident by now, SAP ERP's HCM suite of solutions streamlines HR operations, reduces the average cost borne by a firm to conduct an HR transaction, and brings together HR-related tools and data thereby affording rapid responsiveness to employees, better management visibility into hiring and retentions trends, and greater overall compliance with company standards and regulatory bodies.

Through its Americas' SAP Users' Group (ASUG), SAP conducts an ongoing satisfaction survey with its SAP ERP HCM customers. Recent polling suggested the following reasons why SAP ERP HCM is ideal for HR organizations seeking to best manage and retain their people:

▶ HCM is integrated into other business processes by virtue of its connection with SAP ERP Financials, Manufacturing, and so on.

▶ World-class enterprisewide talent management functionality gives an organization the ability to proactively manage its most precious assets—its people.

▶ HCM gives leadership and line managers alike the ability to enable and empower the global team.

▶ The ability to connect a firm's workforce to a single system of record and accountability facilitates smooth internal transfers and other career development activities around the world.

▶ HCM's built-in business intelligence capabilities provides powerful company-wide HR reporting.

▶ The ability to run SAP ERP HCM as an outsourced business process (also called Business Process Outsourcing, or BPO) gives HR organizations a choice.

▶ SAP's extensive partner network helps ensure supportability.

▶ SAP ERP HCM's superior technology platform and functionality not only are inherently innovative, but invite further innovation through easy integration, extended business processes, and computing platform choice.

SAP ERP HCM is rather amazing. Its power is found in its touchpoints to SAP's other solutions, as explained previously—financials, sales, workflow, managerial accounting, asset accounting, services, operations, and analytics all tie directly to SAP ERP HCM. In the end, it is this integration and cross-company visibility that makes HCM such a solid and safe solution. SAP's SAP ERP HCM customers cited "safe choice" as a key differentiator as well. After all, SAP has a proven track record, has the resources to continue developing and supporting SAP ERP HCM, and has the global reach and influence to assure its customers that their needs will be taken into account for years to come.

SAP Manufacturing and ERP Operations

SAP ERP provides several solutions that assist firms in achieving operational excellence through process efficiencies, business agility, and streamlined business operations. Essentially logistics, these solutions encompass all processes related to a firm's purchasing, plant maintenance, sales and distribution, manufacturing, materials management, warehousing, engineering, and construction. SAP Manufacturing and SAP ERP Operations (an aging but still useful term) include the following solutions:

▶ Procurement and logistics execution, allowing end users to manage their end-to-end procurement and logistics business processes as well as optimizing the physical flow of materials

▶ Product development and manufacturing, from production planning to manufacturing, shop floor integration, product development, and so on

▶ Sales and service, which range from actual sales to managing the delivery of services and all the processes necessary to pay out commissions and other sales incentives

SAP Manufacturing's goal is to fully connect a firm's manufacturing processes with the rest of its business functions: logistics, financials, EH&S requirements, and more. It also allows a firm to manage its manufacturing operations with embedded Lean Sigma and Six Sigma, both of which are critical to creating and improving competitive advantage.

Lean Sigma and Six Sigma speak to increasing the quality of a process. The difference between the two is generally seen as one of improving process flow or speed (Lean Sigma) versus reducing process variation or increasing quality (Six Sigma). Ultimately, Lean Six Sigma will bring these two approaches together in the name of advancing continuous improvement.

SAP Manufacturing allows discrete and process manufacturing firms to better plan, schedule, resequence, and monitor manufacturing processes so as to achieve higher yields and greater profitability. This is accomplished through partner and supplier coordination, exception management, embracing Lean and Six Sigma, complying with EH&S requirements, and so on—all facilitated by SAP Manufacturing. Through continuous improvement, SAP seeks to provide management and shop floor teams alike the ability to view and optimize real-time operations. SAP Manufacturing's powerful analytics support the firm's ability to make changes on the fly. Thus, SAP Manufacturing allows a company to transform itself through enhanced manufacturing capabilities like the following:

▶ **SAP Lean Planning and Operations**—Useful for accelerating and maintaining lean operations (through high throughput, high quality, and low overhead)

▶ **SAP Manufacturing Integration and Intelligence**—Essentially the data that a manufacturing team needs to take the proper action at the proper time

▶ **SAP Supply Chain Management**—Enables the kind of supply chain optimization that brings together and empowers the team

▶ **SAP Solutions for RFID**—A set of customized solutions that help optimize supply chains through more efficient asset tracking and management

▶ **SAP ERP Operations**—Enables the manufacturing team to gain greater visibility into its operations and in turn increase control and business insight

The latter solution, SAP ERP Operations, has been a mainstay of SAP ERP for many years. In fact, the bulk of SAP ERP Operations' core functionality hails from the days of SAP R/3 and its logistics-related modules, some of which are covered next.

Production Planning and Control

Within SAP ERP Operations, the focus of SAP's Production Planning and Control module is to facilitate complete solutions for the following:

▶ Production planning

▶ Production execution

▶ Production control

Production Planning and Control encompasses the comprehensive production process from its inception with the initial creation of master data through the production process, including control and costing. The Production Planning module includes a component called Sales and Operations Planning, which is used for creating realistic and consistent planning figures to forecast future sales. Depending on your method of production, you can use SAP's Production Order processing, Repetitive Manufacturing, or KANBAN Production Control processing. KANBAN is a procedure for controlling production and material flow based on a chain of operations in production and procurement. Overall, then, Production Planning and Control helps manage the following:

- ▶ Basic Data
- ▶ Sales and Operations Planning
- ▶ Master Planning
- ▶ Capacity and Materials Requirements Planning
- ▶ KANBAN
- ▶ Repetitive Manufacturing
- ▶ Production Orders and Product Cost Planning
- ▶ Assembly Orders
- ▶ Production Planning for Process Industries
- ▶ Plant Data Collection
- ▶ Production Planning and Control Information System

As you can see, the implementation of the Production Planning and Control module makes it possible to eliminate routine tasks for the end users responsible for production scheduling. The related reduction in time allows for additional time to be dedicated to more critical activities within the company.

Materials Management

A firm's inventory and materials management business processes are essential to the success of the company. Streamlined day-to-day management of the company's consumption of materials, including company purchasing, managing warehouses and their inventory, tracking and confirming invoices, and so on, are all part of the Materials Management module. Its components include the following:

- ▶ Inventory Management
- ▶ Warehouse Management
- ▶ Purchasing
- ▶ Invoice Verification
- ▶ Materials Planning
- ▶ Purchasing Information System

The result? Materials Management saves time and money, and conserves resources while helping to optimize the company's supply chain.

Plant Maintenance

The main benefit to SAP's Plant Maintenance module is its flexibility to work with different types of companies to meet differing designs, requirements, and work forces. The Plant Maintenance module also contains a graphical interface, which makes it very user friendly and enables it to cater to a larger population of your work force.

Different management strategies are supported within the application, including Risk Based Maintenance and Total Productive Maintenance. Some benefits that your company will derive from the implementation of the Plant Maintenance module involve reduced downtime and outages, the optimization of labor and resources, and a reduction in the costs of inspections and repairs. Components of Plant Maintenance include the following:

- Preventative Maintenance
- Service Management
- Maintenance Order Management
- Maintenance Projects
- Equipment and Technical Objects
- Plant Maintenance Information System

On the whole, the integration of the Plant Maintenance module supports a company in designing and executing its maintenance activities with regard to system resource availability, costs, materials, and personnel deployment.

Sales and Distribution

The Sales and Distribution module, which enables sales and services, arms a firm with the necessary instruments to sell and manage the sales process. SD provides a wealth of information related to a company's sales and marketing trends, capabilities, and so on. An SD end user can access data on products, marketing strategies, sales calls, pricing, and sales leads at any time to facilitate sales and marketing activity. The information is online up-to-the-minute support to be used to service existing customers as well as mine for potential customers and new leads.

Also included within the Sales and Distribution module is a diverse supply of contracts to meet every type of business need. Agreements concerning pricing, delivery dates, and delivery quantity are all supported within this module.

SAP ERP Corporate Services

The final SAP ERP business solution, Corporate Services, assists companies with streamlining internal lifecycle processes. Modules of Corporate Services include the following:

▶ **Global Trade Services (GTS)**—Intended to manage international trade activity complexities, from regulatory compliance to customs and risk management. (GTS was discussed in much more detail earlier this hour.)

▶ **Environment, Health and Safety (EH&S)**—EH&S compliance and occupational health management is intended to assist firms with managing how they comply with matters of product safety, hazardous substance management, waste and emissions management, and so on.

▶ **Quality management**—Reflects the controls and gates necessary to proactively manage the product lifecycle.

▶ **Real estate management**—Used to manage the real estate portfolio lifecycle, from property acquisition through building operations, reporting, maintenance, and disposal.

▶ **Enterprise asset management**—Addresses design, build, operations, and disposal phases.

▶ **Project and portfolio management**—Used to manage a firm's project portfolio (including tracking and managing budget, scheduling, and other resource-based key performance indicators).

▶ **Travel management**—Ranges from processing travel requests to managing planning, reservation changes, expense management, and specialized reporting/analytics.

Several of these services and modules are explored in more detail, next.

Real Estate Management

SAP's Real Estate module integrates real estate processes into your company's overall organizational structure. The Corporate Real Estate Management model is divided into the following two components:

▶ Rental Administration and Settlement

▶ Controlling, Position Valuation, and Information Management

In order for your company to successfully use the Real Estate component, necessary configurations are required in your Plant Maintenance, Materials Management, Project System, and Asset Accounting modules.

Quality Management

The Quality Management module is directed at improving the quality of your products and to some extent processes. In order to produce high-quality products, a well-managed Quality Management system needs to be in place that ensures the integrity of your products, which in turn helps foster good client relations while enhancing your firm's reputation relative to its products as well as the company in general. Services contained in the Quality Management module include the following:

▶ Quality Planning

▶ Quality Inspections

▶ Quality Control

▶ Quality Notifications

▶ Quality Certificates

▶ Test Equipment Management

▶ Quality Management Information System

As should be apparent, the Quality Management module gives a company the capability to analyze, document, and improve upon its processes across several dimensions.

Project and Portfolio Management

Once simply called the Project System module, this important component of SAP ERP Corporate Services assists a company in managing its portfolio of projects. Such high-level cross-project insight allows for outstanding planning, execution, and financial oversight, facilitating true project management in the process. As such, it is centered on managing the network of relationships within the system and establishing project management links.

You can use Project and Portfolio Management in many areas, including investment management, marketing, software and consulting services, research and development, maintenance tasks, shutdown management, plant engineering and construction, and complex made-to-order production. The components of the Project System module include the following:

▶ Basic Data

▶ Operational Structures

▶ Project Planning

▶ Approval

▶ Project Execution and Integration

▶ Project System Information System

Like most project management approaches, the system is based on Work Breakdown Structures (WBS). A WBS is a structured model of work organized in a hierarchical format; work or tasks are managed in a stepwise manner during the course of conducting a project, where large tasks are broken down into key elements that represent the individual tasks and activities in the project.

Summary

This hour provided background into SAP R/3 and how it evolved into what is known as SAP ERP today. SAP ERP consists of several high-level solution offerings, including Financials, Operations (itself composed of three logistics offerings), Human Capital Management (HCM) and its various solutions, Corporate Services, and Analytics. An introduction to these core solutions areas was further bolstered by discussions into specific functional solutions and modules underpinning each SAP ERP solution offering.

Case Study: Hour 8

Consider this SAP ERP case study and the questions that follow, the answers to which may be found in Appendix A, "Case Study Answers."

Situation

MNC Global is implementing SAP HCM and several SAP ERP logistics solutions. As a member of the development team, you have been asked to answer a number of questions held by several of MNC's stakeholders.

Questions

1. What does the acronym SAP ERP HCM stand for, and why is it a compelling solution for organizations today?

2. What are the components of Plant Maintenance?

3. What kind of business solutions does SAP ERP Operations address?

4. Why is there so much overlap among SAP ERP's business solutions, modules, and business processes?

5. For the most robust yet targeted set of SAP ERP analytics, what should MNC consider implementing?

The SAP Business Suite

What You'll Learn in This Hour:

▶ What makes SCM, CRM, SRM, and PLM unique

▶ How SAP CRM affects the bottom line

▶ Different venues for using SAP SRM

▶ How to gain business insight through SAP PLM

▶ Insight into SAP Manufacturing and SAP Service and Asset Management

Outside of SAP ERP, SAP offers several additional business applications or components. These components, along with SAP ERP, constitute a family of tightly integrated business solutions under the umbrella of the SAP Business Suite. In Hour 8, "SAP ERP: SAP's Core Product," we looked at SAP ERP. In this hour, you will learn about the other components, how they fit into the big picture, how they are used, and the value they provide.

SAP Supply Chain Management

SCM is the most mature component within SAP's Business Suite. By transforming your supply chain into a dynamic customer-centric supply chain network, SAP Supply Chain Management (SCM) enables you to plan for and streamline your firm's network of logistics and resources that come together to form a supply chain. Generally speaking, a supply chain comprises three areas—supply, manufacturing, and distribution. The supply portion of a supply chain focuses on the raw materials needed by manufacturing, which in turn converts raw materials into finished products. The distribution aspect of a supply chain focuses on moving the finished products though a network of distributors, warehouses, and outlets. Thus, SCM opens the door to cross-company collaboration as a firm gains visibility into its suppliers, vendors, and customers. SCM empowers a firm by creating a more predictable supply chain capable of capitalizing on circumstances, minimizing costs, and maximizing profitability through the following:

▶ Improving responsiveness via real-time insight into the entire supply chain

▶ Improving inventory turns by synchronizing inputs with outputs (that is, balancing supply with demand)

▶ Encouraging collaboration by providing visibility into trends as seen through supply chain monitoring, analysis, and business analytics

Leveraging the same SAP NetWeaver platform used by all of SAP's Business Suite components, SCM streamlines operations without taxing a firm's IT organization or SAP support team—the solution foundation and integration technologies are the same as those employed by other NetWeaver components, including WebAS, Web Services, and so on. This combination of capability and mature technology makes for a true win-win: better service, increased productivity, and improved profitability, all within the umbrella of standards-based and mature technologies. As of SCM release 4.1, SAP supports creating and maintaining an adaptive supply chain network through three components—SAP Advanced Planner and Optimizer (SAP APO), SAP Inventory Collaboration Hub (SAP ICH), and SAP Event Management (SAP EM), all of which are outlined next.

SAP APO

SAP's Advanced Planner and Optimizer (APO) supports supply chain network-oriented planning, decision making, execution, and optimization. It integrates supply planning with the other SAP components discussed this hour—CRM, PLM, and SRM—giving a firm complete 360-degree visibility of its supply chain network. APO is really the core of SCM, and is a mature solution by any standards. By providing a flexible and adaptive engine for managing your planning processes, APO enables you to make smart decisions through central planning and execution. Finally, note that the newest releases of SAP APO also include SAP Business Information Warehouse (SAP BW) to enable reporting.

SAP Inventory Collaboration Hub

SAP's Inventory Collaboration Hub (ICH) enables a firm to collaborate with its suppliers, jointly approving and easily tweaking the best mix of inventory necessary to meet production demands. This is accomplished through supply chain visibility focused on the firm's manufacturing facilities: knowing what each plant needs, what they consume and at what rate, and when each facility's stock needs to be replenished. With tight integration into an organization's back-end ERP or R/3 system, ICH integrates naturally into a firm's planning system and its subprocesses.

Though functionally it looks to be a seamless solution, bridging ERP and SCM, from a technical perspective SAP ICH is complex. SAP Process Integration (PI, formerly known as SAP Exchange Infrastructure or SAP XI) enables this integration. ICH leverages its own web user interface based on Business Server Pages (BSP) technology. Finally, integrating master data SAP ICH requires an ERP or R/3 plug-in. Read through the relevant Master Guide to determine your unique requirements.

SAP Event Management

SAP's Event Management (EM) enables a firm to monitor the supply chain, including creation and escalation of alerts based on specific conditions and thresholds. This enables end users to identify and proactively resolve process exceptions and potential supply chain issues before they become show-stoppers. More simply, EM makes it possible to notify supply chain owners of critical situations or exceptions, which in turn enables fast turnaround and thus improved process quality and customer satisfaction.

SCM Business Purposes and Benefits

Through APO, ICH, and EM, SAP Supply Chain Management tremendously impacts a firm's bottom line. Companies can literally shave millions in cost and drive improved margins in the process. Benefits include the following:

▶ Better supply/demand responsiveness, enabling your organization to see and respond to new opportunities

▶ Improved customer satisfaction, given the improved underlying communication and collaboration made possible

▶ Improved regulatory compliance, essential in today's world of Sarbanes-Oxley and EH&S requirements

▶ Better coordination and synchronization between you, your suppliers, and your other business partners, which help keep your supply chain well optimized and aligned with your priorities

▶ Improved cash flows, given the reduction in inventory levels in conjunction with the improved number of inventory turns made possible

All the aforementioned items enhance profitability through lower costs made possible by timely planning, execution, and supply chain coordination, particularly APO. Typical applications of SAP APO, using different APO applications, are outlined next:

▶ From the Supply Chain Cockpit (SCC), a firm can use APO to launch a query comprising company-specific supply chain elements. This might include products, resources, locations, transportation lanes, and other variables. Query results can be displayed in a map, in lists, or in any number of table-based or graphical formats.

▶ Using APO's Demand Planning application, a firm can also forecast market demand for its products or services, and then follow this up through the creation of a demand plan. Different models can be created, too, changing the balance of supply and demand to affect profitability, minimize inventory turns, and so on. In doing so, the firm feeds not only its sales forecast, but also its sales analysis processes.

▶ From APO's Production Planning application, a firm can create a production schedule that balances and reflects a supply plan with its point-in-time manufacturing capacity.

▶ From APO's Purchasing Planning application, a firm can model and develop various plans for balancing raw materials and other resources against the demand for its products, and generate a well-thought-out supply plan as a result.

▶ Leveraging APO's Transportation and Handling capabilities, a firm can also plan for, optimize, and manage the transportation and handling processes surrounding a particular product group.

▶ Finally, using APO's SNP Planner, a firm can schedule the people, products, and other resources that need access to its internal facilities.

Through these sample real-world scenarios, you can see how using SAP SCM can help to maximize your company's return on assets, increase its profitability, and help your business unit become more competitive than ever.

SAP Customer Relationship Management

SAP's Customer Relationship Management component has found great acceptance in the CRM marketplace. In its traditional role, SAP CRM supports customer-related processes end-to-end. It enables a firm to obtain a 360-degree view of its customers and their various touchpoints into the organization. SAP CRM also augments typical back-end functions such as order fulfillment, shipping, invoicing, and accounts receivable. And it folds in and enables enterprisewide customer intelligence, or business intelligence specific to the firm's customers and their needs.

By bringing this functionality together, CRM facilitates better and faster decision making, lending itself to improving profitability per customer while helping address the business's strategic priorities. Exactly how this is all accomplished is covered next.

How CRM Extends SAP ERP

Through the functionality mentioned previously, SAP CRM effectively extends SAP ERP and SAP ECC in particular. It brings together and integrates industry-specific processes to better support a firm's customers; customer-facing organizations benefit from insight obtained across many different touchpoints, from marketing and sales to service, support, back-end financials, and more. And because SAP CRM is tied to these essential touchpoints, the solution collapses field interactions, Internet-based transactions, and even channel- and partner-based transactions into a single powerful customer-centric view. Within this view lies the true power of SAP CRM—powerful analytics let a firm capitalize on what it knows about its customers so as to not only retain them but maximize profit per transaction and expand revenue in the process.

SAP CRM Features

A number of the core features and support for specific business processes outlined previously are worth exploring further:

▶ **Marketing support**—Use SAP CRM to enhance your marketing effectiveness, maximize resource use, and empower your team to develop and maintain long-term profitable customer relationships. From a user's perspective, this includes marketing resource management, campaign management, trade promotion management, market segment management, lead/prospect management, and marketing analytics.

▶ **Sales support**—Maximize your sales efforts by removing barriers to productivity and working with your customers in a consistent manner. CRM Sales is geared toward your sales force, empowering them and providing the tools they need to close deals. For example, territory management, account and contact management, lead and opportunity management, and sales planning and forecasting help your sales force identify and manage prospects. Then, by leveraging quotation and order management, product configuration, contract management, incentive and commission management, time and travel management, and sales analytics, you can retain customers all the while growing sales volume and margins and managing the expenses associated with sales.

▶ **Service support**—Through CRM, you can maximize the value both you and your customers obtain from post-sales services. This enables you to profitably manage a broad range of functions geared toward driving successful customer service and support, including field service, Internet-enabled service offerings, service marketing and sales, and service/contract management. After they are entrenched, customers benefit from improved warranty and claims management, and effective channel service and depot repair services. Your service team benefits from service analytics, enabling it to maximize profit per touchpoint.

▶ **Web channel** (formerly Internet-based e-commerce)—Use Web channel to increase sales and reduce transaction costs by turning the Internet into a service (or sales and marketing) channel for businesses and consumers. This makes it possible to increase profitability of existing accounts while also reaching new markets in the process.

▶ **Interaction Center (IC) management support**—With support for marketing, sales, and service vehicles such as telemarketing, telesales, customer service, e-service, and interaction center analytics, SAP CRM IC complements and arms your field-based sales force.

▶ **Partner channel management**—Use this to improve processes for partner recruitment, partner management, communications, channel marketing, channel forecasting, collaborative selling, partner order management, channel service, and analytics. In this way, a firm can attract and retain a more profitable and loyal indirect channel by managing partner relationships and empowering channel partners.

▶ **Business communications management**—Enable inbound and outbound contact management across multiple locations and communications channels. Business communications management integrates multichannel communications with a firm's customer-facing business processes to create a seamless communications experience across any number of mediums (such as voice, text messaging, email, and more).

▶ **Real-time offer management**—Manage the complexities of offers in real time using SAP's advanced analytical real-time decision engine, and optimize the decision-making process on all customer interaction channels, thus enabling your firm to quickly accept, intelligently modify, and across-the-board enhance its customer relationships.

CRM Industry-Specific Processes

CRM processes are typically very customer focused, built around the needs of a particular business unit or organizational entity. SAP CRM takes these fundamental capabilities and brings them up a notch, helping firms manage and deliver customer-focused value within their unique industry vertical. And because SAP CRM is easily adapted to different industries, it's uniquely positioned to service multiprovider organizations. Several additional industry-specific features round out SAP CRM. For example, SAP CRM enables trade promotion management, which allows account and trade managers the ability to improve control and visibility into the trade promotion process (another method of providing brand awareness). Here are some other examples of the power that SAP CRM delivers relative to industry-specific CRM processes:

- **Professional services industry**—Use SAP CRM to manage prospects, opportunities, client relationships, project resources, and the development of client deliverables.

- **Automotive industry**—SAP CRM can also manage the automotive sales cycle from start to finish, including vehicle market planning, sales, financials, distribution, and post-sales management.

- **Leasing entities**—CRM's Leasing capabilities address end-to-end lease management, from identifying financing opportunities for new leases or loans, to remarketing existing leases, to lease termination.

- **Consumer products industry**—Manage customer trade promotions, including brand management, activity planning, demand planning, budgeting, program execution, evaluation, and subsequent analyses of each phase.

- **Media industry vertical**—SAP CRM can manage intellectual property (IP), help you leverage this IP to your financial benefit, and manage any resulting royalties or other payments.

- **Utilities vertical**—Manage both commercial and industrial customers from a sales perspective, including opportunity and quotation management, cross-system contracts, and key revenue-producing accounts.

- **High-tech industry**—From managing and measuring business volume to viewing customer demand, managing channel inventory, and splitting commissions, SAP CRM addresses high-tech partner and channel relationship needs.

- **Public sector**—Through constituent services and tax and revenue management, SAP CRM can help a public sector organization manage and address tax administration, service programs, and more.

▶ **Pharmaceutical industry**—Use SAP CRM to manage and support the stages of drug commercialization, from strategy definition through sales planning and execution, on to measuring the success of each drug's respective sales and marketing programs.

▶ **Manufacturing vertical**—Manage orders, the manufacturing process, fulfillment, and more through SAP CRM's lean batch-management capabilities.

SAP CRM's business benefits are indeed as far-reaching as they are diverse. And with visibility into customer data effectively spread across a firm's enterprise (from financial systems to its supply chain, ERP, and HR repositories), CRM expedites decision-making just as much as it enables strategic objectives to be balanced against tactical needs. In this way, SAP CRM is one Business Suite component where measurable return on investment is not only fairly easy to calculate, but nearly as easy to achieve.

SAP Product Lifecycle Management

Still the least popular Business Suite component, Product Lifecycle Management (PLM) is nonetheless valuable to organizations tasked with managing product lifecycle. PLM is focused on helping companies develop new products by helping those organizations embrace and facilitate creativity and innovation. Further, SAP PLM helps companies identify and remove productivity-robbing organizational constraints. It serves as the foundation for successful new product development and introduction (NPDI). Using NPDI, you tie people and information together, effectively interconnecting your sales, planning, production, procurement, maintenance, internal service provider, and other organizations together. And outside of a firm's own internal organizations, PLM enables you to easily bring together partners, suppliers, contract manufacturers, external service providers, and even customers under the umbrella of developing better products.

PLM's IT Platform

Like its counterparts, PLM is built on the NetWeaver technology stack. In this way it takes advantage of industry-standard communications protocols to maximize its capability to connect and operate with other solutions. Specifically, PLM's use of HTML, XML, and the Wireless Application Protocol (WAP) enables a firm that has deployed PLM to access it from desktops or laptops as well as through handheld and mobile devices. Its open architecture also means PLM may be customized for specific company and industry verticals, allowing anytime, anywhere access regardless of industry business process specifics.

Business Insight Through PLM

Product Lifecycle Management (PLM) facilitates rapid development and delivery of the products upon which your business depends for its revenue. PLM's technology platform sets the stage for usefulness, but in itself does not solve any business problems. Only by affording a holistic view into the processes and resources that come into play during a product's lifecycle does PLM become a comprehensive problem solver. With it, you can take care of your product conception, design, engineering, production ramp-up, product change management, post-sales service, and maintenance needs. With PLM, the benefits are many:

▶ Enjoy a faster time to market as a result of rapid development capabilities.

▶ By tying together your supply chain with procurement and PLM, manufacturing operations are streamlined; delivery and production are sped up.

▶ Capitalize on core competencies while outsourcing non-core tasks, thereby minimizing your overall costs.

▶ Measure and evaluate the progress of discrete product-oriented projects across different product lines.

▶ By integrating with your operational systems, you can lower your total cost of ownership relative to planning for and deploying a new product.

▶ Leverage PLM's modular approach to product development and ramp-up, so as to incrementally meet your product's needs as it evolves through the product lifecycle.

▶ Realize improved product quality.

▶ Maximize your product workers' productivity through the use of a role-based enterprise portal front end.

▶ Reduce the waste and inefficiency that surrounds typical product lifecycle management processes.

▶ Make better and faster business decisions, taking advantage of powerful analytics across the product lifecycle (portfolio management, quality, occupational health and safety, maintenance management, and others).

Ultimately, the greatest business benefit of PLM is found in the improved business results a firm will enjoy as a result. PLM enables a company to pursue and develop new products; innovate, explore, and analyze new markets; penetrate those new markets; gain a higher market share in existing markets; and increase customer satisfaction throughout the entire product lifecycle.

Using PLM

At the end of the day, SAP's comprehensive solution for product lifecycle management aids a company in its day-to-day execution surrounding product management. Use PLM to enable collaborative product development, engineering, and associated project and quality management. Plug in your partners as you all seek to meet environmental, health, and safety requirements. Gain visibility across your enterprise by extending PLM via the entire SAP Business Suite—from CRM and SCM to SAP ERP and more. In doing so, you can tie in every intercompany and partner-provided department or organization, which enables you to optimize communications, strengthen marketing and sales efforts, and include the necessary post-development service and support organizations. Through all this, you maintain a low cost of ownership as you push new products through their development and engineering phases into manufacturing, and ultimately into the hands of your customers—thus reaping better margins and faster turnarounds than ever possible before.

SAP Supplier Relationship Management

SRM is SAP's venerable solution for managing the procurement and support of the goods and services a company needs day in and day out. Just as SAP CRM manages the relationship between a company and its customers, SAP SRM helps to optimize and manage the relationship between a company and its suppliers. As another one of SAP's more mature offerings, it's no surprise that SAP's Supplier Relationship Management is well integrated with other SAP Business Suite components. For example, SRM integrates seamlessly with PLM, enabling a high degree of collaboration between product buyers and parts suppliers. Bidding processes are streamlined as well. All this naturally impacts SAP ERP as well, because financial and logistics data are updated and shared between systems. SRM also ties into SAP SCM, extending and enabling tight integration with your supply chain while leveraging the open standards-based SAP NetWeaver platform.

SRM-to-PLM Integration Benefits

With this tight integration into NetWeaver, the SAP Business Suite, and specifically PLM, SRM users benefit in terms of the following:

- ▶ Improved design collaboration and therefore time-to-market.

- ▶ Streamlined access to engineering documentation and other materials useful in optimizing product quality, manufacturing processes, and more.

- ▶ Better visibility into ERP back-end data, such as materials management processes, financial documents, and bills of materials (BOMs).

▶ The capability to mark up and "redline" computer-aided drawings.

▶ By the same token, SAP PLM users benefit from PLM's tight integration with SRM's sourcing capabilities.

▶ A high degree of collaboration made possible during the design and engineering phases of a product, because workers focus on technical specifications and the development of requests for proposals (RFPs) and requests for quotes (RFQs).

How SRM Impacts Your Enterprise

SRM enables a firm to lower its costs through its integration with the other components found in the SAP Business Suite. This is especially so with "operational" systems such as ERP, CRM, computer-aided design, and supply chain systems. Through this integration, Supplier Relationship Management enables an organization to improve its product and sourcing strategies, shorten sourcing cycle times, and effectively reduce procurement costs. By reducing the costs of goods sourced and used throughout your company, yet improving supply efficiencies, SRM enables a firm to manage its bottom line. Business benefits are many:

▶ Sourcing strategy improvements, which include improved access to each supplier's performance, improved management of supply, and therefore decreased supply-related risk

▶ Compressed cycle times made possible through faster RFP-to-receipt processes, use of online approvals to speed up the procurement cycle, and improved supplier responsiveness

▶ Reduced process costs facilitated through simplification, process automation, low-cost integration and connectivity with other systems, and the elimination of maverick buying

▶ Lower overall unit prices in light of the consolidation made possible for all your departments, along with reduced costs for carrying inventory and as a result of competitive bidding

Using SAP SRM

With your understanding of SRM from a business benefit and technology perspective, a final look at how you can use SRM is in order. Most obviously to those who have already deployed it, SRM is used by those responsible for internal procurement, which includes the following:

▶ Employee-driven self-service, whereby employees are empowered to procure materials and services necessary to the completion of their organization's goals. Administration and processing are accomplished through one interface using web-based tools that not only make the process a simple one, but also facilitate corporate spending and procurement compliance.

▶ Automated materials procurement performed as part of an organization's supply-chain workflow (essentially integrating your purchasing function with your supply chain management system).

SRM enables strategic purchasing and sourcing by supporting a host of management, development, and analysis functions as well. For example, use SRM to do the following:

▶ Manage contracts relative to overall compliance with each contract's terms and conditions, and more.

▶ Create, manage, and administer your procurement catalog, using built-in tools to import new product detailed data from external sources, to manage your product hierarchy or schema, and to index your products so that search capabilities are enabled.

▶ Manage your supplier-selection process, thereby creating a base of supply and inherently improving process repeatability. Use electronic auction and bidding tools to analyze each supplier's performance, to collaborate with your suppliers, and to minimize procurement risks.

▶ Develop strategies for supply, again using built-in tools to aggregate the demand for particular materials and services across your enterprise. In the same way, manage and analyze your product portfolio, conduct product management tasks, and control the purchasing process.

▶ Analyze your spending patterns through global spend visibility; conduct analytics related to your products and suppliers, and then share this data across your enterprise (populate data warehouses, data marts, other procurement systems, as well as electronic catalogs, supply chain management systems, and other internal systems).

Last of all, SRM makes it possible to collaborate with suppliers and thus streamline procurement processes, provide better information access to a firm's purchasers, make better sourcing decisions, as well as the following:

▶ **Collaborate with product developers**—Share data between trading partners and your own purchasing team to enable faster product development cycles.

▶ **Collaborate with your suppliers**—Give them access to your inventory and replenishment data so they can help you maintain your minimum required inventory levels.

▶ **Connect and integrate your suppliers with your team**—Use standard XML-based document exchange technology to gain real-time access into the lowest prices, best volume discounts, and so on.

By using SRM's breadth of capabilities, a firm can truly optimize, integrate, and automate procurement processes into its own day-to-day workflows. This helps the organization never to miss out on supplies essential to conducting business.

SAP Manufacturing

Though the previous SAP Business Suite offerings reflect standalone products, SAP offers several solutions that are an amalgamation of existing products assembled to provide a particular service or capability. As briefly outlined last hour, SAP Manufacturing is one of these components or products. It allows a firm to fully connect the manufacturing process—and insight into the process—with the rest of the business. SAP Manufacturing integrates manufacturing with other operations, too, all while enabling manufacturing quality control through embedded lean and Six Sigma processes. Through the SAP Manufacturing solution, a firm's management and production departments can gain real-time visibility into key data, enabling them in turn to act quickly. Managers can document, track, and interpret quality and performance using rich analytics capabilities as well. Finally, manufacturing capabilities may be extended and augmented with the complete set of solutions for manufacturing, including:

▶ **SAP Lean Planning and Operations**—Accelerate lean transformation, and sustain lean operations.

▶ **SAP Manufacturing Integration and Intelligence**—Deliver actionable intelligence to production personnel.

▶ **SAP ERP Operations**—Gain control and insight, and create value.

▶ **SAP Supply Chain Management**—Connect and empower your organization.

▶ **SAP Solutions for RFID**—Enable agile supply chain execution, efficient asset management, and adaptive manufacturing.

SAP Service and Asset Management

SAP Service and Asset Management is used to manage service delivery, service parts, and track asset maintenance and performance. As such, it is really an extension or combination of SAP's other applications, particularly SCM, SRM/Procurement, and CRM solutions; the specifics surrounding SAP Service and Asset Management depend on a firm's business scenarios to be implemented. As SAP shares with its customers, though (whether a manufacturer, third-party service provider, utility or telecommunications provider, or involved in an asset-intensive business), SAP Service and Asset Management helps improve service delivery and better maintain assets. Consider the basic solution's capabilities as outlined by the SAP Service Marketplace:

▶ **Service management**—Manage, optimize, analyze, and continuously improve your entire service operations.

▶ **Service parts management**—Reduce company investment in service spare parts while ensuring that you have the right parts in the right place at the right time.

▶ **Enterprise asset management**—Gain real-time visibility into asset performance and maintenance to reduce operating costs, manage capital expenditures, and improve asset productivity.

▶ **IT service and asset management**—Optimize your IT service support and delivery processes and keep track of your IT assets throughout their lifecycle.

This targeted solution provides the tools necessary to increase service revenues all with margins. Service becomes a competitive differentiator as a firm learns to reduce service and maintenance costs, enhance asset reliability and availability, improve productivity, and increase its return on assets. Regulatory compliance is maintained as well; requirements from agencies such as the FDA and OSHA and regulations such as Sarbanes-Oxley are taken care of transparently through SAP Service and Asset Management. In fact, everyone from the firm's employees and partners to its customers may be provided with a well-thought-out, consistent, and integrated view of the firm's service activities, including the following:

▶ Handling service sales and marketing

▶ Managing service-level agreements

- ▶ Overseeing service call centers

- ▶ Tracking warranties and claims

- ▶ Providing customer self-service over the Web

- ▶ Performing field service, in-house maintenance and repair, and depot repair

- ▶ Addressing service parts management, including execution and planning along with providing mechanisms for managing service performance and conducting financial analysis

Thus, SAP Service and Asset Management provides asset owners and operators a method for managing assets, equipment, and facilities, unlike anything SAP has provided in the past. SAP Service and Asset Management is comprehensive, addressing the complete asset lifecycle—from design specification and procurement, to installation and start-up, maintenance and operations, and finally decommissioning and disposal.

Summary

As you can imagine, the complexity of the SAP business solutions discussed in this hour are much greater than reflected here. Indeed, each SAP component within the broader SAP Business Suite umbrella constitutes an SAP implementation in its own right. However, the skills and knowledge you have gained in the past hour have equipped you with a wide-ranging understanding of how each solution can be of benefit.

Case Study: Hour 9

Consider this hour's case study regarding the SAP Business Suite and the questions that follow, the answers to which may be found in Appendix A, "Case Study Answers."

Situation

In your new role as Director of Strategic Applications at MNC Global, Inc., you have tasked your team with assessing and making a number of observations about SAP's Business Suite components or applications.

Questions

1. Which features in SAP CRM augment your capability to support new customers?

2. Can you buy SAP Manufacturing in the same way you buy SAP CRM or SRM?

3. How does SRM's tight integration with PLM benefit your SRM users?

4. Which of the Business Suite components or products is the most mature in terms of years of availability?

5. What are the three general areas of a supply chain?

PART III

Implementing SAP

Implementation Overview: A Project Management Perspective

What You'll Learn in This Hour:

▶ How the project management roadmap is embodied in SAP's ASAP methodology

▶ Insight into the ASAP methodology

▶ How contemporary methods and tools aid effective project management

▶ The role and makeup of the SAP project team

Just as there are business and technical roadmaps for implementing an SAP application, there is also the need for a project management roadmap and resulting project plan. Most implementation experts would argue that the project roadmap is actually most important, in fact, because it comprises the other roadmaps and reflects the high-level overall project view by which low-level project plans are built. The project roadmap is indeed the overarching blueprint.

SAP and the ASAP Methodology

SAP found long ago that without a sound implementation roadmap, its customers would often fail to realize their business process reengineering goals and in the process of failure often blame SAP's software. Truth be told, SAP's software is indeed complex and typically time-consuming to implement. But the reasons lie nearly exclusively outside of SAP's control; SAP is difficult to implement for the following reasons:

▶ Business is innately complex.

▶ Business users are typically uninterested in embracing the changes associated with conducting business in a new way.

▶ Executive buy-in and ongoing support are historically spotty.

▶ IT computing platforms can serve to artificially limit innovation or fail to enable the kind of technical agility needed by business applications.

▶ Implementation teams have historically lacked fundamental project management and change management skills necessary for a successful project.

▶ The ERP implementation process itself is cumbersome, subject to reinvention, and therefore inordinately expensive.

Researchers looking at ERP implementations have found the last two items most responsible for the cost overruns that continue to find their way to the front pages of *The Wall Street Journal*. The Gartner Group noted more than half of all ERP implementations—nearly half of which were built around SAP's products—required double what was originally budgeted. Further, more than half of all ERP implementations were deemed less than successful (Gartner Group, 1998, "Implementing SAP R/3: Avoiding Becoming a Statistic"; Landauer, 2000, "Agencies Piece Together Sprawling Systems"). Clearly, to help ensure its software lived up to its customers' expectations, something had to be done.

> Did you know that SAP projects have a significantly greater chance of failure due to weak change management processes? To remedy this, initiate your project with strong alignment and commitment among all stakeholders as to how changes will be controlled, managed, and enforced throughout the project. This not only facilitates project success, but also helps maintain focus on the project's value and business problems the project seeks to resolve.

Introduction to ASAP

For the reasons noted, SAP developed a basic implementation methodology tagged ASAP, or AcceleratedSAP. Envisioned initially for smaller SAP projects, ASAP eventually became something of a de facto standard for describing an implementation roadmap from a project management perspective. It helped organizations get their arms around what it meant to reengineer the current operating environment, structure, systems, and processes—from both business and IT perspectives.

ASAP continues to help firms today design their SAP implementation roadmap in a manner that's both efficient and comprehensive. It helps steer a project team to optimize the time, people, and other resources necessary to implement SAP. Focused on leveraging reusable templates, tools, and training, and wrapped up in a five-phase process-oriented roadmap for guiding implementation, ASAP has found great success in the real world even 10 years after its introduction. The ASAP project management roadmap is composed of the following sequential phases:

▶ Phase 1: Project Preparation

▶ Phase 2: Business Blueprint

▶ Phase 3: Realization

▶ Phase 4: Final Preparation

▶ Phase 5: Go-Live and Support

See Figure 10.1 for the ASAP roadmap.

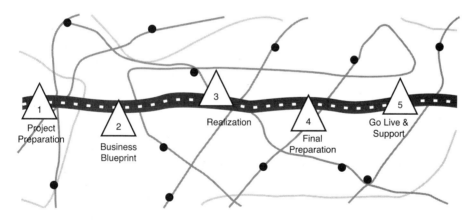

FIGURE 10.1
SAP's ASAP roadmap remains a valuable tool even today.

Phase 1: Project Preparation

Phase 1 comprises many of the steps necessary to start an SAP implementation on the right foot. During this phase, the team is initially structured and assembled. The team then begins the process of identifying, collecting, and managing all the resources necessary for the implementation. Several important milestones occur in Phase 1:

▶ Obtaining senior-level management/stakeholder support

▶ Identifying clear project objectives

▶ Architecting an efficient decision-making process

▶ Creating an environment suitable for change and reengineering

▶ Building a qualified and capable project team

The remaining four phases of ASAP are covered in the next hour, "Implementing SAP: A Business and Functional Perspective." The project matter explored throughout the remainder of this hour relates to an implementation from a project management perspective.

Senior-Level Management Support

One of the most important Phase 1 milestones is obtaining the full agreement and cooperation of the most important company decision makers and other key stakeholders. As you read earlier, their backing and support are crucial for a successful implementation.

Clear Project Objectives

An SAP implementation requires well-defined objectives and expectations. Vague or unclear notions of what a firm hopes to obtain through deploying SAP only handicap the implementation process. Ensure the firm's expectations are aligned to the company's resources, too. Unclear resource requirements is one of the biggest reasons behind the enormous cost overruns that are often talked about in large ERP implementations. Clearly define, communicate, and subsequently refine all ideas, goals, and project plans well before attempting to moving the project forward.

An Efficient Decision-making Process

One obstacle that often stalls implementations is a poorly constructed decision-making process. Before embarking on an implementation, key decision makers need to be clearly identified. Decide now who is responsible for different decisions along the way, being careful to include executive as well as local decision makers and project leaders from each area of the business affected. In the same way, don't forget to identify the IT decision makers as well. And be sure to communicate the need for rapid decision making; identify timelines and escalation plans to help ensure your project doesn't stall while awaiting a key decision along the way.

Environment Suitable for Change and Reengineering

The team must be willing to accept that, along with the new SAP software, things are going to change—the business will change, the information technology enabling the business will change, and the methods of testing and communicating changes will change as well. By implementing SAP, you will essentially redesign your current practices to model more efficient or predefined best business practices. Use education to help gain momentum and avoid resistance to change.

Building a Qualified Project Team

Probably the most important milestone early on is assembling a project team for the implementation. Your project team must be a representative sample of the population of your company. If you are implementing the Materials Management and Plant Maintenance modules in SAP ERP, for example, you need to include people from both of these departments, as well as from your Information Technology department, on the implementation team. The team should also represent management as well as the business or "functional" personnel. After all, management is often less aware of the day-to-day functions of an organization, including how implementing SAP will tactically influence those functions.

Beyond Phase 1, ASAP comprises Business Blueprinting (phase 2), Realization (phase 3), Final Preparation (phase 4), and Go-Live and Support (phase 5). Each of these critical phases reflects the business and functional roadmap more so than the project management roadmap, however, and are therefore outlined in detail in Hour 11. Before turning to Hour 11, though, look through the final pages of this hour.

More Contemporary Implementation Tools and Methodologies

Because ASAP has proven itself effective, most SAP implementation partners continue to embrace ASAP or a customized version of it. Several years ago, though, ASAP evolved into GlobalSAP and later ValueSAP. ASAP was intended to be limited in terms of rigid phases; the fact that implementation phases in the real world often overlapped, or that businesses found themselves in the midst of multiple ASAP phases as a result of a geographically phased rollout, was contrary to ASAP. The new SAP deployment methodologies therefore added Evaluation and Continuous Business Improvement to their core focus on implementation. These changes help overcome some of the previous shortfalls, although not all of them. During this time, the roadmap changed a bit as well, shrinking from five to four phases.

In 2001, SAP AG released an improved delivery vehicle—SAP Solution Manager, or SolMan—when it introduced Web Application Server (WebAS) 6.10. By the end of 2002, Solution Manager had matured considerably, offering not only multiple roadmaps to implementation but also improved content. Some of this content included sample documents, new templates, a repository for canned business processes, and better project-management tools.

SAP Solution Manager has built upon ASAP's groundwork. Robust project monitoring and reporting capabilities have been recently augmented with Learning Maps, which are role-specific Internet-enabled training tools featuring online tutoring and virtual classrooms. In this way, the project team can more quickly get up to speed. With training and related support of the ASAP and ValueSAP methodologies replaced by SolMan, project teams do well to transition from ASAP-based and other methodologies to those facilitated by SAP Solution Manager.

It's important to remember, though, that at the end of the day these approaches all amount to little more than frameworks or methodologies with supporting templates. Even SolMan only facilitates an implementation—there's still much real work that needs to be done. But if you are seeking to deploy well-known and mature SAP functionality, and are focused on avoiding too much custom development, SolMan is a wonderful tool in your implementation arsenal. Let's now turn our attention to the project team.

Overall SAP Implementation Project Structure

A typical project structure for SAP implementation consists of an executive steering committee or project board headed by a project sponsor. The cross-bundle project lead is answerable to this committee. In turn, the core project team itself is headed by the cross-bundle project leader. He is supported by the different bundle/project leads and their respective senior representatives. Reporting to each bundle lead are project leads for the different SAP "rows." Examples of common SAP rows are the Order Management row, Purchasing row, Warehouse Inventory row, and so on. As you can see, rows equate to functional business areas and form the core functional deliverable team for each SAP implementation. To read more about row leaders, see Hour 11.

The Executive Steering Committee or Project Board

The executive steering committee (often called a project board) consists of the SAP project's key stakeholders, executive decision makers, senior business and IT leaders, and other stakeholders with a keen interest in seeing the SAP implementation through to completion. It is this committee's ability to steer the project, given the inevitable changes both inside and external to the project, that makes it vital. The project sponsor is nearly always a key member of the committee, along with the SAP cross-bundle project leader (the company-internal SAP Project Manager outlined later this hour).

Important committee members include the following:

▶ The committee chair, a senior executive tasked with making SAP a reality.

▶ The project sponsor, who may or may not chair the committee.

▶ The chair or lead of the firm's Project Management Office (PMO).

▶ The firm's cross-bundle project leader (the company-internal project manager as opposed to other project managers who are often appointed from consulting and integration partners and SAP itself), who may or may not chair the PMO.

▶ Functional area or workstream leaders, each of whom is a high-level representative of his or her respective business areas, such as Finance, HR, Manufacturing, Logistics, Worldwide Sales, and so on.

▶ The firm's Chief Information Officer (CIO) or another senior IT representative, who typically has the final say in IT-related decision making.

▶ The Director of Enterprise Computing (or someone holding similar responsibility and authority); this person is usually responsible for the systems currently in place, systems that will be retired when SAP is introduced.

▶ A senior-level chief architect or chief technologist (who may also be SAP AG's appointed project manager); this person acts as the SAP technical liaison to the steering committee and is responsible for setting strategic technical direction and to some extent making IT-related decisions.

The steering committee meets daily in many cases to review status, quickly work through issues, and publish decisions, recommendations, and overall opinions. Tasks crucial to the executive steering committee include the following:

▶ Identifying and approving the scope of the project

▶ Prioritizing the project among all corporate projects

▶ Providing the necessary funding and resources from the business to ensure project success

▶ Setting priorities

▶ Settling disputes

▶ Committing resources to the project

▶ Monitoring the progress and impact of the implementation

▶ Empowering the team to make decisions

The importance of upper management's buy-in and other influence cannot be underestimated—they have a direct impact on the success of the implementation. Not surprising, the SAP implementation projects that have the most problems are often the ones where upper-management support is unclear or divided.

Project Sponsor

At this point, certain senior-level executives have already been convinced that implementing SAP is right for the firm and its stakeholders. Typically, others must still be convinced that the business units are on the right track and that the investment in SAP is not only warranted, but in the organization's best interests long term. This is where the project sponsor spends his or her time initially, gaining consensus within the impacted business areas, executive circles, and various IT organizations that will ultimately contribute to supporting the project.

The project sponsor also plays a key role in initially guiding the project board or steering committee, discussed later in this hour. The project sponsor builds momentum, gaining buy-in and "talking up" the project throughout the company. When the project sponsor works with the various business units to help them understand how important they will be to the project, and how much better the project will address their needs, excitement and buy-in around the project naturally grows in these early days.

As the head of the project board or steering committee, the project sponsor has the following responsibilities:

▶ Providing the business leadership required for ensuring the project is carried through

▶ Leading the project board in resolving issues

▶ Being the champion of the board, linking end-user organizations and their functional areas to the SAP project, and the SAP project to the firm's executive management team

▶ Helping drive much of the initial decision making regarding who the firm will partner with to implement and oversee SAP

The project sponsor is also typically involved in selecting the candidate within the firm who will lead the SAP implementation on behalf of the firm—the cross-bundle (or company-internal) project leader, discussed next.

Cross-Bundle Project Leader: The SAP Project Manager

One of the most absolutely critical roles in an SAP implementation is held by the cross-bundle project leader (so called because this person manages and leads the various functional area workstreams or bundles them together to make the project what it is—a complex collection of people, teams, and other resources). Because this position is almost exclusively held by an employee of the firm implementing SAP, the position is often ubiquitously referred to as the SAP Project Manager. Regardless of title, this leader does the following:

▶ Chairs and manages the PMO and thus the project's diverse leadership team (composed of representatives from each bundle or functional area, various subteams within the IT organization, and key members of partner organizations)

▶ Acts as a single point of accountability and contact into the project board

▶ Controls and oversees the project from a resource synchronization and staffing perspective, ensuring high-level project activities fall in place within the larger scope of the project

▶ Manages issues across the various functional areas and teams

▶ Acts as the final voice and point of escalation when business needs and IT realities fail to work together

▶ Maintains the pulse of the project in regards to risk management, issue escalation, and overall project milestones and status

The Project Management Office

An organizational structure with executive visibility and extensive relationships with both the business and the IT group needs to be tasked with overall project management of your SAP implementation. Often labeled the Project Management Office (PMO), this team is responsible for developing and coordinating a cooperative environment among all the different team members, so that together the team may be successful. This PMO's leader typically reports to the project sponsor or steering committee, and must be familiar with the inner workings and politics of the firm for which SAP is being implemented. Alternatively, a triumvirate of PMs representing PMO leadership can be assigned, one each from the company, primary SAP consulting or integration partner, and SAP itself.

The PM, like the project sponsor, must tailor his or her language and other communications skills to the audience, be it the boardroom, shop floor, IT group, or any number of functional organizations, such as Accounts Payable or the Supply Chain team. The PM must also be aware of the politics surrounding the various organizations. This includes determining who the informal decision makers are, as well as the ones granted this authority through formal leadership positions. Key tasks include the following:

▶ Scope and resource planning, as well as validating and aligning resources and budgets to the project's goals and objectives

▶ Developing and maintaining the overall project plan, including task scheduling

▶ Developing and maintaining the project's other PM-related tools, including the project's quality plan, risk assessment, contingency plan, communications plan, escalation process, and more

▶ Escalating issues to the stakeholder committee or project board when necessary

▶ Monitoring and improving upon the project's progress via regular reporting and stage-wise or phase-specific scheduled meetings

▶ Providing direction to the project team when priorities are in conflict

The PMO is usually comprised of the firm's senior project management leaders, along with representatives from SAP's consulting group and your SAP alliance partners—including the Big 4 and any number of hardware-oriented and boutique SAP consulting and support organizations. It is their job to direct the implementation team's day-to-day efforts to help ensure the SAP implementation is a success.

Scope Management

Managing scope is particularly important for the PMO. Allowing "the sky is the limit!" mentality serves neither the firm introducing SAP nor the IT delivery team well. Without an agreed-upon scope, there's simply no hope that any party will walk away happy at the conclusion of the project (if indeed a conclusion can be arrived at, given the ongoing scope creep implied by "the sky is the limit"). Other PMO tasks are detailed next.

Scheduling

Effective and efficient projects are founded on accurate task duration estimates and balanced by controls and active (rather than passive) management. Schedules created at the project's onset will change; thus, it's imperative that stakeholders from across the project team meet regularly to discuss what-ifs and other potential impacts to the project's schedule. Maintaining a well-thought-out and regularly updated schedule will give stakeholders an idea of what to expect throughout the project's execution. It will communicate milestones, critical path activities, and the relative importance of resource commitments. The affects of project constraints and other potential issues gives further weight to scheduling's importance. Effective time scheduling requires risk assessment; buffer time needs to be allocated to tasks where the risk of overrun significantly impacts the project. Scheduling is therefore worthy of daily reviews and corrective action, particularly when a task's output directly initiates or affects a subsequent task or phase.

Quality Planning

Sound quality planning helps ensure the various project tasks and overall project itself achieve their intended result. Note the difference between *quality assurance* and *quality control*. The former speaks to the processes used by the PMO to ensure execution of the project's tasks are wrapped in quality planning and systematic evaluation activities. Quality control, on the other hand, determines how well the project's results are aligned to a published set of quality standards. This is accomplished through regular process-monitoring activities. Together, quality assurance and quality control help ensure that problems with quality may be addressed early on by the project's leaders.

Communication Planning

In any project, a project manager needs to constantly communicate the project's progress and activities to the proper stakeholders. Especially in the case of complex, multistaged, and collaborative projects, a good communication process needs to be in place.

Communication pathways, medium, and presentation are crucial in project planning. A breakdown in communications can negatively impact the smooth flow of the project.

Contingency Planning

Risks are inherent in every project. Any number of activities or resource losses can occur to affect the project's schedule, dependencies, ability for a task to be completed, and so on. Therefore, it is incumbent on the project manager to identify key risks as soon as possible. In this way, contingencies may be weighed and developed prior to any real emergencies. All of these "what-if" items are then placed in the project's contingency plan.

Assembling the Overall Project Team

The design, makeup, and skill sets embodied in the SAP project team are critical to an implementation's success. Team participation must encompass executive management support, underlying IT support, and especially all the firm's various business units transitioning to SAP. When structuring the project team, consider the following:

▶ Assess all the business areas that will be affected by the SAP installation (such as the Finance department, Accounting department, Warehousing group, Plant Maintenance organization, executive decision makers, and so on).

▶ Identify the skills required of each team member, from managerial and leadership to professional and technical skills.

▶ Assess the subteam of the IT organization (sometimes called the SAP support team) tasked with supporting SAP.

When you determine what areas will be affected and what skill sets will be needed by the various project team members, you also need to look for individuals who either possess or can be enlightened to possess the strategic vision required by those tasked with implementing SAP. More specifically, the vision of change and the reengineering of your current processes is essential to a successful implementation.

Your company's project team also needs to comprise individuals from all levels of the business who will be impacted by the SAP implementation. Even more importantly, upper-management support is required for efficient decision making and project direction. And throughout the project team, members must be focused on results as much as on satisfying a long-term vision. To this end, an ideal initial project team structure is illustrated in Figure 10.2.

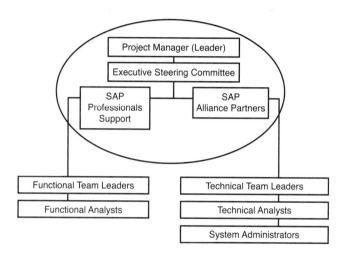

FIGURE 10.2
An SAP project team's structure should reflect these fundamental design and role tenets.

Regardless of the specific role a member in the project team might hold, there are five key characteristics the team overall (and individuals where it makes sense) should embody:

▶ The aptitude to assess how the new system will enable or affect individual and collective business processes companywide

▶ The ability to identify the impact on current business processes

▶ The ability to comprehend the requirements for reengineering identified business processes hosted by SAP

▶ The knowledge to design and complete the integration of the SAP structure, hierarchies, and business process configuration across the enterprise

▶ The ability to provide an efficient transfer of knowledge throughout the implementation and serve as a willing and available body of knowledge well after Go-Live

With the team assembled and ready to go, the cross-bundle project leader is finally positioned to manage the project's execution. Control and execution is covered next.

Project Execution and Control

Project plan execution for an SAP implementation is a full-time job for several people, if not an entire team. Although the cross-bundle project leader has overall project execution responsibility, it is not uncommon for several other PMs to help manage portions of the project schedule. After all, watching over timelines, preserving resource availability, managing scope and quality, and tracking costs is no small undertaking. In the context of an SAP project, execution and control equates to the following iterative activities:

▶ System configuration and development—Includes establishing the blueprinting and business requirements foundation.

▶ Testing—Includes unit/functional testing, systems integration testing, user acceptance testing, and eventually load/stress testing (refer to the "By the Way" box for more details).

▶ Issue management—The process of opening, tracking, documenting, resolving, closing, and communicating the status of issues.

▶ Change management or change control—Refers to the process where changes are evaluated through the lenses of business need, priority, risk, and project impact. After evaluation, changes may be implemented as-is, revised and implemented, put on hold, or rejected.

▶ User training—The training attended by the end-user community who will eventually use SAP in the course of conducting their day-to-day work.

By the Way

There are many different types of SAP testing, depending on the scope of a project. However, four types are prevalent throughout all SAP implementations:

▶ **Unit/functional testing**—Validates each step of a business process or functional transaction

▶ **Systems integration testing**—Involves walking through all the steps in a business process to verify it operates as expected

▶ **User acceptance testing**—Useful in verifying that the overall system works as a whole

▶ **Load/stress testing**—Used to ensure the system scales as required

During project execution, the cross-bundle project leader will spend a great amount of time managing and tracking the following:

▶ Risk management plan

▶ Business blueprint process

▶ Project schedule

▶ Quality management plan

▶ Various test plans

▶ Development and delivery of training materials

▶ Development and use of the project's contingency plan

▶ Development of the production support plan

▶ Development of the production cutover plan

Once project execution has been concluded, the team can turn its attention to project closeout tasks, addressed next.

Project Closeout

Eventually the project will come to a conclusion—the new system will be turned on, the old one shut down, and the work of the project team will come to a close. After production cutover and Go-Live, it is important to clearly indicate that the project has been completed. Review the following to capture lessons learned and document the SAP project's closeout:

▶ Project objectives versus what was achieved

▶ Actual delivered quality of the project versus the level of quality requested

▶ The status of project issues

The executive steering committee, project sponsor, or cross-bundle project lead should pose the following questions to validate whether the SAP project is ready to be officially closed. Ensure the following questions can be answered affirmatively:

▶ Project documentation—Have all project documents been accepted and signed off by the responsible customer party?

▶ Financial health of the project—Have all payments been made or negotiated?

▶ Financial outcome—Has a final report been developed and shared with the stakeholder committee regarding the project's budget and financials?

▶ Project team evaluation—Has an evaluation for each project team member been written and delivered?

It is also important to capture what the team learned as the project progressed. Project issues and resolutions, the status of change orders, installation and configuration check sheets, and more all constitute some of the knowledge to be managed. Also be sure to track and return all assets used by the project team, to file or dispose of confidential or restricted materials, and other housekeeping matters.

Summary

In this hour, we covered the fundamental project methodology ASAP, developed by SAP in response to the need to consistently manage SAP implementations and do so in a repeatable manner. We also outlined the structure and development of the executive steering committee, the Project Management Office, the overall project team, the cross-bundle project leader, and more. Then we explored project execution and control, followed by the project closeout process.

Case Study: Hour 10

Consider this case study, which focuses on preparing for an SAP implementation from a project management perspective. Read the situation and address the questions that follow, the answers to which may be found in Appendix A, "Case Study Answers."

Situation

MNC Global is seeking to transition its old Human Resources Management system to SAP ERP HCM. With your 20 years of experience and excellent network of business and IT relationships in MNC, you have been selected as the cross-bundle project leader and need to make a brief presentation to the steering committee regarding the initial viability of this project. A quick assessment reveals the following:

▶ The project must be completed in less than a year.

▶ You have no one available to lead this project from a technical oversight or technical leadership perspective.

▶ MNC has a strong Project Management Office.

▶ You understand that the Vice President of Human Resources has personal history with a failed SAP implementation, and openly shares his distaste for SAP in general.

Questions

1. Given the timeframe, is SAP's ASAP methodology a good starting point for going live in less than a year?

2. With your IT team's lack of technical leadership regarding SAP, where should you turn for help?

3. How will MNC's PMO work toward the project's advantage?

4. What challenges do you face given the VP of HR's past history with SAP?

5. Considering the whole situation, what initial recommendation should you make to the steering committee regarding this project?

Implementing SAP: A Business and Functional Perspective

What You'll Learn in This Hour:

▶ Business perspective relative to implementing SAP

▶ Business-to-functional translation

▶ Functional perspective relative to implementing SAP

▶ The SAP project lifecycle: a business perspective

Spanning manufacturing and mining to industries such as high-tech, banking, and finance, SAP arguably provides the most comprehensive business solutions on the market today. Implementing these solutions requires knowledge of the business, to be sure, but also insight into what SAP functional consultants spend their time doing—translating a firm's business requirements into functional specifications, which are used as a guide in configuring SAP to functionally execute the firm's business processes.

SAP Implementation Methodology

Regardless of the specific methodology employed, an implementation must reflect a firm's business roadmap to actually meet the firm's needs. The ASAP methodology and it successors touched upon in the previous hour allow for developing and maintaining a business roadmap through a process called *blueprinting*, which is explored next.

Phase 2: Business Blueprint

As outlined in other hours, SAP defined a business blueprint phase in its ASAP methodology. The intent of this phase is to help extract pertinent information about the firm seeking to implement SAP. Such blueprinting information is collected via templates, which are essentially questionnaires designed to probe for business-specific data describing how a company currently or should be conducting business. As such, these questionnaires also serve to document the essence of the implementation. Each business blueprint document essentially outlines future business processes and business requirements. The kinds of questions asked are germane to the particular business function, and reflect data points such as the specific information necessary to complete a purchase requisition or pull together information for a particular financial report.

AcceleratedSAP Question and Answer Database

Despite its age, the Question and Answer Database (QAdb) continues to be useful. It is designed to facilitate the creation and maintenance of your business blueprint. This database stores questions and their answers, and serves as the heart of your blueprint. Customers are provided with a Customer Input Template for each application that collects the data. The question-and-answer format is standard across applications to facilitate easier use by a project team.

Issues Database and Its Successor

Another tool historically used in the blueprinting phase is the Issues Database. This database stores any open concerns and pending issues that relate to the implementation. Centrally storing this information assists in gathering and then managing issues to resolution, so that important matters do not fall through the cracks. You can then track issues in the database, assign them to team members, and update the database accordingly.

Today, the implementation team has SAP's Solution Manager (SolMan) at its disposal. Much more robust and ubiquitous, SolMan tracks issues and resolutions just as the Issues Database does.

Phase 3: Realization

With the completion of the business blueprint in Phase 2, "functional" experts are now ready to begin configuring SAP in what is the longest and most complex phase of the ASAP roadmap—realization. The realization phase is divided into two parts:

▶ **Baseline configuration**—The SAP consulting team configures the baseline system for starters.

▶ **Fine-tuning configuration**—Addressed by the implementation project team as it seeks to fine-tune the system to meet all your business process requirements identified during blueprinting.

The initial configuration completed during the baseline configuration is based on the information you provided in your blueprint document. The remaining approximately 20% of your configuration that was not tackled during the baseline configuration is completed during the fine-tuning configuration. Fine-tuning usually deals with the exceptions that are not covered in baseline configuration. This final bit of tweaking represents the work necessary to fit your special needs.

Configuration Testing

With the help of the SAP consulting team, you can segregate your business processes into workstreams or cycles of related business flows. The workstreams serve as independent units that enable you to test specific parts of the business process. You can also work through configuring the SAP Implementation Guide (IMG), a tool used to assist you in configuring your SAP system in a step-by-step manner (covered later in Hour 13, "Development Tools and Methodologies"). During this configuration and testing process, the project team will benefit from extensive component-specific, functional area–specific SAP training. Such in-depth instruction will provide the team with the SAP expertise needed to translate the business's unique requirements into SAP configuration.

Knowledge Transfer

As the configuration phase progresses toward a close, ensure the firm's very own functional leads and other business process owners will be left knowledgeable of how the system is configured and to some extent how it can be maintained; don't let all your business process knowledge walk out the door when the lead systems integrator and other partners have concluded their work. The team left on the ground and responsible for ongoing systems maintenance needs a formal handoff, sure, but also detailed knowledge transfer. Take this opportunity to also begin formally training the end users tasked with actually using the system for day-to-day business purposes.

Phase 4: Final Preparation

As Phase 3 transitions to Phase 4, you should find yourself not only in the midst of SAP training, but also in the midst of rigorous functional and stress testing. Phase 4 is all about conducting the necessary final preparation and fine-tuning of the configuration prior to Go-Live. More importantly, Phase 4 also includes migrating data from your old system or systems to SAP.

Workload testing (including peak volume, daily load, and other forms of stress testing), integration testing (between modules or functional areas), and final functional testing (within a functional area) are executed at this time to ensure the accuracy of your data and the stability of the soon-to-be-productive SAP system. Because you should have begun testing back in Phase 2, you theoretically should have enough time to complete all these activities before Go-Live. In reality, the team will be under tremendous pressure as last-minute issues are uncovered and functionality is found that fits less well than intended. Save any real rework for post-Go-Live; there will be plenty of time to introduce new functionality in subsequent releases or change waves. Now is the time to ensure the system actually delivers well what it was intended to deliver—focus on core business functionality. Also take this time to perform preventative maintenance checks to ensure the system performs adequately, if not optimally; performance of your SAP system is critical to end users' perceptions as to whether the project has been a success.

Give yourself plenty of time within Phase 4 to plan and document your Go-Live strategy. Preparing for Go-Live means preparing for your end users' questions as they start actively working on the new SAP system. Be sure to staff and train your SAP help desk, for example, during Phase 4. The help desk needs to be armed with solutions to the most frequently asked questions—questions your prime integrators and partners will have no problem putting together.

Phase 5: Go-Live and Support

The Go-Live milestone itself looks straightforward to achieve on paper—with a flip of a switch, everyone will begin working on the new system. Orchestrating a smooth and uneventful Go-Live is another matter altogether, though. Preparation is the key, including attention to what-if scenarios related not only to the individual business processes deployed but also to the functioning of the technology underpinning these business processes. Business processes need to be proactively monitored for performance, just as the technology platform needs to be monitored relative to how well the system is meeting the business's Service Level Agreements (SLAs) it made with the SAP IT support organization. And preparation for ongoing support, including maintenance contracts and documented processes and procedures, is essential. Fortunately, with literally thousands of successful Go-Live "non-events" to their name, the support professionals at SAP and in the partner community have a wealth of information to share. Additional resources are available—from websites hosting blogs, wikis, and whitepapers, to conferences, SAP publications, SAP's own online support site, and more. Turn to Hour 24, "SAP Resources," for all the details.

Translating Business Requirements to Functional Specifications

The job of converting a firm's business requirements to functional specifications that may in turn be used to configure SAP appropriately is the responsibility of a special collection or matrix of people and teams. Often composed of a mix of both company-internal and prime integrator or other third-party contractors, these functional business area or "row" leaders and their roles are outlined next.

Functional Business Area or "Row" Leaders

The concept of row leaders was touched upon last hour. Rows are equivalent to functional business areas; a typical implementation has between five and more than 20 rows that together form the core functional team for the SAP implementation. Row leaders, the functional business area experts tasked with translating business requirements into functional specifications, are normally divided into two groups. Some row leaders handle the different rows of SAP strictly from a functional perspective; there is a row leader for ERP's Materials Management (MM) and another for the Controlling (CO) module, for instance. These are functional row leaders. Master data row leaders, on the other hand, are primarily responsible for the data to be used in the SAP project implementation. This data includes things such as the firm's stock numbers assigned to products, employee records, customer and vendor records, names assigned to plants and storage locations, and so on. Further differentiation between functional and master data row leaders includes the following:

▶ Functional row leaders are responsible for delivering the overall solution (consisting of work processes brought together to form systems) for their row. As they go about their work, functional row leaders help ensure that end-user site requirements are addressed (such as verifying desktop and laptop configurations meet the SAP GUI's minimum requirements and the network connection between the sites is robust enough to carry all the "SAP traffic"). The functional row leaders are also tasked with introducing and leading work process change with site leadership; how well change is introduced into an organization is directly related to how well the organization embraces the changes.

▶ Master data row leaders work with end users and leadership as well, but from a different perspective. They are responsible for data cleanup and rationalization efforts, first of all. This means working through the data to remove old data no longer relevant to the business, to consolidate data (such that the same product code or identifying number is assigned to the same part or component regardless of site), and to develop a taxonomy that helps bring all the data together under a single unified umbrella. Master data row leaders also assist in work process development and deployment, helping functional teams understand how a business process changes based on the site, plant, or company code associated with the data being processed (for instance, creating a sales order for a particular site might require special shipping and handling data not needed for sales orders created for other sites). The master data row leader also has a hand in end-user training and creating the documentation needed for both the business processes and data.

Though the functional and master data row leaders get the most visibility, another team of specialists tends to do most of the work. These are the functional configuration specialists, many of whom work for the prime integrator and subsequently contract to the firm implementing SAP. Other specialists work for the firm itself, too, as discussed next.

Company-Internal Functional Configuration Specialists

Apart from the aforementioned, other key resources exist who are really customers to the project team but play a role within the project. They are the mirrors to the prime integrator's configuration specialists. These employees and other company-internal representatives help ensure the prime integrator achieves what is described in the business blueprint. They are involved in helping define and validate the business blueprint, typically to the point of actually configuring functionality alongside their integration partner counterparts. They also play an important role in user acceptance testing, act as SAP component business liaisons, and provide other expertise from the business (primarily) and IT (occasionally) perspectives.

The company-internal functional specialists are important, but it is rare for a single person to hold enough knowledge to single-handedly design and implement all the business processes germane to a particular functional area (such as Finance, Logistics, or Human Resource/Capital Management). The company-internal functional specialists therefore lean heavily on other key experts in their various roles—namely, power users.

The Role of Key or "Power" Users

Within each functional business area or "row" may be found power users. Power users are typically known as the business experts in their field inside the company. Joe Smith in Accounting might be "the guy" when it comes to understanding the intricacies of how the firm handles accounts payable, for instance. In the context of an SAP implementation, the importance of power users can't be underestimated:

▶ They participate with the technical team in defining and reviewing how the implementation's technical solutions will solve the firm's business problems.

▶ They help define and refine business processes alongside the functional specialists, leading business blueprinting, reviewing and approving identified solution gaps, and prioritizing potential changes.

▶ They are the experts in how the firm leverages and deploys global standards, where and how it maintains documentation, and so on.

▶ They serve as internal consultants to the "real" consultants, coaching the implementation team in terms of how business is currently conducted.

▶ They provide on-going support to the site's business group or department, often acting as a single point of contact relative to nagging final questions or clarifications around their business area.

As the experts in a site's or department's work habits and more formal business processes, power users are engaged in the implementation project throughout most if not all of the project lifecycle. They work with their respective teams to build buy-in for SAP, help in testing and validating the system from functional and performance perspectives, assist with training end users, and help ensure documentation is accurate and complete. Power users need not only possess the required business knowledge and expertise to affect authentic change, but also must be open-minded as new approaches to addressing the functional area's work are introduced, weighed, and potentially implemented. "Business as usual" has no place in a power user's attitude towards adopting SAP.

At the conclusion of the SAP implementation, you might think that the power users' importance would be diminished as they return back to their old job (admittedly using a new system to get their work done). This is far from true. By the end of the implementation, power users have learned so much more about how their functional area fits and integrates into the firm's larger business scope that they're more valuable than ever. Power users become the experts in SAP functionality as well; with their combination of business and SAP skills, power users will be looked to as the experts long after Go-Live. Probably the greatest challenge organizations face after Go-Live is retaining their power users.

The SAP Project Lifecycle

Earlier this hour we concluded our discussions around the ASAP methodology. However, when it comes to business professionals and the IT projects that support business applications, looking at matters from a lifecycle point of view rather than steps in a methodology can make more sense. A lifecycle approach does a good job of illuminating the broad-brush tasks associated with ASAP's blueprinting phase.

The SAP project lifecycle is often divided into seven phases or steps:

1. Project initiation

2. Matching and prototyping

3. Design and construction

4. System integration testing

5. Business acceptance testing

6. Cutover preparation

7. Stabilization

In terms of blueprinting, steps 2 through 5 are most useful to dissect. Deliverables or outputs are associated with each step and act as input into the subsequent step. Each step is also associated with particular objectives and goals. A timeline illustrating the SAP project lifecycle is shown in Figure 11.1.

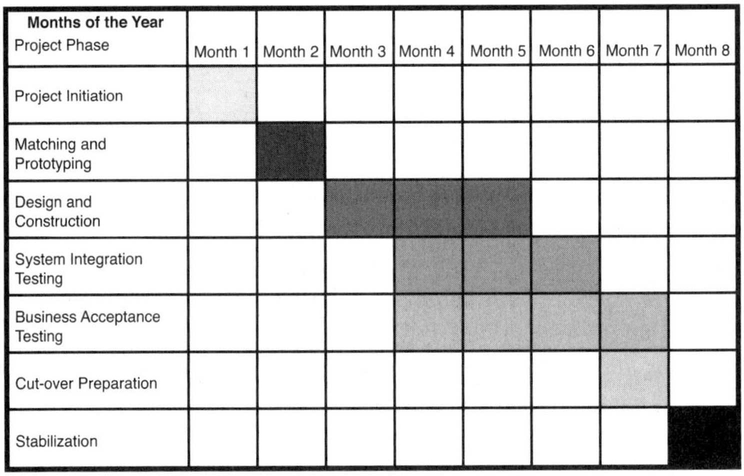

FIGURE 11.1
The SAP project lifecycle comprises seven sequential phases or steps.

Months of the Year Project Phase	Month 1	Month 2	Month 3	Month 4	Month 5	Month 6	Month 7	Month 8
Project Initiation	▓							
Matching and Prototyping		▓						
Design and Construction			▓	▓	▓			
System Integration Testing				▓	▓	▓		
Business Acceptance Testing					▓	▓	▓	
Cut-over Preparation							▓	
Stabilization								▓

Step 1: Project Initiation

Project initiation commences the SAP project lifecycle in terms of driving the planning and overall strategy of the project—how it will be staffed, executed, managed, and evaluated. This involves several tasks similar to ASAP's Phase 1:

- Establishing objectives and scope

- Designing and staffing the implementation team

- Training the team

- Establishing controls and other project management processes

- Conducting the project's formal kickoff

Outputs include publishing a defined scope of work (project scope), filling out the team's roster of resources, aligning business units and their respective power users, establishing measurable success criteria, and creating the initial business templates to be used for prototyping.

Step 2: Matching and Prototyping

In prototyping, functional experts and other row leaders work with power users and SAP component specialists to review SAP's solutions. Through this exercise, each functional team prototypes a workable, albeit limited, business-specific SAP solution. Some of the tasks associated with prototyping include the following:

- Developing and sharing a complete set of business scenarios

- Mapping the firm's unique business processes and workflows to the SAP solution being adopted

- Identifying gaps relative to the previous task

- Conducting initial integration testing (also called *shakedown testing*)

Outputs from these prototyping activities include a complete list of agreed-upon in-scope business scenarios, a document mapping work processes to SAP functionality and solution sets, a list of gaps in required and desired business functionality, and an initial set of integration test results showing the potential viability of the proposed solution sets.

Be careful to manage the time spent prototyping; without a clear scope of work and meticulously managed marching orders, a team of expensive consultants and a slew of company-internal resources can be quickly consumed by prototyping that may never bear fruit. Carefully align this activity and manage it closely.

Step 3: Design and Construction

In Step 3 of the SAP project lifecycle, the new functionality required by SAP's systems to meet a firm's business requirements are outlined from both technical and business perspectives. From a technical point of view, the teams responsible for design and construction do the following:

▶ Conduct a set of reviews focused on the scope and design of all development items.

▶ Document and complete all functional configuration and programming work required to meet a firm's business requirements.

From a business perspective, the design and construction teams perform the following tasks:

▶ Align new or updated business processes with row leader expectations.

▶ Train power users in the workflows and business processes developed for SAP.

▶ Publish standard operating procedures for those workflows and business processes.

Step 3 outputs are primarily published documents reflecting technical solution scope and design, standard operating procedures, and the entire process surrounding training power users.

Step 4: System Integration Testing (SIT)

The objective during system integration testing is to demonstrate and prove that the system is capable of supporting the business requirements. This is a massive undertaking and thus warrants its own step or phase. A detailed SIT schedule needs to be developed and used. The SIT is necessarily complex; simple unit or functional testing is followed by testing with all necessary master data (itself a daunting task to assemble, as you saw in Hour 10, "Implementation Overview: A Project Management Perspective"). Then tasks are combined into business processes and tested, culminating in a system integration test.

The SIT schedule represents an important interim output for this. Final outputs include the deployment of a "rollout system" capable of supporting the new SAP-derived business processes.

SAP Project Testing

There are many different types of SAP testing, depending on the scope of a project. However, four types are prevalent throughout all SAP implementations, upgrades, and migrations:

▶ **Unit/functional testing**—Validates each step of a business process or functional transaction to ensure it operates as expected.

▶ **System integration testing (SIT)**—Involves walking through all the steps in a business process to verify the entire business process works as expected, and then taking the tests up a notch to determine how well they work for a business group or entire site. An example might include testing the sales-to-cash business process from ordering through procurement, shipping, delivery, and final billing.

▶ **User acceptance testing**—This type of testing is more detailed than system integration testing because it should include all real-world as well as what-if test case scenarios. Rather than being performed by the business configurators (as is the case with SIT), row leaders and power users tend to drive the bulk of user-acceptance testing. Such testing might include ordering a mix of products from various sites and with various payment terms and shipping requirements to various distribution centers around the world—just as real users would presumably do one day.

▶ **Load or stress testing**—Also called *volume testing*, this form of testing is required to ensure that business processes run well with other business processes—all under the load placed by hundreds or thousands (whatever is realistic) of users doing their work, just as they will one day do in production. This will validate whether database locking becomes a problem when the system is under load, and at what point the system no longer responds well (also called *smoke testing*). As you can imagine, load testing is especially useful to the technical teams tasked with ensuring SAP performs well.

Step 5: Business Acceptance Testing

Business acceptance testing demonstrates that the SAP system, as configured, is capable of supporting the firm's business requirements. An extension of both SIT and user acceptance testing, business acceptance testing involves the following:

▶ User acceptance signoff

▶ End-user training signoff

▶ Standard operating procedures signoff

Outputs from business acceptance testing include verification that all users are indeed trained and ready to work on the new system, that the new system and its business processes work as intended (that is, they work as described by the scope of work outlined initially, including the impact that subsequent change orders would have had on the system), and that all business test cases and other real-world scenarios are tested and signed off by the business.

Step 6: Preparation for Production Cutover

Production cutover requires preparation like any other phase. Once all the preceding activities have been signed off on, a series of business-oriented and technology-oriented "checks" should be conducted. Only once all issues have been resolved or deemed noncritical can the system be cut over and Go-Live achieved. The following constitute several such checkpoints:

▶ Completed "transports" of all configuration and development changes, which are initiated in the development environment and tested in QA/Test, and upon signoff are transported from development directly into the production system.

▶ Master data integrity check, to ensure all master data is up to date, consistent, validated by the business, and present (like configuration and development changes, master data is transported across the SAP system landscape, too).

▶ Transaction data migration from legacy and other systems to the SAP system landscape, which gives SAP's end users the ability to look at recent albeit pre-SAP transactions (useful when accounts or shipping status needs to be validated shortly after Go-Live and the old systems have been retired).

▶ Stress/load testing, to ensure the system scales well under the load of hundreds or thousands of users (see the "SAP Project Testing" sidebar).

▶ SAP EarlyWatch reporting, which entails SAP AG or a local SAP-approved partner connecting to the SAP system and running through a series of technical checks intended to validate stability, availability, and performance.

Watch
Out!

Make no mistake, just like the development and configuration aspects of developing a new system, transports will also consume a huge amount of time during an SAP implementation. Don't underestimate the manpower required, not to mention the timing and coordination necessary between the functional consultants, row leaders, power users, and others. It's more work than you think.

The SAP support team also needs to develop and publish an SAP production support plan in preparation for production cutover. This comprehensive plan provides the framework defining how issues are captured, escalated, and managed, how performance is monitored, how business processes are monitored to ensure their performance meets established Service Level Agreements, and so on. The production support plan also includes a contingency plan—the firm's backup plans in case something goes horribly wrong and the system crashes or key functionality failure represents critical business disruption. Outputs are numerous and generally reflect the items listed earlier.

Step 7: Operational Stabilization

Step 7 is actually post-Go-Live and therefore the step or phase of longest duration in the SAP project lifecycle. It maps quite well to ASAP's Phase 5. The team will be busy on several fronts during this time. Simply initially supporting the end-user community and their respective business groups will consume many resources. Other team members will be busy planning for the first several change waves (where new functionality will likely be introduced that didn't make the cutoff time for production Go-Live). Developers will continue doing their work of developing, transporting, and testing changes and bug-fixes alike, while the firm's PMO will publish its conclusions and lessons learned, measure and report against the project's success criteria, obtain final signoffs for all outputs and other deliverables, and close out the project. Still others will focus on refining the tools used for monitoring and maintaining the system—from the lowest levels of the SAP technology stack to the applications, integration points, and bolt-on products necessary to run a business.

Operational stabilization outputs include finalizing and publishing all project documentation, publishing all end-user and technical team training materials, handing off operations support to the appropriate post-Go-Live teams, and finalizing all project actuals, resource status, and other communications mechanisms, including the project's lessons learned.

Summary

In Hour 11, we completed our study of the ASAP methodology, explored the roles of various row leaders and power users, and walked through the SAP project lifecycle. In this way, we covered much of what an SAP implementation entails from a business perspective.

Case Study: Hour 11

Read the following case study, which reflects business and functional perspectives of an in-process SAP implementation. After reading the situation, attempt the questions that follow, the answers to which may be found in Appendix A, "Case Study Answers."

Situation

As MNC Global continues to deploy SAP ERP, it has discovered just how important its power users are; the project initially undervalued these long-time experts in their respective functional areas. You are responsible for identifying prospective power users across MNC's various accounting teams spread out over 10 different sites, each of which represents a different MNC business group.

Questions

1. Given MNC's late start in identifying and taking advantage of the knowledge held by its power users, what might be some risks related to the actual SAP technical solutions being deployed?

2. Explain how power users help the prime integrator's functional specialists get their job done.

3. List the four types of testing that the power users will support in one form or another.

4. With regard to the company's power users, what might be the biggest challenge faced by MNC's management team after Go-Live?

5. Though power users play an important role in an SAP implementation, who owns the job of converting a firm's business requirements to functional specifications that may in turn be used to configure SAP?

Implementing SAP: A Technical Perspective

What You'll Learn in This Hour:

▶ How the Technical Project Team dovetails with other functions

▶ Key Technical Project Team constituents

▶ Important pre-installation tasks

▶ Technical implementation lessons learned

Technically implementing SAP is a very large and expensive undertaking, spanning upward of a year if not longer. As such, it usually comes at the culmination of an in-depth "needs analysis" and subsequent SAP vendor- and partner-comparison processes. Equally as important as the SAP application being implemented is the functional team responsible for configuring the application, the SAP Technical Project Team; this team will ultimately install and manage the SAP system. Hour 12 underscores some of these technical implementation details and provides recommendations for technically implementing SAP into your organization.

Assembling the Technical Project Team

The design, makeup, and skill sets embodied in the SAP Technical Project Team are critical to the success of your implementation. The design and structure of this team must dovetail into several other structures and efforts:

▶ Ensure the team has representation with the company's executive leadership team, including the overarching SAP Steering Committee.

▶ Tie into the overall project management umbrella described in Hour 10, "Implementation Overview: A Project Management Perspective."

▶ Encompass all technology areas or technical disciplines described in Hour 5, "Developing a Technical Roadmap for Deploying SAP."

▶ Support the business' needs for SAP functionality as highlighted previously in Hour 11, "Implementing SAP: A Business and Functional Perspective."

The Technical Project Team also needs to have representation with the various business units that will ultimately use the SAP system being implemented. This will become especially important shortly before Go-Live, when the system's availability for functional and end-to-end business process integration testing must be closely coordinated between the technical and functional teams.

The individual responsible for assembling this team thus has a great responsibility. Not only must the Technical Project Team reflect a gamut of technical skills, it must also comprise individuals who either possess or can be enlightened to possess the strategic vision held by the various stakeholders and other teams tasked with implementing SAP.

Technical Project Management

Technical project management is so important to the SAP implementation's success that there are usually two such project managers—an internal or customer PM and an external noncustomer PM (that is, a PM from a partner organization). The external PM is often one of the SAP implementation project managers who are also closely aligned with the project's overall Project Management Office (PMO).

By the Way

Technical representation in the PMO helps ensure scheduling, coordination, and key technical constraints are not only shared widely but communicated just as widely throughout the project's lifecycle. The external Technical Project Manager often hails from SAP itself or one of the SAP alliance partners—either the Big 4 or one of the primary SAP hardware/services partner organizations. It is the Technical Project Manager's job to work in conjunction with the larger team to ensure that SAP is implemented and operationalized correctly.

Like other SAP PM roles, there's usually a Technical PM that comes from the customer side of the house as well. This person brings knowledge and experience of the customer to bear; with his or her unique insight into the customer's existing IT team, competencies, and relative weaknesses, this PM helps keep the overall Technical Project Team grounded.

SAP Consulting

The support you receive from SAP Consulting is intended to let you more quickly navigate SAP project issues across the many different constituencies that come into play. SAP Consulting typically plays a support or subcontractor role, though the organization has led or "primed" projects in the past. Regardless of how they fit in, your SAP support professionals are crucial to accelerating your teams' learning process through onsite education and instruction. And their unparalleled SAP knowledge, experience, and far-reaching contacts into the backrooms of SAP engineering and SAP Labs are critical when the inevitable issues arise. SAP Consulting can assist your team with everything from project organization to planning for new technology and product deployments, and will happily provide a certain amount of oversight throughout the project's duration as well.

SAP Alliance Partners

SAP's Alliance partner community is enormous nowadays, and consists of the many different SAP-certified partner companies that play various support roles for your SAP system. This includes general SAP consulting and integration specialists, hardware support specialists, any number of functional and programming experts, and experts aligned with SAP-certified third-party products such as bolt-on utilities, management or security options, scheduling products, and much more. It should come as no surprise that literally thousands of such people are readily in the SAP ecosystem available to be contracted. For a complete list of SAP's Alliance partner community, see http://www.sap.com/usa/ecosystem/partners/index.epx.

Team Leaders

The Technical Project Team consists of team leaders as well as individual consultants, contractors, and members of the customer's IT and other technology support organizations. It is the responsibility of the team leaders to work with the project manager with regard to planning and managing scope, schedule, and resources. Team leaders identify the impact on, and the requirements for, technology that supports the business processes being configured in SAP. Just like the Functional Team's leaders, the Technical Project Team's leaders are experts and role models in their respective fields, and are an integral part of the knowledge-transfer mechanism between the team's members—the various technical analysts and other specialists—and the company-staffed teams and other various teams of partners, consultants, and contracted help.

Technical Specialists

The technical specialists or analysts are the skilled IT professionals on the Technical Project Team. From SAP Basis or network infrastructure specialists to individuals holding specialized knowledge in a particular technical tool or technology discipline, these are the folks who really get most of the work done. They are responsible for designing and customizing interfaces between SAP and your legacy or other remaining systems, for example. They might be the folks who spearhead your technical customizations necessary for SAP to actually work in your company's unique business environment. These technically inclined associates also own the task of designing the Go-Live plan and migrating data from the old system into the new SAP system. As such, the technical specialists hold key enabling positions within the larger scope of the implementation. Armed with the computer skills and savvy necessary to plan for and deploy SAP, the best of these specialists eventually rise into team leader roles.

System Administrators

Unlike the technical specialists who plan for and deploy systems, tools, or interfaces, the system administrators are responsible for maintenance of your actual hardware and software technology stack along with your specific SAP application installation. It is their duty to administer, maintain, and protect your SAP data. This includes preparing and verifying scheduled backups, maintaining spools, installing upgrades, and applying hot packages, legal change packages (LCPs), and so on. System administrators often begin managing the systems for which they will be responsible months before Go-Live, and then carry on with this responsibility ad infinitum.

Hot packages are collections of updated code or functionality that you download or otherwise receive from SAP on a periodic basis. Also called *enhancements*, they are designed to correct or enhance your current SAP version. Hot packages include any tweaking done to the SAP system that can be installed as a fix before the next big release of the product. Legal change packages are enhancements that are issued occasionally to accommodate legislative and governmental regulation changes required before the next official release of the software. As such, they serve the same role as a hot package but tend to have a more formal purpose.

Pre-Installation Planning

Before SAP can be installed (see Hour 15, "Technical Installation of SAP" for a step-by-step example), the technical specialists outlined earlier need to coordinate with the system administrators several key matters, discussed in the next few sections.

Hostname Naming Conventions

A server "host naming scheme" needs to be developed. Good hostnames or machine names—like AEPQVDB01—will reflect where a system physically resides (for example, A for Arizona), which SAP software component is being hosted (for example, EP for Enterprise Portal, BI for Business Intelligence, SR for Supplier Relationship Management), the host's role in the environment (for example, D for development, Q for quality assurance, or P for production), whether the server is physical or has been virtualized (P or V), the host's function (for example, DB for database server, MS for message server, or AP for application server), and the number of the SAP instance (00, 01, and so on). Having such a standard is very useful to administrators both before and after Go-Live; such an intuitive naming convention makes it easier to identify servers and thus more reliably schedule maintenance or plan for future outages, perform troubleshooting on the "right" server, and so on.

Operating System Installation

Many companies have dedicated IT teams responsible for Linux, Windows, or various UNIX server "builds." These teams are typically given an IP address by the network team, provided disk space by the SAN/Disk team, and are assigned a hostname by the Server team. The server system administrators may then be responsible for installing the OS and developing various standards in this regard. For example, assigning drive letters or mount points and subsequently formatting the storage that will eventually be used by the SAP installation process are several important OS-specific matters that should reflect a standard approach. Developing a standard for drive letters or mount points serves the same purpose as the hostname standard process just outlined; it aids in troubleshooting and maintenance. And the consistency is certainly appreciated as well when it comes time to administer, maintain, and eventually update the systems.

Unicode or Non-Unicode

Before an SAP system is installed, it's paramount that the decision be made as to whether the new SAP application will be installed as a Unicode or a non-Unicode system. For new SAP customers and projects, the decision is fairly easy today—SAP requires all new SAP installations (though not functional upgrades) from this point forward to be Unicode.

By the
~~Way~~

SAP introduced support for Unicode in SAP R/3 Enterprise (sometimes referred to as SAP R/3 4.7). Unicode is basically an encoding scheme where each character in the database is stored in the system in *two* bytes (where a byte is simply a unit of space). In contrast, non-Unicode systems typically store characters in a single byte. The Unicode method allows complex character sets (such as Mandarin, Kanji, and Japanese) to be easily represented, which in turn aids an organization in supporting a global end-user community.

The advantage of Unicode is that in global SAP installations, every character from every language can be represented as a single (albeit two-byte) Unicode character. This enables SAP to support multiple languages without adding any codepages (special constructs required in non-Unicode systems that complicate such installations; codepages are like "band-aids" when Unicode isn't used). The downside to Unicode is that it does require more system resources such as disk, processor, and memory. If you need to support multiple languages or are installing a new SAP product in your landscape, Unicode is probably the way to go despite the increased need for disk space and horsepower. For single languages, though (except new installations), non-Unicode is probably a safe choice as long as you do not envision supporting additional languages in the future.

SAP Solution Manager

Finally, before SAP can be installed, it is necessary to generate an installation key. This is done today via an SAP Solution Manager installation. Solution Manager (SolMan) is an SAP system used to support your other SAP systems. SAP has integrated support into Solution Manager. For example, Solution Manager can be used to create or "open" support messages with SAP corporate. It can also be used to download SAP Notes. Solution Manager provides much more functionality as well (including the ability to generate SAP EarlyWatch reports and provide technical monitoring or business-oriented support to your end users).

Again, though, in the scope of this particular hour, the most important function played by Solution Manager is its ability to generate an installation key, which is subsequently required to complete an SAP installation. Some have argued that this is SAP's way of gently coercing customers to implement SolMan (which can admittedly play other valuable roles in the course of an implementation).

Technical Implementation Lessons Learned

Like business-related and project management lessons learned, new implementations are rife with technology-specific lessons and other gotchas. Such lessons learned impact the success if not the very nature of an implementation, as described next.

Service Level Agreements

Just as the business has expectations of IT in general to deliver a highly available and well-performing system, so too must the SAP Technical Project Team hold itself accountable to deliver a robust SAP platform for the functional and development teams. This is accomplished by drafting Service Level Agreements (SLAs) between the IT groups and the business groups. Oftentimes, the SAP Basis Team might require SLA from the lower-level infrastructure teams, too (for example, a certain amount of availability, support, and raw performance might be required by the SAP Basis Team from the Server, Network, and SAN/Disk teams).

Lack of Technical Buy-In

Although one of the greatest benefits of SAP is its open approach to supporting various hardware, OS, and database platforms, this is also an area that requires a great amount of attention. Different factions of an organization's IT team may rally for a particular solution stack, for example, based on what the team knows and is comfortable with. Similarly, biases may come to light that preclude successful deployment on a particular technology platform. For these reasons and more, it is paramount that the SAP implementation team garner buy-in of the proposed SAP solution from technical as well as executive and end-user stakeholders.

> Long-term buy-in is important to gain up front. And it is just as important to manage and nurture this buy-in throughout the project's deployment lifecycle. Buy-in not only means gaining executive-level approval, but also the approval and a sense of ownership on the part of the end users who will ultimately use the system. This includes functional organizations, organizational leadership, and the myriad of end-users themselves. Pay particular attention to the super-users or power-users distributed across most organizations. These well-respected and often very senior users tend to have great informal power and influence within their respective organizations. They can therefore help make or break an SAP project.

By the Way

Start Small, Think Big

Instead of biting off more than you can chew, avoid project-stalling technical issues by starting small. Divide large tasks into smaller, more manageable ones. In doing so, you will be positioned to make true progress, all the while working toward your overall goal of implementing SAP.

This method of dividing and conquering has another advantage as well. By sub-dividing tasks into more manageable pieces, it becomes possible to spread the work out among more team members and in many cases complete high-level milestones faster than otherwise possible.

Big Bang or Phased?

Another process-oriented lesson learned involves whether to deploy SAP "all at once" in a big-bang manner or to deploy SAP in phases (such as by geography, by business unit, or by functional area). If you are leaning toward a big-bang implementation to quickly transition the company from an old way of doing business, you might consider running the old system concurrently with the new SAP system for some period of time. This helps to ensure no surprises with the new system will impact the business, for example. If your goal is to phase in different plants, facilities, or SAP components, though, a phased approach makes sense; it's proven to be most manageable but requires additional coordination.

Learn and Move On

Mistakes happen, and schedules can be impacted dramatically. Nonetheless, the lesson here is to learn from mistakes so as not to repeat them, and then move on. Implementing SAP is an iterative process, in that implementing the various system landscapes and working on the various development and test clients offers an opportunity to improve upon the IT and other processes already in place. The fact that SAP is deployed by first deploying Development, and then Test/QA, and then perhaps Training, and finally the Production system also lets you learn from your mistakes, so as to be prepared to circumvent known issues as each new implementation wave begins. Learn from your mistakes, document how you resolved your issues, communicate all this broadly, and move on.

Beware of Long-term Consultants and Contractors

Relying too heavily on third-party consultants is problematic on many fronts. Whether technology or development-focused, this seemingly obvious problem is quite common. Third-party consultants and contractors serve a wonderful purpose, bringing much-needed expertise to bear. Keeping these same people engaged too long only wastes money, though. Keeping them in key positions or roles might not be the best idea, either—they hold too much knowledge and power, and therefore too much leverage. Knowledge that third-party consultants acquire during an SAP implementation needs to be documented and shared with the home team, not hoarded and hauled away at Go-Live.

Manage Technical Scope Creep

It is reasonable to assume that some scope creep will occur in an SAP implementation, whether functional in nature or technical. Priorities and situations change, after all, and scope change is the natural response to this. However, scope creep and bolt-on "madness" (adding extra features, bells and whistles, or other nice-to-haves to your originally trim SAP project plan) have pushed many projects beyond their originally intended Go-Live dates. Not only does the add-on to the project lengthen the time to implementation, it also impacts day-to-day operations as well as future support and maintenance needs. In all of this, then, the key is to stay focused. Identify the critical path, establish priorities, and focus on executing against the project plan's tasks, taking care to document exceptions and in all cases communicate and transfer knowledge in the process.

Summary

In this hour, we have looked at assembling the Technical Project Team, including taking a closer look at several of the main players, hailing from the customer themselves, SAP itself, and any number of SAP's partners. The important role of the Technical Project Team's leaders, technical specialists, and system administrator was also covered, followed by discussions of key pre-installation planning tasks. The hour concluded with a quick review of SAP implementation lessons gleaned from real-world technical deployments.

Case Study: Hour 12

Consider this technical implementation preparation case study and questions that follow, the answers to which may be found in Appendix A, "Case Study Answers."

Situation

MNC Global continues to prepare for its upcoming Human Capital Management implementation. As a newly hired technical specialist focused on HP ProLiant server builds and related infrastructure, you have been tasked by your Project Technical Team's customer PM (to whom you essentially dotted-line report) to continue preparing for the SAP-on-Linux/Oracle platform installations. Answer the following questions.

Questions

1. With no idea where to begin, you remember at one of your project meetings that MNC Global has invited several partner organizations to participate in the Project Technical Team; who might some of these partners be, given your limited knowledge of the project?

2. What are several key tasks the other technical specialists on your team may be asked to spearhead?

3. List some general pre-installation planning tasks.

4. List several technical implementation lessons learned.

5. What are some system characteristics that should be reflected in a well-thought-out SAP server hostname?

Development Tools and Methodologies

What You'll Learn in This Hour:

- ▶ The differences between programming tools and configuration tools
- ▶ Reviewing your implementation options
- ▶ Reviewing the role of SAP Solution Manager (SolMan)
- ▶ Viewing the SAP procedure model
- ▶ Tracking tasks in the IMG

Given the complex business processes involved, along with the equally complex information technology requirements, implementing SAP is no easy task. In response, SAP has developed options for rapidly deploying and enhancing SAP. This hour discusses SAP programming tools as well as configuration tools and methodologies, including SAP Solution Manager and the IMG.

Programming Tools

The term *development tools* is often used generically to refer to the various toolsets provided by SAP to enhance SAP systems, code, and configuration. Although a number of different tools are available, they can basically be categorized into two specific groups—programming tools and configuration tools. Our focus in this section will be on the development tools used for programming. In the next section, we will discuss those tools used for configuration.

SAP programming tools were partially introduced in Hour 7, "Laying the Groundwork: SAP NetWeaver," in the discussion of SAP NetWeaver clients. These development tools are basically divided into three major areas: ABAP, Java, and the new Composition Environment.

ABAP

ABAP development dates back to the 1980s and was the core of SAP programming for many years. It can be used for any SAP system for which the SAP NetWeaver ABAP stack is installed. At the heart of ABAP programming is the ABAP Development Workbench, available via transaction /nSE80 (see Figure 13.1). This transaction offers a vast array of functions that developers can use for modifying and creating new SAP programs. Its primary functions include the following:

▶ Object Navigator

▶ ABAP Dictionary

▶ Class Builder/Function Builder/ABAP Editor

▶ Screen Painter/Menu Painter

▶ Class Tester/Function Tester

▶ Package Builder

▶ Class Browser, Information System, Data Browser

▶ Modification Browser, Business Add-Ins

FIGURE 13.1
Transaction
/nSE80 gives
developers an
assortment of
tools for devel-
oping SAP
applications.

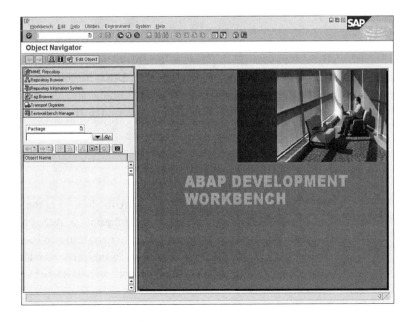

In addition to these capabilities, the ABAP Workbench also includes a web application builder for developing SAP Internet Transaction Server and Business Server Page

components, test tools such as the ABAP Debugger and Runtime Analysis, and the newer Web Dynpro for ABAP. Web Dynpro for ABAP is the future of SAP ABAP development, which is to replace the older SAP GUI–based screen development over time.

Java

Java development for SAP's NetWeaver Application Server is based on the current Java EE 5 standard and was adopted by SAP as a platform-independent open-source development framework to allow customers to leverage existing non-SAP development resources.

SAP offers the SAP NetWeaver Developer Studio (NWDS), briefly discussed in Hour 7, as its Java development environment. Developer Studio, as it is also referred, is based on Eclipse and includes the following features:

▶ Built-in Java EE 5 design-time support based on WTP 1.5

▶ JPA design-time support, based on the open-source Dali project

▶ Web services support

▶ On-the-fly application debugging

▶ Hot deployment

▶ Wizards and graphical tools to speed up development

In addition to the features of Developer Studio, SAP offers new options for distributing Java changes through the SAP landscape. Although Java objects can still be deployed locally via manual processes, SAP's NetWeaver Development Infrastructure (NWDI) allows customers to manage Java development with a robust, change management tool built on similar principles as SAP's Transport Management System (TMS) of the ABAP stack.

Composition Environment

The SAP NetWeaver Composition Environment (CE) was introduced in Hour 7. CE bundles SAP NetWeaver Studio with SAP NetWeaver Application Server and provides a model-based architecture for building SAP applications. Using CE, customers can leverage both SAP and proprietary services to build business applications.

Although ABAP, Java, and the Composition Environment provide the core toolsets for SAP development, a number of other development areas are worth mentioning. SAP "front-end tools" such as Microsoft Duet, referenced in Hour 16, "Integrating SAP with Microsoft Office," and Adobe interactive forms allow developers to enhance the user experience by customizing the presentation layer of business applications. SAP NetWeaver Process Integration (PI), Business Application Programming Interfaces (BAPIs), and the SAP Java Connector facilitate the development of interfaces for SAP or non-SAP applications. Finally, SAP Adobe Document Services (ADS), Smart Forms, and SAPscript all allow for the customization of SAP forms.

SAP Configuration Tools and Methodologies

Everyone knows that introducing SAP into your business will be challenging. After all, it's nothing like installing Microsoft Word or some other desktop application. It entails a reengineering of your current environment, structure, systems, and processes across both business and IT organizations. In this section, we will discuss SAP's AcceleratedSAP (ASAP) Roadmap, its evolution into SAP Solution Manager, and more.

ASAP—AcceleratedSAP

As outlined in earlier hours, ASAP is a long-time tool used to help make your business transformation easier by assisting in the implementation of SAP. Its purpose is to help design your SAP implementation in the most efficient manner possible. Its goal is to effectively optimize time, people, quality, and other resources, using a proven methodology for implementation.

At the turn of the century, in response to the need to more rapidly and completely deploy R/3 and a host of growing solutions offered by SAP AG, ASAP began to evolve. The methodology was always limited in that it assumed a very rigid phased approach; the fact that implementation phases often overlapped, or that businesses found themselves in the midst of multiple ASAP phases as a result of a geographically phased rollout, was contrary to ASAP. The new SAP deployment methodologies therefore added Evaluation and Continuous Business Improvement to their core focus on implementation. These changes helped overcome some of the previous shortfalls, although not all of them. See Hour 10, "Implementation Overview: A Project Management Perspective," for much more detail on ASAP.

SAP Solution Manager for Implementation

In 2001, SAP AG released an improved implementation delivery vehicle—SAP Solution Manager, or SolMan—when it introduced Web Application Server (WebAS). By the end of 2002, Solution Manager had matured considerably, offering not only multiple roadmaps to implementation but also improved content. Some of this content included sample documents, new templates, a repository for canned business processes, and better project-management tools to assist with the implementation lifecycle. These tools and when they are used are summarized next; see Hour 11, "Implementing SAP: A Business and Functional Perspective," for more details.

Implementation Tools and Content

As shown in Figure 13.2, the core implementation tools include a four-phased approach, which is a shortened version of the original ASAP methodology.

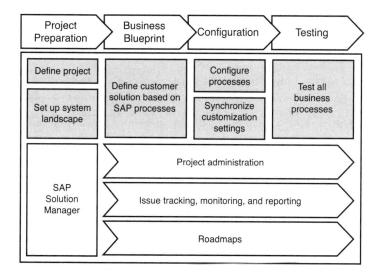

FIGURE 13.2
The four core implementation phases.

Project Preparation

Project preparation initiates with a retrieval of information and resources. It is an important time to assemble the necessary components for the implementation. Some important milestones that need to be accomplished during this time include the following:

▶ Obtain senior-level management/stakeholder support.

▶ Identify clear project objectives.

- ▶ Architect an efficient decision-making process.

- ▶ Create an environment suitable for change and reengineering.

- ▶ Build a qualified and capable project team.

Business Blueprint

SAP has defined a business blueprint phase to help extract pertinent information about your company that is necessary for the implementation. As such, business blueprinting also essentially documents the implementation, outlining your future business processes and business requirements.

To further assist with this process, SAP offers Implementation Content on a variety of products and scenarios, which can be pulled in to Solution Manager from the Business Process Repository (BSR). This content from the BSR provides predelivered documentation, transactions, and configuration support to assist customers with specific relevance to the business scenario being implemented.

Configuration

With the completion of the business blueprint, "functional" experts are now ready to begin configuring SAP. The configuration phase is broken into two subphases:

1. Your SAP consulting team helps you configure your baseline system, called the baseline configuration.

2. Your implementation project team fine-tunes that system to meet all your business and process requirements as part of the fine-tuning configuration.

The initial configuration completed during the baseline configuration is based on the information you provided in your blueprint document. The remaining approximately 20% of your configuration that was not tackled during the baseline configuration is completed during the fine-tuning configuration. Fine-tuning usually deals with the exceptions that are not covered in baseline configuration. This final bit of tweaking represents the work necessary to fit your special needs. During this phase, you also work through configuring the SAP Implementation Guide (IMG), the tool used to actually configure SAP in a step-by-step manner.

Testing, Final Preparation, and Go-Live

From a tools perspective, final preparation and Go-Live equates to testing. Workload testing (including peak volume, daily load, and other forms of stress testing) and integration or functional testing should be performed to ensure the accuracy of your data and the stability of your SAP system. Now is an important time to also perform preventative maintenance checks to ensure optimal performance of your SAP system. Preparing for Go-Live means preparing for the inevitable end users' questions, for example, as they start actively working on the new SAP system.

Preparation is the key to a successful Go-Live, including attention to what-if scenarios related not only to the individual business processes deployed but also to the functioning of the technology underpinning these business processes. And preparation for ongoing support, including maintenance contracts and documented processes and procedures, is essential. Fortunately, a wealth of information and additional resources are available.

Additional Implementation Roadmaps

As discussed earlier, the ASAP Roadmap evolved over time and is still a major component among the variety of roadmaps available with Solution Manager. In addition to the ASAP Roadmap, the Run SAP Roadmap focuses on a methodology for operational efficiencies. In includes "how-to" and best practice documentation for management and administration tasks.

SAP continues to grow the number of roadmaps as new products are developed. A few additional roadmaps available today include the following:

- ▶ ASAP Implementation Roadmap for SAP Enterprise Portal

- ▶ ASAP Implementation Roadmap for SAP Exchange Infrastructure (now renamed Process Integration, though the roadmap still retains the old label)

- ▶ Solution Management Roadmap

- ▶ Global Template Roadmap

- ▶ Upgrade Roadmap

- ▶ Methodology for accelerated transformation to Enterprise SOA

It is important to remember that at the end of the day these approaches all amount to little more than frameworks or methodologies with supporting templates. Even SolMan only *facilitates* an SAP implementation—there's still much real work that needs to be done. But if you are seeking to deploy well-known and mature SAP functionality, and are focused on avoiding too much custom development, SolMan is a wonderful tool for your implementation arsenal.

The SAP Implementation Guide (IMG)

If you return to the configuration phase, you will remember that the Implementation Guide (IMG) plays a central role in assisting you with configuring SAP. The IMG is essentially a large tree structure diagram that lists all actions required for implementing SAP, guiding you through each of the steps in all the different SAP areas that require configuration. For each business application, the SAP Implementation Guide (IMG) does the following:

▶ Explains all the steps in the implementation process

▶ Communicates the SAP standard (default) settings

▶ Describes system configuration work (tasks or activities)

The guide begins with very basic settings, such as "What country are you in?" It ultimately drills down into very specific matters such as "What number do you want your purchase orders to begin with?" Everything said, it is nearly impossible to complete an SAP implementation without SAP Implementation Guide familiarity. To begin, execute transaction code /nSPRO or follow the menu path Tools, AcceleratedSAP, Customizing, Edit Project. The main screen appears similar to the one shown in Figure 13.3.

By the Way

It is important to note that the screens depicted in this hour might not appear exactly as the screens appear on your system. The SAP components and modules being implemented, your SAP version number, the progress in the implementation, and your specific user/authorization access all affect the way the screens appear.

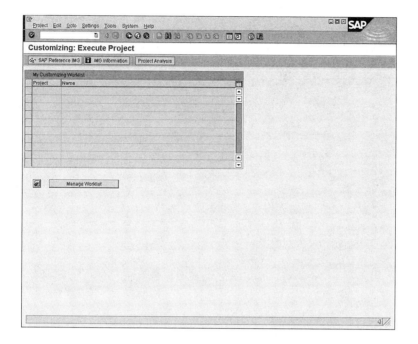

FIGURE 13.3
The Implementation Guide main screen varies depending on your SAP component, installation, and the amount of configuration that has been completed.

Different Views of the IMG

You can view and use the Implementation Guide (IMG) within SAP in different ways. Each of these perspectives is called a *view*. Depending on the type of information you want to see and the order in which you want it presented on the screen, you select a different view of the IMG. You can also create your own custom views of the IMG. Note that there are four levels of the SAP Implementation Guide (IMG):

▶ The SAP Reference IMG

▶ SAP Enterprise IMGs

▶ SAP Project IMGs

▶ SAP Upgrade Customizing IMGs

The SAP Reference IMG

The SAP Reference IMG contains documentation on all the SAP business application components supplied by SAP and serves as a single source for all configuration data (see Figure 13.4).

FIGURE 13.4
Using the SAP
Reference IMG,
you can cus-
tomize your
entire SAP
implementation
from a single
console.

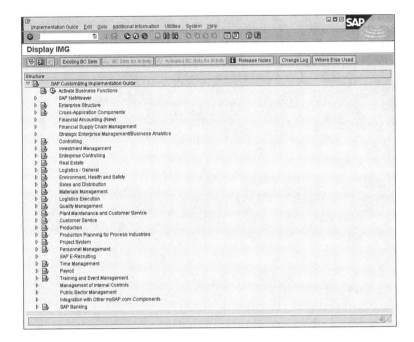

The SAP Enterprise IMG

The SAP Enterprise IMG is a subset of the SAP Reference IMG, containing documentation only for the components you are implementing. It appears the same as the Reference IMG but lists only the configuration steps necessary for your company's implementation. For example, if you are implementing only logistics within SAP ERP, your IMG would not contain any information on configuring payroll from the Human Resources module (see Figure 13.5).

The SAP Project IMGs

SAP Project IMGs are Enterprise IMG subsets that contain only the documentation for the Enterprise IMG components you are implementing (such as a Customizing project). For example, if you are implementing ECC Logistics exclusively, but have divided the implementation into two projects—one for Sales and Distribution and a second for Materials Management—you can set up two different projects. This can make the projects much easier to manage and configure.

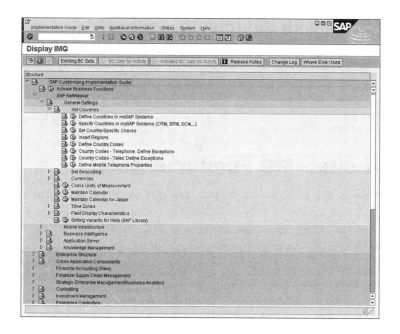

FIGURE 13.5
This display structure in the Enterprise IMG provides for the configuration of your country global parameters.

The SAP Upgrade Customizing IMGs

SAP Upgrade Customizing IMGs are based either on the Enterprise IMG or on a particular Project IMG. They show all the documents linked to a Release Note for a given release upgrade (see Figure 13.6).

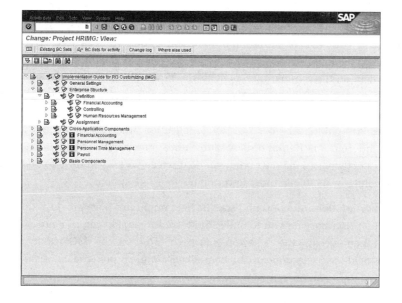

FIGURE 13.6
The SAP Upgrade Customizing IMG enables you to specify a configuration based on specific SAP releases.

Integration with Solution Manager

With the latest features of SAP Solution Manager, you can now create projects within SolMan and link it to one or multiple IMG projects in component systems. This allows you to navigate configuration for one or more projects from a central location as well provide a single configuration repository within SAP Solution Manager.

Additional IMG Fundamentals

With the transaction code /nSPRO, the initial view of an IMG structure is always a tree diagram with symbols shown to the left. You can use the plus (+) sign to the left of each item (for older SAP releases) or the triangle (for newer SAP releases) in the tree structure to expand a branch of the tree to view its substructure. You can also expand a branch by placing your cursor on a line item and then following the menu path Edit, Expand/Collapse or by placing your cursor on a line item and pressing the F5 key on your keyboard. To expand all possible branches, place your cursor on the highest level and select Edit, All Subnodes.

Looking at the IMG with the subnodes expanded gives you a good idea of the IMG's purpose—to configure basic settings for SAP. Taking a look at each of the line items, it is easy to see how this tool facilitates implementation.

Help in the IMG

The first thing you should learn about the IMG is how to retrieve help for any individual line item. Just by looking at the description of each line item, it is not always clear exactly what the configuration of that item entails. You can access selection-specific help by double-clicking any activity (line item) in the IMG. This brings you detailed help on the configuration activity you have selected. In some cases, it launches a small window describing the reasons for the activity and what it entails, including actual examples of what the activity is used to configure. In other instances, it might launch your SAP Help application, thus enabling you to search for more information. Help is also available after you execute a line item in the IMG. Most activities in the IMG bring you to a screen where you need to add or modify values in a table in order to configure your SAP system.

The field descriptions and selection-specific help might not have provided all the information necessary for you to understand what to do. Placing you cursor in any field and then selecting the F1 key on your keyboard from any IMG activity screen launches field-level selection-specific help. The Help file is presented as a small window describing the possible values for entry in that field. Using the Help in the IMG is essential in obtaining additional information on the activities required for configuring your SAP system.

Documentation in the IMG

The Implementation Guide is usually your main source for configuration. That is essentially why it is the ideal location for documenting your configuration. Use the Status Information icon to navigate to the Memo tab of the Status Information screen. From there, record your comments, notes, or configuration information on the appropriate configuration step provided in the IMG. Alternatively, use your cursor to select the documentation symbol, and your screen launches into a screen like the one shown in Figure 13.7.

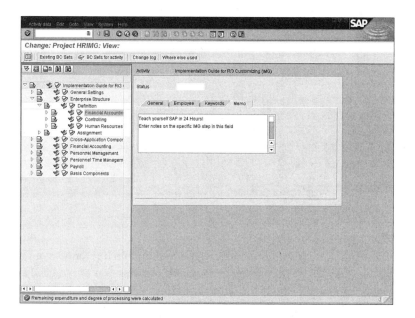

FIGURE 13.7
The IMG's Memo tab in the Status Information screen is an ideal resource for writing configuration notes documenting particular activities.

For each line item in the IMG, you can enter text in this way and, in doing so, document the system as you go along. This is therefore a very helpful tool, not to mention a great reference to use after your implementation is complete or during SAP upgrades and changes. You can type configuration notes into the space provided in the Memo tab and save them with that line item in the IMG. You can then use the Read Note symbol to review any of these notes at a later time.

Status Information

Selecting the Status Information symbol brings you to the General tab, as shown in Figure 13.8. This tab allows you to record the status and progress of your configuration for a particular line item, including planned versus actual start and end dates, and more. Other tabs include the Employee tab, Keywords tab, and the aforementioned Memo tab.

FIGURE 13.8
The Status Information screen records the status of the item, planned versus actual start and stop dates, the percentage complete, and much more.

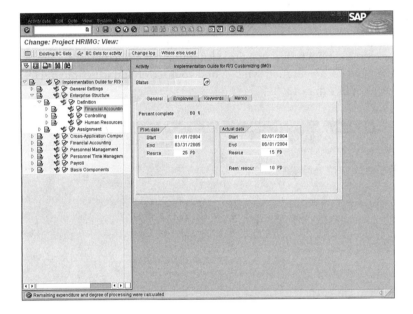

Status

One purpose of the Status Information screen is to maintain a record of your configuration to date, and to track your implementation progress. It is also a good place to see who is working on what. One of the first things you need to assign on this screen is the Status field. Sample Status types include the following:

▶ In Process

▶ In Q/A Testing

▶ Completed

You set up the different status levels, as determined by your company's specifications. This Status designation segregates your configuration tasks into different completion categories.

Percent Complete

The Percent Complete field is used to display a processing status for an activity expressed as a percentage. Sample percent completed values include 25%, 50%, 75%, 100%, and so on. At one time, these values were up to the individual to maintain. In newer releases of SAP, though, the percent complete is actually calculated by SAP.

Plan Start and End Dates

The Plan Start Date field is where you record the initial projected date on which this particular activity should commence. Select the Possible Entries Help button on this field to display a calendar that enables you to select the date rather than entering it directly. The date is selected using the calendar control by selecting the month, date, and year and then double-clicking or by selecting the green check mark.

The Plan End Date field is where you record the projected completion date for this particular activity. The SAP calendar is also available on this field.

Plan Work Days

The Plan Work Days field records the planned duration of an activity in days. The planned expenditure can be maintained manually. If neither actual expenditure nor processing status is maintained, the remaining expenditure is calculated.

Actual Start and End Dates

In the real world, things do not always go as planned. The Actual Start Date field records the actual date that an activity was started. Similarly, the Actual End Date field records the actual date that an activity was completed. These fields are maintained when the planned start date and the actual start date differ.

Actual Work Days

The Actual Work Days field records the actual duration in days of an activity. This field is usually maintained only when the planned start and end date conflict with the actual start and end date.

Remaining Work Days

The Remaining Work Days field records the remaining expenditure for an activity in days. The remaining expenditure is calculated from the actual expenditure and the processing status, or from the planned expenditure, if these fields are not maintained. You can also set the remaining expenditure manually.

Using the Employee Tab for Resource Assignments

For each particular task in the IMG, you can assign resources (or people) responsible for that task. Use the Employee tab in the Status Information screen to denote these resource assignments. By using the Possible Entries Help button in the resource field, you can select the resources responsible for performing an activity. As the multiple resources boxes depict, you can assign multiple resources to a single task.

Release Notes

Release Notes contain specific relevant information on changes to the SAP system since the last release. They contain functionality and screen changes, as well as menu path and table structure changes. Release Notes are helpful when you are migrating from one SAP version to another. They are also a good tool for retrieving additional information about how something works in the SAP system.

You can turn on an indicator in your IMG that displays a marker next to each activity, thereby revealing whether the Release Notes are available for that particular activity; see Figure 13.9 for a sample Release Notes screen.

FIGURE 13.9
Selecting the Release Notes symbol brings you to a screen containing documentation about the line item and how it has been changed since earlier releases.

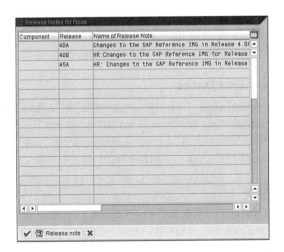

Summary

Decisions concerning the development tools and implementation strategy affect the time, cost, and path you follow in your SAP implementation. SAP rapid deployment options are effective and efficient solutions that might not be the best fit for your company. Because no two companies are alike, you should discuss your company's individual needs with your SAP representative before deciding what tools and methodologies you should employ, and take it from there. When an "empty" shell of SAP is installed, the Implementation Guide is the tool used to assist you in customizing and implementing your SAP system. The Implementation Guide is designed to pinpoint the configuration activities you are required to perform in order for your SAP implementation to be a success. It also enables you to tweak your SAP system to ideally suit your company's individual needs through custom configuration.

Case Study: Hour 13

Consider the following SAP development and resource-oriented case study and the questions that follow, the answers to which may be found in Appendix A, "Case Study Answers."

Situation

You are selected to participate in a development team meeting. Upon your return to your business unit, you have been tasked with answering several questions from junior colleagues anxious to understand more.

Questions

1. What is the transaction code to launch the ABAP Development Workbench?

2. What is the name of the development environment for creating SAP Java applications?

3. What are the four consecutive phases of the SAP Solution Manager Implementation Tool?

4. Besides ASAP, what are some alternative methodologies or tools for SAP implementation.

5. Which view of the IMG contains only the relevant documentation for the SAP components your company is implementing?

6. What are three different project views of the IMG?

7. What is the transaction code to launch the IMG?

HOUR 14

SAP and Enterprise SOA

What You'll Learn in This Hour:

▶ Differentiating between SOA, Enterprise SOA, and Web Services
▶ Benefits and challenges of SOA
▶ How SAP leverages SOA for NetWeaver

According to SAP, Enterprise SOA is like a blueprint used to create an adaptable, flexible, and open IT architecture, which in turn may be leveraged to create services-based business applications. To realize its own vision of such applications, SAP engineered NetWeaver to provide the required technical platform. The result is SAP's ability to create real-time enterprise applications that benefit from both rapid prototyping and deployment, and high reusability/low development costs.

Introduction to Enterprise SOA

Service-Oriented Architecture (SOA) is nothing more than an approach to designing a more innovative computing platform that takes advantage of reusable services to build powerful business processes. As such, it's a distinct departure from systems that are custom designed and developed from the ground up (sometimes called "custom apps"), and is just as much a departure from prepackaged client/server applications. SOA provides for definitions and methods of building an IT infrastructure that makes it possible not only to exchange data between different systems and other data repositories, but to build and extend business processes. As such, SOA is necessarily tied to both the underlying operating systems as well as the development/programming languages native to an application. But the link is a loosely coupled one; in this way, it is possible to support different operating environments spanning traditional UNIX offerings, Linux, Windows, and even mainframes.

If you're a programmer, you've known for years the value of modular programming, where chunks of code can be easily reused. This approach takes a bit more time up front, but saves a huge amount of time in the long run, particularly with regard to ongoing maintenance and when changes need to be made. SOA takes the same approach but from an architecture perspective. SOA segregates functionality into modular services, which in turn can be combined and reused to create and change business applications. Services communicate with one another by passing data or by coordinating interservice activities.

Thus, it's services, Web Services in particular, that make an SOA architecture actually useful. A Web Service encompasses some kind of business function or application logic that may be accessed and used over and over again in support of a business process. SAP speaks of aggregating Web Services into business-enabling enterprise services. Before we explore how Web Services enable automated enterprise-scale business scenarios, we need to step back and look more closely at SAP's adaptation of SOA, called Enterprise SOA.

Differentiating SOA from Enterprise SOA

From an Enterprise SOA perspective, SOA is more generic; any computing architecture that allows for reusable services describes SOA. In the same way, any system that uses Web Services is SOA compliant or enabled. SOA's concept of creating composite complex business applications through bundling reusable services is fairly broad. Reusable services might include Web Services or might also encompass open services such as those described by WSDL, SOAP, and UDDI. As you can see, SOA is a set of technical specifications—an architecture—rather than a methodology for creating business applications.

On the other hand, Enterprise SOA has a definite business focus. Built on SAP's Enterprise Services Architecture (ESA), Enterprise SOA is decidedly SAP inspired as well; Enterprise SOA is SAP's version of the more generic SOA. Enterprise SOA enables composite applications to be built by assembling enterprise services (similar concept to Web Services, though more generic in nature), while SAP NetWeaver's Enterprise Services Repository (ESR) serves as the central building block for creating SAP Enterprise SOA applications. It is actually these enterprise services that really differentiate SAP's Enterprise SOA from its more general counterpart. SAP has engaged not only its internal development team but countless partners as well to develop a robust collection of enterprise services. SAP calls this its "inventory of enterprise services," more formally described as SAP's Enterprise Services Inventory (ESI). As Enterprise SOA's foundation, these enterprise services occupy the ESR and do the job of fulfilling a specific business need. Further, each enterprise service in turn passes data and triggers another enterprise service.

Not surprisingly, SAP continues to engage its development teams and partners to build new services, engaging its customers in the process to help identify or initiate and then vet out new potential enterprise services. SAP created the Enterprise Services Community (ESC) to give credence to its concept of enterprise services; the ESC busies itself with defining and refining enterprise services as well. Another SAP tool, the ES Workplace, provides initial access to SAP's customers and partners to newly published enterprise services. SAP also published business maps that essentially map services to business processes and solutions. In this way, SAP effectively promulgates its concept of Enterprise SOA while simultaneously giving its approach the legs it needs to prove effective in the real world.

> Open services require structure and description. WSDL, or Web Service Description Language, is used to describe a SOAP (Simple Object Access Protocol) message in terms of encoding and transport. SOAP in turn is essentially an HTTP-capable XML carrier protocol. Combined with the API for interacting with Web Service registries, UDDI (Universal Description, Discovery, and Integration, at least as it relates to Web Services), these three components make up the Web Service Interoperability profile, or WS-I.

Did you Know?

Principles of Enterprise SOA

SAP describes five principles of Enterprise SOA. In doing so, SAP hopes to create a loosely controlled set of development precepts for its enterprise services. These principles include the following:

- ▶ **Abstraction**—Serves to mask unnecessary or otherwise puzzling details.

- ▶ **Modularity**—An essential property of enterprise services that enables the development of reusable components or building blocks by breaking down services into fundamental units.

- ▶ **Standardized connectivity**—Necessary to describe and enable data sharing and triggering, which in turn can be used to build and combine flexible services into full-fledged enterprise business processes and business solutions or scenarios.

- ▶ **Loose coupling**—Another necessary property that enables individual services to grow and evolve without requiring a rewrite. Loose coupling preserves reusability as well as integration and connectivity between services.

- ▶ **Incremental design**—The ability to enable changes to a service's composition and configuration without requiring a rebuild.

Through these five principles, SAP AG is quickly becoming the market leader in enterprise application software built on Service-Oriented Architecture. These principles make it possible for SAP to continue developing world-class enterprise services that will ultimately incent if not enable SAP's thousands of legacy R/3 customers to finally move away from their trusted though increasingly inflexible client/server architecture. Enterprise SOA's flexible and standardized architecture supports business better than its older architectural counterparts because it simplifies a firm's ability to innovate, connect to partners and vendors, and better service its customers. Enterprise SOA unifies business processes and simplifies their deployment and maintenance by structuring complex business applications as merely ad hoc collections of enterprise services. SAP's particular approach is explored in more depth next.

Enabling SOA Through SAP NetWeaver

As briefly mentioned earlier this hour, SAP NetWeaver enables SOA—SAP helps customers leverage the power of a business-driven, service-oriented approach to business application architecture through Enterprise SOA. SAP NetWeaver lays this foundation through several technologies or constructs, enabling cross-functional business processes at the end of the day. As the enabler of Enterprise SOA, SAP NetWeaver combines the power of its Web Application Server with the previously described ESI and ESR to enable enterprise services.

Web Application Server

Although not originally envisioned as NetWeaver specific, SAP's Web Application Server or WebAS—the "new" and more comprehensive Basis layer developed for mySAP at the turn of the century—was designed to simplify installation, integration, and ongoing maintenance. Additionally, SAP wanted to give its developer community a choice, adding Java/J2EE support to SAP's programming mainstay ABAP/4. Eventually SAP integrated its web server (Internet Transaction Server, or ITS, available since 1996) into this new powerful platform.

Within a few short years of introduction, SAP's WebAS made for a powerful Web-enabled SOA-compliant technical platform capable of helping firms completely transform how they conducted business in a world that continued to demand greater nimbleness, more flexibility, and ever-increasing business and therefore underlying technology agility. WebAS provided enhanced support for XML and Web Services technologies, including early support for SOAP and WSDL. With support for Unicode offered as of WebAS 6.30, the capability to standardize on a particular companywide technology platform relative to matters as diverse as language support also made a compelling argument for deploying what ultimately morphed into the platform undergirding NetWeaver—the same platform that made Enterprise SOA possible as well.

Enterprise SOA Is Already Here

Skepticism is human nature, and for what appears to be the end-all solution to so many business and technology challenges faced by firms around the globe today, Enterprise SOA naturally invites its share of skeptics. As recently as 2007, there seemed to be more slideware and marketing fodder on Enterprise SOA than anything resembling service-oriented architecture solutions. But much has changed, and the truth of the matter is that SAP ERP is already delivering enterprise service-enabled business processes today, in industries as diverse as those serviced by SAP. Enterprise services can be found in systems such as the following:

- ▶ Invoice processing systems (more precisely, the electronic bill presentment and payment functionality found in SAP ERP Financials)

- ▶ Recruiting and enterprise learning systems (SAP ERP HCM)

- ▶ Shop floor integration systems (SAP ERP Manufacturing)

- ▶ SAP SRM supplier collaboration (procurement) systems

- ▶ Process collaboration solutions as found in SAP cFolders

- ▶ Solutions leveraging radio frequency identification (RFID) for SAP ERP inventory and warehouse management systems

- ▶ Document exchange systems (via self-service procurement and requisition services)

- ▶ Collaborative project management systems

Enterprise services continue to grow and mature, making it possible to construct more and more capable and complex yet easily decipherable business solutions and scenarios. In a process called *orchestration*, business process experts link and sequence these enterprise services to create new services and full-fledged enterprise solutions and business applications.

Benefits of Enterprise SOA

If not for the benefits of SOA and its SAP-specific counterpart Enterprise SOA, these architectures would quickly fade away alongside other well-intentioned though ill-timed or incomplete initiatives. Enterprise SOA is different, though. Not only does it deliver, but it is real and holds real appeal to technology and business folks alike. Enterprise SOA–enabled SAP applications built from a mix of reusable and extensible services deliver the flexibility, agility, and uniformity required by enterprises seeking to spend less time maintaining code and more time innovating. Building SAP applications from a single suite of enterprise services makes this not only achievable but less costly than preceding client/server and monolithic architectural approaches to deploying enterprise applications.

Underlying and making possible these enterprise services is metadata that describes each enterprise service's characteristics and the data that comprises and passes between them. XML is typically used extensively to create and package the data, which in turn is wrapped and then described by WSDL and communicated about by the SOAP protocol. To be sure, these standards are open and subject to change; for now, though, they will suffice for our argument for Enterprise SOA–enabled SAP enterprise services and their respective business solution sets.

Why SOA? Reusability

Often cited as the number-one reason for adopting SOA is SOA's innate reusability. Services broken down into their constituent tasks naturally lend themselves to fewer integration problems, less code overhead, and so on. Reusability makes for lean applications in the same way as reusability's next of kin—modular design.

Why SOA? Modular Design

It has been pondered whether SOA is really unique and therefore any better than its predecessors. For those of us with a couple of decades of IT experience, it's easy to understand from where this questioning arises. SOA looks like the reinvention of modular programming hailing from the 1970s and 1980s. It also smacks of event-oriented design, a systematic design and development model also from the 1980s. Regardless of what it looks like, though, you can't argue that a modular approach to *anything*—from building cars to erecting skyscrapers or developing business processes—makes sense on most levels. SOA's modular design makes it possible to separate core services from one another, enabling an organization the ability to then compile the exact functionality it needs without introducing a lot of extra capabilities and therefore extra integration, overhead, and maintenance headaches down the road. In this, SOA helps businesses respond quickly and more cost-effectively to changing markets and industry conditions. SOA's modularity enables the agility businesses need to compete better.

Modular design also equates to lean design, a universal tenet of good code. The fact that enterprise services can run so efficiently on various distributed platforms, and can therefore be effectively constructed and accessed in the form of business processes running across networks spanning the globe, makes SOA that much more compelling. Modular design maximizes a service's reusability as well. This in turn reinforces SOA's usefulness in helping to create custom business processes.

Why SOA? Cost Effectiveness

SOA requires investment up front, to be sure. But down the road, its modular design and innate reusability will prove SOA more cost effective than legacy architectures. And for businesses that need special or custom services, industry trends are revealing a new twist. An increasingly greater number of SAP partners and other software development companies are building SOA services and selling them for a fee. This should not only help drive the costs down over time, but provide firms with more incentive to use SOA in general and Enterprise SOA in particular, further driving development of new services.

In the end, companies will have at their disposal a greater variety of purpose-built as well as general services, and more industries will be serviceable through SOA. Businesses might construct enterprise business processes composed of SAP-provided, partner-provided, and partner fee-based services. Innovative customers will even develop their own services and either maintain them as part of their competitive advantage or sell them for reusability by other firms. By spreading development costs out across a much greater breadth than SAP's own development community, such developer independence will continue to increase SOA's usability and adoption, further decreasing costs in the process.

Differentiating SOA and Web Services

Although SOA might prove both business-enabling and cost effective, a significant investment is still required to create an SOA architecture. Beyond this investment, an IT shop interested in adopting SOA must embrace Web Services (or in the case of SAP, enterprise services). A Web Service provides the platform-independent service-based functionality that is eventually combined with other services to create a business process. In a nutshell, Web Services provide the legs for SOA (in the same way enterprise services enable Enterprise SOA); Web Services gives life to an SOA-compliant architecture.

Here are a few things to remember about SOA and Web Services:

- ▶ Services are standalone; by definition, a service is not required to know how an application functions.

▶ In the same way, applications are not required to know how a particular service operates; they are completely independent from one another.

▶ The interface definition ascribed to a particular service hides its unique programming language and logic details; again, an application does not need to know anything about the service's internal operations.

In this way, a service written in C# (pronounced *see-sharp* for the non-programmers among you) and a service written in Java may both be used to create a business process. More compelling (to mainframe IT shops held captive by programs coded tens of years ago), even COBOL programs can be encapsulated and presented as a service. Thus, Web Services facilitate the kind of business and technology domain alignment necessary for truly open and extensible solutions. By extending a computing platform's usability and indeed its useful lifecycle, IT shops are no longer constrained by their particular computing platform's innate shortcomings and thus are free to innovate and better meet the business's needs.

Challenges to Adopting SOA

Several significant challenges exist relative to adopting SOA, as explored next.

IT Organizational Silos and Ownership

No question about it, SOA is a strategic enabler. Yet many existing IT departments are organized by platforms and business applications and therefore present a simple organizational challenge to firms otherwise interested in adopting SOA. Although such a decentralized organizational approach might seem advantageous from a support perspective, in reality it creates silos or stovepipes of knowledge. More to the point of SOA adoption, contemporary IT structures fail to leverage shared skills and experience, much less shared services. Thus, adopting SOA runs counter to the organization's design—no single entity can "own" SOA, so developing buy-in and encouraging the actual use of SOA is naturally problematic.

However, a company implementing or upgrading SAP is in a good position to drive the adoption of SOA. As a natural initiator and owner of SOA (at least initially), an SAP project normally has the executive buy-in and attention of the business and other key stakeholders to put an SOA adoption strategy on good footing. Why is this important? Implementing SOA amounts to an enterprise undertaking rather than a local task; SOA is all about sharing services and service definitions across a company and not just a single application. Because SAP tends to impact most if not all of how a firm goes to market and conducts business, its implementation creates a logical entry point for a service-oriented architecture. To this end, SAP speaks of an enterprise architecture, as discussed next.

Need for an Enterprise Architecture

A range of additional technology challenges arise for strategic deployments of SOA across the whole company and all of its IT silos. The ideal way to address these enterprisewide challenges is to adopt a business-driven enterprise architecture (EA) approach. An EA methodology not only sets the stage for SOA, but can validate the SOA approach for a particular firm.

The most popular EA methodology for AMR Research clients is The Open Group Architecture Framework (TOGAF, pronounced *toe-gaff*). SAP has built an EA framework that extends TOGAF to include SAP Solution Architecture. A number of software vendors and systems integrators have developed specialist tools to aid analysis, modeling, and documentation of EA. Virtually all of them support the TOGAF methodology, and some of these can also link to SAP Solution Manager.

> Based on TOGAF, SAP introduced an SAP-branded enterprise architecture framework. Co-created with Capgemini, SAP's EAF supports and integrates SOA. SAP EAF 1.0 was introduced at SAPPHIRE 2007 and already boasts more than 60 customers. It is based on the AcceleratedSAP (ASAP) methodology, and similar to ASAP includes roadmaps, steps, reference architecture documentation, and accelerators. These components are maintained by SAP Solution Manager 4.0, SAP's enterprise application lifecycle management tool for implementation and ongoing operations.

By the Way

Moving Away from Client/Server Architectures

Client/server-based enterprise solutions still prevail today despite the presence of SOA and similar architectures, and SAP's installed base is no exception. To transition today from a proven solution that meets a client's core needs to an architecture that promises greater rewards but may require significant retooling is simply not palatable to everyone. SAP and its partners can talk of increased business agility and flexibility that comes from Enterprise SOA, for example, but the pain of functional upgrades and technical replatforming costs money, incurs downtime, and is generally disruptive for months. Add to this the need to embrace a new architectural approach and train both IT and an organization's SAP end-user community, and it's no wonder that the transition to SOA is anything but slow and deliberate. Finally, given the fact that most organizations tend to upgrade mission-critical applications such as SAP at 5-to-10-year lifecycles means we have yet to see what will eventually become a true groundswell of SOA adoption activity in the world of SAP. But it's coming...

Summary

This hour provided background into SOA from a generic perspective and SAP's Enterprise SOA in particular. You learned from where SOA evolved, advantages and challenges relative to adopting SOA, and the difference between Web Services and Service-Oriented Architecture.

Case Study: Hour 14

Consider this Enterprise SOA case study and the questions that follow, the answers to which may be found in Appendix A, "Case Study Answers."

Situation

MNC has been struggling to adopt a new business-enabling architecture, and with the advent of its SAP program has determined that the new SAP ERP implementation will lead the way with Enterprise SOA. At an early stage still, the project's steering committee has been tasked with building awareness around SOA and its advantages to MNC. Assist the committee with answering several fundamental questions.

Questions

1. What is the difference between SOA and Enterprise SOA, and from where did Enterprise SOA come?

2. How does Web Services differ from SOA?

3. What are several challenges to adopting SOA?

4. What are the advantages of Enterprise SOA as implemented by SAP?

PART IV

SAP Technical Considerations

HOUR 15

Technical Installation of SAP

What You'll Learn in This Hour:

▶ The SAP technical installation phases
▶ The planning and pre-planning phases of an installation
▶ The basic steps of an SAP installation

We've come a long way on our path toward implementing SAP, and finally we've reached the point where it is time for the actual technical installation. In this hour, we will walk through a fairly straightforward installation of an SAP Solution Manager 4.0 central system (where the database and all SAP elements are installed on a single physical server) installed atop a Linux operating system with an Oracle database.

Installation Overview

Let's set the stage before we get too far down our installation path. First, we are going to assume that the SAP solution has been architected and sized appropriately—our installation will represent nothing more than a technical sandbox used by the IT team to gain familiarity with the entire technology stack and overall SAP system. Further, we have been told and therefore know exactly which software components we need to install based on our business scenario (as explained in the SAP master installation guide). And we have a physical server in our hands configured with the necessary processors, memory, and disks. With all this behind us, let's get started with the technical implementation!

Installing SAP can be broken down into three phases: planning, pre-installation, and installation. In addition, some post-installation tasks need to be completed before the installation is truly finished. We have already covered the initial planning stages in Hour 12, "Implementing SAP: A Technical Perspective." The pre-installation phase involves making sure the server is ready for the SAP installation to take place. Careful planning in the first two phases should result in a smooth installation.

In a typical SAP implementation, the initial technical installation is either a development system or a sandbox (that is, technical "test" system).

Planning

The first phase in an SAP installation is planning. We have already covered the high-level planning needed to get to the point of server installation, but more planning and reading are required for the SAP software technical installation. The first step in any SAP installation should be obtaining the SAP installation guides and associated notes. The installation guides are available from the SAP service marketplace under keyword instguides (http://service.sap.com/instguides).

The first step is to download the master guide. For example, to install SAP Solution Manager 4.0, you would download "SAP Solution Manager 4.0 Master Guide." The master guide provides a wealth of valuable information, including notation of the media required for your installation. It also covers scenarios—which are basically the different ways you can use an SAP software component. For example, your company might choose to implement Employee and Manager Self-Services. The master guide would explain the installation sequence for your scenario and detail the requirements.

We also want to make sure we get the related installation and configuration guides. In our case, we would want to make sure we have "SAP ERP 2005 SR2 ABAP on Linux: Oracle" and "SAP Web Application Server ABAP 7.0 on Linux: Oracle" Parts I and II ("Planning and Preparation" and "Installation and Post-Installation," respectively). Finally, we need to download and review the notes associated with our installation. There will almost always be a note associated with the installation from an OS perspective (Linux, in our case) and the platform/database combination (Linux and Oracle). We cannot overstate the importance of planning—in our experience, following the procedures in the installation guides along with the associated notes is the most critical step to a smooth installation.

For example, to install Solution Manager on Linux/Oracle, we would first download the following manuals and SAP Notes:

▶ SAP Solution Manager 4.0 SR1 on Linux: Oracle—Installation Guide

▶ SAP Web Application Server ABAP 6.40 SR1 on Linux: Oracle Part I—Planning and Preparation Manual

▶ SAP Web Application Server ABAP 6.40 SR1 on Linux: Oracle Part II—Installation and Post-Installation Manual

▶ 171356—SAP Software on Linux: Essentials

▶ 958253—SUSE Linux Enterprise Server 10: Installation Notes

▶ 980426—Oracle 10.2 Software Installation on New Operating Systems

▶ 861215—Recommended Settings for the Linux on AMD64/EM64T JVM

▶ 1090932—IBM Download Site for Special JDK Builds—iFix

Pre-Planning

In order to install SAP, we first need to have the corresponding infrastructure in place. This would include the network, storage, and server infrastructure. Again, the assumption is that the infrastructure has already been planned for, including storage, network, and server considerations:

▶ Storage requirements have been determined, disk space has been allocated, and the SAN infrastructure is in place.

▶ The network requirements have been determined, and the network infrastructure is in place.

▶ The server has been sized, racked, and connected to the network and storage infrastructure.

Believe it or not, from a technical perspective getting the infrastructure in place and optimized for the actual installation is most of the battle—the SAP installation itself is the easy part.

SAP Infrastructure Review

With the infrastructure in place, we need to validate and document our SAP standards and conventions. Keeping a single spreadsheet with all the pertinent information grouped onto different worksheets (Network, SAN, Operating System, Database, SAP, and so on) makes it easy to complete the installation (having all the information in a central location makes installation a snap). Let's spend a few minutes further reviewing the infrastructure requirements.

Network

For the SAP install, all we need are the server to be on the network and an IP address. But for the network team, things aren't quite this simple—a network architecture has to be developed before this happens. One of the major considerations in a network design for SAP is whether each environment (production, quality assurance, and development) will have its own network segment. It is also possible for customers to create separate network segments for user access and data (database access and backups). The availability of SAP components through the Internet (if applicable) must also be addressed. The goal of all this is to provide a secure environment for the SAP servers without impacting the functionality. Depending on the company, the network team usually cables up the server and assigns the IP address, leaving the SAP installer oblivious to all this behind-the-scenes complexity.

Storage Area Network (SAN)

For capacity and performance reasons, SAP databases typically require SAN storage—another task typically handled behind-the-scenes. For the SAP install to proceed, the storage team needs to allocate the storage from the SAN. New storage (typical for new SAP implementations) must be designed for performance and availability. There are many considerations for storage design. For example, with an HP EVA, disk groups must be configured (including RAID level), LUNs must be created and assigned to hosts, and so on. Finally, the fiber must be run to the host and connected to the SAN infrastructure (SAN switches). The end result is that the host operating system has access to the required storage.

Hostname Considerations

One of the pre-install decisions that must be made is the hostnaming convention. It is really useful to know where a system resides, which SAP software component(s) it is running (ECC, Enterprise Portals, BI, and so on), its role in the environment (development, quality assurance, or production), and its function (database application server or message server). Having such a standard aids administrators by making it easy to identify servers for maintenance or troubleshooting.

Operating System Installation

Many companies have separate teams responsible for Linux or Windows server builds. These teams are typically given an IP address by the network team, the necessary SAN storage from the storage team, and assign the hostname based on the naming convention. The administrators may also be responsible for assigning drive letters and formatting the storage. Having a standard for drive letter assignment also aids in troubleshooting and maintenance. For example, for consistency the database log files should always be installed on the same drive letter.

Note that the file allocation unit size is determined during the formatting of a drive and can have a significant effect on performance. For example, for Windows/SQL and Linux-based systems on x64 hardware, the data drives should be formatted with 64K blocks for best performance.

CD/DVD Media

You normally receive the installation DVDs as part of the installation package from SAP. However, it is also possible to download the required media as determined from the installation guides from SAP at http://service.sap.com/swdc. In most cases, you will want to copy the media to a central location (you will need the same media for the quality assurance and production installations). In our simple example, we need the following media based on the SAP Solution Manager 4.0 master guide:

▶ 51032955: SAP Solution Manager 4.0 Support Release 3 Installation Master
Location: /dvd/SAP_Solution_M._4.0_SR3_Inst._Master

▶ 51032956_2: SAP Solution Manager 4.0 Support Release 3 Installation Export
Location: /dvd/SAP_Solution_M._4.0_SR3_Inst._Export

▶ 51031676_1: Oracle 10.2 64-Bit RDBMS Linux on x86_64 64bit
Location: /dvd/51031676

▶ 51033032: SAP NetWeaver 2004S SR2 Kernel 7.00 Linux on x86_64 64bit
Location: /dvd/NW_2004s_SR2_Kernel_WINDOWS__LNX_X86

▶ 51033272: Oracle 10.2 Client
Location: /dvd/ORACLE 10.2 Client

▶ 51031811: Oracle 10.2 RDBMS Patch 10.2.0.2 Linux_X86_64
Location: /dvd/DVD_ORACLE_10.2.0.2_Patches_LINUX

▶ 51032958: SAP Solution Manager 4.0 Support Release 3 Java Components
Location: /dvd/51032958

▶ JCE policy files (available at https://www6.software.ibm.com/dl/jcesdk/jcesdk-p; note that you will need to register with the site to download these policy files)

We will document the purpose of the CDs/DVDs as we proceed through this hour.

SAP Solution Manager Keys

SAP requires a Solution Manager key be generated for the installation of the latest SAP software components, including ERP 6.0, which necessitates a Solution Manager installation. Solution Manager (SolMan) is an SAP system used to support your other SAP systems. SAP has integrated support into Solution Manager—for example, Solution Manager can be used to open messages with SAP and download notes. Solution Manager provides much more functionality as well (including the ability to generate EarlyWatch reports and provide support to your end users), but the important thing to remember is that you must have a Solution Manager instance in order to complete the installation—some would argue this is SAP's way of gently coercing customers to implement SolMan (though it is in everyone's best interest to do so).

Installation

From a solution stack perspective, installing the SAP central server can be viewed as a four-step process:

- ▶ Operating system installation/configuration
- ▶ Validate prerequisites
- ▶ Database installation configuration
- ▶ The actual SAP software installation

Operating System Installation

The operating system installation for SAP systems is similar to that of any other application. For Windows systems, SAP makes some recommendations for the page file size and a few settings to optimize performance in the install guide. Linux has page file and package requirements also found in the install guide. The customer is always responsible for licensing and obtaining the OS media. The final step in the operating system installation should be going through a prerequisite checklist, as detailed next for the Solution Manager on SUSE Linux/Oracle installation.

Prerequisite Checklist

In this case, our prerequisite checklist is for a Linux-based system. A similar checklist can be developed for other operating environments.

- ▶ Check network teaming and other network interface properties.
- ▶ Install Java Runtime Environment (JRE).
- ▶ Verify the following Linux SUSE RPMs have been installed: SAP Application Server Base (sapinit) and C/C++ Compiler and Tools.

▶ Verify the saplocales RPM attached to SAP Note 171356 is installed. (Note: Do not install the Oracle server init package.)

▶ Select MD5 password encryption as the default encryption method used.

▶ Verify swap space—the SAP recommendation is 2× RAM (20GB maximum).

▶ Verify that the file systems are laid out as described in the respective master guide.

▶ Verify that you have downloaded the updated RUNINSTALLER (see SAP Note 980426 for specifics relative to an Oracle-based installation).

A prerequisite checklist is a great way to ensure that the operating system is ready for SAP to be installed.

A Linux RPM actually refers to an RPM Package Manager, the rpm program (used to manage installed software), or the file format used for such files (rpm file format). In the latter case, the rpm file format is used for distributing software in a "packaged" format, either as a precompiled binary or in its source code format.

By the Way

The swap file (Linux and UNIX) or page file (Windows) size should be twice the size of the physical RAM in the server, or 20GB, whichever is smaller for a 64-bit operating system. At this point, you should only be installing SAP on 64-bit operating systems, too, as 32-bit operating systems are no longer recommended by SAP.

Watch Out!

Database Server Software Installation

The installation process for the database depends on the SAP software release and the database software. Two common options are explored next. (Although remember that SQL Server is only supported on Windows, whereas Oracle can be installed on Windows, Linux, and all SAP-supported UNIX variants.)

Microsoft SQL Server

Microsoft SQL Server is always installed "outside" of the SAP installation procedure. SAP provides installation instructions for SQL Server, too, although for the most part it is a standard SQL Server database install.

Oracle

In some earlier releases of SAP's applications, the Oracle database software was installed from a "normal" Oracle CD obtained from SAP. The installation of the database software is normally accomplished by a running batch file provided by SAP that contains answers to all the configuration questions asked by the Oracle installer. In recent releases of SAP, the Oracle Server software comes in .SAR files, which are unzipped during the SAP installation process. Interestingly, the SAP install process still stops and requires the installer to complete the Oracle install before proceeding by running RUNINSTALLER. After the Oracle installation completes, the current Oracle patch set must be installed. Oracle Enterprise Edition is required for all applications.

By the Way

In both cases, it is important to remember that Oracle or another database is simply the vendor's standard database software configured for SAP.

SAP Software Installation

The following needs to be done before commencing on the SAP software installation:

▶ Plan your SAP system according to the master guide.

▶ Choose your basic system variants.

▶ Identify basic SAP system parameters.

We have reached the point where we need to choose the basic system variants and identify the basic SAP system parameters.

System Variants—Different "Kinds" of Installations

SAP can be installed in several different ways, depending on the requirements gathered in the planning phase. These include the following:

▶ Central Services Instance for ABAP (ASCS)

▶ Central Services Instance (SCS)

▶ Database Instance

▶ Central Instance

▶ Dialog Instance

For a high-availability installation of Solution Manager, all but the Dialog Instance is required; the Dialog Instance (also known as an *application server*) is optional. We will complete the four separate installations on the same host for demonstration purposes (we could achieve the same results by choosing a Central System installation). We will identify the SAP system parameters as we proceed through the installation.

The SAP installation is started from the master installation media using the SAP installation utility, sapinst. Let's walk through an SAP Solution Manager 4.0 installation together—we'll choose the high availability option so you can see several installations.

SAP Central Services Instance for ABAP (ASCS) Installation

Perform the following steps to install SAP Central Services for ABAP (ASCS):

1. As user "root," log on to server linux-test1.

2. Start SAPINST:

```
$ export DISPLAY=<workstation ip address>:0.0
$ export SAPINST_JRE_HOME=/opt/java1.4
$ cd /dvd/SAP_Solution_M._4.0_SR3_Inst._Master
$ ./sapinst
```

3. On the SAP Installation Master window, select SAP Installation Master, SAP Solution Manager 4.0 Support Release 3, SAP Systems, Oracle, High-Availability System, Based on AS ABAP and AS Java, Central Services Instance for ABAP (ASCS), as shown in Figure 15.1.

   Click Next.

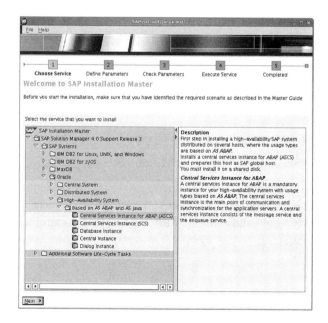

FIGURE 15.1
The Central Services Instance for ABAP (ASCS) is the first of four installations that need to be completed in order to create a highly available Solution Manager system.

4. On the SAP System, General Parameters window, enter the following:
   SAP System ID (SAPSID): **TST**
   SAP System Mount Directory: **/sapmnt**
   Click Next.

5. On the SAP System, Administrator Password window, enter the following:
   Password of SAP System Administrator: **"xxxxxxxxx"**
   Confirm the password and then click Next.

6. On the SAP System, ASCS Instance Number, enter the following:
   ABAP ASCS Instance Number: **02**
   Click Next.

7. On the SAP System, ASCS Instance Number window, enter the following:
   ABAP SCS Messaging Service Port: **3602**
   Internal ABAP SCS Messaging Service Port: **3902**
   Click Continue.

8. On the Media Browser, Software Package Request window, enter the following:
   Location of Kernel NW70: **/dvd/NW_2004s_SR2_Kernel_WINDOWS_**
   LNX_X86
   Click Next.

9. On the SAP System, Unpack Archives window, check Unpack box for Archive
   "DBINDEP/SAPEXE.SAR" and then click Next.

10. On the Parameter Summary window, review the choices to ensure they are
    correct.
    Click Start.

11. On the Task Progress window, click OK when you see the message "Execution
    of Service has been completed successfully."

SAP Central Services Instance (SCS) Installation

Perform the following steps to install SAP Central Services (SCS):

1. On the SAP Installation Master window, select SAP Installation Master, SAP
   Solution Manager 4.0 Support Release 3, SAP Systems, Oracle, High
   Availability System, Based on AS ABAP and AS Java, Central Services
   Instance (SCS).
   Click Next.

2. On the SAP System, General Parameters window, enter the following:
    SAP System ID (SAPSID): **TST**
    SAP mount directory: **/sapmnt**
    Click Next.

3. On the SAP System, SCS Instance window, enter the following:
    SCS Instance Number: **02**
    Click Next.

4. On the SAP System, SCS Instance window, enter the following:
    Internal SCS Messaging Service Port: **3902**
    Click Next.

5. On the Parameter Summary window, verify the parameters and then click Start.

6. Click Cancel in the message box "Your system does not meet some prerequisites...."

7. When you see the message "Execution of Service has been completed success-fully" on the Task Progress window, click OK.

SAP Database Instance Installation

Perform the following steps to install a SAP Database instance:

1. On the SAP Installation Master window, select SAP Installation Master, SAP Solution Manager 4.0 Support Release 3, SAP Systems, Oracle, High Availability System, Based on AS ABAP and AS, Database Instance. Click Next.

2. On the Media Browser, Software Package Request window, enter the following:
    Java Component SOLMAN40SR3: **/dvd/51032958**
    Click Next.

3. On the SAP System, Java Development Kit window, enter the following:
    JDK directory: **/usr/lib64/java**
    Click Next.

4. On the SAP System, JCE Unlimited Strength Jurisdiction Policy Archive window, enter the following:
    JCE Unlimited Strength Jurisdiction Policy Archive: **/dvd/jce_policy-1.4.2.zip**
    Click Next.

5. On the SAP System, General Parameters window, check the box "profiles are available" and then enter the following:
Profile Directory: **/sapmnt/TST/profile**
Click Next.

6. On the SAP System, Master Password window, enter the following:
Password for all users of this SAP system: "**xxxxxxx**"
Confirm the password and then click Next.

7. On the SAP System, Database Parameters window, enter the following:
Database ID (DBSID): **TST**
Database Host: **linux-test1**
Click Next.

8. The SAP System, Database Administrator Password window should be filled in already. Click Next.

9. On the Media Browser, Software Package Check window, enter the following:
Location of the Installation Export DVD: **/dvd/SAP_Solution_M._4.0_SR3_ Inst._Export/Export1**
Click Next.

10. On the Media Browser, Software Package Check window, enter the following:
Location of the Installation Export DVD: **/dvd/SAP_Solution_M._4.0_SR3_ Inst._Export/Export2**
Click Next.

11. On the Oracle, Database System window, enter the following:
Instance Memory: **16384**
ABAP Schema: **SAPSR3**
Password of ABAP Schema
Confirm the password.
Java Schema: **SAPSR3DB**
Password of Java Schema
Confirm the password.
Click Next.

12. On the Oracle, Database System window, enter the following:
Database Advanced Options
MaxDatafilesize: **10000**
Check the Advanced DB configuration option and then click Next.

13. On the Oracle, Standard Database Users window, you can change the passwords or simply keep the master password, as follows:
Password of sys: "**xxxxxxxxxx**"
Confirm: "**xxxxxxxxxx**"
Password of system: "**xxxxxxxxx**"
Confirm: "**xxxxxxxxx**"
Click Next.

14. On the Media Browser, Software Package Check window, enter the following:
Location of Oracle RDBMS: **/dvd/51031676**
Click Next.

15. On the Oracle, Listener Configuration window, enter the following:
Listener Name: **LISTENER**
Listener port: **1540**
For the Network Configuration Files, check the following:
Keep listener.ora
Keep tnsnames.ora
Click Next.

16. On the Oracle, Advanced Configuration window, check the following:
Sapdata Directory Mapping
Database Instance File Systems
Autoextend
General Storage
Click Next.

17. On the Oracle, Database System window, highlight sapdata2 through sapdata19 and then click Remove.
You are left with only sapdata1 on the screen.
Click Next.

18. On the Oracle, Database Instance File System window, enter the following:
$ORACLE_HOME Directory: **/oracle/TST/102_64**
Oracle Stage Directory: **/oracle/stage/102_64**
Sapdata Home Directory: **/oracle/TST**
Click Next.

19. On the Oracle, Tablespace Extensions window, make sure all options are set to Autoextend and then click Next.

20. Click Next on the Oracle, General Tablespace Storage window.

21. On the SAP System, Database import window, enter the following:
SAP codepage: **4103**
Number of Parallel Jobs: **8**
Click Next.

22. On the SAP System, Secure Store Settings window, enter the following:
Key phrase: "**xxxxxxxxxx**"
Confirm: "**xxxxxxxxxx**"

23. On the ABAP System, Create Database Statistics window, click the "create statistics at the end of import" option and then click Next.

24. On the SAP System, Unpack Archive window, check the following:
ORA/SAPEXEDB.SAR
ORA/DBATOOLS.SAR
OCL10264.SAR
Click Next.

25. Review your choices on the Parameter Summary window and then click Next.

26. Enter the parameters of the SAP database system on the Oracle, Database System window. Change the sapdata path for all instances of SAPDATA listed to "SAPDATA1" and then click Next.

27. SAPinst now stops the installation. Install the Oracle database as follows:
    a. Log in as oratst.
    b. Set the DISPLAY variable.
    c. Change to directory /oracle/stage/102_64/database/SAP.
    d. Start ./RUNINSTALLER.

28. On the Specify Inventory Directory and Credentials window, verify the full path of the inventory directory (/oracle/oraInventory) and then specify the operating system group name (dba).
Click Next.

29. Click Next on the Available Product Components window.

30. On the Product-Specific Prerequisite Checks window, change the status of Warnings and Not Executed to User Verified.

31. Click Install on the Summary window.

32. Perform the following actions on the Execute Configuration Scripts window:

    a. Open a terminal window.

    b. Log in as "root."

    c. Run the scripts.

    d. Return to this window and click OK to continue.

33. Run orainstRoot.sh.

```
linux-test1:~ # /oracle/oraInventory/orainstRoot.sh
Changing permissions of /oracle/oraInventory to 770.
Changing groupname of /oracle/oraInventory to dba.
The execution of the script is complete
```

Run the root.sh script:

```
linux-test1:~ # /oracle/TST/102_64/root.sh
Running Oracle10 root.sh script...
The following environment variables are set as:
    ORACLE_OWNER= oratst
    ORACLE_HOME=  /oracle/TST/102_64
Enter the full pathname of the local bin directory: [/usr/local/bin]:
/usr/local/bin
    Copying dbhome to /usr/local/bin ...
    Copying oraenv to /usr/local/bin ...
    Copying coraenv to /usr/local/bin ...
Creating /etc/oratab file...
Entries will be added to the /etc/oratab file as needed by the
Database Configuration Assistant when a database is created
```

Finish running the generic portion of the root.sh script; product-specific root actions will be performed.

Click OK.

34. Click OK on the Execute Configuration Scripts window.

35. On the End of Installation screen, click Exit.

36. Install the Oracle 10.2.0.2 patch.

37. Click OK on the message box "SAPinst now stops the installation."

38. When you see the message "Execution of Service has been completed successfully" on the Task Progress window, click OK.

SAP Central Instance Installation

Perform the following steps to install an SAP Central Instance:

1. On the SAP Installation Master window, select SAP Installation Master, SAP Solution Manager 4.0 Support Release 3, SAP Systems, Oracle, High Availability, Based on AS ABAP and AS Java, Central Instance. Click Next.

2. On the Media, Software Package Request window, enter the following:
   Location of the Java component: **/dvd/51032958**
   Click Next.

3. On the SAP System, Java Development Kit window, enter the following:
   Location of the JDK directory: **/usr/lib64/java**
   Click Next.

4. On the SAP System, General Parameters window, enter the following:
   Profile directory location: **/sapmnt/TST/profile**
   Click Next.

5. On the SAP System, Master Password window, enter the following:
   Master password for all users for this SAP system: **"xxxxxxxxxx"**
   Confirm: **"xxxxxxxxx"**
   Click Next.

6. On the Oracle, Listener Configuration window, enter the following Listener information:
   Listener Name: **LISTENER**
   Listener Port: **1527**
   Check "Keep listener.ora" and "Keep tnsnames.ora" and then click Next.

7. On the SAP System, Central Instance window, enter the following:
   Central Instance number: **00**
   Click Next.

8. On the SAP System, ABAP UME window, enter the J2EE engine user names:
   Administrator User: **J2EE_ADMIN**
   Guest User: **J2EE_Guest**
   Communication User: **SAPJSF**

9. On the SAP System, ABAP UME window, enter the J2EE engine user passwords:
   Password of administrator user: **"xxxxxx"**
   Confirm: **"xxxxxx"**
   Password of communication user: **"xxxxxx"**
   Confirm: **"xxxxxx"**
   Password for SDM: "xxxxxx"
   Confirm: **"xxxxxx"**
   Click Next.

10. Click Next on the SAP System, DDIC Users window.

11. On the Media, Software Package Request window, enter the location of the following:
Kernel NW 70: **/dvd/NW_2004s_SR2_Kernel_Windows_LNX_X86**
Oracle Client: **/dvd/Oracle_client**
Click Next.

12. On the SAP System, Unpack Archives window, check the Unpack box for the following:
DBINDEP/IGSEXE...
DBINDEP/IGSHEL...
Click Next.

13. Click Next on the SAP System, NWDI Landscape window.

14. On the SAP System, System Landscape Directory window, check "Configure a local SLD" and then click Next.

15. On the SAP System, Local SLD window, enter the following:
Object server name: **cijciTST**
SLD Data supplier user: **SLDDSUSER**
Password of SLD data supplier user: "**xxxxxx**"
Confirm: "**xxxxxx**"
SLD ABAP ASI user: **SLDAPIUSER**
Password of SLD ABAP API user: "**xxxxxx**"
Confirm: "**xxxxxx**"
Click Next.

16. On the SAP System, ADS Users window, enter the following:
Password for ADSUSER: "**xxxxxx**"
Confirm: "**xxxxxx**"
Password for ADS_AGENT: "**xxxxxx**"
Confirm: "**xxxxxx**"
Click Next.

17. Review your choices on the Parameter Summary window and then click Next.

18. When you see the message "Execution of Service has been completed successfully" on the Task Progress window, click OK.

This concludes the sapinst portion of the SAP Solution Manager 4.0 install.

Post-Installation

The installation of SAP is almost complete, but you still need to carry out the following tasks before the system is ready to use:

▶ Stop and start the system using stopsap and startsap, respectively.

▶ Log on to the system (user SAP* or DDIC in client 000, 001, or 066 [SAP* only]) using the master password.

▶ Install the permanent SAP license. The temporary license key valid for weeks is created during the install. You can obtain a permanent license key for the installation from http://service.sap.com/licensekeys.

▶ Apply the latest kernel and support packages. After the installation, apply the most current support package stack available for download from the SAP Software Distribution Center (http://service.sap.com/swdc).

▶ Perform a client copy.

▶ Modify the SAP profiles based on recommendations from SAP Notes as well as recommendations from your Basis lead (such as the number of work processes memory configuration parameters, and so on).

This concludes our successful installation of a Solution Manager 4.0 system. Congratulations!

Summary

In this hour, we outlined the steps necessary for a successful technical installation. With careful planning and preparation, the actual installation should be a breeze. Finishing the post-installation phase marks the end of the technical implementation. At this point, the system is ready for the functional team. Keep in mind that although the technical installation is over, this is really just the beginning of the SAP implementation; much business configuration work remains to be done to make the system actually useful!

Case Study: Hour 15

Consider this following SAP installation case study and the questions that follow, the answers to which may be found in Appendix A, "Case Study Answers."

Situation

MNC has standardized on SQL Server and has decided to implement Solution Manager. You have been tasked by MNC's SAP Basis teamleader with installing a Solution Manager 4.0 sandbox so your colleagues can begin "playing" with the new features/functionality. You have worked with your implementation partners to architect and size the solution, and the infrastructure is in place. With all necessary planning behind you as well, you are ready to begin the installation process.

Questions

1. What is the first thing you should do?

2. What is the name of the media from where you start the SAP installation process (sapinst)?

3. Atop what operating system will you be installing Solution Manager?

4. In case you can't find one of the CDs/DVDs, where can you go to download SAP media?

HOUR 16

Integrating SAP with Microsoft Office

What You'll Learn in This Hour:

▶ Using SAP's %pc functionality to save SAP data
▶ Moving SAP data into Microsoft Excel, Word, and Access
▶ Review of Duet
▶ Microsoft Active Directory Integration

Integration between SAP and Microsoft products continues to be important to most end users. Through Object Linking and Embedding (OLE) it has long been possible to drop your SAP data into a Microsoft application. In this way, additional analysis of your SAP ERP list-based and report-based SAP data sources can be easily accomplished through Microsoft Excel, Access, and so on. And with the latest joint product development between SAP and Microsoft—Duet—this integration continues to grow deeper and more valuable, adding Microsoft Exchange, Outlook, other database sources, and more to the list of Microsoft products that afford better integration with SAP.

SAP Integration with Desktop Applications

The first layer of integration between SAP and the Microsoft desktop hinges on the use of OLE, a common and standard technology for transferring and sharing information among applications. With OLE, you can take data out of your SAP system and place it into another system, all the while maintaining the format and integrity of the data. For example, you can view data residing in any number of SAP database tables as a series of columns and rows in Microsoft Excel—an easy way to view and manipulate data otherwise trapped in the SAP database.

The SAP Assistant is the OLE interface used for calling SAP functions and transactions from other non-SAP applications. The SAP Assistant exposes both ActiveX controls and OLE object classes, for logging in to SAP, managing data and tables, calling functions and transactions, and more. SAP systems are therefore designed today so that you can share data with any OLE-compatible application. Sample OLE-compatible applications include

▶ Microsoft Office, including Visio and other products

▶ Corel Office, including Paradox

▶ Star Office

▶ Lotus SmartSuite

▶ Many web server development environments, such as Microsoft FrontPage

Additionally, nearly all modern application development languages in use today support OLE. This includes the old-school C++ programming language, the latest and greatest Microsoft .NET Visual Basic offerings, IBM's WebSphere Information Integrator, as well as PowerBuilder by Sybase. In this way, the developer of a non-SAP application can create objects that can access information in SAP.

Using %pc **to Download Data**

There are many ways to share data between SAP and Microsoft. As mentioned in previous hours, executing %pc in the transaction dialog box is an excellent and expedient way of moving data from SAP lists into other formats. Transactions that display their data via OCX controls—in various panels, each with its own data sources, constructs, and so on—are generally not good candidates for %pc. That is, OCX-based output typically does not lend itself to being downloaded into a PC format such as XLS, RTF, and so on. But transactions that are displayed in list format—most of them, to some degree—are excellent candidates.

To save SAP list-based output to a file on your desktop or the network, enter the characters %pc in the transaction dialog box and then press Enter. A print window pops up (see Figure 16.1), which defaults to saving the screen's contents in an unconverted file format. Choose the format most appropriate for your immediate needs, press Enter, browse to the desired directory path, type the name of the output file you want to create, and then click Save to save the list data to the filename you specified.

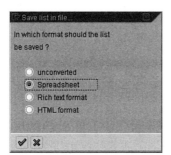

FIGURE 16.1
Saving SAP data in a number of formats is easily and quickly accomplished by using %pc.

Exporting SAP Data to Microsoft Excel

Microsoft Excel provides a user-friendly format and helpful tools to assist you in the process of analyzing and presenting data. To get your SAP data into Microsoft Excel, you can employ several methods. The most basic method involves the System List function, which enables you to save lists displayed on your SAP screen.

> If you want to save your downloaded SAP list in Microsoft Excel, be sure to select File, Save As and then select the Microsoft Excel Workbook (*.xls) option in the Save As Type box of your spreadsheet; otherwise, by default, it is saved in a text format.

By the Way

You can also use the SAP Query tool to export data to Microsoft Excel, as follows:

1. Execute an SAP Query (SAP Query, InfoSet Query, Ad Hoc Query, and QuickViewer).

2. The options listed on the selection screen enable you to designate the type of output you want for your report. For a basic transfer to a Microsoft Excel spreadsheet, select the Display As Table radio button.

3. From here, select List, Save, Local File to download this table into Microsoft Excel. A Save As box appears, enabling you to select the download file format. Be sure to select the spreadsheet option.

4. After the download is complete, start Microsoft Excel and open the data you have just saved (see Figure 16.2).

5. Return to the SAP Query output screen displaying your table.

> You can use the same method detailed later in Hour 22, "Reporting and Query Basics," to download InfoSet or other "ad hoc" queries.

Did you Know?

FIGURE 16.2
Your Microsoft Excel spreadsheet containing your SAP Query data looks the same as the data in your original query output.

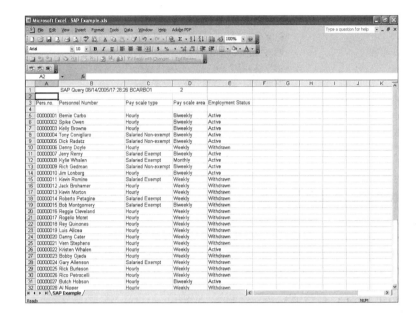

Creating SAP Form Letters in Microsoft Word

SAP has a great interface for creating form letters using Microsoft Word. This tool has endless possibilities for your company. For example, let's assume you need to output SAP Human Resources employee data into Microsoft Word so that you can create a form letter to all employees. Follow these steps:

1. Select a query to execute.

2. From the selection screen, use the Display As Table option and then execute your report.

3. When the output appears, rather than saving this file to Microsoft Excel, select the Word Processing button at the top of your Query Output screen. Doing so opens the Word Processor Settings dialog box shown in Figure 16.3. Press Enter to continue.

FIGURE 16.3
SAP's Word Processor Settings dialog boxes enable you to download your SAP data into Microsoft Word.

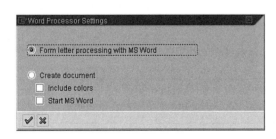

4. The dialog box that is displayed presents you with a number of options. You can designate whether you want to create a new Word document, use a current Word document (one that is currently "open" on your system), or use an existing Word document (one that is saved on your computer). Click the green check mark to begin the merge between SAP and Microsoft Word. Upon execution, SAP opens Microsoft Word (see Figure 16.4).

The mail merge toolbar containing
a link to your SAP fields

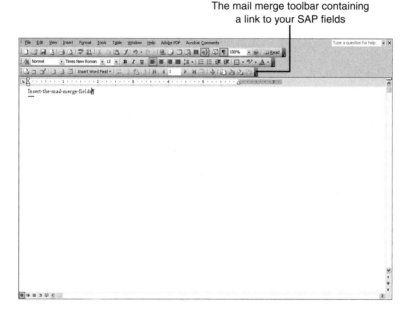

FIGURE 16.4
A Microsoft Word application launches with a new document.

5. An important thing to note is that your Microsoft Word application now contains a new mail merge toolbar that gives you the capability to insert your SAP fields into your Microsoft Word form letter. In Microsoft Word, press the Enter key to begin at a new line, and then select the Insert Merge Field button on the toolbar. In the drop-down list (or the Insert Merge Field pop-up window, in the case of Microsoft Office 2003), shown in Figure 16.5, you see all the SAP fields contained in your original SAP query.

6. As appropriate for your needs, select one of your SAP fields. It appears in brackets in your Microsoft Word document. Press Enter and insert another SAP field. Type some text into your Microsoft Word document and then insert another SAP field (see Figure 16.6).

FIGURE 16.5
The Microsoft
Word Insert
Merge Field but-
ton contains the
names of your
SAP fields from
your SAP query.

SAP fields appear in brackets

FIGURE 16.6
Your Microsoft
Word form letter
contains the
inserted fields
from your SAP
query in addi-
tion to any text
you typed
manually.

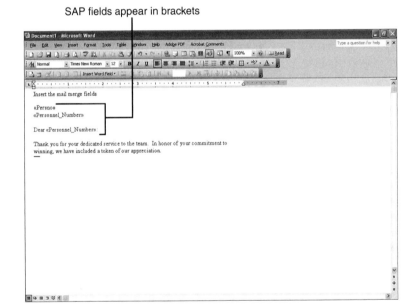

7. To preview the output of your form letter, click the ABC (View Merged Data) button from the mail merge toolbar, shown in Figure 16.7.

8. Use the record selector (forward and backward) buttons on the mail merge toolbar to view the various records.

View Merged Data button

Actual SAP data | Record selectors

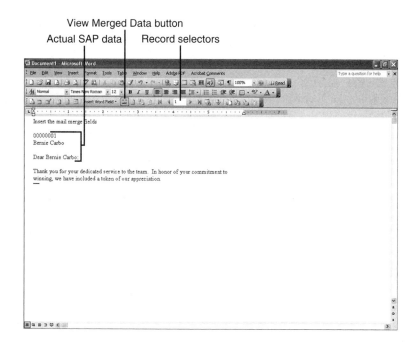

FIGURE 16.7
A sample
Microsoft Word
form letter con-
taining the SAP
fields from your
SAP query, in
the View
Merged Data
view.

You can save your Microsoft Word merge document for repeated use. The next time you want to use the same form letter (but with the latest data from SAP), you need to reopen the SAP query that serves as the source of the document, select the List, Word Processing option from the menu, and then select the Existing Word Document radio button. You are then prompted to enter the name of your Word document where you saved the file. Microsoft Word will launch, displaying your existing form letter containing the latest data from your SAP system.

Did you Know?

Exporting SAP to Microsoft Access

As you have seen, exporting SAP data to Microsoft Excel and Word is useful when it comes to performing further offline manipulation of your data, for creating reports and graphs, or for drafting form letters. Exporting data to a Microsoft Access data-base is quite useful, too, when it comes to general reporting.

Exporting to Microsoft Access is helpful when you want to compare data among multiple systems. For example, if your company stores your vendor master data in SAP and also stores this vendor master data in a non-SAP application (implying you have not implemented SAP Exchange Infrastructure with Master Data Management...), you can use Microsoft Access as a tool to quickly compare the two sources relative to overall data consistency.

Did you Know?

The initial steps to export data into Microsoft Access are the same as the steps to download a file into Microsoft Excel—the idea is to get the data into Excel's XLS format. Verify this is the case before proceeding.

> Depending on your Microsoft Excel configuration, you might have to perform a few extra steps:
>
> 1. Launch Microsoft Excel and open the spreadsheet you saved earlier.
> 2. In Excel, use the menu path File, Save As—as if you were going to save the file again.
> 3. Take a close look at the Save As Type box; ensure that the file is saved as a Microsoft Excel worksheet and not any other format. Alternatively, view and verify the extension of the file using Microsoft's Explorer utility.

Importing SAP into Microsoft Access

After the XLS file resides on your local system or an accessible file share, you need to import this file into Microsoft Access (the following steps assume Access has been installed on your system; given that Access is not included with all versions of Microsoft Office, this might not be the case by default):

1. Launch Microsoft Access on your system.

2. From this initial window, select the Blank Database option and then click OK. You are prompted to create a name and to select a location for your database. In this example, the C:\My Documents directory was selected and the database named mySAP.mdb, as shown in Figure 16.8.

FIGURE 16.8
The Microsoft Access File New Database window prompts you to create a new database file.

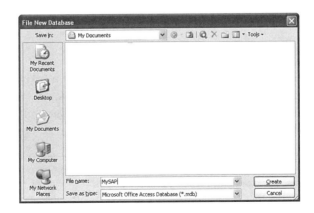

3. Click the Create button; you then see the main Microsoft Access window, which appears in Figure 16.9.

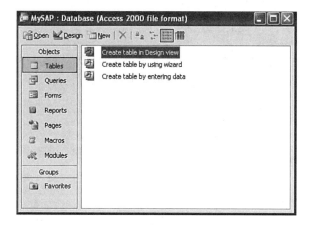

FIGURE 16.9
The Microsoft Access database main window displays the different database elements.

4. To bring the SAP data into Microsoft Access, use the Microsoft Access menu path File, Get External Data, Import. You are then prompted with a window similar to the one shown in Figure 16.10. This is where you have to input the location and filename of the output file you saved earlier. By default, the Files of Type box lists Microsoft Access (*.mdb). You have to change this to Microsoft Excel (*.xls).

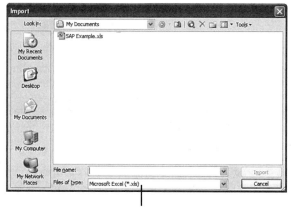

FIGURE 16.10
Select your import file location in the Microsoft Access Import window.

Be sure to change the Files of type drop-down box to reflect Microsoft Excel

5. After changing the Files of Type box and selecting your file, click Import. Just as in the Microsoft Excel import, in Access you are presented with an Import Spreadsheet Wizard similar to the one shown in Figure 16.11.

FIGURE 16.11
The Microsoft Access Import Spreadsheet Wizard assists you in importing your file.

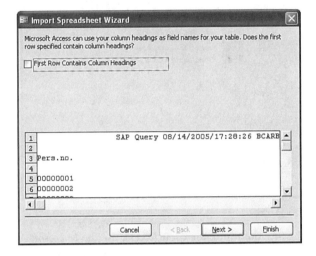

6. On the first screen of the Import Spreadsheet Wizard, click the Next button to continue. On the second screen, it asks whether you want to create a new table or add the data to an existing table. To create a new Access database table containing your SAP data, click Next. The next window, shown in Figure 16.12, gives you an opportunity to name each of your fields.

7. By selecting each column (use your mouse to do so), you can type a field name for each. After you have named all your fields, click Next.

8. The following screen enables you to assign a unique identifying number for each of your records; click the Next button to continue.

9. The last screen asks you to provide a name for your table. Type **MySAP** and click Finish. Microsoft Access then presents you with a confirmation window similar to that shown in Figure 16.13.

10. Click OK in the final Import Spreadsheet Wizard confirmation window; you are returned to the Microsoft Access main window, and your new table is now listed under the Table tab.

Type in a name for your column

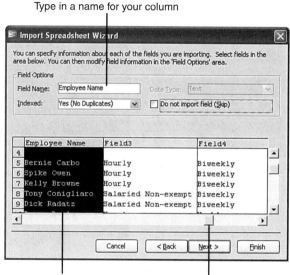

FIGURE 16.12
The Microsoft
Access Import
Spreadsheet
Wizard field
enables indi-
vidual field
specification
and more.

Select a column by using your mouse to highlight it

Use the scrollbar to
navigate through your file

FIGURE 16.13
The Microsoft
Access confir-
mation window
declares that
your data
has finished
importing.

11. To take a look at your table, select it and then click the Open button. Your SAP
list now appears as a Microsoft Access table (see Figure 16.14); it includes an
additional primary key field as well.

This process is certainly a few steps longer than exporting your SAP data into
Microsoft Excel. However, Microsoft Access is a sound reporting tool used by a large
number of SAP customers as their primary reporting tool—especially when other
applications or tools such as SAP NetWeaver BI 7.0, Strategic Enterprise
Management, Cognos, and Crystal Reports are unavailable. Its prevalence also
speaks to the fact that Microsoft Access is both popular and easy to use, as you'll
see next.

FIGURE 16.14
Your SAP data now appears in a Microsoft Access database table.

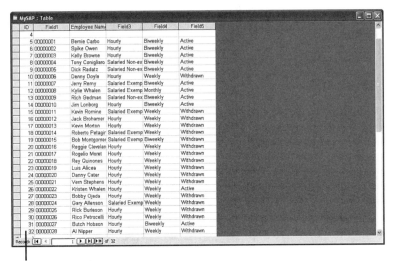

Note the additional primary key field

The Microsoft Access Report Wizard

Creating reports in Microsoft Access is easy using a tool called the Microsoft Access Report Wizard. The use of report wizards simplifies the layout process of your fields by visually stepping you through a series of questions about the type of report you want to create. The wizard walks you through the step-by–step creation of a report, while behind the scenes Access is formatting, grouping, and sorting your report based on the selections you make.

Instead of you having to create a report from scratch, Microsoft Access provides a number of standard report formats. Some of these, such as tabular and columnar reports, mail-merge reports, and mailing label formats, lend themselves to meeting basic reporting requirements. Reports created using the Microsoft Access Report Wizard can also be customized to fit your needs. To use the Report Wizard, perform the following steps:

1. Close any open Access databases by using the menu path File, Close.

2. In the main Microsoft Access database window, click Reports.

3. From here, click the New button to launch the Microsoft Access Report Wizard (or choose the option to create a report in Design view).

4. Assuming you are running the Report Wizard, select the Report Wizard option in the top box and your table name in the second box. Click OK to proceed.

5. You are presented with a field selection screen. From this screen, you can select which fields are output to your report. Select a field by highlighting it with your mouse, and then use the Next button to include it in the report. In Figure 16.15, the Employment Status field was selected.

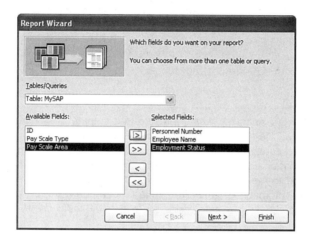

FIGURE 16.15
The Microsoft Access Report Wizard field selection window enables you to specify which fields you want to include in your report output.

6. After you click Next, the Report Wizard asks whether you want to add any grouping levels to your report. This is a helpful step when you are creating a report where you might want to group and subtotal portions of the output. For this example, you don't need grouping or subtotaling, so click the Next button to continue.

7. Now identify your sort order criteria. In Figure 16.16, we have sorted according to Employee Name.

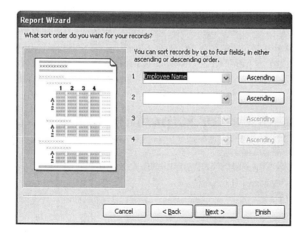

FIGURE 16.16
The Microsoft Access Report Wizard enables you to select multiple sorting criteria.

8. The Report Wizard enables you to specify formatting criteria. The orientation of the report (portrait or landscape) and the layout of the report (columnar, tabular, or justified) are designated on this screen. After making a selection, click Next.

9. You can choose from a selection of predefined formats for your report. After making a selection, click Next.

10. The last step asks you to type a name for your report. Do so, and click Finish to complete the creation of your report.

For advanced users, consider writing a macro that automatically retrieves the latest SAP download file and imports it into your existing Microsoft Access table—replacing the old data and thus automating the Microsoft Access import process. For more information on this function, search the Microsoft Access help for "automate importing." In the same way, advanced ABAP or Java programmers can write a program that automatically generates a file that can be used for the download portion of this process, thus automating the entire SAP-to-Access reporting process.

Microsoft Access is a great reporting tool that enables users with minimal Microsoft Access skills to create reports. Using Access, you can also include graphics in your reports, or you can create graphs and charts of your SAP data. If you take a few minutes to investigate the types of reports you can create using Microsoft Access, you will surely discover the value of this reporting tool for SAP.

Quick References

The following sections provide simple step-by-step instructions for executing many of the reporting processes just discussed. Use the following sections as a quick reference to speed you through each respective reporting process. And remember, if you need more information, refer to each process's respective detailed sections provided earlier in this hour.

Quick Reference for Exporting Lists to Microsoft Excel

The following is a recap of the steps required to use the System List function to export SAP lists to Microsoft Excel:

1. Navigate to the SAP screen containing the list you want to output.

2. Follow the menu path System, List, Save, Local File.

3. Use the possible entries help button to change the location and filename of your new file.

4. Click the Transfer button.

5. Launch Microsoft Excel and open the file.

Quick Reference for Exporting SAP Query Reports to Excel

The following is a recap of the steps required to output SAP Query reports to Microsoft Excel:

1. Execute the SAP Query report that contains the data you want to include in your report.

2. On the selection screen, select the Display As Table option and then execute the report.

3. Select the List, Download to File menu option.

4. Use the possible entries help button to change the location and filename of your new file.

5. Click the Transfer button.

6. Launch Microsoft Excel and open the file.

Quick Reference for Creating Form Letters with Microsoft Word

The following is a recap of the steps required to create SAP form letters using Microsoft Word:

1. Execute the SAP Query report that contains the data you want to include in your report.

2. On the selection screen, select the Display As Table option and then execute the report.

3. Select the List, Word Processing menu option.

4. Click the Enter button on the Word Processing Settings dialog box.

5. Select your required options from the MS Word Settings dialog box and then click the Enter button.

6. Type your document and insert merge fields using the Insert Merge Field button on the Microsoft Word mail merge toolbar.

7. Use the ABC view merged data button to review your document and the record selection buttons to navigate between records.

Quick Reference for Exporting Lists to Microsoft Access

The following is a recap of the steps required to use the System List function to export SAP lists into Microsoft Access. The initial steps of this process are the same for downloading files to Microsoft Excel:

1. Navigate to the SAP screen containing the list you want to output.

2. Follow the menu path System, List, Save, Local File.

3. Use the possible entries help button to change the location and filename of your new file.

4. Click the Transfer button.

5. Open your file in Microsoft Excel, and use the menu path File, Save As to save it as a Microsoft Excel worksheet. Close Excel.

6. Launch Microsoft Access and create a new database.

7. Use the menu path File, Get External Data, Import, and select your Microsoft Excel file to import the file into Microsoft Access using the Import Spreadsheet Wizard.

Quick Reference for Exporting SAP Query Reports to Access

The following is an explanation of the steps required to output an SAP Query report to Microsoft Access. The initial steps of this process are the same for downloading files to Microsoft Excel.

1. Execute the SAP Query report that contains the data you want to include in your report.

2. On the selection screen, select the Display As Table option and then execute the report.

3. Select the List, Download to File menu option.

4. Use the possible entries help button (down arrow) to change the location and filename of your new file.

5. Click the Transfer button.

6. Open your file in Microsoft Excel, and use the menu path File, Save As to save it as a Microsoft Excel worksheet. Close Excel.

7. Launch Microsoft Access and create a new database.

8. Use the menu path File, Get External Data, Import, and select your Microsoft Excel file to import the file into Microsoft Access using the Import Spreadsheet Wizard.

Duet

Formerly known by its code name *Mendocino*, Duet is a suite of products jointly developed by Microsoft and SAP. The product suite consists of server components, client components, tools, and applications that present SAP processes and data to the Microsoft Office 2003 suite. Version 1.0 of Duet brings many common business processes into the familiar Microsoft Outlook interface. These business processes include Time Management, Leave Management, Team Management, and Budget Monitoring.

At the front-end client tier, Duet consists of a client component that extends the functionality of SAP into Microsoft Office 2003, specifically Microsoft Outlook. At the middle tier, Duet runs a server, a request handler, and a metadata service. Finally, running on the back end (in the SAP application layer) is an ABAP add-on and a Java add-on; Web Application Server Java 6.40 SP19 as well as SAP ERP 2004 are required at a minimum. We take a closer look at each tier next.

Client Tier

A Duet client requires Windows 2000 or XP Professional. Windows Tablet Edition is supported as well. The following components are prerequisites: Microsoft .NET Framework 2.0 and the Microsoft Visual Studio 2005 Tools for Office Runtime. Finally, Microsoft Office Professional or Enterprise Edition 2003 is required. The core client functionality extends the reach of the Outlook 2003 user interface (UI) into

SAP by adding an SAP-specific smart panel. Outlook 2003 synchronization with SAP is also included. Finally, business analytic functionality is added to Microsoft Excel 2003, while the viewing and creation of smart business documents is included via Microsoft Word 2003.

Middle Tier

At the middle tier, a server is required that hosts the Duet Server services. The Metadata service defines and controls data flow between Duet, SAP, and Outlook. The Metadata service requires a Microsoft SQL Server 2000 or 2003 instance and a set of web services hosted by IIS. IIS must be installed on the same host as the Metadata Server. Microsoft SQL Server, on the other hand, can be installed on the same host or a separate dedicated server. In the event that you do not have Microsoft SQL Server 2000 or 2003, you can use Microsoft SQL Server 2005 Express Edition.

The Request Handler server component is provided by Microsoft and controls the flow of requests from SAP to Microsoft Outlook 2003 via Microsoft Exchange Server. The opposite flow of data, from Outlook back to SAP, utilizes a web service hosted on IIS. The request handler itself also must be hosted by Microsoft Internet Information Services (IIS). This requires the SAP component "Item Handler" to be configured to communicate with the Request Handler web service. SAP sends updates to the Outlook client using SOAP-based calls. When SAP sends a request, the request handler forwards the request to a trusted Exchange Server, where the information is stored before ultimately being delivered to the Outlook client. The request handler is the only point of entry into Duet for an SAP system request. The Request Handler service must validate the SAP system and user before accepting the connection and forwarding to Exchange.

Backend Tier

The Duet server itself is provided by SAP as a Java add-on and an ABAP add-on. As noted earlier, the Duet Java add-on must be installed on an SAP Web Application Server Java instance, version 6.40 SP19 or later. This component facilitates the use of SAP business packages through Service-Oriented Architecture (SOA). Web services allow the component to communicate with SAP applications and their data.

The Duet ABAP add-on is also provided by SAP and enables business entities within SAP ERP 2004 to be available for use with Microsoft Office 2003 clients. This add-on is installed in the SAP system ABAP stack via the traditional SAP transaction SAINT (SAP Add-On Installation Tool).

Configuration and Scalability

Although the Duet server and services can all be loaded on the same server, even on the same server as the SAP Web Application Server Java instance, Duet is scalable and can be distributed across several servers for load distribution and high availability. Exchange Server and SQL Server can be—and in most cases should be—loaded on separate servers, whereas IIS has to be loaded on the Duet server host computer. Although you can load Duet Server on the same host as SAP Web Application Server Java, special care must be taken to avoid conflicts in the SAP instance. The Request Handler service can be load-balanced on IIS in a typical web service load-balancing cluster. Although the metadata database can be loaded on the same server or any SQL Server instance, it is a single database and cannot be distributed for load. However, it can be clustered for high availability using native SQL Server 2000 or 2005 Enterprise cluster capability and Microsoft Cluster Server.

Microsoft Active Directory Integration

SAP provides additional integration points into the Microsoft infrastructure right out of the box. Although this functionality is integrated at more of a technical and administrative level and is not functional in nature, this "free" integration is very useful to SAP customers. Microsoft Active Directory (AD) is at the heart of every Microsoft infrastructure and provides a single security context for all users and servers. The security domain concept emulates a Lightweight Directory Access Protocol (LDAP) directory, allowing SAP servers to register as objects into the directory, which are then searchable via an LDAP client. One useful function this serves is to allow SAP GUI clients to automatically populate their SAP logon pads (covered in detail in Hour 19, "Logon, Session, and SAP GUI Basics") with available SAP servers culled from the AD directory.

Single Sign-On (SSO)

Once the first level of AD integration has been performed, Single Sign-On (SSO) can be enabled. SAP SSO allows a clients' Windows AD user account to be mapped to a respective SAP user account, thereby enabling direct entry into SAP (once logged in to a Windows workstation, for example) without having to log in to SAP again. If the user has accounts in multiple SAP clients on an SAP system, it is only necessary to click once on the client he wishes to log in to. The SSO integration is rather simple and only requires a Generic Security Service API v2 DLL (which is free of charge from SAP) to be distributed to each server and client computer participating in SSO.

This technology uses Microsoft NTLM Security Service Provider or Kerberos, and SAP's SNC or Secure Network Communications. Unfortunately this SSO technology is only available in a pure Microsoft environment; for explicit SSO installation and configuration instructions, look to one of the SAP install guides for Windows located at http://service.sap.com/instguides.

Summary

Many tools on the market are designed to assist an end user with creating SAP reports. Yet with the integration naturally afforded by SAP for Microsoft's core suite of products, much of what amounts to typical reporting can be handled natively by SAP. Hour 16 provided insight into how Microsoft Excel, Word, and Access could be used for such reporting purposes. Additional easy-to-use functionality was outlined as well; SAP's %pc functionality makes it easy to dump data from SAP into any number of other application formats, for instance. And the joint effort between SAP and Microsoft culminating in Duet has been shown as the next great step in integrating SAP and the Microsoft Office suite of applications. With its business process integration hooked into Outlook, and an enhanced reporting mechanism available through Word and Excel, Duet continues on SAP's promise to deliver enhanced value and integration with the Microsoft platform. This hour concluded with a discussion of SAP's technical integration with Microsoft's Active Directory and Single Sign-On mechanisms. The advantages and no-cost delivery of these tools leave no doubt that Microsoft-based IT shops should certainly pilot these methods if not employ them fully.

Case Study: Hour 16

Review and address the SAP-Microsoft integration-related case study questions posed next. Answers may be found in Appendix A, "Case Study Answers."

Situation

MNC Global runs SAP ERP 2005 purely on the Microsoft OS and database platform. The implementation is very new, and currently only a limited level of functionality has been enabled. Two of the modules implemented by MNC include Time Management and Budget Monitoring. The IT budget for further SAP enhancements is limited, but automation and ease of use have been communicated as the project's keys to implementation success.

Questions

1. How can MNC Global's end users generate low-cost reports using only their desktop PCs and no special software tools?

2. How can MNC Global leverage the functionality of SAP and Microsoft's joint application suite Duet, while keeping infrastructure costs down?

3. MNC Global is looking for ways to cut IT support costs. Currently MNC's IT help desk spends an inordinate amount of time changing and resetting passwords. What low-cost technology can be implemented that will immediately provide relief to the IT help desk?

After Go-Live: System Administration and Operations

What You'll Learn in This Hour:

- ▶ Discovering system monitoring
- ▶ Introduction to the SAP system logs
- ▶ Introduction to SAP CCMS
- ▶ Reviewing basic authorization concepts

Administration, maintenance, and ongoing management of your SAP system are crucial. Administration includes monitoring for availability, performing user administration and basic authorizations, and addressing other fundamental technical administrative functions.

Monitoring the System

Monitoring your SAP systems is essential for good performance and no surprises. SAP provides a number of easy-to-use monitoring tools available through the Computing Center Management System (CCMS), several of which are outlined next.

Available SAP NetWeaver Application Servers (SM51)

System monitoring designed to ensure the availability of SAP to its end users is a primary function of the system administrator. In the course of system monitoring, the system administrator watches over a list of the active SAP instances and their services, looking to ensure that these resources are indeed "up" and available (see Figure 17.1).

You can view the SAP Servers System Monitoring screen following the menu path Tools, Administration, Monitor, System Monitoring, Servers, or by using transaction code /nSM51. This screen displays all available instances in your SAP system, including the core services (hosted by specialized work processes) provided by each instance—services earmarked for online users, batch jobs, performing database updates, and so on.

FIGURE 17.1
SM51 monitoring needs to be regularly performed by an SAP system administrator.

An *instance* is typically an administrative unit used to logically describe the set of SAP system components that together provide one or more services (for example, a "Production Instance" of SAP). An instance can also refer to the services provided by a single SAP server (for example, an SAP Application Server instance).

Did you Know?

> SAP provides three different options when installing and operating an SAP NetWeaver Application Server: ABAP, Java, and ABAP + Java. Figure 17.1 shows that this instance runs the J2EE service, which indicates that it is a dual-stack environment running an ABAP + Java instance and can therefore execute ABAP as well as Java programs.

SAP System Logs (SM21 and More)

SAP maintains system logs that record important events that occur in your SAP system. Which system log and which tool to use to display the events depends on whether the SAP NetWeaver Application Server consists of the ABAP, Java, or ABAP + Java stack.

System Log for ABAP Stack

You can view the SAP System Log screen by executing transaction code /nSM21. The selection screen that appears—similar to the one shown in Figure 17.2—enables the system administrator to sift through and select certain criteria from what can ultimately be a very large and very complex log of events and occurrences.

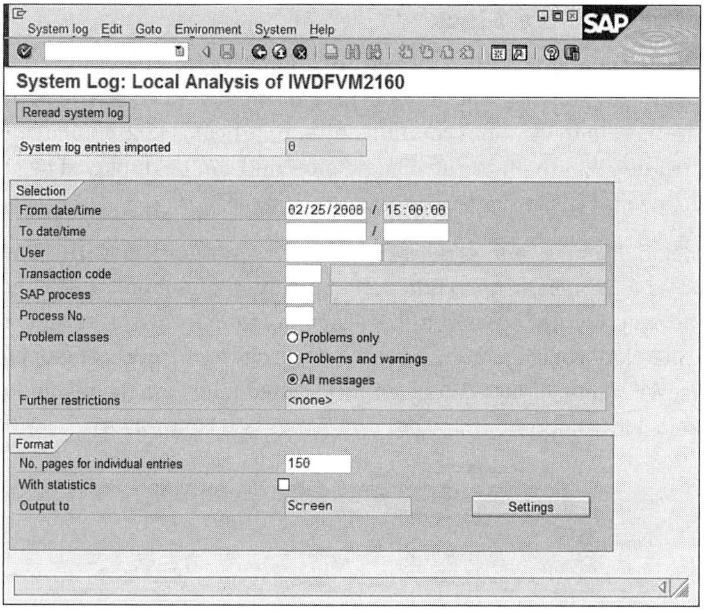

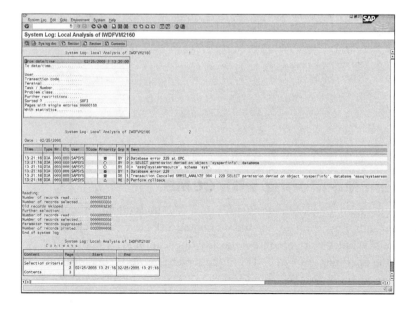

FIGURE 17.2
You can specify certain system criteria to be displayed on your system log by using the System Log: Local Analysis screen.

After identifying key search criteria such as dates, user IDs, and so on, the administrator then selects the Reread System Log button to generate the specified subset of the entire log. Refer to Figure 17.3 for just such an abbreviated log.

FIGURE 17.3
After specifying specific selection criteria, you can display a subset of the SAP system log.

System Log for Java Stack

SAP provides several different Log Viewers to display events. The Visual Administrator, for example, offers the Integrated Log Viewer. Logs written from the J2EE engine and all applications running on that particular J2EE engine are automatically registered in the Integrated Log Viewer and can be displayed by clicking through the menu Cluster, Server, Services, Log Viewer.

Another tool to display events is the SAP NetWeaver Administrator. This Web Dynpro–based tool offers, among other administration and monitoring capabilities, a central access point for logs and traces generated from local SAP systems and/or the entire SAP NetWeaver system landscape. The Logs and Traces component of the SAP NetWeaver Administrator can be easily accessed following the menu path System Management, Monitoring, Logs and Traces (see Figure 17.4).

FIGURE 17.4
The SAP NetWeaver Administrator provides various so-called pre-defined views (filters) for displaying logs and traces. In this case, SAP Logs is the chosen pre-defined view.

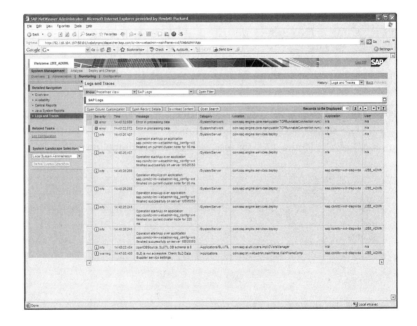

System Monitoring with CCMS

SAP's Computing Center Management System (CCMS) is a built-in monitoring tool used for controlling, configuring, and managing SAP across much of the technology stack. This includes everything from the SAP application layer to the database, the underlying operating system, and even the servers, networks, and disk subsystems underpinning all of SAP. You can access the CCMS tools by following the menu path

Tools, CCMS (and in releases before R/3 4.6C, by using transaction code /nSRZL). CCMS covers a great deal; the following represent key capabilities of CCMS, relative to system administration:

▶ Systems management (called "Control/Monitoring")

▶ User/workload distribution and balancing (through "Configuration")

▶ Database administration

▶ Print management

▶ Background processing

You also use CCMS to monitor your installation. CCMS executes the SAP OS Collector, which collects basic performance and availability data via an SAP operating system service or daemon. You can then use CCMS to sort through and display this data. Detailed information relative to the configuration and basic responsiveness of your SAP system can be displayed. Although traditionally limited to single instances, SAP CCMS has evolved over the last few years into a much broader and more capable systems-management tool—it serves as a key source of data for full-fledged systems management and other utilities, too, such as SAP NetWeaver Administrator, SAP Solution Manager, HP OpenView, BMC Patrol, and more. In this capacity, CCMS represents an ideal starting point to help you identify problems early on and characterize potential or existing performance bottlenecks.

Alert Monitor (RZ20)

One of the CCMS tools is SAP's Alert Monitor. It provides an entry point to the CCMS system repository, the database storing data about your SAP system. A capable and customizable tool, SAP's Alert Monitor features the following:

▶ Comprehensive, detailed status of any number of SAP systems, host interfaces, underlying database and OS layers, and more.

▶ Easy-to-read color-coded status indicators (green, yellow, and red) for all your SAP components, interfaces, and so on.

▶ Proactive alerts, based on whether the threshold of a particular status indicator has been exceeded.

▶ Analysis and auto-reaction methods can be assigned to alerts such as reports, SAP transactions, function modules, and more.

▶ Monitor sets, monitors, thresholds, and more can be customized to your needs.

Spend time getting comfortable with the Alert Monitor—it is powerful, capable, and free (in the sense that it's paid for with the purchase of the SAP license). To use this tool, follow the menu path Tools, CCMS, Control/Monitoring, CCMS Monitor Sets, or execute transaction code /nRZ20. An example of an Alert Monitor screen is displayed in Figure 17.5.

FIGURE 17.5
The Alert Monitor can display and monitor the status of multiple SAP functions and parameters.

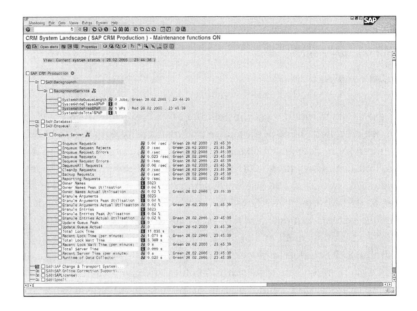

It may make sense to declare one CCMS environment as the central monitoring system (CEN) for all SAP system landscapes in your firm. The monitoring architecture of the CEN allows you to gather and, with the Alert Monitor, to display all available alerts of SAP ABAP, Java, dual-stack, standalone components, and non-SAP components in one CCMS environment.

Response Time and Workload Performance (ST03)

Another CCMS tool is the so-called Workload Monitor. Monitoring your unique user-driven and batch job workload is one of the most important components of performance management. Execute the Workload Monitor by running /nST03 or /nST03N. This enables you to display the workload of your ABAP stack in total, or broken down by dialog, batch, update, or other task types. From each type, click the Transaction Profile button and then sort the results by response time. Here, you can analyze your top transactions—the programs that consume the most database time (DB Request Time), CPU time, and other core components of response time. You can also look at aggregate totals over various periods of time, from 15 minutes to a month's worth of data at a time. It's also common to view and track the total number of dialog steps processed each day, broken down hour-by-hour so as to get a feel for how each hour in a day holds up when it comes to workload.

Finally, ST03G gives you the capability to view and analyze the load associated with external systems such as J2EE engines, Internet Transaction Servers, and more, as well as the capability to analyze the performance of systems underpinning business processes that span multiple systems. It's a powerful addition to ST03N. For SAP IT organizations responsible for multiple systems, ST03G has no equal.

Other Important CCMS Tools

Many other monitoring tools prove useful in the day-to-day administration of an SAP system. At the high end is SAP's Solution Manager, a tool that among other things allows for cross-business-process monitoring (systems management encompassing multiple SAP and other systems tied together to execute complex business processes). However, SAP CCMS provides much in the way of administrative support as well. Run the following transaction codes to get a sense of the built-in management capabilities SAP offers:

▶ ST06, the Operating System Monitor, is ideal for analyzing the performance of the entire SAP technology stack.

▶ SMLG is used to monitor how well SAP's logon load balancing is performing; use F5 to drill down into group-specific performance data.

▶ AL08 is useful in reviewing the end users logged in to particular SAP application servers (and the transactions they are executing).

▶ ST07 is useful in reviewing end users logged in to the entire system, sorted by functional areas (such as SAP ERP FI, MM, PM, PS, SD, and so on).

▶ SM66 is ideal for looking at systemwide performance relative to processes executing on every application and batch server within an SAP system.

▶ ST22 is used to review ABAP dumps and therefore identify program errors (to aid in escalating ABAP programming issues to the responsible programming team).

SAP Authorization Concepts

Although a detailed treatise on SAP security is beyond the scope of this book, it would be unfair to not include a brief discussion on SAP authorizations and the role they play in securing your data. The data stored in SAP needs to be secured not only from outside intrusion, but also from within your end-user organizations as well. Assume that your company has implemented SAP ERP Materials Management and Human Resources; you would not want individuals from your Materials Management department accessing confidential HR data, nor would you like to see HR employees mucking around in your warehouses. To avoid this, SAP uses the concept of assigning "authorizations" to users based on the job or role the users hold in their organization.

User Authorizations for ABAP-Based Application Servers

SAP user authorizations are stored in the master record of each user. Users, in theory, might be assigned one or many authorizations, depending on their role in an organization.

The *master record* is a data record containing the principal employment and authorization data on a user that usually remains unchanged, including the user's system authorizations, standard printer settings, and transaction settings.

The following are a number of the fields a user master record generally contains:

User name	Personal printer configuration
Assigned client	Time zone
User password	Activity group
Company address	Authorizations
User type	Expiration date
Start menu	Default parameter
Logon language	

Authorization Profiles

To simplify the administration of security authorizations, authorization profiles are established. Such profiles are assigned to specific SAP user IDs (remember from previous hours that your user ID is your user name in the user master record). Your user ID refers exclusively to profiles when designating access privileges in SAP. In turn, these profiles grant (or by their exclusion, deny) a certain level of system access on behalf of the user. Examples of ERP Authorization Profiles are listed in Table 17.1.

TABLE 17.1   SAP ERP Authorization Profiles

Authorization	Abbreviated Authorization Description Profile Name
SAP_ALL	All SAP system authorizations
S_ABAP_ALL	All authorizations for ABAP/4
S_ADMI_ALL	All administration authorizations
S_A.ADMIN	Operator
S_A.CUSTOMIZ	Customizing (for all system setting activities)
S_A.TMSADM	Authorization for system user TMSADM
S_A.TMSCFG	Authorization to maintain CTS configuration
S_A.SYSTEM	System administrator (superuser)
S_ADDR_ALL	All authorizations for the central address management
S_ADMI_SAP	Administration authorization except spool administration
S_ADMI_SPO_A	All spool administrations
S_ADMI_SPO_D	All spool device administration
S_ADMI_SPO_E	All extended spool administration
S_ADMI_SPO_J	All spool job administration for all clients
S_ADMI_SPO_T	All spool device type administration

You should assign your SAP user profiles specific to the job functions performed by individuals in your organization. For example, Human Resources Administrative Clerks require access to the basic data-entry screens to enter and maintain new employees' personal data; however, they might not need access to your company's organizational chart and reporting structure. Use transactions /nSU56 and /nSU53, respectively, to review authorizations you currently have and to check authorizations you are missing.

> Your SAP system contains some preinstalled standard authorization profiles. Although these might seem like a fast solution for security configuration, it is not a good idea to try to mold your organization into these limited standards. Also, instead of manually creating, changing, and assigning authorization profiles, we recommend you use the SAP Profile Generator. This tool lets you generate and assign profiles automatically based on roles. Creating specific roles reflecting your organization's structure will serve you much better in the long run. Be prepared, though—such work will consume a significant amount of time.

Watch Out!

SAP Profile Generator (PFCG)

The Profile Generator (PG) was introduced long ago in SAP R/3 3.1G to assist in the implementation of your company's application-layer security model. Based on the concepts of authorization objects, authorizations, and authorization profiles, the Profile Generator is the recommended tool to use. Using the Profile Generator, the authorization profiles you develop are not typically (but might be) assigned to individual users (an activity that all too often would consume the bulk of an administrator's time); instead, users are assigned to one or more roles (called *activity groups* in the earliest releases of PG), and these roles are then assigned authorizations. With the roles, you assign to your users the user menu that is displayed after they log on to the SAP system. Roles therefore reflect the authorizations needed by users to access and run their reports, transactions, and web-based applications. Execute PG by running transaction PFCG.

Combined, all your various roles set up in SAP should map back to the various departments and teams spread across your user base. Authorizations can naturally become very detailed and complex; certain users might require additional capabilities based on their specific job within a department, for instance. As you can imagine, manually setting up these roles is very time-consuming, and managing and updating them as your business needs evolve is equally time-consuming. It was precisely for this reason that SAP developed the Profile Generator. For more detailed information, refer to SAP's online help (http://help.sap.com) or one of the many excellent texts on security administration and support.

User Authorizations for Java-Based Application Servers

Just like ABAP-based Application Servers, user access to applications and resources predicated on the Java-based Application Server needs to be controlled. The Java Application Server supports two types of authorizations: roles and access control lists (ACLs). Whereas roles define and assign activities to users, ACLs control the use of objects on the Java-based Application Server. Users and authorizations are managed with the User Management Engine (UME). It provides centralized user management for all Java applications and lets you access user management data from various data sources, such as LDAP directories, user management of ABAP-based Application Servers, and more.

Authorizations are assigned to users through User Management Engine (UME) roles. UME roles reflect a user's function within the company. To create, change, and assign UME roles, use either the SAP NetWeaver Administrator, the Portal, or the standalone console. When using the SAP NetWeaver Administrator, enter **http://<AS_hostname>:<AS_HTTP_port>/nwa** in your web browser and follow the menu path System Management, Administration, Identity Management. To receive a list of all available roles, select Roles in the search area, choose Go, and review the search results, as shown in Figure 17.6.

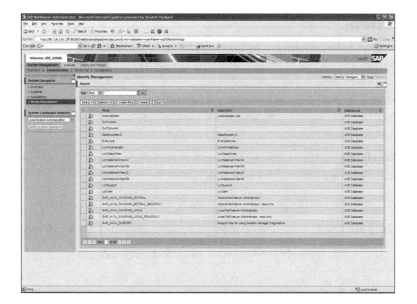

FIGURE 17.6
The SAP NetWeaver Administrator serves as the user interface for the User Management Engine (UME).

Summary

SAP system administration is central to maintaining a highly available and well-performing system. As such, system administration in the broadest sense cannot exist in a vacuum—it must be tied to tools and approaches that facilitate proactive maintenance and management by exception. SAP's very own CCMS represents an ideal starting point for such system administration. This type of work is often performed by system administrators designated within your IT organization to manage and monitor SAP. These individuals are critical in holding and managing the responsibility that comes with maximizing system availability day in and day out.

This hour was designed to provide an overview of some of the system administration tools and techniques used to manage your SAP system from a technical perspective. As a regular SAP end user or programmer/developer, such material provides grounding in what it takes to administer SAP; however, it is unlikely that anyone but an administrator will regularly use most of the material found in this hour.

Case Study: Hour 17

Consider this SAP systems administration and operations case study, and questions that follow, the answers to which may be found in Appendix A, "Case Study Answers."

Situation

MNC Global's SAP environment has been growing and consists now of about 50 different SAP instances. Part of your team's responsibilities is to monitor proactively the entire SAP environment, particularly the core SAP ERP ECC 6.0 dual-stack environment along with MNC's latest addition, an Enterprise Portal (Java only) system landscape.

Questions

1. What does the acronym CCMS stand for?

2. Which CCMS tool helps you to proactively monitor your SAP instance?

3. Is the Alert Monitor limited to monitoring only SAP ABAP stack instances?

4. How can you centrally monitor your entire SAP environment?

5. Where can you find other CCMS tools related to monitoring?

After Go-Live: SAP Upgrades and Enhancements

What You'll Learn in This Hour:

- ▶ Upgrade, enhancement, and migration terminology
- ▶ What constitutes an SAP OS/DB migration
- ▶ Differences between technical and functional upgrades
- ▶ Upgrade and migration project requirements

The reality of running a well-oiled SAP system is remembering that change is always in the air. Keeping up with the latest technology, enhancing business process functionality, and staying ahead of SAP's breakneck release schedule is no easy task. Once an SAP customer has finally gone "live," it is never too early to begin thinking about the future. Enhancements, upgrades, and even migrations are admittedly a key part of this future.

Enhancement, Upgrade, and Migration Terminology

A discussion of terminology is in order before we dive into this hour. There are many similar and therefore confusing terms when it comes to making changes to a live SAP environment, especially when it comes to upgrading or migrating SAP. We have been involved in many situations where a customer or someone in sales asks us to develop a scope of work surrounding an SAP project we have been told comprises an upgrade or migration. Usually we find the project to be only partially accurate; once we find representation on the technical team we eventually find out what is really needed. Many times the first 15 minutes of such a meeting focuses on level-setting everyone in the room on terminology.

The terms *migration* and *upgrade* are general, vague, and confusing. So is the term *enhancement*. For these reasons, standard SAP terminology is outlined next.

Enhancement Terminology

SAP *enhancements* are modifications or updates to existing SAP systems; enhancements modify or extend current functionality. Enhancements can be SAP driven (such as those done through SAP support packages) or customer driven, meaning they are developed in-house and transported through the SAP landscape. Enhancements in many cases can be a combination of these two methods, too. For instance, to enhance a current SAP financial business process, you may need to update the system to a required support package level and then make subsequent custom modifications to adapt the new functionality to an SAP system's specific business process.

Enhancements can also be delivered through specific SAP enhancement packages. Enhancement packages differ from support packages in that they add functionality on top of the SAP application stack rather than providing it through modifying existing functionality. Surprisingly, SAP makes it possible to install enhancement packages without impacting the system—no downtime is required to actually implement them. However, to actually make the enhancements or changes to the system, they must be activated in the SAP Implementation Guide or IMG (see Hour 13, "Development Tools and Methodologies," for a discussion of the IMG). In this way, through enhancement packages, SAP customers have the ability to modularly upgrade functionality. This makes it possible to extend the lifecycle of your SAP systems by pushing off full-blown functional upgrades. However, although enhancement packages can extend the product lifecycle for a season, there will come a time when an upgrade indeed is necessary, which leads us to our next discussion.

Upgrade Terminology

The term *upgrade* is confusing, because an upgrade can speak to many things—very different things, as it turns out. The key is to ask what is actually being upgraded. Is it a server hardware upgrade, an OS upgrade, an Oracle or SQL Server database upgrade, an SAP kernel upgrade, an SAP support pack upgrade, or a full-blown SAP functional release or version upgrade? When using the term *upgrade*, be as specific and detailed as possible to avoid confusion. When upgrading non-SAP components in the SAP landscape, it is pretty easy to say, "We are upgrading our SAP servers" or "We are upgrading the database to Oracle 10*g*." However, when you're upgrading SAP R/3 4.6C to SAP ERP 6.0, the lines can get a bit blurry, as oftentimes an upgrade so high in the technology stack assumes lower-level technology stack upgrades.

Generally speaking, talk of SAP upgrades implies an upgrade to the functionality of the SAP system—an SAP functional upgrade. These are major undertakings, nearly akin to a new implementation in the worst cases. We also talk of SAP technical upgrades, though, which are upgrades to the Basis layer or WebAS underpinning the SAP application. Technical upgrades include an update to the kernel, and often drive other updates to the technology stack (for support reasons, primarily; not every SAP Basis or WebAS release is supported by every operating system version or hardware platform, for example). Suffice it to say here, then, that it is paramount to understand the scope and magnitude of an SAP upgrade prior to tossing the term about.

Migration Terminology

Because the term *migration* is often thrown about interchangeably with the term *upgrade*, it is necessary to differentiate between the two. The term *migration* is confusing, to be sure. We have often heard customers make comments such as, "We are migrating our SAP R/3 4.6C environment to SAP ERP 6.0." This statement is generally incorrect. However, in some cases, it actually could be partially correct! How confusing is that? What's more, SAP has released a tool called TDMS (or Test Data Migration Server), which has nothing to do with traditional migrations but rather is more aligned with copy functionality (specifically, TDMS allows SAP customers to essentially copy a portion of an SAP database and build a new system around the smaller, condensed database, thus enabling rapid prototyping for new projects). Again, it is for all these reasons that we find it necessary to differentiate between different types of migrations.

Traditionally in the SAP world, *migration* has referred to what is more correctly labeled an *OS/DB migration* (operating system/database migration). An OS/DB migration is when a customer decides to move an SAP instance, usually a whole landscape, to a new operating system or database platform. An OS/DB migration is a fairly complex endeavor, requiring the services of one or more SAP certified OS/DB migration consultants. To invoke this term properly, we should use the complete phrase SAP OS/DB migration.

With products such as SAP TDMS and the like, the term *data migration* takes on a new meeting. Data migration might comprise moving data from a non-SAP system such as PeopleSoft into an SAP system, for instance. Products such as TDMS also move data between SAP systems in the form of client copies, a project correctly labeled as an SAP data migration. But the "real" migration—the term as it is generally known in the technical circles of SAP implementation and administration—is an OS/DB migration, which is discussed in more detail next to better set the stage for functional enhancements and upgrade discussions.

SAP OS/DB Migrations

An SAP OS/DB migration is a project requiring several very key skill sets to perform properly and ensure a smooth Go-Live. This type of migration may be between one of the various flavors of UNIX and Windows, or vice versa. It also could mean moving to a different database platform, such as from Oracle to DB2. In any case, either the operating systems are not binary compatible (meaning the database data files cannot be mounted and read on the new platform), or the database change requires reloading the SAP data into the new database.

Customers execute OS/DB migrations for a few different reasons. One of the primary reasons, of course, is cost. The cost of running SAP on an older version of one of the big UNIX platforms can be tremendous. When these big UNIX boxes are out of support, a customer is required to pay handsome support costs. Another big cost factor tends to be outsourcing. For some customers, it can make sense to outsource their SAP environment to one of the many hosting providers. However, other shops are better suited to support SAP in-house. An OS/DB migration is the method used to move to that cheaper platform or new hosting provider. Another name for an OS/DB migration is *heterogeneous system copy*, as opposed to its cousin the homogenous system copy, where the OS or DB platform do not change.

To execute an OS/DB migration, SAP requires the customer to solicit an SAP-certified OS/DB migration consultant. For an SAP consultant to obtain this certification, he or she must first acquire an SAP Basis certification, such as SAP Technology Consultant 2002. SAP then requires the consultant to take their course TADM70, which is a 3-day class usually held in Walldorf, Germany at SAP's headquarters. The best type of consultant for this work tends to be someone who understands the source and target platforms from a system administration perspective, and is skilled at installing SAP. In many cases, it is wise to have two consultants—one who intimately knows the OS and the other who knows the DB platform. Most importantly, the consultant should know the target platform. Additionally, the customer's Basis staff should be involved to take on the post-installation tasks, similar to what would be required after a homogenous system copy.

SAP also requires a licensing change to support the new OS/DB combination. It sells an OS/DB migration check Go-Live service. With this service, the OS/DB migration consultant must register his or her SAP ID to validate certification and a project plan describing the various phases of the migration, showing multiple test iterations. A typical OS/DB migration project will consist of five heterogeneous system copies: one of DEV, one or more for QA, and three for production. The production migration should consist of a test run, a dress rehearsal, and a final Go-Live. This ensures a smooth Go-Live by allowing the technical team to work out any issues in the migration process.

A typical SAP OS/DB migration project of a three-system landscape of SAP R/3 or SAP ERP runs roughly 3 months in length to get through all the planning, testing, and downtime windows required. It is not uncommon for a project of this type to run to 6 months in length. The technical team required for a project of this nature should include system administrators for both the source and target platforms, SAN administrators, database administrators, SAP Basis, bolt-on administrators, SAP external interface administrators, and functional testers.

Most importantly, though, C-level executive management sponsorship, business and IT management buy-in, and overall technology team leadership support are required to rally the troops and drive a project like this. Many times corporate politics can play a big roll in a platform change. System administrators and DBAs can feel betrayed when their beloved platform is thrown out for a faster, albeit cheaper alternative.

SAP Upgrades

As previously stated, *upgrade* refers to a major version change of SAP, such as 4.6C to SAP ERP 6.0 . More specifically, this is referred to as a *technical upgrade*, meaning the project is more about the version change and not about adding functionality.

A *functional upgrade*, on the other hand, does not necessarily mean a major version change, but refers to adding functionality to an SAP system. Adding functionality many times requires individual components of the SAP system to be upgraded. For instance, an SAP add-on or support packages may need to be added to the system using either the SAP transaction SPAM or SAINT. Some individuals may refer to this upgrade as just a project or functional rollout. Although this may hold true to from the end users' point of view, many times this functionality change requires a back-end component upgrade of one type or another.

There are many reasons why an existing SAP customer would want to upgrade an SAP R/3 4.6C system to SAP ERP 6.0, for example. The best one is simply that SAP is ending support for R/3 4.6C, so to stay in support, you must upgrade the version to SAP ERP 6.0. (Conversely, you might determine that the incremental cost is acceptable and stay put another several years.) This type of upgrade is called a *technical upgrade*, because no new functionality is being added. However, if you are upgrading your version of SAP to take advantage of new functionality, maybe when you upgrade you will add a new module such as FSCM 6.0 (Financial Supply Chain). This changes the dynamics of the upgrade, the scope, and the team requirements.

Before where you were just making technical changes, you needed only limited functional and ABAP support for the upgrade. Now you require multiple new team members. This is called a *functional upgrade*. Keep in mind that a functional upgrade does not necessarily mean you need to go to a new version of SAP. These types of upgrade projects can be complex and confusing, with vastly different team requirements depending on what component is being touched.

SAP Enhancements

Once your organization has "gone live" with SAP, you might be inclined to think all the real work in terms of developing and maintaining functionality has been done and little follow-on work remains. To some extent this is true for the IT team; the stress of implementation and late-into-the-night testing will be replaced with steady state maintenance, occasional technology stack patches, and so on. But for the development team and business analysts tasked with representing the business's needs to the SAP support team, much work remains to be done well after Go-Live. After all, the business will continue to evolve, and new functional needs will come to light in the wake of these changes. Even more common, bug fixes and other updates to existing business processes will need to be tested and introduced as well. This is where enhancement planning will pay great dividends for the organization. The entire process is very planning intensive, which brings us to the next section—high-level planning for upgrades, enhancements, and migrations.

High-Level Project Planning

Planning for upgrades, migrations, and enhancements is very important simply due to the magnitude of change and therefore risk. Better said, changes of such great consequence to mission-critical SAP systems deserve nothing less than careful planning. In return, the IT team will avoid unplanned outages and unsatisfied unproductive users. The next several sections outline key planning considerations for all three types of system changes.

Project Planning for Enhancements

Enhancements are often implemented in quarterly "waves" or phases comprising multiple SAP user groups and therefore multiple functional areas and business processes. Complicating matters further, each wave typically takes one to two quarters to plan for and test. And beyond the functional updates, there might be technology changes required to support the new functionality. In fact, it is not uncommon for a quarterly implementation of enhancements to include one or even all of the following:

► Hardware refresh

► DB patches or upgrades

► Operating system and security patches

► SAP kernel updates

► SAP support package stacks (ABAP and Java)

► SAP modification transports

► Customer transports

As you can imagine, this scope of changes can require significant team coordination and project management expertise. In some cases, the better part of an IT department can be absorbed while implementing a wave of SAP enhancements, especially when you consider that these changes have to be moved through multiple environments as part of the SAP landscape (development, quality assurance, production, and so on).

Once these changes are implemented, one or more testing cycles have to be performed to ensure that all the changes do not break any existing processes, and to ensure that the changes are ready for the move to production. This is usually performed by a combination of SAP experts and business users who (either manually or via automated scripts) test at minimum the core pieces of changed SAP functionality to ensure they still work properly. As errors are encountered in testing, fixes have to be developed that are then applied after the enhancements to subsequent environments. For example, it may be discovered in testing that an SAP support package caused a particular SAP transaction to abort, also called a *short dump* (because an SAP short dump is created in the process of aborting). During the troubleshooting process, the tester may find a relevant SAP OSS note that has been released by SAP that purportedly resolves the problem. This note is then downloaded into the development environment and a corresponding transport is created. In the next phase of testing, it is confirmed that this fix indeed resolves the problem with the SAP transaction. This transport is then added to the post-enhancement transport list scheduled for production and then moved into production.

Project Planning for SAP Upgrades

Technical upgrades are more common than functional upgrades, and certainly more common than OS/DB migrations. Nonetheless, they still only occur every 3 to

5 years or so. In a technical upgrade, the actual release of SAP is changed, though the functionality related to the release remains the same. An SAP technical upgrade is similar in nature and duration to a migration (outlined later this hour); although the same types of resources from the infrastructure support folks up through the SAP Basis layers are required, it is also necessary to add ABAP programmers, SAP functional analysts, and business end users (for heavy business process testing) to our list of project resources. A functional upgrade takes this complexity one step further and combines functional changes with technical platform changes.

Most upgrade projects require new hardware and therefore a new underlying infrastructure on which to implement. In fact, it's becoming more common to find combination OS/DB migration and SAP technical upgrade projects where the migration and upgrade are performed sequentially over the same (very long!) weekend. In the recent past, SAP AG would not support a migration and upgrade performed as one project with a Go-Live in a single weekend. However, in many environments today this is a requirement. Pressure on SAP has found its way into making such a complex project supportable.

During the planning stages of an SAP upgrade, it is wise to evaluate whether the existing database should be converted to Unicode. Unicode is a prerequisite to MDMP (or multidisplay multiprocessing code page). Single code page customers do not have to convert to Unicode, although it is the stated direction of future SAP products. SAP recommends all customers convert to Unicode.

Once the new SAP infrastructure is implemented, a system copy must occur from one of the source SAP systems. Typically a copy of production is used for the first test upgrade; however, some customers choose to start with an upgrade of development. Once the first development system is upgraded, this begins a dual support path for changes throughout the project. Any changes put into development and promoted through the system to production on the source environment must also be pushed and promoted through the upgraded environment. This keeps the environments functionally synchronized.

The Basis team will use two SAP tools—prepare and Upgrade Assistant—to perform the technical upgrade. The first, prepare, does a thorough evaluation of the SAP system and recommends changes, fixes, and service packs that must be applied to the system before the upgrade can begin. Once the changes are made and prepare completes successfully, the upgrade can begin. The Upgrade Assistant is a graphical display of the upgrade process; it is menu driven, allowing the Basis team to choose one of several options as to how to proceed with the upgrade. Options such as Downtime Minimized and Resource Minimized help determine how long the upgrade will take and at what point in the upgrade the system must be shut down.

Downtime Minimized allows the team to do much of the upgrade work while the system is still in production, thus reducing the overall system outage. Resource Minimized forces the system to go offline at an earlier phase. However, it reduces the overall time it takes to run through the upgrade process. The only time it is feasible to run the Downtime Minimized option is when an in-place upgrade is being performed and the hardware that would otherwise cause a system outage is being retained.

One critical Prepare phase allows the Basis team to bind support packages and add-ins to the upgrade process. In many cases, a certain support package level is required to be bound to the upgrade. In most cases, it makes sense to put in all the latest support packages during the upgrade, rather than waiting until the upgrade completes to apply them. The reason a certain support package level may be required is due to the level of the support packs on the source system. If the source system is at a support package level that introduced functionality that was not included in the base target system, but was included for the target version as a support package, then the upgrade must apply the same level of functionality through support packages. Otherwise, data will be lost.

After the first development upgrade, the system needs to be handed over to the functional and ABAP teams for remediation and testing. SAP tracks problems to upgraded objects with transactions /nSPAU and /nSPDD. SPAU tracks repository objects, whereas SPDD tracks dictionary objects. SPAU and SPDD allow the developer to look at objects affected by the upgrade and gives options on how to proceed with remediation. Once the objects are repaired, the changes are saved to a transport and can be used to quickly repair the problems as they appear in the upgrades to the quality and production systems. Optionally, the Reset to Original option with SPAU or SPDD allows a developer to revert to the standard SAP code applied by the last upgrade or support pack. Version control is handled in SPAU and SPDD so the developer can call up previous versions of the object in question.

ABAP code remediation efforts depend on the amount of customization done to an SAP system. SAP estimates (and we concur) that most customers spend about 30% of the upgrade project testing and fixing their custom code. Many IT consulting companies have developed tools that analyze an SAP system before an upgrade to accurately estimate the effort required for code remediation. Such an investment is an excellent idea for all but the most vanilla of installations.

Planning for an OS/DB Migration

Very infrequently, an IT organization might determine that the platform underpinning SAP requires a fundamental computing platform change, particularly if the potential for greater business application innovation or reduced cost is desired. Other reasons for such *replatforming* abound as well. Perhaps the database upon which SAP runs is being retired (as was the case with Informix after the company was purchased by IBM). Maybe the operating system itself is being retired, too (DEC Unix/Tru64), or the hardware platform is at its end of life (EOL). In these cases, it makes a lot of sense to step back and reassess the SAP technical landscape while simultaneously looking ahead at where the business might be in the next 3 to 5 years. For instance, perhaps a higher level of performance or availability beyond the current platform's capabilities will be in order soon, given the growth expected in user counts, M&A activity, or other business acquisitions. In such cases, IT will be tasked with performing an OS/DB migration.

The SAP OS/DB migration plan lends itself to being more technical and infrastructure-heavy when it comes to resource planning. The underlying platform or foundation of the SAP environment will be changing, after all. People familiar with the new servers, operating system, network and security requirements, and storage systems will be a "must" for project success. Furthermore, one or more database administrators (DBAs), SAP Basis specialists in both the current and the new OS/DB combinations, and one or more SAP-certified OS/DB migration consultants will be required (the latter of which is a requirement by SAP AG itself). Functional testing, although certainly required, will be minimal on this type of project compared to projects where the functionality is actually changing; an OS/DB project does not change the functionality or release/version of SAP ERP (or CRM, PLM, and so on) itself. Rather, what actually must be validated from a functional perspective is the myriad of technical connections, interfaces, scripts, and other entrances into and exits out of the SAP application.

The duration of an OS/DB migration varies. For planning purposes, give yourself a minimum of 3 or 4 months. For a standard three-system landscape, this will provide you with adequate testing, validation, and planned outages time. It is recommended to divide the 3 to 4 months into several phases, the most important of which are listed here:

- ▶ Project planning, including proof-of-concept testing if the perceived risk of a new platform potentially outweighs its rewards

- ▶ Target infrastructure build (building out the "to be" system)

- ▶ Source system export preparation

- ▶ Initial test migration, followed by a test cycle

- ▶ Migration of the development system, followed by testing

▶ Migration of the QA system, following by testing

▶ Validation of all bolt-on systems (such as tax software, fax utilities, external job schedulers, and so on)

▶ A "dress rehearsal" for the production migration process

▶ The actual migration of the production system

Unsure of what "exporting" comprises? In SAP's terminology, it is simply the process of unloading a database. The unloaded database itself (called an export) is an ASCII dump of an entire SAP database that may in turn be reloaded into another system. By converting the database into ASCII, the SAP export process gets around the specific OS file system's uniqueness and current database's formatting, thus enabling it to be reconverted into another database format sitting atop a different OS file system. Exporting (followed by importing) is what makes it possible to convert an SAP application's database from Tru64 UNIX running the Informix database to Windows 2008 running Oracle 11g, for example.

Did you Know?

The planning phase includes covering the build-out of the new SAP landscape, the export of the source SAP system, interfaces and scripts that must transition to the new landscape, and the import of SAP and overall installation of the target platform. The infrastructure build includes addressing data center readiness (such as rack infrastructure, power, and cooling requirements), servers, OS, network, storage, backup, high availability, and disaster recovery plans. Source system export preparation simply means installing the migration tools, performing an SAP Basis (technical) health check, and procuring file system space on the storage system to ensure enough space is available for the exported databases.

Next, the first or initial test migration is just that: a test migration. This helps validate the overall migration process, obtain a general idea of what issues will be faced during the remainder of the migrations, and gauge system throughput for estimating the overall downtime for future migrations. This latter point is critical because several methods are available to speed up the export and import process, but these take time and extra preparation to pull off. For the most accurate timing, it is recommended that you migrate a copy of the production system's database, because this tends to be one of the largest and certainly the most important database to be migrated. After the test migration has been completed, and the technical foundation and functional capabilities of the system have been validated by all interested parties, the copy of the production database may be deleted or used for additional testing and process refinement.

The next step, migrating development, is not much different from the first test migration, except that the exported and newly imported data will be retained as the new development system.

Once the development system has been migrated, the SAP support team will be required to maintain what is termed "dual support paths" to production. One path will start with the old or original development system, and work its way through the old landscape to the current premigrated production system. However, the new development system will need the same set of development updates, enhancements, and so on applied to it. In this way, on the day it becomes the sole development environment (after the old production system has given way to the newly migrated one), it will be in sync with the original development, QA, and production environments in terms of functionality, patches, and so on.

Interestingly, the QA system migration can be handled in one of two ways—either copied from production after the migration project is over or migrated as one of several nonproduction databases that require such migration. The quality system is often migrated next, as we have suggested. This allows you to have another migration run, which is good practice for tweaking and speeding up the migration process in preparation for the production migration. Clearly, by the time you get to migrating production, it is paramount to have a well-documented, detailed checklist reflecting a step-by-step flawless migration process. Once production is migrated and cut over at Go-Live, the source development and quality systems may be retired or retained as "reference systems."

During this general stage in the project, it is also necessary to begin addressing any OS-specific scripts and interface mechanisms that will need to be recoded for the new platform. For instance, in a UNIX environment, an SAP environment often includes a set of shell scripts that perform certain actions. If you are migrating to Windows, you will have to retool these UNIX scripts to run in a "command" or CMD shell. Although tools such as cgywin give you the ability to execute shell scripts and UNIX commands in a Windows environment, it is good practice to rewrite the scripts in a language the native OS can interpret, thereby limiting third-party tools on the new or target SAP systems. In the same way, any critical bolt-on applications tied to SAP must be tested and verified prior to migrating SAP. It is very common to find it necessary to update or replace a particular bolt-on utility or application simply due to its inability to interface with the target OS/DB combination.

> Examples of bolt-on systems include tax software, faxing software, email/workflow utilities, banking and other financial linkages, SAP Solution Manager, file sharing utility servers, systems management agents, ecommerce and other business connectors, job scheduling utilities, and so on.

Next, let's move to the dress rehearsal migration of the production system. Dress rehearsal is designed to mimic Go-Live. It requires the same level of involvement by all the resources in the project, including business end users for testing of key business process, as will the actual production migration. The outcome of this migration drives a key go/no-go decision relative to performing the migration on the production system. In the dress rehearsal, it is paramount that the documented and validated migration process checklist be followed to a T. After all, it's too late in the project to uncover and subsequently try to address new issues. By the time the weekend outage is scheduled and the production system is migrated, cutover should resemble a long weekend at best and be nearly a nonevent in the eyes of the system's end users.

Summary

SAP enhancements, migrations, and upgrades are significant project undertakings, requiring specialized skill sets. With your understanding of the correct definitions and terminologies for each, in conjunction with knowledge of how each project is pursued to completion, you should be well prepared to consider these options as they naturally arise in the SAP deployment and maintenance lifecycle.

Case Study: Hour 18

Review and address the upgrade and migration-based case study questions posed here. Answers may be found in Appendix A, "Case Study Answers."

Situation

Today, MNC Global runs SAP R/3 4.6C as its core ERP application for Financials and HR. The system is hosted by a provider, and ongoing support costs are astronomical. Additionally, the SAP system runs on an out-of-support version of UNIX and Oracle. MNC Global is planning an upgrade to the latest release of SAP ERP 6.0.

Questions

1. MNC Global has employed a recruiter to help hire a project manager for the project. The online advertisement reads, "Project Manager with migration skills, requires experience migrating from R/3 4.6C to SAP ERP2005." Is this ad technically accurate? How should it read?

2. How can MNC Global potentially lower the support costs for the SAP system during the upgrade project?

3. What other technical business-enabling change should MNC Global consider along with the upgrade project?

PART V

Using SAP

Logon, Session, and SAP GUI Basics

What You'll Learn in This Hour:

▶ Logging on and off the system

▶ Session management and multitasking

▶ Menu path navigation

▶ Transaction code navigation

This hour helps you understand the basics necessary to actually *use* SAP. First, we guide you through setting up your initial connection and logging on to the system. Once you are logged in, we cover the basics regarding how to navigate SAP using menu paths, transaction codes (T-codes), the SAP menu bar, and the standard and application toolbars.

Accessing the System

As we have discussed, SAP applications can logically be divided into three tiers: application, database, and presentation. The presentation tier is the user interface to the SAP systems. The user interface connects to the SAP application server (the SAP "executables"), which in turn talks to the back-end database holding all the programs, data, and so on. The key advantage of separating the presentation logic from the other tiers is that users can access the system from anywhere—you aren't tied to a particular desktop or even a single type of client. What this means is that you have the freedom to operate the system from any computer that has the SAP GUI (SAP's user interface, also called *presentation software* by the folks at SAP AG) or Internet Explorer (in most cases). For example, if you happen to be visiting your warehouse and realize that you forgot to perform an important task back at the office, you can perform it from this site (assuming the computer is connected to SAP via the company network or intranet). SAP recognizes who you are and what activities you are allowed to perform through your SAP user ID.

The SAP Logon Pad

Until a few years ago, it was common to log in to SAP by double-clicking an SAP icon that the system administrator set up on each user's desktop. Although simple in approach, it was a bit limiting—especially for companies that deployed multiple SAP systems. Each user's desktop could crowd up quickly with SAP GUI icons. And additional icons set up on each user's desktop to log in to Disaster Recovery systems and so on added to the complexity.

Therefore, SAP developed the SAP Logon Pad, a simple utility with a straightforward yet powerful interface designed to help you manage access to your SAP systems. The SAP Logon Pad is delivered as part of the SAP GUI client. As shown in Figure 19.1, the SAP Logon Pad enables you to organize the various systems you need to use.

FIGURE 19.1
The SAP Logon Pad is useful for organizing and simplifying access to multiple SAP systems.

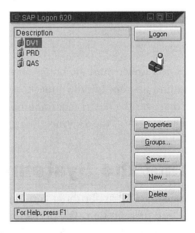

Configuring the SAP Logon Pad

To configure the SAP Logon Pad, you can either manually enter all the systems (using the buttons to add individual servers or groups of systems) or copy the saplogon.ini file from another person's personal computer to your own and then customize its contents (many companies deploy standard saplogon.ini files via desktop management software). The saplogon.ini file usually resides in the C:\windows directory. To modify the entry for an existing system in the SAP Logon Pad, right-click the SAP system's description and then select Properties. Enter the SAP application server you connect to (either the computer's hostname or its TCP/IP address) and its system ID (or SID, a three-character identifier assigned by the system administrator). You'll also need to include the system number (a two-digit number) and click the R/3 button (which actually comprises all systems except SAP's old mainframe-based R/2 system). You should also edit the description to reflect something meaningful, such as the system ID. See Figure 19.2 for an example. Click the OK button when you're finished.

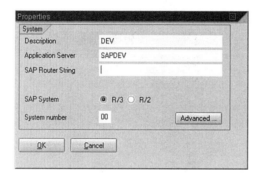

FIGURE 19.2
For each system you intend to log in to, specify at minimum a description, SAP application server, system ID or system number, and SAP system type.

Low-Speed Connections

One of the most useful features of the SAP Logon Pad is its capability to support low-speed connections. For instance, if your worksite is physically far away from the SAP system, or you use a slow connection method, such as modem dial-up or a slow WAN (wide area network) link, you can instruct SAP to skip sending you all the pretty graphics and other such constructs that can really slow down an already bogged-down network connection. By giving yourself this extra network bandwidth, you'll be in a position to get your SAP work done that much faster. Click the Advanced button from within the SAP Logon Pad's Properties dialog box, and a new Advanced Options box is displayed. Simply click the Low-Speed Connection check box and save the new setting by selecting OK.

For SAP GUI users at remote sites or using slow modems or networks to connect to SAP, the Low-Speed Connection option can really help speed up system response times. Feel free to change it as often as you need to, based on the SAP connection you have or from where you are connecting.

Initial SAP Logon

The initial screen you see when first connecting to SAP is the SAP R/3 Logon screen. See Figure 19.3 for an example, keeping in mind that the Logon screen associated with different SAP products or components might look a bit different.

On this screen, you need to provide the client number, your user name, and the initial password assigned to you. Enter the information provided to you on this screen and then select the green check mark (or press the Enter key on your keyboard) to continue.

FIGURE 19.3
The first screen
you see when
starting the
logon process is
the SAP Logon
screen.

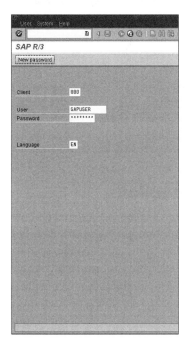

SAP User ID

All SAP users are assigned a user name (although it is not uncommon to see infrequent factory, distribution site, and warehouse workers sharing a single SAP user ID). In most cases, it is your own name or initials, similar to the PC logon name you're accustomed to using. When you connect to SAP using your initial password, you are forced to change it immediately upon logging in, thus securing your user ID even from system administrators and others tasked with maintaining security.

SAP Client

The concept of a client within SAP is quite different from the traditional information technology usage of a personal computer or workstation. In SAP, a *client* is a logical and separate business entity within the SAP system—typically a company or a major division within a company. A system may have a number of different clients, each one assigned a unique three-digit number to make it easy to distinguish between them. A developer might log in to client 100 in the development system to do training, client 200 to review and approve new business logic, and client 500 to conduct actual development activities for the company. In the same way, an end user might log in to client 300 in the production system to do his day-to-day work, and occasionally client 900 in the QA or test system to check on the status of new functionality being developed for production.

Logon Language

It is not necessary for you to enter your logon language on the initial logon screen (refer to Figure 19.3). Your system will likely be configured to default to a standard language for your organization, such as "EN" for English. If your organization requires global (multilingual) logon capabilities, and those particular languages have been set up for your system, you can specify a two-digit language code in the language box. Check with your administrator or business lead for the language-specific codes you might need in your specific case.

Changing Your Password

After your first login to SAP, you are prompted to change your password. Keep in mind the following five rules to create your password (with the caveat that some of these rules can be changed by your system administrator):

▶ Rule 1: A password must consist of at least three characters (most companies go with between five and eight characters at a minimum, however).

▶ Rule 2: The first character cannot be !, ?, or any other special character.

▶ Rule 3: The first three characters may not be identical.

▶ Rule 4: The first three characters should not be contained in the user name.

▶ Rule 5: The password is generally limited to excluding **SAP*** and **pass**, along with anything that the system administrator assigns as a "no-no" password in database table USR40. Most sites do not allow their company name to be used as a password, for instance.

In addition to the standard rules for governing passwords, your company will almost certainly define a set of rules that pertains to its own operations. A particular minimum length and the use of special characters or numbers within the body of the password both serve to create stronger passwords and a more secure environment for SAP.

On the Change Password screen, shown in Figure 19.4, enter your new password on both lines and select the green check mark (or press Enter) to continue.

FIGURE 19.4
Upon first logging in to SAP, you are required to change your password. In the same way, if your system administrator ever resets your password, you are also required to change it the next time you log in. This applies to each client for which you have a user ID.

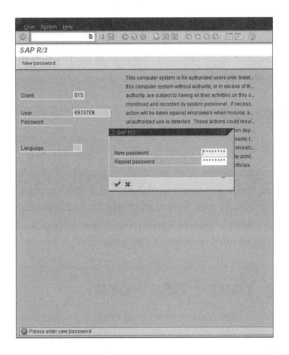

Session Basics

Each time you connect to SAP via the SAP GUI user interface, you begin a user session. You can have multiple sessions open with multiple SAP components—such as SAP ERP, BI, CRM, and so on—or you can open one or more sessions with a single system. The number of the current session is displayed in the status bar, which you will see in a few minutes. Because each session uses system resources, your company will normally set limits to the number of sessions that you and your colleagues can create. Alternatively, your company might encourage the SAP user community to limit itself to only one or two sessions.

One of the benefits of this multiple session option is that you can multitask. Assume that you are processing a new customer order and your boss asks you to generate a report. There is no need to stop processing the order. You can leave that session (screen) open on your computer and begin a new session. With this new session, you can request and generate your boss's report. By default, you can open up to six sessions at the same time, although the default can be changed by the system administrator.

Creating a New Session

In SAP, you can create a session at any time and from nearly any screen in the system. You do not lose any data in the sessions that are already open with each new session you create, either. Create a new session by following the menu path System, Create Session. You will now have two sessions open on your computer. If you want to determine which session you are currently in, check the status bar on the bottom-right side of your screen (see Figure 19.5).

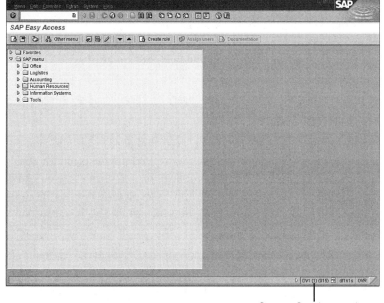

FIGURE 19.5
The SAP GUI window displays the current session number in the bottom-right side of the screen, in parentheses.

Current Session number

Creating a New Session Using the Command Field

Rather than following the menu path, you can also create a new session by typing /O (for open) in the command field at the top-left corner of your SAP GUI window and pressing Enter. You will be prompted with a window like the one shown in Figure 19.6—similar to the window shown when you enter transaction SM04, although with the added benefit of the Generate button.

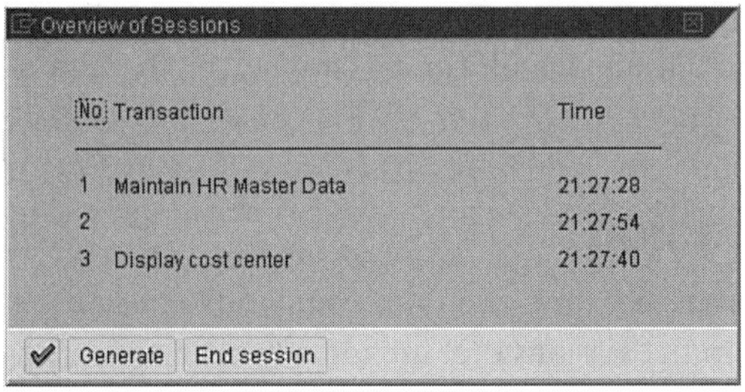

FIGURE 19.6
The Overview of Sessions window displays the number of open sessions and enables you to create a new session or end any existing sessions.

From this box, you can create a new session by selecting the Generate button or terminate an existing session by selecting the End Session button. This box also provides an overview of all the sessions you currently have open, making it easy to determine what you are doing in each session, for example.

When you generate a session in this way, the system displays the initial SAP R/3 or SAP Easy Access system screen in the new session. But you can change this by changing what you type into the command field, as explained next.

Creating a New Session and Starting a New Task at the Same Time

Instead of creating a new session and then executing a desired transaction or task, you can combine these two steps into one. Again, you use the command field. By entering transaction codes in the command field, preceded with /o, you can quickly call a task or proceed to a specific screen. A transaction code is a unique sequence of between three and eight alphanumeric characters that identify a transaction in the SAP system.

To execute or call a transaction, enter the transaction code in the command field at the top-left corner of your SAP GUI window and press Enter. Give it a try using the transaction code SE38. Type /oSE38 in the command field and press Enter. This should not only open a new session, but should take you to the ABAP Editor Initial screen as well.

Transaction codes are not case sensitive, which means you can enter them in lowercase or uppercase. We provide more information on finding and using transaction codes later in this hour.

Depending on your system's security authorization, you might not be able to enter certain transaction codes or navigate to certain screens. Work with your system administrator to understand your personal user ID authorizations and limitations.

Also, it is important to note that, when using transaction codes from any screen except the initial screen, you need to add the prefix /N before the transaction code or /O to create a new session and start a new transaction (neither of which is case sensitive; feel free to use upper or lower case).

Ending a Session

After you are done using a session, it is a good idea to end it. Each session uses system resources that can affect how fast the SAP system responds to your requests, and that of your colleagues. Before you end a session, you must save any data you want to keep. When you end a session, the system will not prompt you to save your data if you are in the middle of a transaction, for instance.

Ending a session is similar to creating a session. You follow the menu path System, End Session (or enter /O as previously discussed). From the Overview of Sessions box, you can selectively close a session by selecting it and then selecting the End Session button. Give it a try. Assuming you've followed along and opened a number of SAP GUI sessions, select number 2 by single-clicking it, and then select the End Session button. It might not initially appear that anything has happened, but the session was indeed closed. To verify this, return to the Overview of Sessions box by typing the transaction code /O in the command field. Transactions 1 and 3 should still be listed, but number 2 is no longer open. Follow the same steps to end session 3, leaving only session 1 open.

Logging Off of SAP

To terminate your SAP session or connection, you can select the System, Logoff option from the main menu or select the Windows "X" icon in the top-right corner of your SAP GUI window. You may also execute /nex from the SAP GUI command field. SAP will prompt you with a window confirming the shutdown of your connection to SAP.

SAP GUI Basics

The SAP GUI window is the user interface to most SAP systems available today. At the very top of the window is the title bar, which gives the screen (or transaction) description for the window that is displayed. The standard elements of an SAP GUI window are shown in Figure 19.7, and are explained in the following sections.

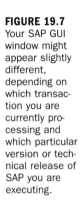

FIGURE 19.7
Your SAP GUI
window might
appear slightly
different,
depending on
which transac-
tion you are
currently pro-
cessing and
which particular
version or tech-
nical release of
SAP you are
executing.

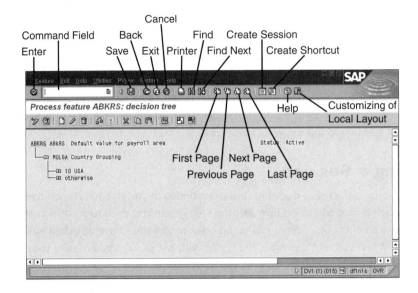

The Menu Bar

The menu bar contains all the menu options available. The menu bar changes from
screen to screen to match the function module that you are currently processing.
The last two items on the menu bar, System and Help, remain constant on all SAP
screens and contain the same submenu options.

The Standard Toolbar

The standard toolbar is easy to identify because of all the buttons. It varies slightly,
but generally contains the same basic components on every screen. The main navigational, printing, page viewing, and help functions are all made available here.
It contains the following elements:

▶ **Enter button**—This button has the same function as the Enter key on your
keyboard and is used to check your entry in a field or your work in a transaction when you have finished entering data on a screen. This button should
not be confused with the Save button.

▶ **Command field**—The command field is located to the right of the Enter
button and is used to enter transaction codes to call a task without having
to choose menu options for navigation.

▶ **Save button**—The Save button saves your work and performs the same
function as selecting Save from the Edit menu.

▶ **Back button**—The Back button is quite similar to the back button used in most web browsers, and it does just as its name implies. It will take you back to the previous screen. If you use this button to return to the previous screen, your data will not be saved unless you save it first using the Save button on the toolbar.

▶ **Exit button**—The Exit button is used to leave the current application. The system returns you to the previous application or to the main menu screen.

▶ **Cancel button**—The Cancel button is used to exit the current task without saving and performs the same function as selecting Cancel from the Edit menu.

▶ **Print button**—The Print button is used to print data from the screen in which you are currently working. (There are some advanced settings that the user should set up in order for the print setting to work more efficiently. These are covered later in this hour.)

▶ **Find button**—This button is used to perform a search for data on the screen in which you are currently working.

▶ **Find Next button**—This button is used to perform an extended search for data on the screen in which you are currently working.

▶ **First Page button**—This page navigation key is generally used in reports. It is used to travel to the top of a screen (or page) if the information on the screen is too long to fit on a single screen.

▶ **Previous Page (Page Up) button**—This page navigation key is generally used in reports. It is used to travel up one screen (or page) if the information on the screen is too long to fit on a single screen. This button is equivalent to using the Page Up key on your keyboard.

▶ **Next Page (Page Down) button**—This page navigation key is generally used in reports. It is used to travel down one screen when the information on the screen is too long to fit on a single screen. This button is equivalent to using the Page Down key on your keyboard.

▶ **Last Page button**—This page navigation key is generally used in reports. It is used to travel to the end of a screen (or page) when the information on the screen is too long to fit on a single screen.

▶ **Create Session button**—Open a new session by clicking this button. Alternatively, execute /0 in the command field.

▶ **Create Shortcut button**—This is handy for creating a shortcut on a user's desktop for any SAP transaction, report, or other task that is executed frequently.

▶ **Help button**—The Help button is used for context-sensitive help. That is, when you place your cursor on any object on the screen and select the Help button, you receive specific help for that item. (You learn more about the Help button and SAP's help system in Hour 24, "SAP Resources.")

▶ **Customizing of Local Layout button**—This customizing button allows a user to customize SAP GUI display options; details are provided in Hour 21, "Customizing Your SAP Display."

The Application Toolbar

The application toolbar is located under the standard toolbar. This toolbar is application specific, and in some cases transaction specific, and varies depending on the screen (or transaction) you are currently processing in. For example, if you are in the Finance module, Create Rental Agreement screen, your application toolbar will contain buttons that enable you to copy or retrieve master data from SAP. But if you are in the ABAP/4 Workbench Initial Editor screen, your application toolbar will contain buttons for the Dictionary, Repository Browser, and Screen Painter.

Navigation Basics

In order to perform the tasks related to your job, you need to understand how to navigate the SAP system. For example, a salesperson would need to know how to enter a sales order or check on the status of an existing order. Menu paths and transaction codes are used to call transactions. The menu bar and toolbars in conjunction with the mouse and keyboard complete the transaction and save the data.

Performing Tasks Using Menu Paths

When you first start using SAP, you are very likely to use the SAP menus to navigate to the transactions required in your job/role. Your SAP user menu (or Easy Access menu) allows you to navigate through all the functions, areas, and tasks in SAP down to the individual transactions. With menus, you can easily drill down into business-specific application transactions and other functions without having to memorize transaction codes.

Navigation Using the Mouse

After starting a transaction, you will use the SAP menu bar as well as the standard and application toolbars to navigate through the screens required to complete the task. To select an entry from the SAP menu bar, single-click the menu to display the various options listed underneath that menu. Menu entries that contain an additional list of objects (submenus) include an arrow (see Figure 19.8).

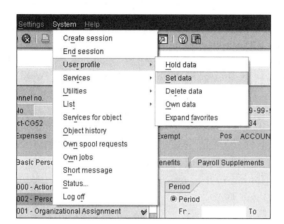

FIGURE 19.8
Menus and submenus can be selected using your mouse.

Navigation Using the Keyboard

Menu bars can also be selected with the keyboard. To select items from the SAP menu bar using your keyboard, press F10 (to activate the menu bar) and then use the navigational arrow keys on your keyboard to select and display the menu. You choose a function by highlighting it with the arrow keys and then pressing Enter.

Performing Tasks Using Transaction Codes

As you learned earlier, you can jump directly to any screen in the SAP system by entering an SAP transaction code into the command field on the standard toolbar. A transaction code is an alphanumeric code, essentially a shortcut, that takes you directly to the screen for the task you want to perform. For most SAP transactions, the last number indicates the purpose of the transaction—1 to create, 2 to modify, or 3 to display SAP data. For example, to display an existing sales order in R/3, you can enter VA03 in the command field and then press Enter. Similarly, to update a vendor's credit limit, you can enter FD32. Such T-codes save a considerable amount of time otherwise spent navigating the menu system.

SAP provides a T-code for nearly every transaction. The alphanumeric codes themselves vary in length, but do not exceed 20 characters. In fact, most are generally less than six or seven characters. And SAP provides you with the ability to create your own transaction codes to augment those that already exist. Such custom T-codes start with the character Y or Z. Use custom T-codes to help you execute custom versions of transactions or reports.

By the Way

> From any SAP screen except the main screen, you need to enter /n (or /N) before the transaction code in the command field to execute a new transaction (for example, /nVA03). Otherwise, you first need to navigate to the main screen, which is time-consuming. To open a new SAP GUI session and execute a new task, use /o (instead of /n) plus the transaction code (for example, /oVA03).

Finding the Right Transaction Code

To find a transaction code for a certain task, begin by using the standard SAP menu or SAP Easy Access menu. It can often be displayed from the main SAP screen by entering /n in the command field and pressing Enter. A screen will appear similar to the one shown in Figure 19.9.

FIGURE 19.9
You can use the SAP Easy Access menu to search for transaction codes.

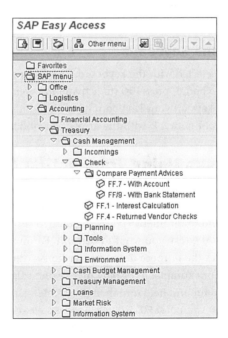

Watch Out!

Depending on the SAP modules you are using, the client you are logged in to, and your system configuration, your SAP Easy Access or other standard menu might be different.

On the screen, you see a list of the SAP application areas, with arrows (or plus signs, in the case of older SAP releases) to the left of every item that has sublists attached underneath it. On the menu bar, select Edit, Technical Name, Technical Name On. This turns on the feature allowing all transaction codes to be displayed next to the tasks. To display one of the application area sublists, double-click it. The sublist appears containing tasks, more sublists, or both. You can identify a task by the fact that no arrow (or plus or minus sign) appears to the left of it, and a transaction code is listed instead.

Continue to drill down until you see the task you want. You can start the function now by double-clicking it. Otherwise, you can use this transaction code to start this task from any screen in the SAP system. When you use a transaction code to start a task, the SAP system closes, or ends, your current task and then displays the initial screen of the new task.

Did you Know?

You can also save frequently used transactions in the SAP Easy Access menu under Favorites.

As you can see, this seems like a lot of work to find a particular transaction code. Fortunately, a number of shortcut methods exist. For example, after you have entered a particular task's screen, there's a simple method of determining its relevant T-code, as explained in the following section.

Finding the Transaction Code for the Current Task

From nearly every screen in SAP, the system allows you to easily determine its relevant transaction code. From the SAP screen, select the menu path System, Status. This displays the System Status screen, which provides a great amount of detail and technical information regarding the screen you are on (see Figure 19.10).

In addition to all the detailed and technical information, the System Status screen gives you the transaction code for the screen. Look in the field under the SAP Data heading called Transaction. This gives you the multicharacter transaction code for the current screen. In the example shown in Figure 19.10, the transaction code is RCATSC01. You can use this method from nearly any screen in the system.

FIGURE 19.10
The System
Status screen
provides useful
information,
including the
transaction
code for the
screen you are
currently on.

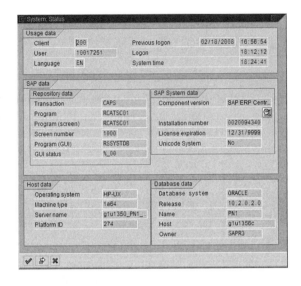

By the Way

In some instances, an SAP action or event consists of a series of screens. Some of the screens within that action might contain the same transaction code as the first screen in the action, in essence telling you that you cannot start this particular transaction midway; it must be started from the beginning.

Using the History List to Find Transaction Codes

The list of all the transaction codes processed since you logged on is called the *history list*. To access the history list, use your mouse to select the down arrow to the right of the command field (see Figure 19.11).

From the history list, select the transaction code you want to execute by highlighting it and pressing the Enter key on your keyboard or clicking the green check mark on the toolbar. The initial screen of the task associated with that transaction code will appear.

Scrolling Techniques

When you view information in reports or view the SAP online help, occasionally some of the information will not fit in your window. To see the additional information, you can use the scrollbars. Your window has a vertical and a horizontal scrollbar.

You use the vertical scrollbar to move (or scroll) up and down through the information in the window. You use the horizontal scrollbar to scroll left and right through the information in the window.

You can also use the scroll (Page Up and Down) buttons in the standard toolbar to view information in windows, as follows:

Destination Shortcut	Toolbar Button	Function Key
First Screen Page		F21 Ctrl + PageUp
Last Screen Page		F24 Ctrl + PageDown
Previous Screen Page		F22 PageUp
Next Screen Page		F23 PageDown

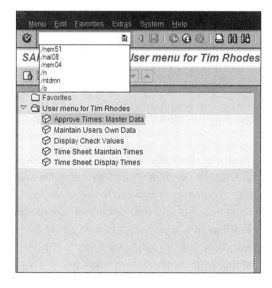

FIGURE 19.11
The history list is quite useful for navigating back and forth between different transactions that you have executed or accessed within your current session.

Did you Know?

To save screen output (like that found in a list) to a file on your desktop or the network, enter the letters %pc on the command line and then press Enter. A print window pops up, defaulting to saving the screen's contents in an unconverted or XLS file format. Choose the format most appropriate (for example, XLS or RTF for Excel or Word-based output, respectively), press Enter, browse to the desired directory path, type the name of the output file you want to create, and then click Save to save the list data to the filename you specified.

Stopping a Transaction

Occasionally you might need to stop a transaction—for example, right after you realize you just accidentally kicked off a long running query. The easiest way to do this is to click the curious little icon in the upper-left corner of the SAP GUI, as shown in Figure 19.12, and select Stop Transaction.

FIGURE 19.12
Use the icon in the upper-left corner of the GUI to stop a long-running transaction or any other inadvertent misstep.

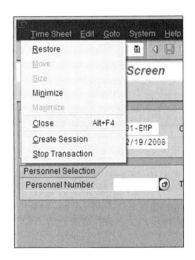

Summary

At this juncture, as a user you should be more comfortable working in the SAP system. We walked through logging on to SAP and exploring the SAP graphical user interface, or SAP GUI. You also were introduced to the concepts of session management. You have learned about the different methods of navigation within SAP. You should now be more familiar with the concept of navigation using transaction codes and how to find a transaction code for any screen within the SAP system. You should also be comfortable with the scrolling concept in reports and screens. The fundamentals you have learned in this hour will serve you well as you work your way through the remaining hours in this book.

Case Study: Hour 19

Consider this case study focused on setting up the SAP Logon Pad and using SAP. Address the questions that follow, the answers to which may be found in Appendix A, "Case Study Answers."

Situation

MNC has just finished the installation of a sandbox system for the upcoming ERP 6.0 implementation. You have just been asked by your boss to log on and test the functionality of the sales order entry and display transactions typically completed by a sales associate on this new system.

Questions

1. What information will you need in order to be able to set up an entry for the new system in your SAP Logon Pad?

2. Assuming you have never entered a sales order, what is the easiest way to find the sales order entry transaction?

3. How would you determine the transaction code for the sales entry transaction while you are running the transaction?

4. You find that the sales order entry transaction code is VA01. Can you determine what the display T-code is?

HOUR 20

SAP GUI Screen and Printing Basics

What You'll Learn in This Hour:

▶ SAP screen objects
▶ Entering data in SAP screens
▶ Printing in SAP

This hour we walk you through using SAP's screens. We cover the fundamental elements of SAP screens and discuss how to interact with them. Printing and several advanced topics are also addressed, all of which you should find helpful as you continue to get more comfortable using SAP.

Understanding and Using Fields

Now that you know how to call transactions to perform tasks in SAP (based on what we covered last hour), it is time to develop an understanding of how to interact with the SAP screens in order to really use SAP. This starts with developing a basic understanding of the elements of the SAP screens. A "screen" in SAP is essentially the window you see in SAP GUI when you call a transaction, which in turn may consist of several screens used to enter, display, or manipulate data.

The SAP system houses a large database of information. This database is composed of tables that store data (master data, transactional data, programs, and more). The tables are composed of columns (called fields) and rows (called records or data). A typical row (record) is composed of many columns (fields). As you enter data into the various fields in an SAP screen (in a create transaction), you are essentially creating a record (row) in the database. For example, from within the SAP ERP 6.0 application, use the command field to navigate to transaction code /nFF7A. This transaction code will take you to the Cash Management and Forecast screen in the Financial Accounting module (see Figure 20.1). SAP screens also display these database fields on their screens for display transactions.

FIGURE 20.1
The Cash Management and Forecast screen gives a good example of an arrangement of fields presented on an SAP screen.

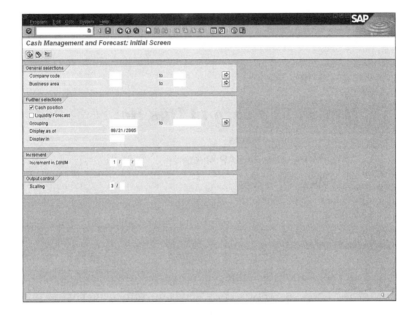

Input Fields

Most screens in the SAP system contain fields in which you enter data. These types of fields are called *input fields*. An example of an input field is shown in Figure 20.2. This screen displays a series of fields that are linked to database tables in the system.

Input fields vary in size: The length of a field determines how many characters you can enter in it. In the example shown in Figure 20.2, the Display As Of date input field is 10 characters long. The length of the rectangular box indicates the length of the longest valid data entry for that field.

By the Way

The *active* field is the field that currently contains the cursor and is waiting for input.

Input fields

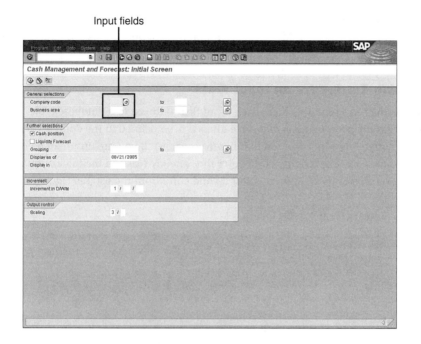

FIGURE 20.2
SAP input fields
accept the entry
of the data and
are tied to
fields in your
SAP Data
Dictionary.

When you place the cursor anywhere in an empty input field, the cursor appears at the beginning of the field, making data entry simple. Remember that the field can only hold data that fits into its rectangular box. After entry, the cursor remains in the input field until you press the Tab key to move it to the next field, press the Enter key to check your entry, or click another input field.

> The initial placement of the cursor in a field is determined by your system settings and can be modified. See the section "The Cursor Tab" in Hour 21, "Customizing Your SAP Display," for more information.

Did you Know?

Replace and Insert Modes

Your computer keyboard has a button called Insert in its top-right area above the Delete button. This Insert key toggles your computer setting between two writing modes. The Insert mode enables you to insert data into an existing field without typing over it. The Overwrite mode enables you to type over existing data in a field. The Overwrite mode is the SAP default.

You can tell which setting your SAP system is using by looking at the bottom-right area of your screen. In the box to the left of the system clock, you will see the abbreviation OVR for Overwrite mode or INS for Insert mode. This setting is based on the user's preference. However, keep in mind that with each new session you create, the default Overwrite mode setting will be active unless you change it.

Possible Entries for an Input Field

As explained earlier in this hour, each input field is linked to a database table. Some fields will only accept entries that have already been defined in the database (either by the system's developers or via another transaction). If you are unsure of a valid entry (that is, the exact name of an entry that already exists in the table), you can use the Possible Entries button to select a valid entry from the list (see Figure 20.3).

FIGURE 20.3
Many fields in the SAP system contain Possible Entries Help, where you can select an appropriate value from a list instead of typing it.

Input field with Possible Entries help

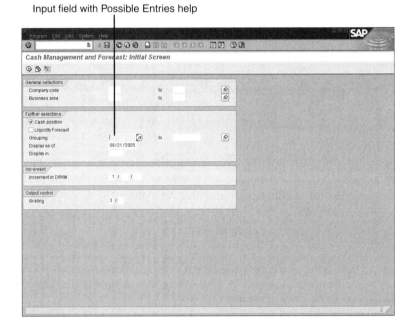

Any field containing a right arrow (like the one indicated in Figure 20.3) on the far-right side has a Possible Entry function. Give one a try. Use the Transaction code /NFK10 to travel to the Vendor: Initial Screen Balances Display screen. This screen contains three input fields. Use your Tab key to navigate between the three fields. You will see that as you travel from one field to another, the Possible Entries down arrow appears only when the field is active. You will also see that the Possible Entries down arrow is not present on the Fiscal Year field. Use your Tab key to return to the Company Code field. Use your mouse to select the Possible Entries arrow as displayed in Figure 20.4 (the Possible Entries Help button down arrow disappears when the Possible Entries window opens).

Not all input fields have lists of possible entries. You cannot determine whether such a list is available for an input field until you place the cursor in the input field. Also, some fields that contain Possible Entries Help do not have a down arrow, even when the field is active. You can select the F4 button on the top of your keyboard to retrieve the Possible Entries Help in any SAP field where it is available.

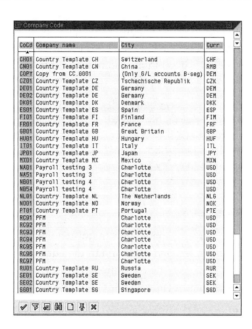

FIGURE 20.4
The Possible Entries Help window displays available company codes.

CoCd	Company name	City	Curr.
CH01	Country Template CH	Switzerland	CHF
CN01	Country Template CN	China	RMB
COPY	Copy from CC.0001	(Only G/L accounts B-seg)	DEM
CZ01	Country Template CZ	Tschechische Republik	CZK
DE01	Country Template DE	Germany	DEM
DE02	Country Template DE	Germany	DEM
DK01	Country Template DK	Denmark	DKK
ES01	Country Template ES	Spain	ESP
FI01	Country Template FI	Finland	FIM
FR01	Country Template FR	France	FRF
GB01	Country Template GB	Great Britain	GBP
HU01	Country Template HU	Hungary	HUF
IT01	Country Template IT	Italy	ITL
JP01	Country Template JP	Japan	JPY
MX01	Country Template MX	Mexico	MXN
NA01	Payroll testing 3	Charlotte	USD
NA51	Payroll testing 3	Charlotte	USD
NB01	Payroll testing 4	Charlotte	USD
NB54	Payroll testing 4	Charlotte	USD
NL01	Country Template NL	The Netherlands	NLG
NO01	Country Template NO	Norway	NOK
PT01	Country Template PT	Portugal	PTE
RC91	PFM	Charlotte	USD
RC92	PFM	Charlotte	USD
RC93	PFM	Charlotte	USD
RC94	PFM	Charlotte	USD
RC95	PFM	Charlotte	USD
RC96	PFM	Charlotte	USD
RC97	PFM	Charlotte	USD
RU01	Country Template RU	Russia	RUR
SE01	Country Template SE	Sweden	SEK
SE02	Country Template SE	Sweden	SEK
SG01	Country Template SG	Singapore	SGD

In this example, after selecting the Possible Entries down arrow for the Company Code field, you are presented with a list of possible entries that are acceptable and valid for that field.

Keep in mind, depending on your system's configuration, that your Possible Entries list might appear slightly different from the one displayed in Figure 20.4.

To select an item from a Possible Entries list, you can double-click it or use your mouse to highlight it once and then choose the green check mark icon. The list will disappear and the value selected will then be present in your Company Code field.

See what happens when you enter a value that is not an item listed in the Possible Entries Help. Return your cursor to the Company Code field, type your initials, and press the Enter key. A warning or error message appears in the status bar area. This error or warning message prevents you from progressing to additional screens until the issue is corrected.

Editing the Data in an Input Field

Now that you have an invalid entry in your Company Code field, you need to return to that field to correct the input. Place your cursor in the Company Code box and then select the Possible Entries Help down arrow for the Company Code field. Select any item from the list of possible entries and click the green check mark. Now your invalid entry is replaced by a valid one. Press the Enter key, and SAP checks your entry to confirm that it is acceptable and removes the warning message from the status bar.

Sometimes the SAP system saves the last value entered in an input field into memory. Even when you replace it with a new value, the old one is retained. To clear the SAP memory for an input box, select the exclamation point key (!) and press Enter; this clears the memory for that input field.

Required Input Fields

In the case of certain SAP screens, some fields might require input data before you can proceed. These are called *required fields* and in the early days of SAP they contained a question mark (?). Today, these required fields contain a square with a check mark inside it, as shown in Figure 20.5. The following are examples of required fields:

▶ A purchase order number field on a Create Purchase Order screen in the Financials module

▶ An employee personnel number on a Change Basic Pay screen in the Human Capital Management module

▶ A date of accepted delivery field in an Inventory Management Control screen in the Logistics module

Generally, if a screen does not contain a square with a check mark, you can navigate to the next screen without entering data in any fields. However, some screens that contain required fields are not marked in this way. For example, this situation can occur when you enter data in an optional field that has required fields associated with it.

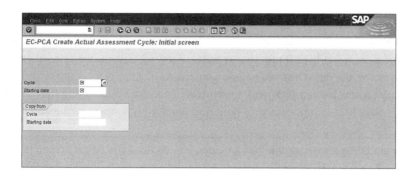

FIGURE 20.5
Required fields
require data
before enabling
you to save or
proceed past
the screen.

If you have not completed all the required fields on a screen and then try to proceed
to another screen, the SAP system displays an error message in the status bar. At the
same time, it returns the cursor to the first required field that needs data entered so
that you can make the necessary changes.

Field Entry Validation

After entering data into input fields on the screen, use the Enter key or the green
check mark on your SAP toolbar to check the validity of your entries. If your entries
are valid, the system will advance to the next screen in the task. If the system checks
your entries and finds any errors—for example, entries in the wrong format—it displays a message in the status bar and positions the cursor in the field that you need
to correct.

Canceling All the Data Entered on a Screen

To cancel all the data you just entered on a screen, use the menu path Edit, Cancel
or use the red X (Cancel) button on the toolbar. In most instances, you will be
prompted with an SAP window confirming that data will be lost if you proceed to
exit the current screen (see Figure 20.6).

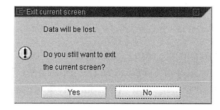

FIGURE 20.6
The Exit Current
Screen box
confirms that
data will be lost
if you choose to
exit the current
screen.

Saving Your Data on the Screen

The SAP Save button appears on the standard toolbar and looks like an open folder. When you are working in a task that consists of several screens, the system temporarily stores the data that you enter on each screen. After you complete all the necessary screens in your task, you need to save your data by selecting the Save button. The Save button processes your data and sends your changes to the database.

> If you are doing a task for the first time and you do not know which screen is the last screen, the system prompts you to save when you reach the last screen.

Replicating Data

No one likes entering data. SAP has a way to simplify the process. Say that you need to enter a handful of new employees into the ERP Human Capital Management (HCM) modules and all the employees have the same hire date. Using the Hold Data or Set Data SAP functions, you can set the hire date to automatically default to the date you set for each of the employees you need to enter, without having to re-key it each time.

Hold Data

To use the Hold Data function on any SAP screen (except the login screen), enter the data that you want to hold in an input field. While your cursor is still in the input field, navigate to the menu path System, User Profile, Hold Data, as shown in Figure 20.7.

The data will be set in memory for that field for each new record you create until you turn the Hold Data setting off. The Hold Data feature also has another advantage: The input field defaults to the data you have set to hold, yet it also allows you to override the data. If you want to hold data and not give the user the capability to change the default, you would use the Set Data setting.

Set Data

The Set Data feature works in the same fashion as the Hold Data setting, but it does not enable the user to override the default in the input field. The advantage to using the Set Data setting is that it gives you the capability to automatically skip fields with held data, so you do not need to tab from field to field during data entry.

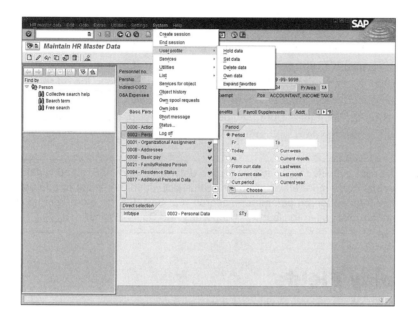

FIGURE 20.7
Hold Data is a
useful tool for
entering data
in SAP.

To use the Set Data function on any SAP screen (except the login screen), enter the
data in an input field that you want to set. While your cursor is still in the input
field, go to the menu path System, User Profile, Set Data, as shown in Figure 20.8.

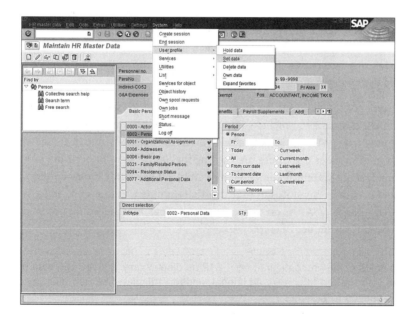

FIGURE 20.8
Using the Set
Data option
restricts users
from changing
the set value
in the field.

Deleting Data That Is Held or Set on a Screen

You can hold data for as many different screens as you like. The data you enter and hold on a screen is held for that screen until you delete it or until you log off the SAP system. If you want to remove the setting without having to log off the system, place the cursor in the input field that you want to delete and follow the menu path System, User Profile, Delete Data. The data will be deleted, and the next time you access the screen the data will not be displayed.

By the Way

You can also simplify the input of repeated data using parameters and variants. Parameters are a more advanced topic that is not within the scope of this book. For more information on parameters, search your SAP Help for more information. Variants are discussed in Hour 22, "Reporting and Query Basics."

Display Fields

Another type of SAP field is a display field. This type of field is not used to enter data, but only to display it. Display fields are always shaded with a gray background to indicate that the field cannot be changed.

Display fields are often used for values that were set according to some configuration in the system or by previous steps in a process. What this translates to is that fields are often assigned values based on configuration that occurs behind the scenes. For example, if you add a new employee to your Human Capital Management module, on the new hire screen will be a display field listing the employee's status as active. This value is assigned by the system and cannot be changed by the user.

By the same token, when system administrators run processes for maintaining the system, their screens often include date fields storing the current date, which are display only. The system does not enable you to change the value in these fields because in most cases the values are used by the SAP system for accurate processing. Using the Human Capital Management example, if you hired a new employee and were able to change his status from active to terminated, the new employee would not be recognized in SAP as an active employee. Therefore, he would not be paid or receive benefits as an active employee.

By the Way

Some fields come preconfigured from SAP as display only, but you can also customize your system to change additional fields to "display only" so users cannot make changes to the data.

Screen Objects

This section covers the different types of items you will see on SAP screens. Regardless of the SAP component's module you are processing in, the same types of screen objects will generally appear on the different SAP screens.

SAP promotes itself as very logically designed and organized; a user can easily navigate through its system. The style of the SAP system is much different from many popular applications available on the market today, such as the Microsoft Office family of products. Often absent in SAP are the friendly pictures, detailed formatted text, and elaborate design. Most screens in SAP are designed in tabbed formats or tree structures through which the user navigates by "drilling down."

SAP Trees

You will soon become accustomed to using SAP trees in navigating through the SAP system (see Figure 20.9). The SAP menus you learned about in Hour 19, "Logon, Session, and SAP GUI Basics," are examples of SAP trees. SAP's logically devised environment centers on a basic tree structure. SAP trees appear similar to the Windows structure you see in Windows Explorer. The tree structure is formulated so that you can drill down in the tree to reach deeper levels (branches) until you reach the endpoint (leaf). To use an SAP tree for navigation, you need to select the arrow sign to expand or compress the tree to view more or fewer selections, respectively. Older versions of SAP used plus and minus signs, respectively, to expand and compress the tree.

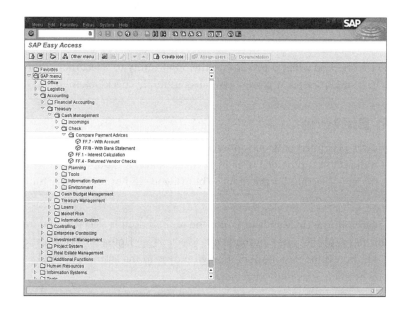

FIGURE 20.9
SAP ERP and similar SAP systems' menus are based on an elementary tree structure.

Check Boxes

When you are working in SAP, entering information sometimes involves selecting options. These options can be in the form of check boxes, like the ones shown in Figure 20.10. A check mark placed in the check box indicates that the box is selected, and an empty box indicates that the box is not selected.

FIGURE 20.10
Check boxes are used to respond with a yes or no to a selection.

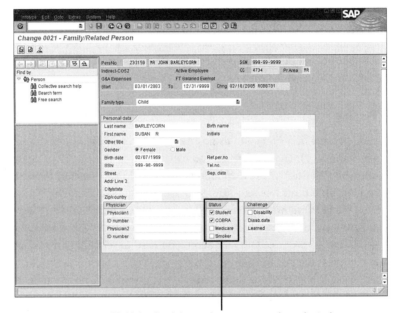

Multiple check boxes in a group can be selected

Check boxes are used when a person has the opportunity to select more than one option. On a single screen, a person can select multiple check boxes.

Radio Buttons

When you are permitted only *one* option among a selection of many, you will see a group of radio buttons provided instead of check boxes. A group of radio buttons accepts only one selection for the group. That is, you cannot mark more than one radio button in a group.

A mark placed in the circle indicates that the radio button is selected, and an empty circle indicates that the radio button is not selected (see Figure 20.11). An example of a radio button is the designation of an employee in the Human Capital Management module as male or female.

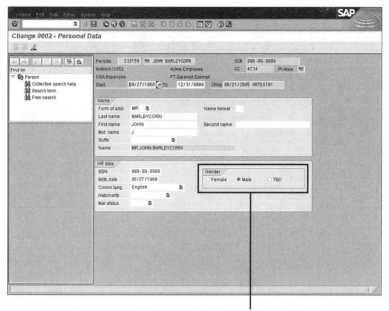

FIGURE 20.11
Radio buttons are always shown in a group of at least two or more; choices are mutually exclusive.

You can only select one radio button in a group

Dialog Boxes

Dialog box is a fancy word for a window that pops up to give you information. These are also sometimes called *information windows*. Here are two situations in which a dialog box appears on your screen:

▶ The system needs more information from you before it can proceed.

▶ The system needs to give you feedback, such as messages or specific information about your current task.

For example, you might receive a dialog box on your screen when you are logging off SAP. If you select the SAP icon in the top-left corner of your screen and then select the Close button, you are prompted with a dialog box confirming that you indeed want to log off the system.

Table Controls

A final object you will see on most SAP screens is the table control, as shown in Figure 20.12. Table controls display data in a tabular format similar to a Microsoft Excel spreadsheet. Table controls are popular for displaying or entering single structured lines of data.

SAP Table Control

FIGURE 20.12
Table controls
are very popular
in SAP for pre-
senting data in
a simple struc-
tured format.

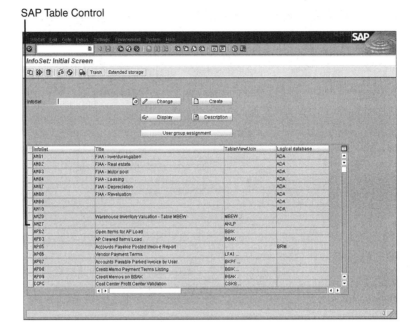

Printing in SAP

Printing enables you to make hard copies of lists, tables, and reports from SAP. The SAP Print button is available on most SAP screens (see Figure 20.13).

Print button

FIGURE 20.13
The Print button
allows you to
create a hard
copy of your
SAP output.

Let's take a look at the printing features in SAP. Even if you are not connected to a printer, you can still follow along.

By the Way

> In order to print from SAP, your workstation needs to be connected to a printer either by way of a network connection or in the form of a printer directly plugged into your workstation.

The SAP Print Screen List

Start with the SAP transaction code /nOS06, the SAP Operating System Monitor screen. If you do not have access to this screen, you can use any SAP screen where the Print button is available. Select the Print button on the standard toolbar. You will be prompted with the Print Screen List window, which is used to enter the output device (printer) you intend to print to—select or type in the name of your printer, make any other updates to the number of copies or pages (see Figure 20.14), and select the green check box to continue.

If you are not presented with this screen or if you receive a warning message saying your system is not connected to a printer, contact your system administrator for assistance in connecting to a printer.

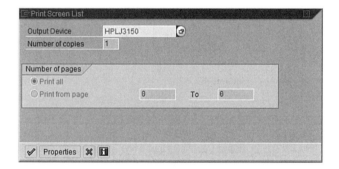

FIGURE 20.14
The Print Screen List window enables you to specify your printer, number of copies, and specific pages to print.

Output Device

This field contains the name of the output device. This could be a printer, a fax machine, or some other hardware device connected to the SAP system. In the example provided in Figure 20.14, it contains my printer name—HPLJ3150. To see a list of available output devices connected to your SAP system, select the down arrow to the right of this field.

Number of Copies

The Number of Copies field is where you specify the number of copies of the document you want to print.

> Sometimes in SAP, your reports might be lengthy. It is always a good idea to determine how many pages your output is going to be before printing one or multiple copies. Use your scrolling options on the toolbar, covered in Hour 19 under the "Scrolling Techniques" sidebar, to navigate through your output to determine its length before printing.

Did you Know?

Spool Request Attributes

In the previous section, we detailed how to print one or more copies of a screen list with the default settings. In order to customize the settings for a spool request, you click the Properties button in the Print Screen List window, and the Spool Request Attributes window appears. The parameters are grouped by function—you simply double-click a parameter line to change the parameter's value, as shown in Figure 20.15.

FIGURE 20.15
The Spool
Request
Attributes
screen allows
you to cus-
tomize your
printer settings.

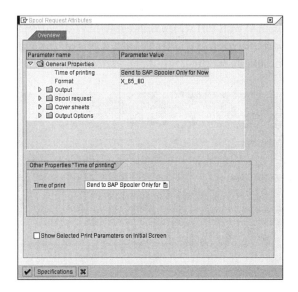

General Properties

We will now walk through some of the more commonly changed spool request attributes, starting with General Properties. The Time of Printing parameter determines when the request is sent to the printer. Send to SAP Spooler Only for Now places the request in the SAP spooler without sending it to the printer. You can choose to print it later by choosing System, Own Spool Requests. The Print Out Immediately option sends the spool request to the output device immediately. This setting is usually selected if you are printing small reports. This option will bypass the standard spool routing and send the request directly to the designated printer. Finally, the Print Later option allows you to schedule the time when the job will be sent to the printer. This option is normally used to schedule the printing of large reports when the printer is less busy.

The Format field contains the spool request format for output. The Rows field determines the number of lines per list page. The Columns field contains the current line width of the list; the maximum line width of a list is 255 characters. It is a good idea to accept the default settings for these fields. It is also a good idea to test the different formats listed to find one that is most acceptable for the output you are printing.

Spool Request

The Name field contains the name of the spool request. As you will learn, everything in SAP is assigned a name or an identifier within the SAP system. This name designates the item (in this case, a print request to the system). For example, if you go to your printer and you do not find your output, you can search in the SAP system by this spool request name and find out what happened to your output. Although you can change the spool request name, it is usually a good idea to accept the name proposed by the system.

You can, however, add a description of your own in the Spool Request Title field. It might consist of any combination of letters, digits, special characters, and blanks. This field can help you to identify your spool request.

Cover Sheets

The SAP Cover Sheet field determines whether to include a cover sheet with your output that is sent to the printer. Information such as recipient name, department name, and format can all be included on your SAP cover sheet. The permitted values for this field are System Administrator: Default Settings, Do Not Print, and Print.

The OS Cover Sheet field determines whether the standard operating system cover sheet is to be sent with the print job and has the same values as the SAP cover sheet.

The Receivers field contains the spool request recipient's name that appears on the cover sheet of hard copy printouts. The default value for the name of the recipient is the current user name.

The Department field contains the name of the department originating the spool request. On hard copy printouts, the name is displayed on the cover sheet.

Output Options

The Delete Immediately After Printing option determines whether to delete the spool request immediately after it has been sent to the output device or only after the spool retention period has expired. The default setting for this option is that the Delete After Printing box is cleared, indicating that the spool requests are saved for the duration of the spool retention period set in the retention period box. This is helpful in the previous scenario we detailed where a printout was lost. If the spool request was immediately deleted, you would not be able to go back and search for the item.

Most users check the Delete After Printing box in an effort to conserve space by not saving a spool request for every item printed. The box is cleared only when the user feels it is necessary to retain the request for very important spool requests.

Setting Default Values for the Printer

Each time you select the Print button in the SAP system, you will be prompted with the SAP Print Screen List. You can set a default value for each field in this screen so that you need not reenter your settings each time you print. You do this by clicking the Specifications button in the Spool Request Attributes windows; this brings up the Maintain Settings dialog box (see Figure 20.16). Next, select the field name and set the field default value and the validity settings—decide if you want the value to be valid for only this report or all reports, reports generated by batch jobs, dialog processing, or both. After you have entered all the settings to your specifications, select the Copy settings button—repeat this for each field name you wish to set a default for, and click the green check box when you are finished.

Don't forget when you select the Print button from the standard toolbar that you will be prompted with the Print List screen. You must select the Print button from this screen in order to send the output to your printer.

FIGURE 20.16
The Maintain Settings screen allows you to set the default value for a field.

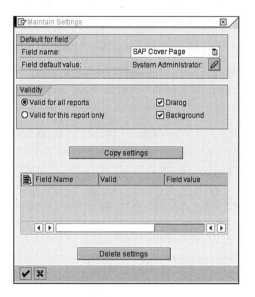

Advanced Concepts

Several advanced concepts and features are available to the SAP end user, particularly those centered around the clipboard and creating screen prints, both of which are addressed in this section.

Using the Clipboard

You can transfer the contents of SAP fields (and in some cases, the entire contents of an SAP screen) onto your Windows Clipboard and then paste the data into other SAP fields, or into other applications such as Word and Excel.

Moving Data

To move data from a field, highlight the text and press Ctrl+X, Ctrl+V.

The Cut (or Move) command is generally used on input fields.

Copying Data

To copy data from a field, highlight the text and press Ctrl+C, Ctrl+V.

The transferred data remains in the Clipboard until you use Cut or Copy again to move or copy new text onto the Clipboard.

Copying Unselectable Data

You are not able to select certain data displayed on SAP screens using your mouse and the methods previously described. To give you an example, return to your main SAP window and use the transaction code /nSE11 to travel to the SAP Data Dictionary Initial screen. Place your cursor in the Object Name field and select the F1 key to launch the field-specific help, as shown in Figure 20.17 (if you do not have access to transaction code /nSE11, place your cursor in any SAP field and select the F1 key on your keyboard.) A window will appear giving detailed definitions and technical information for the field you selected.

> The SAP Help system is covered in more detail in Hour 24, "SAP Resources."

By the Way

Try to use the mouse to select the text displayed on this screen. You will see that you are unable to select the data. In cases like these, you will need to add one more keyboard combination. Use your mouse to tap once anywhere on the screen. Next use Ctrl+Y to change your mouse to a crosshair cursor. Use this cursor to select the desired text and follow the same steps as before: Ctrl+C to copy the text, and Ctrl+V to paste the text.

FIGURE 20.17
Field-specific
help can be
accessed for
nearly any SAP
field by select-
ing the F1 key
on your
keyboard.

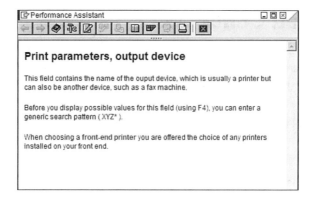

Creating Screen Prints from SAP

There might be times when you want to obtain a print or "screenshot" of an SAP
screen. Although the Print function is available on most SAP screens, there might be
an occasion when you want to print a copy of a status message (that appears on the
bottom-left corner of the window) that would not appear using the standard SAP
Print function.

To take a screen print of an SAP screen, perform the following steps:

1. Select the Print Screen button in the upper-right area of your keyboard. This
   stores a snapshot of your current screen in the Windows Clipboard.

2. Launch the Windows Paint application to paste the file for output. Follow the
   Windows menu path Start, Programs, Accessories, Paint to launch Windows
   Paint (or execute pbrush.exe from Start, Run).

3. On the Edit menu of the Paint application, select the Paste option (if you are
   prompted to enlarge the bitmap, choose OK).

Your screen print will now appear in the Windows Paint application. From here, you
can print or save it to a bitmap file on your computer for later reference. The same
kind of paste process can be applied in Microsoft Word if you simply need to save a
screen print, rather than potentially manipulating the image in Paint.

To save screen output (such as that found in a list) to a file on your desktop or the network, enter **%pc** on the command line and then press Enter. A print window pops up, defaulting to saving the screen's contents in an unconverted or XLS file format. Choose the format that's most appropriate (for example, XLS or RTF for Excel- or Word-based output, respectively), press Enter, browse to the desired directory path, type the name of the output file you want to create, and then click Save to save the list data to the filename you specified. This %pc functionality is also outlined in Hour 16, "Integrating SAP with Microsoft Office."

Summary

At this juncture, as a user you should feel very comfortable working in the SAP system. Many of the once-obscure objects, functions, and concepts should now be familiar. For instance, you should be well equipped to enter data into the SAP system, and you are quite familiar with the SAP objects that you will encounter on the different screens, including dialog boxes and radio buttons. You also should feel more comfortable with SAP terminology as it applies to screens and controls. You should also understand how to use the Windows Clipboard to store data as you move between screens and applications. Finally, a very important topic that we covered in this hour is the concept of retrieving print screens from the SAP system and then setting your preferences for printing using the SAP Print List screen.

Case Study: Hour 20

Consider the case study and questions that follow, which are related to using the SAPGUI and printing from SAP. The answers to these questions may be found in Appendix A, "Case Study Answers."

Situation

One of the SAP system administrators (also known as SAP Basis administrators) is on maternity leave and you have been asked to help out. You will need to run some of the common monitoring transactions as well as record performance data for later analysis.

Questions

1. Navigate the SAP menu to CCMS (Tools, CCMS). What type of screen object is the SAP menu structure?

2. Drill down to /nOS06 (Activity) using the menu path Control/Monitoring, Performance, Operating System, Local. How would you go about saving this information to an Excel spreadsheet?

3. Most basis transactions display data collected in the SAP database. Execute transaction /nST02 (Tune Summary). What type of structure are the buffer statistics displayed in?

4. Execute transaction /nSM04 (User List). How would you copy your terminal name to the Clipboard?

Customizing Your SAP Display

What You'll Learn in This Hour:

▶ How to select the best version of the SAP GUI

▶ How to customize the SAP front end to your specifications

▶ How to customize colors and fonts

▶ How to change the way SAP responds to you

Regardless of whether you are an SAP end user, a system administrator, or a manager of a team tasked with supporting or using SAP day to day, there will come a time when you want to customize the SAP user interface to your liking. With the basics under your belt from Hour 1, "What Is SAP?," and Hour 2, "SAP Basics: What It's All About," along with the knowledge you just gained from Hour 20, "SAP GUI Screen and Printing Basics," you are ready learn how to customize your SAP display. In this hour, we look at how to select the best interface for your needs, and then you'll learn how to manipulate the most popular graphical user interface for SAP, the SAP GUI for Windows, to your custom specifications.

Which SAP GUI Is Right?

With a number of flavors of the JavaGUI, the WebGUI, and the WinGUI at your disposal, a bit of insight is in order so that you can select the best user interface for your purposes (keeping in mind that often this decision is made by your company's IT management or business teams and, therefore, perhaps out of your hands). Take into consideration the following points when choosing a user interface:

▶ The SAP business functionality required by the end users.

▶ The average user's front-end client hardware platform (desktop and laptop specifics, including CPU speed, amount of RAM, and the amount of disk space available).

▶ The average user's front-end client operating system platform (Windows, UNIX, Linux, Mac OS).

▶ The network infrastructure servicing the users. (Don't forget about remote users—do they access SAP over a slow wide area network (WAN) link or even slower dial-up?)

▶ Installation ramifications. (Are there IT resources available to deploy the SAP GUI to each desktop or laptop, and then patch and maintain it?)

The following section describes some of the benefits and drawbacks of each SAP GUI flavor.

JavaGUI—SAP GUI for Java

For users of UNIX, Linux, and Mac OS, the JavaGUI might well be the only choice for connecting to and working with SAP. The JavaGUI supports Windows as well, including Windows Vista. The JavaGUI not only be can run as a standalone application but also as an applet in a web browser, providing the same functionality as the standalone solution. Support for Mac OS was less than desirable until SAP GUI 6.10. This and later versions have been working well, though—they install smoothly and offer the basic and advanced functionality seen in the SAP GUI for Windows.

Installation of the JavaGUI requires a Java Runtime Environment (JRE), which is simply a utility program that needs to be installed before the JavaGUI. After it's installed, the total desktop footprint (that is, disk space required on the desktop) is relatively small—depending on the platform about 20MB to 70MB is required for the JRE and about 40MB is required for the JavaGUI itself. And the product works well. It's as fast as the SAP GUI for Windows, and offers most of the functionality.

You can also run the SAP GUI for Java on 64-bit hardware (such as Itanium2 workstations) if there is a 32-bit Java Runtime Environment available for that specific hardware platform and operating system combination.

If the best description of your company's desktop environment or your own worksite conditions is "variable," you will do well to consider the JavaGUI. It operates in an identical manner on all supported platforms, despite its platform independence. It supports all SAP ERP transactions and it boasts an ultra-thin network protocol (it is very efficient). Other than several limitations such as the Office integration and limited drag-and-drop capabilities, it is comparable to the SAP GUI for Windows.

To obtain the latest version, or pull down older versions, see ftp://ftp.sap.com/pub/sapgui/java/. The .JAR files range from 20MB to 40MB—quite reasonable compared to the SAP GUI for Windows, and thus another reason to seriously consider the SAP GUI for Java.

WebGUI—SAP GUI for HTML

SAP introduced the user interface for HTML at the end of 1996, when R/3 3.1G was released along with another then-new product, Internet Transaction Server. Much has changed in the subsequent years, obviously, but the WebGUI is still an excellent interface to SAP. Originally, the WebGUI supported a number of browsers but supported perhaps only 90%–95% of SAP's user transactions out of the box. Today, the SAP GUI for HTML emulates the full features of the traditional SAP GUI with no real difference, except for the fact that a web browser is used. The latest SAP NetWeaver 7.0 Release supports both Microsoft Internet Explorer (IE) and the Firefox browser.

In the last few years, the SAP GUI for HTML has been much improved. Recent features and enhancements include:

▶ Timer Control is now supported with the SAP GUI for HTML

▶ SAP GUI for HTML can now be used to access Unicode systems

▶ Smaller network bandwidth is required

▶ Support for the vast majority of SAP transactions is included

▶ Improvements in the ALV grid helps match the behavior of the SAP GUI for Windows, creating a very consistent front-end experience for those end-users that find themselves using both

Because the hardware footprint is minimal (no disk space is necessary per se, assuming the web browser is already installed by default), the SAP GUI for HTML makes a lot of sense for many SAP users. Drawbacks exist though. The WebGUI does not support the same level of Microsoft Office integration as the SAP GUI for Windows, nor can it display interactive business graphics or support Drag and Drop mechanisms as supported by the WinGUI. Finally, until recently, the WebGUI moved 3–5 times the amount of network traffic than its Windows and Java counterparts executing the same SAP business transactions, making it the chunkiest (least efficient) member of the SAP GUI family from a network perspective (and therefore a bit slower than the others in terms of overall client performance).

WinGUI—SAP GUI for Windows

Because it is the most mature user interface offered by SAP, it comes as no surprise that a number of SAP GUI for Windows "flavors" are available. For years, the only option was the plain gray screen displayed in Figure 21.1, now called the "classic" SAP GUI for Windows. In typical German fashion, it was very functional. However, it was not known for its good looks.

FIGURE 21.1
The classic
SAP GUI.

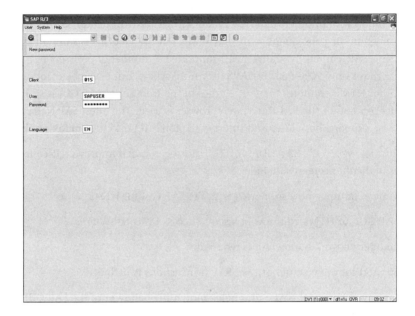

All that changed after Hasso Plattner, one of the founding engineers of SAP AG, toured a customer facility and was given such feedback personally. The result was EnjoySAP—a much more attractive and greatly updated interface, as seen in Figure 21.2. In the meantime, further designs have been added, such as Streamline and Tradeshow.

The space needed for a local installation is between 110MB up to 510MB, depending on whether Microsoft Office and Microsoft Internet Explorer need to be updated. Although the SAP GUI for Windows is quite resource intensive from a desktop footprint perspective, it is resource efficient when it comes down to network resource consumption. Like the SAP GUI for Java, the WinGUI boasts an ultra-thin network protocol as well.

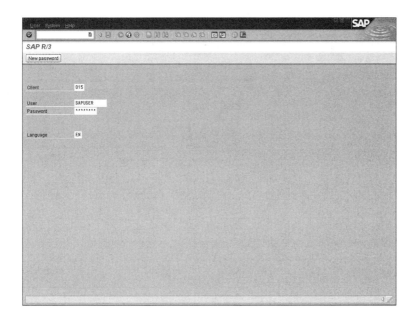

FIGURE 21.2
The EnjoySAP or
simply "Enjoy"
SAP GUI.

To easily obtain the latest SAP GUI for Windows, see ftp://ftp.sap.com/pub/sapgui/ win/. From here, select the version (for example, 710) and then select what you want to download. Typically, the latest compilation is available along with add-ons, patches, and scripting tools. Be prepared to download more than 400MB.

Change Visual WinGUI Appearance

The Tweak SAP GUI is a new tool SAP introduced with the latest version of the SAP GUI for Windows (SAP GUI 7.x). It is a standalone application and has its own icon on the Windows Desktop. The tool lets you change the visual appearance of the WinGUI. You can select from numerous different styles, and it lets you preview the changes you make.

Once you start the Tweak SAP GUI tool, you can see in the top-left corner the menu option Visual Design (see Figure 21.3). The Theme Selection item under Visual Design gives you the option to choose from several themes and lets you set the default theme for the WinGUI.

FIGURE 21.3
The Tweak SAP
GUI tool.

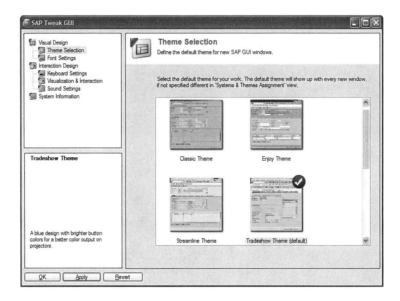

Enjoy

EnjoySAP, also known as Enjoy, has been the most popular SAP GUI flavor. A bit fatter than its predecessor in terms of desktop CPU and network bandwidth consumption, Enjoy initially suffered from performance issues primarily because it required more data to be moved per transaction than the classic SAP GUI. Old network infrastructures struggled with this requirement until SAP provided the option through the SAP Logon Pad to reduce or "throttle" the bandwidth back to a more bare-bones level. It does this by *not* sending bitmaps and other such "extras" that, although pleasant on a screen, require time to download and display. This low-speed connection throttling option is discussed in more detail in Hour 2.

Enjoy is heavier, at least initially, for another reason. Before EnjoySAP, functions such as navigating, scrolling, and searching used to require another network "roundtrip" between the desktop and SAP. With Enjoy, this roundtrip is eliminated, with the downside that a bit more traffic is generated up front. However, because subsequent navigation often requires no extra network traffic (there is more information on each SAP screen, often in tabbed format), Enjoy can be both fast and efficient in the long run. Enjoy is available for the JavaGUI as well as the SAP GUI for Windows. It also used to be available for the SAP GUI for HTML; however, it is no longer supported with the integrated ITS (Internet Transaction Server) 7.0.

Deploying the SAP GUI for Windows does not require special administrative rights; any user can install the product. And with SAP GUI for Windows support of common software management and distribution utilities (such as Microsoft SMS), you can easily deploy it across a globally dispersed enterprise.

High Contrast and Streamline

Intended for visually impaired users, the "High Contrast" theme was introduced to make the SAP GUI easier to read. This mode is helpful when working in dark hotel rooms or ill-lit offices, too, and is equally useful when creating screenshot-based documentation—the high-contrast mode makes for easy-to-read documents, both printed and on the screen.

When SAP GUI 6.30 was released, yet another new theme, called "Streamline," was introduced. Streamline helped create a uniform look and feel between the different GUIs, especially useful when multiple systems and user interfaces were involved. Its green-blue color mocks the default color scheme found in some versions of the WebGUI.

Tradeshow

Another edition to the standard SAP GUI stable of interfaces is called "Tradeshow." Released in 2003, Tradeshow is yet another easily readable interface because its strong SAP GUI controls contrast with a bright background.

It's easy to tell at a glance if you're running in Streamline or Tradeshow mode. Just look at the background color of a button. Light blue (almost gray) buttons indicate Streamline, whereas Tradeshow uses a light yellow color.

XP Design

The SAP GUI for Windows 6.40 introduced, among other new features, the support of the Windows XP desktop theme. As the name of the theme implies, its design is based on the Microsoft Windows XP style. It is quite nice for users with a penchant for desktop consistency.

The Customizing of Local Layout Button

In the top-right area of every SAP GUI for Windows screen, you can see a multi-colored button (next to the Question Mark Help button). Called the Customizing of Local Layout button, and informally referred to as the Customizing or Settings button, it gives you access to the menu options such as (see Figure 21.4):

▶ Options
▶ New Visual Design
▶ Set Color to System
▶ Clipboard
▶ Generate Graphic

▶ Create Shortcut
▶ Activate GuiXT
▶ Script Recording and Playback
▶ Script Development Tools
▶ SAP GUI Help

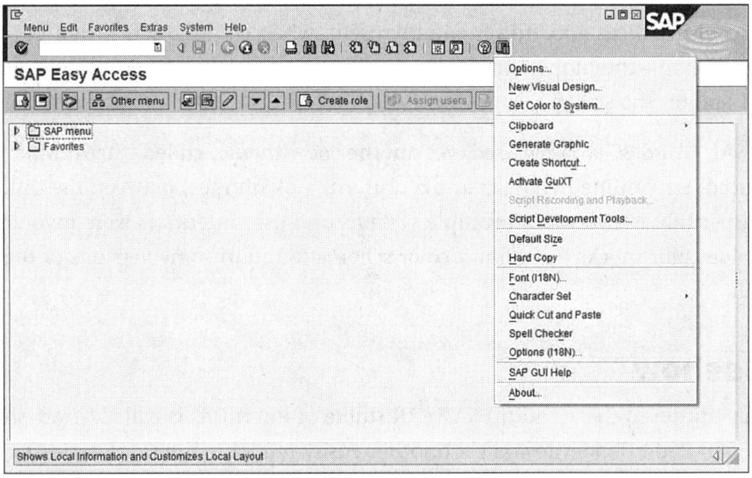

FIGURE 21.4
The Customizing of Local Layout button lets you change the appearance and functionality of your SAP screens, and it provides access to many features, simple tools, and utilities.

A number of the other menu options are self-explanatory, such as the spell checker, the character set selector, the ubiquitous About option, and so on. The About option is especially useful because it not only displays the version and patch level of the WebGUI, but it also identifies the version of each loaded DLL, provides system information details, and provides a button useful for saving this detail into a text file for safekeeping (see Figure 21.5).

From the Customizing menu, select Options. An Options window appears, similar to the one shown in Figure 21.6.

From this Options window, through the use of different tabs, you can perform the following actions:

▶ Define when dialog boxes pop up (with success, warning, and/or error messages) and whether such an action incurs a beep.

▶ Change the cursor width and enable a block cursor (for Overwrite mode).

▶ Specify your default working directory for local data (that is, data that you save from the SAP GUI via %pc or other means, discussed in later hours).

▶ Set Trace options.

▶ Set Scripting options.

FIGURE 21.5
Many valuable options and system insight are available from the SAP Version Information screen.

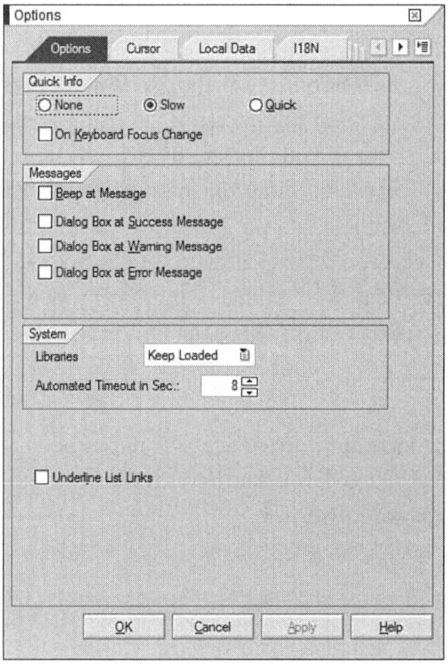

FIGURE 21.6
From the Options window, you can set up messages, adjust cursor settings, specify the directory used to save local data, and more—all through the various tabs.

The Options Tab

From the Options tab, you can change how the system notifies you of certain events and how quickly SAP Help is invoked. These used to be termed "general screen settings" in the days before EnjoySAP. It is important to note the default settings for this tab in case you are unhappy with any changes you make, so that you can easily restore your settings back to the defaults.

Quick Info

The Quick Info option controls how quickly the help information (simple description) launches whenever you place the pointer or cursor over an item in the button bar. For example, if you hover over the Customizing button for a period of time, you'll note that a description displays with the button's full name and its shortcut (in this case, Alt+F12). The Slow setting is indeed pretty slow; we recommend the Quick option. Users who tend to execute the same transactions daily should go with None.

There is also an option to enable On Keyboard Focus Change. With this option enabled, if you tab between buttons, for example, the help information is displayed as each button is highlighted. This setting is also useful when you are in new SAP territory. For users who tend to repeat many of the same functions over and over, this setting will grow tiresome.

Messages

These options enable you to configure how the SAP system presents you with information. The default setting is that any messages from the system appear in the status bar in the bottom-left area of your screen. By default, all messages pertaining to system output, warning messages, and error messages appear in the status bar. You can set these messages to appear in a pop-up box as well by selecting the appropriate box. Experienced users tend to keep none of these checked. Users new to a particular module, or with a critical need to ensure they don't miss an error message, should enable the Dialog Box at Error Message option.

System

This option refers to the location from where SAP retrieves its help files, along with a default timeout. It is best to leave this setting as it is; any changes need to be made and tested by the system administrator.

The Cursor Tab

The Cursor tab enables you to make custom setting changes to the position and appearance of your cursor. The default setting is usually best, as shown in Figure 21.7. In some cases, though, you might want to make modifications. You can change how the cursor is displayed in lists, for example, so that the cursor marks an entire column or simply one character. And the default cursor position or cursor width can be changed as well, as discussed next.

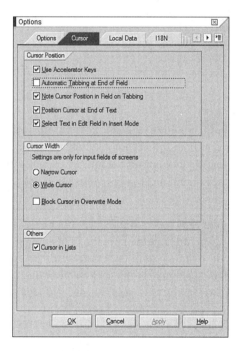

FIGURE 21.7
Your SAP cursor placement can have a big impact when you are doing a lot of data entry in your SAP system.

Cursor Position

With the Automatic Tabbing at End of Field option, you can determine whether the system automatically moves the cursor to the next input field when the cursor reaches the end of the current input field.

> For data entry, Automatic Tabbing (AutoTAB) is useful when you must enter data in many fields and you don't want to press the Tab key to move from field to field.

Did you Know?

In the SAP system, you can determine where you want the cursor to appear when you click in the blank area of an input field. The place where your cursor appears in an entry field is called the *cursor position*. You can change this setting so that your cursor automatically tabs to the end of a field (when you use the Tab key on your keyboard to navigate between fields). You can also set the cursor to appear exactly where you place it in the field, whether or not there are blank spaces. Options such as these and others are designed to make your SAP environment more user friendly and enable you to set the screen and placement of the cursor to your liking.

If you primarily work in tasks that require a great deal of data entry, it is helpful to place the cursor at the end of any text when you click anywhere behind the text. This is the SAP default setting. This way, when the input field is empty, the cursor appears at the beginning, enabling you to freely enter data without worrying about extra spaces in front of the cursor.

Cursor Width

Cursor Width is just what it sounds like: Use it to fatten up or thin down your cursor. And use the check box option in this section to enable Block Cursor in Overwrite mode, which enables you to block out all the text when replacing data in a field. This is handy for users who often must overwrite existing field data, because it saves time compared to pressing the Delete or Backspace key to clear a field.

If you wish to change your SAP system from Overwrite mode to Insert mode, press the Insert key on your keyboard. You then see the abbreviation in the bottom-right corner of your SAP window change from OVR to INS (see Figure 21.8). With each new session you create, the system defaults back to Overwrite mode.

The Local Data Tab

As illustrated in Figure 21.9, the Local Data tab lets you configure history and local cache settings, enable front-end security, and specify the default directory for any local data you choose to save in the course of conducting work with the SAP GUI. We find the defaults to be quite useful, although at times we change the local data directory to suit the needs of various SAP customer systems or sites.

The Trace Tab

The Trace tab has options that enable you to create a file to trace activity in the system. The settings under the Trace tab are managed by your system administrator in an effort to monitor and diagnose system concerns. Traces can be set to keep a record of errors and warning messages a user receives. In addition, traces are used to monitor where a user has been by keeping a file of each transaction code for each screen visited by the user.

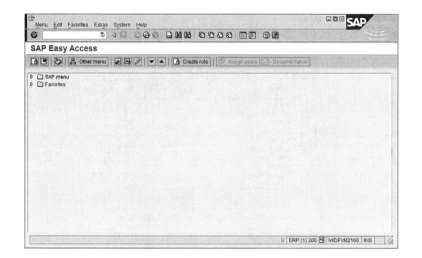

FIGURE 21.8
The Insert and Overwrite modes determine how text entry functions in SAP.

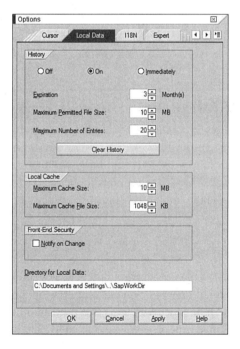

FIGURE 21.9
The Local Data tab is useful in configuring history and local cache settings as well as the default directory for saving local data.

Because such granularity in terms of what is traced is made available, the Trace tool is very powerful. As shown in Figure 21.10, a great number of SAP GUI controls, actions, and conditions can be traced. Use the Select All and Deselect All buttons to work through the list faster, keeping in mind that the more items that are traced, the greater the load placed on the front-end client machine.

FIGURE 21.10
The Trace tab is ideal for diagnosing system problems experienced by a user; its use has a negative performance impact on the speed of the system, however.

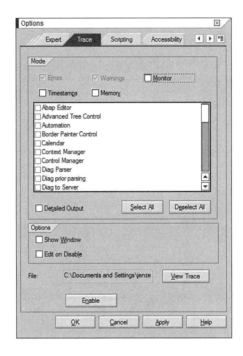

The Scripting Tab

SAP GUI scripting is a robust tool. Besides providing the interface for powerful load-testing tools to simulate real-world workloads, it also gives average users the capability to automate their daily work. SAP introduced SAP GUI scripting with SAP GUI for Windows Release 6.20. SAP GUI scripting is supported on R/3 4.6C and newer ECC and ERP systems, though, making it eminently useful.

Scripts are recorded, saved, and played back later. You can drop a script onto an SAP GUI screen and your script will start running. Scripting is only accessible through the SAP GUI for Windows and SAP GUI for Java interfaces, though. Further, if your screen changes (because of the introduction of a new SAP Support package, for example), your script might very well "break" and therefore need to be re-recorded. Although scripts can be shared between users, if a particular user is not allowed to execute a transaction, any script given him by his colleagues does not work for him.

Use the Scripting tab to first verify that scripting support is indeed available (as seen in Figure 21.11). Then enable it and select one of the two Notify options.

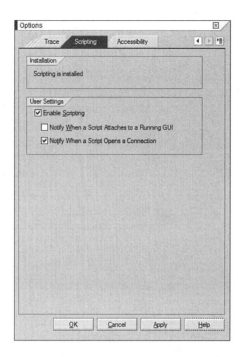

FIGURE 21.11
The Scripting tab lets you verify scripting is installed and enabled for your SAP GUI.

New Visual Design Selection

Beyond the Options selection, the Customizing button offers users great flexibility in configuring SAP GUI settings through the New Visual Design selection. This is accomplished through two tabs:

▶ The General tab

▶ The Color Settings tab

The General Tab

Within the General tab, a number of high-level options are available, as displayed in Figure 21.12. You can select the active theme or mode used by the SAP GUI, for instance. Selections include Enjoy, High Contrast, Streamline, Tradeshow, and System Dependent. You can easily change the font size from here as well (making additional changes to fonts is covered later in this hour). You can also enable or disable audio from the General tab.

FIGURE 21.12
The General tab
lets you make
high-level
changes to
the theme
employed by the
SAP GUI as well
as to the font
size and audio
status.

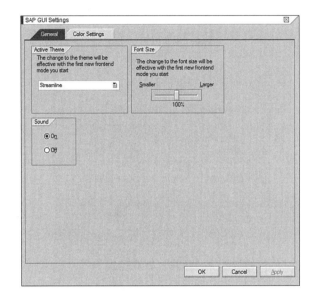

The Color Settings Tab

Like the General tab, the Color Settings tab lets you change the theme. The idea
here, though, is that the display within this particular window is changed in real
time, enabling you to see the impact that different selections and color settings have
relative to each theme. Given its maturity, it comes as no surprise that the Enjoy
option has the greatest number of color settings available. Use it to quickly walk
through different options, and then customize your display.

Clipboard Selection

Although rather simplistic, the Clipboard selection from the Customizing button's
drop-down menu gives you the ability to cut and paste items, and includes the
following commands:

- ▶ Select (Ctrl+Y)

- ▶ Cut (Ctrl+X)

- ▶ Copy (Ctrl+C)

- ▶ Paste (Ctrl+V)

Font Selection

You can make font configuration changes in a number of places. However, this particular selection, from the Customizing button, is the most powerful. Select Font, and from this window you can change the appearance and size of the fonts used in your SAP GUI. This option is most useful when your screen resolution varies from desktop to desktop, or monitor to monitor.

To change the font, perform the following steps:

1. Under the Font section, select one of the possible entries.

2. Under the Font Style section, choose regular, italic, bold, or bold italic.

3. Under the Size section, choose the font size.

As you make changes, a sample of text in the font and size you have chosen appears in the Preview box display. We suggest you document your default settings so that you can easily return to them. Finally, to get a true sense of the impact your font changes have on your screen, select OK.

Status Field's System Information Icon

At the bottom of the SAP GUI for Windows, you can click the small arrow (see Figure 21.13) to display or hide a set of status fields. These fields include the following:

▶ System

▶ Client

▶ User

▶ Program

▶ Transaction

▶ Response Time

▶ Interpretation Time

▶ Round Trips/Flushes

These fields are mutually exclusive, in that only one can be displayed at a time. We normally enable the response time tracker, although we occasionally use the transaction option when documenting a system's configuration or performance, or when working with an end-user helpdesk (so as to automatically capture the current transaction's T-code, such as MM02, in a screenshot).

The status field next to the System Information icon displays the server to which you are connected. Finally, the status field to the rightmost of the screen indicates your data entry mode—Insert (INS) or Overwrite (OVR).

FIGURE 21.13
Clicking the
small arrow at
the bottom-right
corner of the
screen alterna-
tively displays
and hides a set
of useful fields,
including the
System
Information
icon.

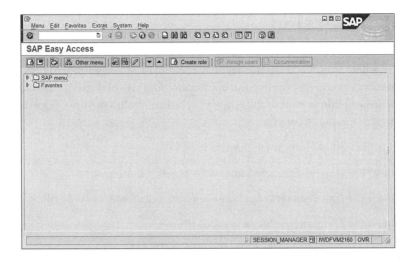

Summary

In this hour, you learned about the three primary flavors of the SAP GUI and how they are alike as well as different. You also learned how to customize your SAP front-end environment to best suit your needs, likes, or personality, including how different front-end themes can prove useful in different situations. From changing your system colors and fonts to customizing your SAP screens and enabling various options, the SAP GUI for Windows offers amazing flexibility. As you become more accustomed to working in your SAP system, you will find certain settings and other configuration changes to your liking.

Case Study: Hour 21

Consider this hour's case study regarding SAP GUI navigation and the questions that follow, the answers to which may be found in Appendix A, "Case Study Answers."

Situation

Congratulations! You have just been hired as the newest SAP Basis administrator for MNC. This is an exciting position in a very dynamic SAP environment because MNC runs nearly the entire SAP Business Suite—from SAP ERP and Enterprise Portal, to SAP Supply Chain Management, and more. After getting settled in, you have been asked to define a new SAP background job (using transaction SM36) in all seven SAP production systems. You have logged in to several of these production systems and currently have many different open WinGUI sessions.

Questions

1. How do you determine which SAP instance and which SAP client you are currently logged in to?

2. Working with several different SAP systems and SAP clients at the same time can be confusing. One option is to use different color settings for different WinGUI sessions in order to better track in which SAP system and SAP client you are working. Where are the color settings for the WinGUI changed?

3. When you make changes through the Customizing button, do they apply only for the current WinGUI session?

4. Which other feature of the SAP GUI for Windows will help you to keep track of in which SAP system and SAP client you are working?

Reporting and Query Basics

What You'll Learn in This Hour:

- ▶ Overview of the reporting options in SAP
- ▶ Introduction to variants
- ▶ Overview of background processing
- ▶ SAP reporting tools

This hour covers basic reporting concepts and introduces the SAP Information System, which contains the General Report Selection Tree. The other reporting options are discussed briefly. At the end of the hour, we wrap up with a more detailed discussion of the SAP reporting tools (SAP Query, InfoSet Query, Ad Hoc Query, and QuickViewer).

Reporting Tools

As detailed in earlier hours, SAP has the capability to support and manage all a firm's business processes and underlying data. Although this data is stored in the SAP system and can be presented on SAP screens, you might still want to produce printed or custom output from the system in the form of SAP reports. You can use reports to extract and manipulate the data from your SAP database; several methods are available to generate reports in SAP, including the following:

- ▶ ABAP List Processing (ABAP programming)
- ▶ ABAP Query Reporting
- ▶ Ad Hoc Query Reporting
- ▶ Structural Graphics Reporting
- ▶ Executive Information System
- ▶ SAP Information System (report trees)

ABAP List Processing (ABAP Programming)

Custom reports can be created in SAP by writing ABAP code to generate lists. This method is called List Processing. Using List Processing, ABAP programmers write statements in the ABAP Editor that query the database and generate reports. Writing reports using ABAP List Processing is therefore rather technical in nature and subsequently relegated most often to the post-Go-Live technical team.

This option becomes viable when you require a report that the canned reports cannot create. This option is also used for creating interface files, or files that provide input to (and thus feed) external systems. For example, if you need your SAP system to connect to an external enterprise system such as an outside third-party bolt-on product, you might consider using the ABAP List Processing method to write a report, the output of which is transmitted to the external system.

ABAP Query

You create custom reports in SAP by creating queries using the ABAP Query tool. ABAP queries are based on logical databases, functional areas, and user groups. Creating reports using ABAP Query is covered in more detail later in this hour.

Ad Hoc Query

The Ad Hoc Query is a reporting tool that was borne out of the original SAP ERP Human Resources functionality. Like the ABAP Query tool, it was initially based on logical databases, functional areas, and user groups. Like the name implies, ad hoc queries are used in an "ad hoc" manner to query your SAP database. The output from the query can then be formatted into a report. Creating reports using the most updated Ad Hoc Query functionality is also covered later in this hour.

Structural Graphics

Structural Graphics is an additional Human Resources tool used in the Organizational Management application component. This method enables you to display and edit the structures and objects in your organizational plan and to select reports directly from the graphical structure for an object.

Executive Information System

The Executive Information System is just what it sounds like: a reporting tool tailored for high-level decision-making. SAP also offers an entire SAP component—Strategic Enterprise Management, or SEM—to cull executive-level information specifically from SAP NetWeaver Business Information (BI). EIS is still useful, however, for users who require quick access to real-time information found in SAP ERP (and do not require the time and expense necessary to deploy SAP NetWeaver BI and SEM, the combination of which could easily consume a year's time and a large budget). Using the Executive Information System Report portfolio, you call up a hierarchy graphic defined for access to your own report portfolio. You can also use the Report selection, in which you call up either the general report tree of drill-down reports or your own custom tree. Or you can use the Report Portfolio report, in which you enter the name of an individual report portfolio and then display it.

The Executive Information System provides you with information that presumably addresses key factors that influence the business activities within your company. It combines relevant data from external and internal sources, providing you with a view into real-time data that can then be quickly analyzed to make sound decisions.

SAP Information System (Report Trees)

Most of the reports you need are available within each module. That is, each module contains its own Information System that houses reports specific to that module. In earlier hours, you reviewed some of these module-specific Information Systems. One example is the SAP ERP Human Resources Information System. Note that you can access all canned SAP reports via the general SAP Information System.

General Report Selection

SAP has many tools within SAP ERP and other components used to extract and then present data in the form of reports. Basic reporting capabilities are afforded through transaction code /nSART or by navigating via the menu path Information Systems, General Report Selection. Note that in the newest SAP releases, SART is not available directly; instead, you must navigate through the menu paths to select a particular functional area, and from there select a particular report.

Report trees are hierarchical structures that can contain standard SAP reports, your organization's custom reports, and lists generated by executing certain reports. General Report Selection is structured as a hierarchy containing the following four levels:

▶ The top level contains the individual SAP system applications.

▶ The second level contains the work areas of each application.

▶ The third level contains the objects of each work area.

▶ The fourth level generally contains the reports and saved lists available for each object.

SAP ERP ships preconfigured with canned reports for every functional area (FI, MM, and so on). You can modify the general reporting structure according to your company's specific needs. For example, if you are installing and configuring only the SAP ERP Financials components, you might want to remove the HR reports from your General Report Selection screen. You customize the General Report Selection reporting tree using the Implementation Guide (IMG). The IMG is discussed in Hour 13, "Development Tools and Methodologies."

Executing Reports

You can execute reports directly from the General Report Selection screen. Depending on the modules currently installed on your system, different reports are available to you. To execute a common HR report within SAP ERP, for example, drill down into the report tree as follows:

1. Expand the Human Resources node.

2. Expand the Payroll node.

3. Expand the Americas node.

4. Expand the USA node.

5. Expand the Payroll node.

6. Double-click one of the reports, such as the Simulation or Start Payroll report.

Double-clicking the report icon launches the selection screen for the report. Selection screens are used by most SAP reports to enable an end user to clarify the output desired by entering precise input data (such as a payroll period, personnel number, reason for running a particular payroll cycle, and so on).

Once the input data is provided, you execute the report by selecting the Execute button from the toolbar. The Execute button is equivalent to the F8 function key on the keyboard. After you click the button or press F8, the report will execute and output will appear on the screen. This output can be viewed, saved electronically in RTF or XLS format by executing %pc in the transaction dialog box, or printed in the more traditional manner.

Depending on your system's configuration and your own set of authorizations or "permissions" within the system, different reports will be available to you. For example, if you have not installed and configured the Human Resources module, or are not authorized to work within the HR system, you will be unable to execute most of the Human Resources reports (if not all of them).

Take a minute to practice executing different reports from the General Report Selection Tree. If you have trouble determining specific input criteria necessary to execute a particular report, work with the functional lead, developer, or power user associated with that functional area.

Report Attributes

To take a look at the attributes of a particular report in the General Report Selection Tree, select the report once using your mouse and then follow the menu path Edit, Node Attributes. A window appears similar to the one shown in Figure 22.1. The window provides basic details about the report, including the report type, technical name of the underlying executable program, report description, and variants (if any).

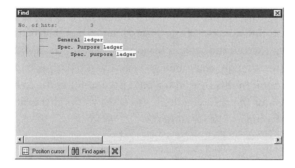

FIGURE 22.1
SAP's Report Attributes window gives you additional information about the selected report.

Searching for Reports

The General Selection Tree has a search function in which you can enter search criteria and search for a report based on its name. From any starting point in the tree, use the menu path Edit, Find, Node. You will be presented with an SAP Find dialog box like the one shown in Figure 22.2. Enter your search criteria (for this example, enter the word **ledger**).

FIGURE 22.2
Use SAP's General Report Selection Tree to search for reports.

After you type your search criteria in the Find box and click the Find button, a new Find window displays the results of your search. The new window includes hot keys (sometimes referred to as *hypertext* in SAP documentation) that link the text to the corresponding reports so that you can jump directly to the report. If no reports matched your search criteria, you receive a message box indicating something to the effect that the search has proven unsuccessful.

Selection Screens

As mentioned earlier, you will be presented with selection screens when you execute an SAP report. The selection screens are quite useful in delimiting precisely which output you are hoping to yield. Otherwise, the data processed in a report often proves so plentiful that the report output becomes too large to be meaningful. For example, if you wanted to generate a list of all open purchase orders in your SAP system, you can execute a report listing your company's purchase orders and indicate on the selection screen that you only want to display orders with the status of Open. In some cases, though, each time you execute a report, you are looking for the same specific data. In this case, you would need to fill in the selection fields on the selection screen for the data you desire. To assist you in this task, SAP makes use of a concept called *variants*, discussed next.

Variants

A *variant* is a group of selection criteria values that has been saved to be used again and again. If you want to run a report using the same selection criteria each time, you can create a variant to save the data that you filled in on your selection screen. The next time you execute the report, you only need to enter the variant name, rather than re-enter the individual values in each of the selection criteria fields.

If you use variants, the selection screen for the report does not appear at all. The report can also be preset to execute with the variant automatically so that no data needs to be filled in at all. A report can have several variants, with each variant retrieving different types of information. For example, a purchase order report might have one variant to retrieve all open purchase orders for your company and another variant used to display purchase orders for a specific vendor only. Use SAP's Save As Variant screen to save your selection criteria as a variant.

Variants are largely used for background execution of reports that tend to run a long time, and therefore are often scheduled to run behind the scenes. Variants are also used simply for convenience; if you tend to look at the same data day in and day out, but require a fresh view into this data, the use of variants can save a considerable amount of time. And with SAP's capability to schedule reports to run at certain times of the day, month, or year, executing a transaction using a variant is simple indeed.

Modifying Variants

From SAP's General Report Selection main screen, select a report that has variants available for it and then follow the menu path Goto, Variants. This brings you to the ABAP: Variants – Initial screen, similar to the one shown in Figure 22.3.

Indicates the report's program name

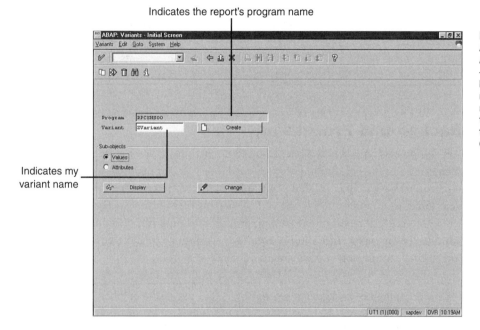

Indicates my variant name

FIGURE 22.3
Access the ABAP: Variants – Initial screen by selecting a report in the report tree and then following the menu path Goto, Variants.

From the ABAP: Variants – Initial screen, you can create new variants and modify existing variants. For example, you can enter the name of an existing variant, select the Values subobject, and then click the Change button. This brings you to the selection screen for the report, which enables you to modify the selection criteria for your variant. You can also select the Attributes subobject and click the Change button, which brings you to the Save As Variant screen for the report. This screen enables you to modify the name, description, and attributes for your variant. On this screen, you can also specify additional variant criteria, some of which is displayed in Table 22.1.

TABLE 22.1   Additional Variant Attributes

Attribute	Description
Only for background processing	Reports can be generated in the background. Selecting this option specifies that the variant can only be executed in the background. Otherwise, if this option is unselected, the variant can be run both in the background and in the foreground (online).
Protect variant	If this field is selected, the variant can be changed only by the person who created or last modified it. This protects your variant from being modified by other people.
Only display in catalog	If this field is selected, the variant name appears in the directory, but not in the general input help.
System variant	This box is reserved for system variants (automatic transport).

Background Processing

You can process reports in the background and, perhaps more important, schedule them to run in the background at predefined intervals. For example, you can have a scheduled background job that prints a list of all the new invoices issued through your Purchasing application at the end of each business day. A background job specifies the ABAP report or external program that should run, together with any variants for the report, including start time and printing specifications. The scheduling of jobs is a function of your system administrator.

Did you Know?

A key advantage of background processing is that the report or job is started in the background by SAP, and therefore does not impact online users in the same way it otherwise might—many of the resources used to execute jobs in the background are distinct and different from those used to host online users. Thus, the performance of both the batch job or report and the online user response time wind up being much improved (compared to executing a long-running report in the foreground).

Lists

After generating a report in SAP, you can save the output as a list. On all report output screens, list options are available that enable you to save the file in Office, a report tree, or to an external file. Saving the report as an external file is covered in more detail in Hour 16, "Integrating SAP with Microsoft Office." In that hour, we discuss how you can work with your SAP data using Microsoft Office products such as Excel and Word.

Saving the list using the menu path List, Save, Office enables you to save the report output in a folder. It also gives you the chance to email the output through SAP's email interface. Finally, you also have the option of saving the generated list to a reporting tree.

Did you Know?

> It is important to note the distinction between a report and a list. A report generated at any time in the system contains real-time data at the time of generation. A list is saved output from a previously generated list and does not reflect the real-time data in your SAP ERP system. In other words, lists are static, whereas reports are dynamic.

SAP Reporting Tools (SAP Query, InfoSet Query, Ad Hoc Query, and QuickViewer)

In the earliest versions of SAP, two tools were delivered for end-user reporting. The ABAP Query was designed for all modules and the Ad Hoc Query was designed exclusively for the Human Capital Management module. The ABAP Query is now called the SAP Query and its features have been enhanced. Additionally, the Ad Hoc Query tool can now be used with all modules in SAP under the name the InfoSet Query (although in the Human Capital Management module SAP still refers to it as the Ad Hoc Query). Both reporting tools enable you to create reports within your SAP environment and neither requires any technical skills. Additionally, SAP introduced another tool called the QuickViewer. In this section, you learn how to create custom reports using these reporting tools, including the necessary configuration and administrative decisions to get you on your way.

The Structure of the Query Reporting Tools

The query tools (SAP Query, InfoSet/Ad Hoc Query, and QuickViewer) are built on the foundation of three main components:

- ▶ Query groups (/nSQ03)
- ▶ InfoSets (/nSQ02)
- ▶ Administrative decisions (company specific)

Each of these components permits a user with no technical programming skills to create custom reports. The overview of the query tool structure is depicted in Figure 22.4.

FIGURE 22.4
The SAP family
of query report-
ing tools gives
users easy
access to the
database via
query groups
and InfoSets.

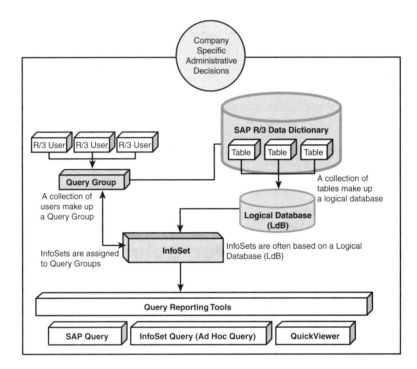

If you think about custom reporting in SAP in layman terms, you picture a programmer sitting down at a terminal and typing lines and lines of ABAP code that go to the core SAP database to collect the information needed for the report. The programmer also has to code to account for security access, output, formatting, and so on. The purpose of the SAP delivered query tools is that all the work is done for you behind the scenes. The use of the three main components holds it all together.

Query Groups

Let's start with the first component, query groups (formerly known as user groups in earlier versions of SAP). The technical definition of *query groups* is a collection of SAP users who are grouped together. A user's assignment to a user group determines which queries he or she can execute or maintain. Additionally, it designates which InfoSets (data sources) the user can access. Basically, query groups permit users to create, modify, and execute reports in a certain area within SAP ERP. For example, you can create a query group for the Finance department that includes your financial users; similarly you can create a query group for the Human Resources department that contains reports specific to Human Resources. Query groups are an easy way to group and segregate your reports.

Query groups are often maintained by the system administrator. Query groups are created on the Maintain Query Groups screen, which you can access using the transaction code /nSQ03. Users can belong to multiple query groups and might, under certain circumstances, copy and execute queries from other query groups (only if the permissions are the same). Any user within a user group has authority to execute queries that are assigned to that group, but only users with the appropriate authorization can modify queries or define new ones. Users cannot modify queries from other query groups. Although the maintenance of query groups is usually a task for your system administrator, we show how to create a sample user group later in this section.

InfoSets

InfoSets (known as *functional areas* in early versions of SAP R/3) are the second component of SAP reporting. InfoSets are created on the Maintain InfoSets screen, which you can access using transaction code /nSQ02. Based on the technical definition, InfoSets are areas that provide special views of logical databases and determine which fields of a logical database or data source can be evaluated in queries. Basically, an InfoSet is the data source; it's where you get your data to use in your reports. InfoSets can be built on a variety of sources, but the most common is the use of what is known as a *logical database (LdB)*. Recall that writing reports without query tools requires a programmer to write code that goes into the main SAP ERP database and retrieves the records it needs. This is no easy skill. SAP's answer to this issue is the logical database.

Logical databases are rational prearranged groupings of data from multiple related tables that are indexed. In layman's terms, logical databases place all the fields you want to report in an easy container from which you simply select the fields you need to include in your report. An overview of the relationship between these different elements is shown in Figure 22.4. Although the maintenance of InfoSets is usually a task for your system administrator, you learn how to create a sample InfoSet later in this section.

Depending on your SAP authorization privileges, you might need to request assistance from your system administrator in creating a test query group, functional area, and query. It is also possible, if you are working with a newly installed SAP system, that you will receive a message saying you must convert objects first. If you receive this message, contact your system administrator. He or she will be required to perform a standard administration function to convert the objects before you can proceed.

Did you Know?

Administrative Decisions

As you will soon learn, creating query groups and InfoSets is an easy task. Before you begin, you must first review the following administrative decisions to see which best applies to your organization:

▶ What is your client/transport strategy?

▶ Will you use the standard or global query area?

What Is Your Client/Transport Strategy?

With custom-coded ABAP reports written by programmers, the traditional methodology for report creation is as follows: A programmer accesses a development environment where the first draft of the custom report is coded. The report is then transported to a testing client where it is tested. Assuming it passes testing, the report then moves on to your production environment for use. This methodology differs from the strategy often used with the query family of reporting tools. The addition of the query tools to SAP enables end users to create reports in real time with no technical skills. It is with this in mind that your organization has to make a decision regarding your transport strategy.

The creation of query objects can be performed in any client. However, there are some best practices you should follow. For starters, end users who will be using the query tools often only have user IDs in the live production environment. Therefore, many companies maintain query groups live in the production client.

Similarly, InfoSets can be created in any client; however, best practice dictates that InfoSets be treated inline with normal programming methodology. It's best to create InfoSets in a development environment and then transport them to a testing client, where they are tested and then moved on to production for use. InfoSets are treated differently because a trained user has the capability to add special coding or programs to InfoSets (outside the scope of this book) that can have an impact on system resources or functioning, and testing them is required in those cases. That leaves the reports (queries) themselves. Unlike custom-coded ABAP reports, query reports are designed to be made in real time in an ad hoc fashion, so the best practice is to create your queries live in your production environment.

Will You Use the Standard or Global Query Area?

Query areas (formerly known as *application areas* in versions earlier than 4.6) contain your ABAP Query elements, queries, functional areas, and query groups. There are two distinct query areas in SAP:

▶ **Standard query areas**—Standard query areas are client specific, which means they are available only within the client in which they were created. For example, if you created a standard query in the production client, it exists only in the production client. You can transport query objects created in the standard area between multiple clients on the same application server via the Transport Truck function on the main InfoSets screen (/nSQ02). This bypasses the customary Workbench Organizer.

▶ **Global query areas**—Queries designed in the global area are used throughout the entire system and are client independent. SAP delivers many of its standard reports in the SAP global query area. These queries are also intended for transport into other systems and are connected to the ABAP Workbench. A common best practice is to allow SAP to continue to deliver reports via the global area and for end users to use the standard query area to create query-related reports. With your administrative decisions completed, you are ready to begin the configuration.

Creating a New User Group

To create a new user group, perform the following steps:

1. Navigate to the Maintain User Group screen using transaction code /nSQ03.

2. Ensure that you are in the standard query area by following the menu path Environment, Query Areas, and then selecting Standard Area (client-specific).

3. Type the user group name that you will be creating, **ZTEST**, and select the Create button (see Figure 22.5).

4. Type a name for your user group on the User Group ZTEST: Create or Change screen, as shown in Figure 22.6, and then select the Save button.

5. A message appears in your SAP GUI status bar stating that the user group ZTEST has been saved.

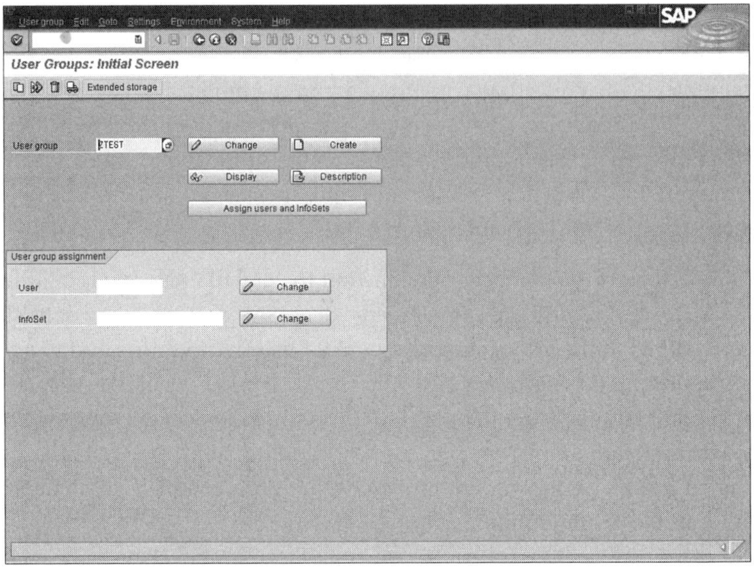

FIGURE 22.5
SAP query
groups are cre-
ated and modi-
fied using User
Groups: Initial
screen.

FIGURE 22.6
Enter the name
for your user
group in the
User Group
ZTEST: Create
or Change
screen.

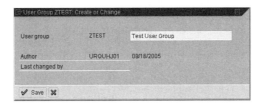

6. Select the Assign Users and InfoSets button. Type the SAP user IDs of any users
you want to include in your test group. Be sure to include your own user ID
(see Figure 22.7).

7. Save the entry by selecting the Save button from the toolbar. A message
appears in your SAP GUI status bar stating that user group ZTEST was saved.

Now that you have created a user group, the next step is to create an InfoSet.

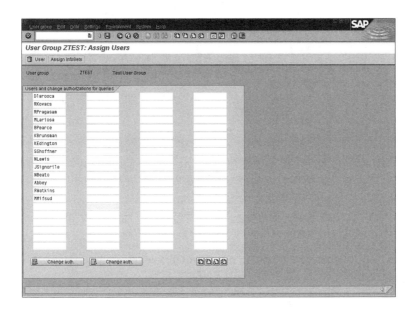

FIGURE 22.7
In your newly created user group, be sure to add your own user name.

Creating a New InfoSet

To create a new InfoSet, perform the following steps:

1. Navigate to the Maintain InfoSets screen using the transaction code /nSQ02.

2. Ensure that you are in the standard query area by following the menu path Environment, Query Areas, and then selecting Standard Area (client-specific).

3. Type the InfoSet name you will be creating, **ZTEST**, and select the Create button.

4. On the InfoSet: Title and Database screen, you are asked to input a description for your InfoSet. This example uses the name Test InfoSet. As mentioned earlier, you can create InfoSets using a variety of sources. The most common is the logical database. On this screen, select the F1S logical database from the drop-down box to be used as your data source (see Figure 22.8).

You can create InfoSets from various data sources, including logical databases, tables, table joins, and so on. The best business practice is to use the SAP delivered logical databases as your data source, because they were created for this purpose and there is at least one logical database delivered with your system for each module within SAP, including Accounting, Personnel Management, and so on.

Did you Know?

FIGURE 22.8
On this screen, select the F1S logical database from the drop-down box.

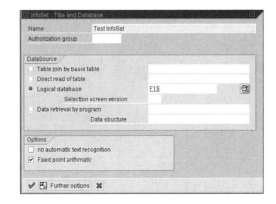

The F1S database used in this example is the training database that SAP uses in its training classes based on a fictional airline scheduling system. It is best to use this database for your test cases.

5. After entering a name and selecting the appropriate logical database from the drop-down list (in this case, F1S), select the green check mark to continue.

6. You are presented with a screen similar to the one shown in Figure 22.9. It lists the tables stored in the logical database F1S.

FIGURE 22.9
The Change InfoSet screen displays a list of all tables stored in your InfoSet.

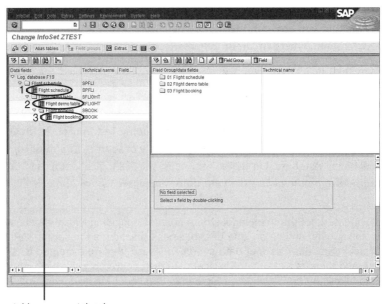

Three tables are contained within the logical database F1S.

7. The logical database F1S selected is a test logical database containing three test tables: SPFLI, SBOOK, and SFLIGHT. To take a look at the fields in these tables, use the Expand Sub Tree button listed next to each table name (see Figure 22.10).

Table names   Field groups

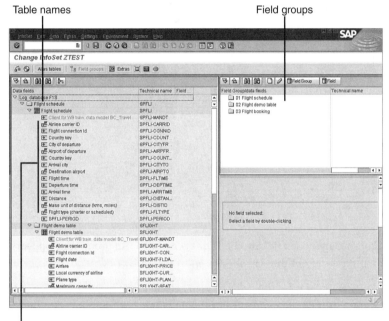

FIGURE 22.10
The Change InfoSet screen with expanded subnodes showing the fields available in each table.

Field names

8. The next step is to assign fields to the field groups (shown at the top-right of your screen) within your InfoSet. These field groups appear in your query tools while reporting. Only the fields that you include in your field groups are available for field selection in your query-reporting tools that use this InfoSet as its data source. By default, these field groups are empty (noted exception follows).

For nearly all modules in SAP, field groups are empty; you need to manually move fields to them. The exception is the Human Capital Management module and the InfoSets that support it. The field groups in this module are created for you with a default set of fields, though you may add additional information if required.

Did you Know?

9. Place your cursor on the first field group, Flight Schedule, and then select fields from the left side of the screen from the Flight Schedule table and add them to the Flight Schedule field group. Place your cursor on a field on the left side of the screen and right-click the option Add Field to Field Group (see Figure 22.11).

FIGURE 22.11
The Change InfoSet screen with expanded tables showing the fields available in each table.

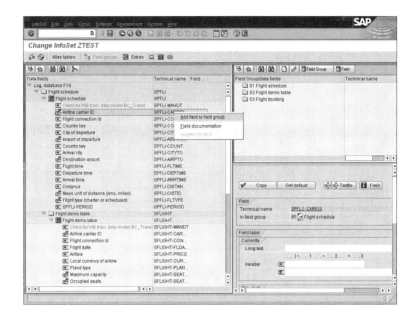

10. Your newly added field to the Flight Schedule Field group now appears at the top-right area of the screen (as seen in Figure 22.12).

11. The next step is to add fields to your selected field group following the procedures outlined previously. Select the field group with your cursor and then move fields from the left side of the screen to the right using the procedure outlined previously. Be sure to add fields to the appropriate field group. For example, you can add the fields in the Flight Schedule table to the Flight Schedule field group, or add fields from the Flight Booking table to the Flight Booking field group.

12. Now that you have added a series of fields to your field groups, select the Save button from the toolbar. A message appears in the status bar saying that the InfoSet ZTEST was saved.

13. Next, you need to generate the InfoSet by selecting the Generate button (the red beach ball) from the application toolbar. A message appears in the status bar saying that the InfoSet ZTEST was generated. The process of generating your InfoSet determines whether any errors are present in the logic of the configuration of the InfoSet.

14. The last step is to exit the Maintain InfoSet screen by selecting the green back arrow.

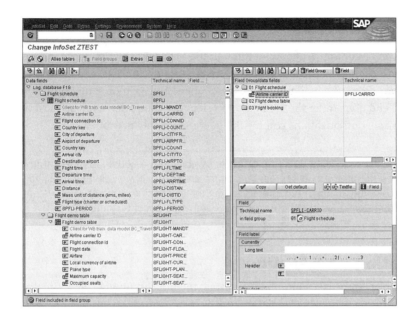

FIGURE 22.12
The field group
Flight Schedule
now has a field
in it that is
available for
reporting with
the query family
of tools.

Assigning the InfoSet to Your Query Group

You have now accomplished the first two configuration steps: You have created both
a query group and a follow-on InfoSet. The last step before you begin creating
reports is to assign the InfoSet to your query group. This is an easy two-step task:

1. From the InfoSet: Initial screen (transaction code /nSQ02), make sure your
   InfoSet ZTEST is present in the InfoSet text box and select the User Group
   Assignment button.

2. From the InfoSet ZTEST: Assign to Query Groups screen, highlight your query
   group name by selecting the gray button to the left of it and then select the
   Save button.

   A message appears in the status bar saying that the assignment of the InfoSet
   ZTEST was saved.

Note that some of the SAP screens and SAP Help text still use the "functional
area" moniker instead of InfoSet or refer to query groups by their old name, user
groups. Just be aware of this. You can also assign the InfoSet to a query group by
using the Maintain User Groups screen (/nSQ03) and by selecting the Assign
Users and InfoSets button from the toolbar and selecting your InfoSet from a list.

Did you
Know?

SAP Queries

Create and maintain SAP queries through the Maintain Queries screen, accessible via transaction code /nSQ01. Unlike query groups and InfoSets, which are often maintained by system administrators, SAP queries are primarily maintained by trained end users (after the configuration steps are complete). Only users with the appropriate authorizations can modify queries or create new ones.

> Security for managing query reporting is available on a couple of different levels. Besides the user group segregation, there are also authorization group specifications. Security configurations are very customer specific; contact your systems administrator to learn more about your company's security configuration.

Creating an SAP Query

With the one-time configuration completed, the fun can finally begin. Creating an SAP query is a relatively elementary task. To begin creating your first SAP query, follow these steps:

1. Navigate to the Maintain Queries Initial screen using the transaction code /nSQ01. A graphical version of the SAP Query is available called the Graphical Query Painter. If you have not used the query tool, this will be set as your default. To turn it off and learn to create easy step-by-step reports, follow the menu path Settings, Settings and deselect the Graphical Query Painter check box.

2. The title bar will list the query group you are currently in. For example, your screen might read Query of User Group ZTEST: Initial Screen. (If you are assigned to multiple user groups, you can see a list of the groups by selecting Shift+F7.)

3. It is always a good idea to ensure that you are in the standard query area by following the menu path Environment, Query Areas and selecting Standard Area (client-specific).

4. In the Query field, type a name for the query you are creating (in this example, **ZMYQUERY**) and select the Create button.

5. The InfoSets of User Group ZTEST window will list all the available InfoSets for your query group. Select the ZTEST InfoSet followed by the Enter key to proceed.

6. You are now presented with the Create Query Title Format screen, which enables you to save the basic formatting specifications for your query, including the name (title) and any notes you want to store for the query. The only required field is the title (see Figure 22.13).

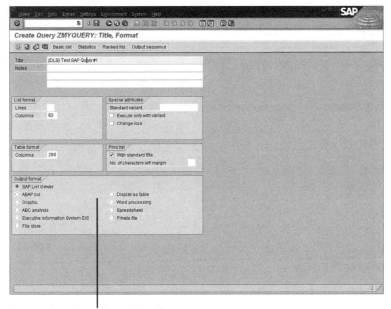

The further processing options listed here are the same as the options that appear on the selection screens when you execute SAP delivered reports.

FIGURE 22.13
You enter the title, format, and processing options for your query on the Create Query Title Format screen.

7. After entering a title, select the Save button on the toolbar. To navigate to the next screen in the SAP query-creation process, select the next screen (white navigational arrow) button from the application toolbar. You can use these navigational arrows to navigate between the different screens of the SAP Query.

8. A screen will appear listing all the field groups available within your InfoSet (in this example, you can see Flight Schedule [SPFLI], Flight Demo Table [SFLIGHT], and Flight Booking [SBOOK]). Place a check mark next to all field groups from which you want to include fields in your report. Select the next screen (white navigational arrow) button from the application toolbar.

9. A Select Field screen will appear (see Figure 22.14), giving you a list of all the available fields within the field groups you selected. Place a check mark next to all fields you want to include in your report. You can use the Page Up and Page Down arrows to navigate between all the fields. Select the next screen (white navigational arrow) button from the application toolbar to continue.

FIGURE 22.14
Use the Page Up and Page Down arrows to navigate between all the fields.

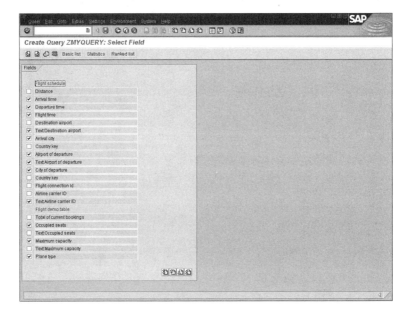

10. You are now presented with the Selections screen, which lists all the fields you have selected. You can now add any of the fields to the selection screen that appears when you execute your report. This enables you to specify your report output when the report is executed. You can add any fields you want to the Selection screen by placing a check mark next to each field. This is the last screen in the basic query sequence; to continue, select the Basic List button from the application toolbar.

11. The Basic List screen shows you a list of the selected fields you want to include for your report. For each field, you can specify the Line and Sequence number as you want them to appear on your report. Additionally, you can use this screen to indicate sort order, totals, and counts, if needed. Start by entering the Line and Sequence numbers like the ones displayed in Figure 22.15.

Line corresponds to the line number
the field appears on in the report.

Sequence determines the order
the fields appear on for the line.

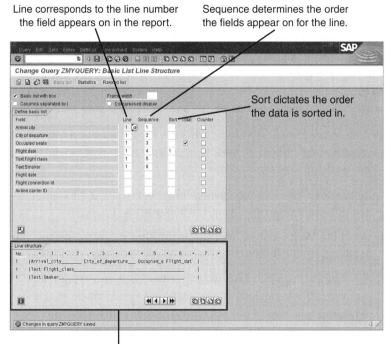

Sort dictates the order
the data is sorted in.

FIGURE 22.15
Basic output
options are
defined on the
SAP Query
Basic List
screen.

After selecting the Save button, a preview of the format
appears in the Line Structure box at the bottom of the screen.

12. For this basic SAP Query example, you will proceed directly to the report.
Select the F8 button from the application toolbar to execute the report.

13. You are presented with the report's selection screen. The selection screen gives
you an opportunity to specify any criteria for the output of your report. Select
the Execute button again to display the report. Your report output should
appear similar to Figure 22.16 (the output of the report corresponds to the
specification entered in the basic list screen).

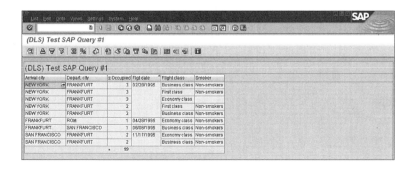

FIGURE 22.16
In version 4.6
and higher, your
report displays
in the SAP list
viewer, as
shown in the
picture.

Advanced SAP Queries

You have created a basic query using the SAP Query tool. Before you start investigating the more advanced options available in ABAP Query, it's a good idea to try creating a few queries using different InfoSets (based on different logical databases). To do this, you need to start from the section "Creating a New InfoSet" earlier this hour, select a different logical database, and then assign it to your query group.

When you become familiar with the SAP Query tool, you will want to try some of its more advanced options. To investigate the advanced options available for processing your queries, follow these steps:

1. Navigate to the Maintain Queries Initial screen using the transaction code **/nSQ01** and select one of your existing queries.

2. Select the Modify button followed by the Basic list button on the application toolbar from the Basic List screen.

3. You can use the next screen (white navigational arrow) button from the application toolbar to navigate to the additional seven screens that house the more advanced functions of the SAP Query, including the following:

   ▶ **Grouping, sorting, and subtotaling**—You can group, sort, and subtotal your SAP data onto reports and modify your subtotal texts. For example, you can create a report listing all open purchase orders and their amounts grouped by vendor and location with custom-named subtotals (see Figure 22.17).

   ▶ **Manipulating colors and texts**—You can manipulate the colors and text styles of the different data presented on reports. For example, your report can contain subtotals in yellow, group totals in green, and individual line items in boldface red text.

   ▶ **Alter the column widths, add colors, hide leading zeros**—You can manipulate the layout of the report output to be used in interfaces or flat file transfers (see Figure 22.18).

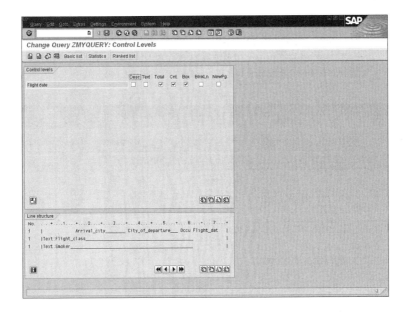

FIGURE 22.17
The Control Levels screen enables you to do sorting and subtotaling, as well as special formatting in your SAP Query report.

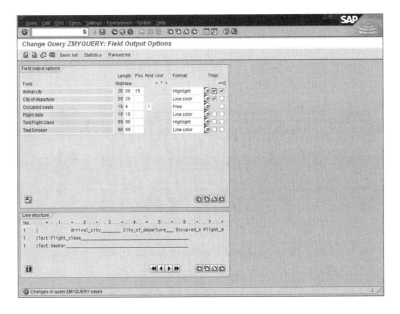

FIGURE 22.18
The Field Output Options screen enables you to vary the column width of your fields or can be used simply to make your report output look better.

▶ **Custom headers and footers**—You can create custom headers and
footers to be shown on each page of your printed reports. Your report
can include the name of the report and the date and time it was created
at the top of each printed page (see Figure 22.19).

FIGURE 22.19
You can use
special symbols
to insert the
current date,
time, and page
numbers in your
custom headers
and footers.

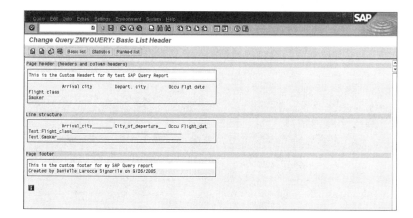

▶ **Charts and graphics**—You can include graphics and create charts of
your SAP data on reports. You can create a bar graph displaying the
open items currently available in your warehouse in comparison to the
items sold (see Figure 22.20).

FIGURE 22.20
Charts appear
in full color
using SAP busi-
ness graphics.

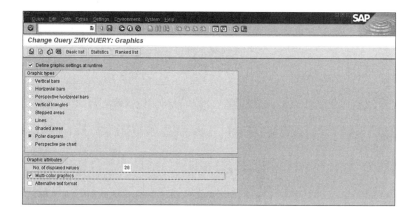

> You can also create calculated fields in your queries to be used in your SAP Query reports. Calculated fields can be used to include variables that are not currently stored by SAP. Examples include a calculated field to store an invoice amount multiplied by a discount percentage or a calculated field to change output based on a number you enter on the Reports Selection screen. You can also create advanced calculated fields using "if-then" type logic. This is performed by using the Local Fields function on the Select Fields screen.

Understanding the InfoSet (Ad Hoc) Query

Unlike the SAP Query, which is a complete reporting solution tool, the InfoSet Query is designed for basic users to retrieve simple single-use lists of data from your SAP ERP database. Using this tool, all query information (including the selection criteria) is available on a single screen. Since version 4.6, the Human Capital Management module-reporting tool, called the Ad Hoc Query, was combined with the technology of the SAP Query and made available for all modules. It's now called the InfoSet Query (although it is still referred to as the Ad Hoc Query when executed for HR reporting). This section refers to it as the InfoSet (Ad Hoc) Query; the functionality is the same regardless of its name.

Unlike the SAP Query (with the seven basic screens and seven advanced screens), all query information—including the selection criteria for InfoSet Query reporting—is available on a single screen.

You can use the InfoSet (Ad Hoc) Query to quickly answer simple questions, such as how many employees received stock options last year, or to create a comprehensive report for printing or downloading to your PC. The InfoSet (Ad Hoc) Query is designed so that users can pose questions to the SAP system and receive real-time answers. Other sample questions you might pose using an Ad Hoc Query include

- ▶ How many employees are over the age of 40?
- ▶ Which invoices are charged to cost center 12345678?
- ▶ How many widgets were available for delivery on 6/26/2008?

The InfoSet (Ad Hoc) Query is a very helpful tool that your functional users can use to retrieve important, comprehensive information in a quick-and-easy fashion.

Your system administrator can control access rights to the InfoSet Query using roles or SAP Query user groups. Exactly one SAP Query user group must be assigned to a role (an InfoSet must be associated with the user group), although the user does not need to be listed in the user group. If users want to save their reports, they need authorization object S_QUERY, field ACTVT, value 2; otherwise, they can only create and execute reports.

Like SAP queries, InfoSet (ad hoc) queries are built on the foundation of query areas, query groups, and InfoSets. Earlier in this hour, you created an InfoSet based on the test logical database F1S, which corresponds to SAP's test system. You can use the same data source used in earlier examples for creating an InfoSet (ad hoc) query or you can create a new InfoSet using an HR logical database. The following example uses the one created earlier in the hour.

Creating an InfoSet (Ad Hoc) Query

When the one-time configuration is completed, creating an InfoSet query is a relatively elementary task. To begin creating your first InfoSet (ad hoc) query, follow these steps:

1. You can access the InfoSet Query in three ways: through an application-specific role using the Easy Access menu, using the SAP Query (transaction /nSQ01) and then selecting the InfoSet Query button, or by using transaction code /nPQAH.

2. You are prompted to select your query group and InfoSet (data source) from a dialog box and then to press Enter. The main screen of the InfoSet (Ad Hoc) Query appears in Figure 22.21.

3. The main screen contains three areas: the actual InfoSet from which you select and choose your fields, the sample report display, and the Selection screen values.

4. To start creating your report, simply check the Output box next to each field you want to appear in the report. In this example, only a few fields are selected (see Figure 22.22).

5. Next, choose fields for the Selection screen by marking each field's Selection check box.

6. The Selections section works just as a standard Selection screen does, by enabling you to input values to specify your reporting output.

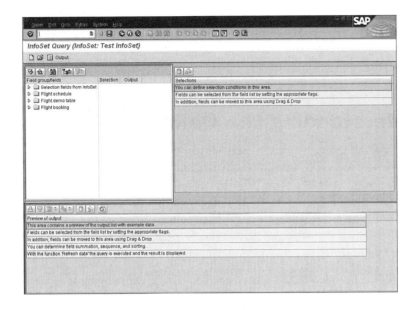

FIGURE 22.21
The main screen of the InfoSet (Ad Hoc) Query.

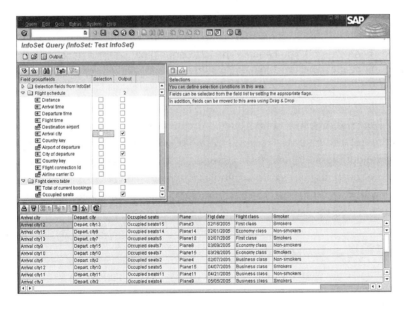

FIGURE 22.22
The three main areas of the InfoSet (Ad Hoc) Query perform a different function.

7. After selecting all the fields you want to include, press the F8 key to execute the report. By default, your report displays in the SAP ALV grid, from which you can easily drag and drop the columns and/or manipulate the look of the output.

The difference between reporting using the test logical database F1S and the
Human Capital Management (HCM) module is that data in the HCM module is displayed by InfoType and not by table name. This makes it easier for the end users.

Understanding the QuickViewer

Unlike the SAP Query, which is a complete reporting solution tool, the SAP
QuickViewer tool is a "what-you-see-is-what-you-get" utility for quick collection of
data from your SAP ERP system. To define a report with the QuickViewer, you simply
enter text (titles) and select the fields and options that define your QuickView.
Unlike with SAP Query, whereby you create queries, you create QuickViews.
QuickViews are not queries and they cannot be exchanged among users. The good
news is that they can be converted to queries to be used with the SAP Query.

Like with the InfoSet (Ad Hoc) Query, you can use the QuickViewer to quickly
answer simple questions.

In contrast to using the SAP Query and InfoSet (Ad Hoc) Query, you do not need to
configure user groups and InfoSets to use QuickViewer. However, if they have
already been created, you can use them. Users simply select a data source
(table, database view, table join, logical database, or InfoSet) when building their
QuickView.

Like SAP queries, InfoSet (ad hoc) queries are built on the foundation of query areas,
query groups, and InfoSets. Earlier in this hour, you created an InfoSet based on the
test logical database F1S, which corresponds to SAP's test system. You can use the
same data source used in earlier examples for creating a QuickView, or you can create a new InfoSet using an HR logical database. The following example uses the one
created earlier in the hour.

Creating a QuickView

After the one-time configuration is completed, creating a QuickView is also a relatively elementary task. To begin creating your first QuickView, follow these steps:

1. Like the SAP queries explained earlier, QuickViews can be run in Basis or
Layout (Graphical) mode. In Basis mode, the system automatically renders the
report from parameters. In Graphical mode, a user can tweak the report's
interface via a visual tool. Like SAP queries, QuickViews are easier to work
with in Basis mode.

2. You can access SAP ERP QuickViewer in three ways: by using transaction /nSQVI, by using the QuickViewer button on the main screen of the SAP Query (transaction /nSQ01), or by using an application-specific role from the Easy Access menu.

3. On the main screen, enter a name for your QuickView and click the Create button. You will be prompted to select a data source. This example uses the F1S data source.

4. There are three main tabs you use to specify your QuickView. The QuickViewer appears in Figure 22.23.

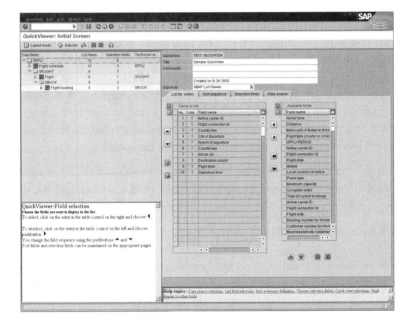

FIGURE 22.23
The main screen of the QuickViewer.

5. The first tab is your list of output fields. Simply select fields listed in the Available Fields column and select the arrow keys to move them to the output column. The second tab enables you to dictate the sort sequence for your selected fields. The third tab enables you to indicate selection fields for specifying your final output.

6. Note in the middle of the screen that you have different export options for your QuickView. Select one from the drop-down box and then select the Execute button to see the Reports Selection screen. You can further specify your selections. Next, select the Execute button to see your completed QuickView.

If you have created a QuickView and you want to convert it to an SAP Query report, simply follow these three quick steps:

1. Navigate to the main screen of the SAP Query (/nSQ01).

2. Follow the menu path Queries, Convert QuickViews.

3. Select your QuickView from the drop-down box and press the Enter key. You are prompted to type a name for the query; press Enter again to convert the QuickView.

Summary

SAP offers a host of reporting capabilities, ranging from dedicated components such as BI and SEM to built-in capabilities found in SAP ERP and other SAP Business Suite components. This hour provided an introduction to the basics of reporting in SAP, including the concepts of variants and background processing. One of the biggest concerns of using a new system is your ability to retrieve output from the system in a manner that is relatively easy to do, in an equally easy-to-use format. Having all the data stored in your SAP system is good, but to be able to output that data into meaningful reports is crucial—SAP reporting makes this possible.

The skills you learned in this hour might be the most meaningful to you as an end user because they will empower you to extract data from your own SAP system. Keep in mind that trial and error is usually the best method for getting accustomed to working with queries in SAP. To this end, seek to "test" your queries in non-production systems.

You have also read how to create ad hoc queries, truly valuable to those who otherwise must rely on the system administration and programming staff to generate reports from the system. Using the simple InfoSet tool, you can pose complex questions and enjoy the output you need in just minutes. You also have the capability to perform further analysis of the data within the query, or you can save or download the report to a local spreadsheet.

Case Study: Hour 22

Consider the case study and questions that follow related to SAP reporting and query basics. The answers may be found in Appendix A, "Case Study Answers."

Situation

MNC Global Inc. has just hired a new Director of Finance who is also an SAP novice. He has asked for someone on the MNC Enterprise Reporting team to help him review the reporting options within the SAP ERP Financials module. Luckily for you, the Enterprise Reporting Manager has selected you to assist on this task. Answer the following questions to help get the new director up to speed.

Questions

1. What reporting mechanism is used to pose "ad hoc" queries to the database?

2. What is the menu path to view a report's attributes from the General Report Selection screen?

3. What is the menu path used to search for reports in the General Report Selection Tree?

4. Define the term *variant*.

5. What is the transaction code to access the Create InfoSets screen?

6. What is the transaction code to access the Create SAP Queries screen?

7. What does a query area include?

8. What are the two different query areas?

9. What must you always do after creating or modifying an InfoSet?

10. What is the transaction code to access the QuickViewer?

PART VI

Developing a Career in SAP

Where Do I Start?

What You'll Learn in This Hour:

▶ Where to find SAP career opportunities

▶ The various job roles available in the SAP market

▶ How to position yourself for a career in SAP

Now that you have learned so much about SAP, its products and technologies, and how you can use SAP, you may be thinking about how you can pursue a career in the SAP market. SAP, its partners, and its customers create an ecosystem of literally thousands of jobs worldwide in a variety of technical and functional disciplines. Working with SAP can prove to be a challenging and rewarding career path, but finding the right opportunity can be a daunting task, especially if you have little direction. In this hour, we will provide much-needed direction and attempt to shed some light on the art of finding a career in SAP. As you read this hour, keep one thing central in your mind: It's *your* career; manage it.

Where Do I Look?

The first question you may ask yourself when seeking a career in SAP is, "Where do I look?" The Internet is a valuable resource to be sure, and in the next hour we will outline popular SAP resources and job websites; however, such resources fail to provide a well-rounded perspective on where SAP career opportunities actually exist. In this section, we will take a closer look at some of those other areas in detail.

Right Where You Are

The first obvious choice when searching for a career in SAP is to look right at home at your current employer. Search your employer's job boards and (as funny as it might sound) search popular websites using your company's name as your search criteria.

If your company is an SAP customer or has plans to become an SAP customer soon, the potential advantage you have as a current employee can make this an ideal method for uncovering an SAP opportunity.

By the
Way

> Be sure to do some due diligence before assuming that your company does not use SAP. At large companies, certain divisions may have implemented SAP whereas others have not, especially if mergers or acquisitions have occurred. Also, if your company is a supplier or vendor of an SAP customer, you may be interfacing with an SAP system and not even know it, missing an opportunity to pick up valuable SAP experience in the process.

Of course, once you are certain there are no SAP opportunities available at your current company, it may be time to take a look outside. Let's review some of these options.

SAP

When looking for a career in SAP, starting right at the source is not a bad idea. With over 50,000 employees in more than 50 countries, SAP AG and its worldwide subsidiaries create a long list of job prospects on their own. A quick search on SAP's career site (http://www.sap.com/careers/index.epx) reveals over 400 job openings in the U.S. alone at the time of this writing, and hundreds others around the globe. Whether it is SAP Labs in Palo Alto, California or one of the many SAP opportunities worldwide, SAP offers a variety of job positions for those seeking employment. Of course, many of these jobs will be internal, administrative, and nontechnical positions within the SAP organization. However, although they may not all be the type of technical or functional position for the SAP career you are seeking, working for SAP still provides a valuable opportunity to get exposure to the SAP product line and eventually work toward your goal.

SAP Partners

Beyond working at SAP, your next option may be to pursue an SAP job at one of the many SAP partners that provide software and services for SAP and SAP customers. These partners include the full gambit, from large multibillion-dollar corporations such as SAP that employ thousands of workers, to outsourcing providers like Accenture, CSC, EDS, HP, and IBM, to small specialty companies that provide more discrete services. SAP partner categories include the following:

▶ Business process outsourcing (BPO) providers

▶ Channel partners

- ▶ Content partners

- ▶ Education and training partners

- ▶ Hosting and outsourcing partners

- ▶ Services (consulting) partners

- ▶ Software solution partners

- ▶ Support partners

- ▶ Technology (hardware) partners

These different partners, along with SAP and the SAP customer base, form what SAP calls its ecosystem. To get an idea of the SAP partners available, execute a partner search at http://www.sap.com/ecosystem/customers/directories/SearchPartner.epx. Note that you will have to enter one set of criteria, such as name, country, or category to get a set of results back.

Within this partner network are also the elite groups of global services partners that provide SAP consulting opportunities across business sectors. Combined, these companies employ thousands of SAP professionals worldwide and help support the growing SAP customer base. The current list of global services partners includes the following (for more information on these partners, see http://www.sap.com/ecosystem/customers/directories/services.epx):

Accenture	Atos Origin
BearingPoint	Capgemini
CSC	Deloitte
Fujitsu	HCL Technologies
HP	IBM Global Business Services
IDS Scheer	itelligence
LogicaCMG	Siemens Business Services
Tata Consultancy Services	Wipro Limited

These companies are SAP's "Who's Who?" for global SAP opportunities and offer prime settings for the serious SAP professional. Whether you are looking for a position in technology at one of the global technology and services partners such as HP or IBM, or seeking an SAP financial auditing position (a great way to learn a lot about SAP, by the way) at Deloitte or Accenture, these partners can offer a quality career path in SAP with the security of working for a large enterprise.

SAP Customers

Although many SAP career settings have been presented, the most likely alternative is that you will find an opportunity with one of SAP's almost 50,000 customers. What types of customers, you may ask? The SAP customer base spans many industry segments as outlined in Hour 1, "What Is SAP?" As a refresher, remember that SAP breaks these industry segments into several major categories, each of which comprises many specific industries:

▶ Financial and Public Services (for example, Banking, Healthcare, Public Sector)

▶ Manufacturing (for example, Automotive, Chemicals, Oil and Gas)

▶ Service (for example, Media, Retail, Utilities)

Moreover, these are just a small subset of the industry segments available. Chances are, no matter where you live, you are not very far from a company that runs SAP. In the next hour, "SAP Resources," you will find information on popular job search engines where SAP customers post hundreds if not thousands of available employment positions at any given time.

What Types of Opportunities Are Available?

As you may recall from Hour 10, "Implementation Overview: A Project Management Perspective," in our discussion on SAP project management, SAP projects create a variety of roles and job functions both in the technical and business arenas. Whether a company is planning an SAP implementation or maintaining an existing SAP landscape, a support network is required to keep the systems technically running, functioning well, and in a state where the requirements of the business may be met. In this section, we will look at the types of opportunities available in more detail.

Business and Functional Positions

On any SAP implementation or in any SAP environment, individuals are needed who can bridge the gap between the business requirements and business processes and the technology. In Hour 11, "Implementing SAP: A Business and Functional Perspective," and Hour 12, "Implementing SAP: A Technical Perspective," we briefly discussed the roles of functional and technical analysts, which are broad categories that can translate into a wide variety of positions. Although the actual job title for these positions can vary greatly, we will discuss a few of them here.

On the business side of the house, every SAP implementation needs personnel who can champion SAP business solutions for their team. For this reason, and rightly so, they are often called *super users*. They are usually the IT-savvy business-knowledgeable folks within their respective departments who can communicate well and have the ability to bring those along who are challenged by new technology. Super users are often the first trained on a given SAP project, and they work most closely with their SAP functional configuration counterparts to resolve issues. This puts super users in a prime position to gain priceless SAP knowledge.

In the SAP technology arena we have functional analysts, often called configuration leads, business analysts, or business process owners. We also have technical analysts, who can be referred to as functional developers or configuration experts. All of these roles are generally aligned with a particular SAP module or modules, such as FI, HR, MM, and so on. These individuals have to work with their business-side counterparts to make the company SAP vision a reality. This is important to note because the more SAP modules a company has implemented, the more people they will require to fill these areas of expertise.

For example, a functional analyst may work with a team leader or super user to gather business requirements for an enhancement to the SAP system. The functional analyst will then work with the technical analyst and potentially other members of the technical team to have SAP configuration activated or modified to meet the business requirements.

As you can see, business and functional roles can be very involved and require tremendous coordination and expertise. All of these roles are vital to an SAP implementation and require motivated, competent individuals to be successful.

Technical Positions

Similar to the business and functional positions, there are wide varieties of technical positions required to keep an SAP landscape running effectively. In Hour 7, "Laying the Groundwork: SAP NetWeaver," we talked about the Basis or NetWeaver expert role as the system administrator for SAP systems. Experienced or senior Basis personnel often take on team lead or architect roles and are responsible for designing the overall SAP technical strategy for their enterprise. SAP security, which is also a Basis component, has become specialized enough that it now stands as its own job function in the majority of companies. SAP security experts work closely with the functional teams to make sure end users can do their job while at the same time maintaining the system's business process integrity.

In addition to system administration roles, a team of developers and programmers are required to manage SAP configuration and code. At one time, these individuals were known as ABAPers (pronounced *ah-bop-ers*) when there was only a simple Basis layer with which to contend. Today, with the Web and Enterprise SOA, this term has broadened. Development can now include ABAP, Java, .NET, SAP Business Intelligence, SAP Process Integration, SAP Enterprise Portal, and many other development niches in or around the core SAP ERP environment.

With the array of SAP products available, technical positions are becoming more and more specialized. Basic, "jack of all trade" system administrators might become SAP Enterprise Portals experts. In addition, ABAP programmers are learning Java and Web Dynpro to keep up with changing technology. All of these role-expanding trends bode well for those looking to find a career in SAP.

Project Management

As you can imagine, bringing together all the preceding functional and technical roles to achieve a common goal can be challenging. For this reason, good project and program managers, especially those with experience on SAP projects, are in high demand. With new SAP product releases, upgrades, and migrations occurring every day, the demand is only getting stronger. Many companies and consulting organizations have established Project Management Offices (PMOs) to coordinate groups of project managers working across disciplines. And as you have read previously, it is not uncommon for an SAP project to require a number of project managers to direct a set of SAP initiatives or represent different stakeholder bodies. Again, this provides a prime opportunity for those looking to break into the SAP arena as a PM.

Trainers and Testers

Although they do not receive the same recognition as other SAP positions, SAP trainers and testers are noteworthy and critical to the success of SAP implementations and projects. As companies learn to carry out their business processes on SAP, trainers take on the difficult challenge of carrying out the new vision to end users who may or may not be completely on board with the new changes. This takes talented trainers and training leads to develop training classes, organize students, and deliver a variety of training modules to an enterprise perhaps unwilling to change.

Likewise, the SAP testing process is a never-ending cycle. Whether it is project-related enhancements to the system or quarterly patches and updates, SAP systems have to be tested to ensure changes are ready for production. This requires people who can create and exercise test scripts either manually or via automated testing tools.

Although tester may not always be the most high profile of positions, you can gain valuable experience on SAP configuration and SAP business processes that can lead to other rewarding positions.

Positioning Myself for a Career in SAP

Now that you know where SAP positions are available and have an idea what types of jobs are out there, how do you get one? In this section, we will focus on just that. You will find out how you can be on your way to a career in SAP.

Again, Right Where You Are

As we discussed in the first section this hour, if your current employer is planning an SAP implementation or currently runs SAP, there is probably no better place to look than right where you are. Generally, companies that kick off a new SAP project are looking for volunteers from the business willing to take on the new challenge and champion the project. If your company does have an SAP initiative planned, there is no time like the present to put your name in the hat as an interested party. New projects are also ideal because there are a variety of positions needed and very little in-house expertise. This means a motivated individual can take advantage of the situation and take the opportunity to develop a new career path.

Although it can be more challenging to move from a non-SAP job to an SAP role at a company already running SAP, you should pursue it as diligently as you possibly can. Leverage your current experience and knowledge of your company to put your potential move in a positive light. Also, if your dream SAP career position is not available yet, do not be afraid to tackle less appealing SAP positions. They can serve as stepping-stones to a more rewarding position later.

Of course, if your current company does not use SAP, has no plans to use SAP, or refuses to give you an opportunity, you will need to search elsewhere.

Leverage Existing Business Experience

As mentioned in the last section, SAP creates many positions built around business modules and business processes. Just as important as it is to know how to configure business processes in SAP, it is equally important to understand the detailed inner workings of the business process itself. If you have that kind of knowledge, you can be a valuable asset to the SAP team. In fact, it is very common for business process experts to become SAP configuration experts, and vice versa.

If you have significant experience in a particular business area but your company does not use SAP, do not be discouraged. This kind of expertise often translates within your industry. For instance, if you worked in the materials management area in the chemicals industry for 15 years, you may be able to leverage that experience to find a job at another chemicals company with a similar business model that uses SAP. This concept applies to all SAP modules across industry segments. Simply identify your role, find a company using SAP, and then pursue that role at the new company!

Similarly, if you pick up new technologies or business solutions quickly, think about becoming an SAP super user or taking on stretch assignments to become the "go-to" person in your business area for all things SAP. Alternatively, consider using your knowledge to become a trainer! Use your business experience and learn how your business processes run on SAP. Then teach others in your department or elsewhere to become educated end users of the system. With a bit of luck, one of these interim training roles will open the door to the SAP career opportunity you *really* want down the road.

Leverage Existing Technical Expertise

If you are an IT professional but SAP technology is all "Greek" to you, do not worry. SAP technology touches almost every facet of the IT industry. In the past, many technical SAP professionals got their start in another area of IT and transitioned over. There is hope for you yet, regardless of where you might be today. In fact, one of our authors got his start in an IT operations position, whereas another started off as a self-taught programmer. Years and many SAP projects later, they are both seasoned SAP professionals with impressive careers. With this in mind, let us now look at various IT positions and how they line up with potential careers in SAP.

Hardware/Infrastructure Specialists

If you currently support server hardware and understand enterprise computing topics such as storage area networks, high availability and clustering, or virtualization, you might be in a good position to add SAP experience to that foundation. Hardware architecture and sizing are critical to the performance of SAP systems, and as such, SAP NetWeaver and Basis professionals have to work closely with their hardware expert counterparts to design and implement SAP systems. As part of this collaboration effort, valuable SAP experience can be gained and leveraged for a career in SAP.

In addition, if you have specific hardware experience for a certain vendor, you might want to consider talking to them about an in-house position. Both HP and

IBM, for example, are SAP technology partners and have server, storage, and systems management platform experts specifically assigned to SAP and SAP customers.

OS/DB Administrators

In Hour 4, "Infrastructure Technology Basics: Hardware, Operating Systems, and Databases," we discussed operating systems (OSs) and databases (DBs) as well as the platform combinations available for SAP. If you are already an administrator on one of these platforms, you might be able to leverage that experience as well. Microsoft Windows Server, UNIX, or Linux administrators and Microsoft SQL or Oracle database administrators can have an advantage over the rest of the competition. If your company or another company runs SAP on the platform with which you are an expert, it might present just the right opportunity at the right time. If not, consider a position at Microsoft or Oracle Corporation, for instance, where the company may be looking for individuals with existing skill sets on their products to work on their SAP teams.

In addition, you should network with your SAP NetWeaver peers whenever possible. Ask questions about how SAP runs on your OS or DB and what aspects affect performance. Find out why your company selected this specific platform to meet its business needs; computing patterns differ in terms of innovation. These types of questions can be the source of priceless knowledge and can also show interest on your part, which can be equally valuable if the right person is listening.

Developers/Programmers

As mentioned in an earlier section, SAP development and programming has gone from the more one-dimensional fourth-generation language of ABAP to a suite of options with object-oriented languages, Java, and Web Services among others. This shift to provide more web-based open access to SAP development could play right into your strengths, for instance, if you are an experienced Java or .NET developer. As you learned in Hour 7 on NetWeaver, many of the IT scenarios now call for the Java stack as a required component. Likewise, Microsoft and SAP continue to collaborate on tools such as the .NET connector for SAP, the .NET PDK for SAP Enterprise Portal, and Microsoft Duet. These changes present an assortment of opportunities for those willing to put in the time to adapt their programming knowledge to SAP.

Content management is also a popular topic in today's SAP environments. If you are a web developer, consider picking up SAP Enterprise Portal and applying your web development and design expertise to the SAP world. SAP Enterprise Portal integrates with existing company portal strategies and products such as Microsoft Office SharePoint Server (MOSS) or IBM WebSphere. Experience in one or more of these technologies can make you a valuable resource and put you in a position to broaden your skill set with SAP.

SAP NetWeaver BI also presents a host of development opportunities. It brings the best of both the technical and functional worlds as it is somewhat of a hybrid. SAP NetWeaver BI developers become the information management experts in a given enterprise. For this reason, technical experience in data mining, database administration, and so on, and functional experience in specific business processes such as FI, HR, and MM are equally important. Therefore, experience in either of these facets may have you well positioned to pick up some SAP BI experience and enhance your career in the process.

Other Options

If you do not have experience that makes one of the preceding options feasible, do not give up yet. There are other nontechnical options for breaking into the SAP market. As we have discussed, project managers are in high demand. Certification from the Project Management Institute (PMI) and the right timing could land you just the SAP opportunity for which you are searching. As a PM, you can pick up multitudes of information about SAP functional design or technical architecture as you work with project team members, which can lead to a career change into a technical or functional role in the future if you so desire.

As we discussed in the prior section, SAP integrates with almost every area of IT, so you have the prospect of working your way into SAP over time. For instance, one of our peers started out as an IT change management analyst and handled change management documentation for her company's SAP team. She eventually took on the job of managing and sending SAP transports throughout the system landscapes and today works as an SAP Basis technician at a large corporation. Just by being a team player and making the most of her opportunities, she advanced her skill set and career.

Similar prospects exist in other IT areas. An SAP bolt-on or complementary product may end up integrating with your IT or business area of expertise and open a window of opportunity. So pay attention, and be ready to take advantage of your skills and experience when the opportunity presents itself.

Working on the Intangibles

Although skill sets and expertise will certainly help in your pursuit of an SAP career, do not underestimate the multitude of soft skills and other intangibles that can make the difference between developing the career you want and being stuck in an unsatisfying J-O-B. As we wrap up with this hour, let us look at some of the little things that normally make all the difference.

Get Educated!

SAP professionals are just that—professionals—and as such, SAP jobs have similar minimum qualifications as other IT and business experts. Many of the positions you see posted at SAP, its partners, and customers require at least a bachelor's degree, if not an MBA or other master's degree. That is not to say that certain years of experience will not get you the job, but advanced education certainly helps plant you at the head of the pack (or resume stack).

Likewise, SAP certification can give you a great advantage as you search for your SAP career. Although it is expensive and may not be as accessible as some certifications, for these same reasons it offers you more exclusivity and regard in the SAP industry. SAP currently has three levels of proficiency: associate, professional, and master (find out more about SAP certification at http://www.sap.com/services/education/certification/index.epx). Any of these certifications can put you well on your way to an SAP career, and the professional and master certifications really raise the demand.

If you are not in a financial position to advance your degree or pay for SAP classes, keep striving. In the next hour on SAP resources, you will learn about a host of helpful sources, most of which are available on the Internet, where you can pick up a wealth of information on SAP and its products. Though you still have to find the right opportunity, do not miss out because you are not prepared and knowledgeable. Terminology, architecture, and standards available in presentations, PDFs, video-based training, and so on, are just a click away. What are you waiting for?

Focus on *Your* Presentation Layer

As we discuss the intangibles, it is worth mentioning that how you present yourself is key. You may have heard the line, "Dress for the job you want, not the job you have." In most corporations, especially the more conservative brands, this is very much a reality. SAP positions, both technical and functional, invariably interact at all levels of management and with all manner of business and IT professionals. As a senior Basis engineer or SAP Financials expert, you may be called upon to do a technical presentation for the CIO or a business presentation for a group of stakeholders. So, if you are serious about advancing your career, you will want to invest in your wardrobe, consider losing the soul patch for a short time, and essentially separate yourself in terms of professional appearance from your peers (meanwhile, we seasoned professionals will keep wearing our shorts and flip-flops, but that's another matter you don't need to worry about just yet).

Also as part of your presentation layer, you should improve your communication skills. Study the culture and primary language reflected by the company, and work not only to fit in but to excel in communication. Your communication skills reflect who you are more than anything else. Many senior-level SAP professionals are not where they are necessarily because they are the most technical analyst or most knowledgeable business process expert but rather because they are able to communicate well across technology and business departments. Simply broadening your vocabulary or improving your pronunciation and articulation with a self-help book to prove you are a strong communicator can boost your career advancement quickly.

Don't stop at verbal skills. Make sure you're a consummate professional when it comes to email and other written communications. You may also want to think about familiarizing yourself with Microsoft PowerPoint. The ability to deliver a solid presentation can say a lot on its own because it lets upper management know you are capable of communicating in both written and verbal forums as well as through group presentations. The ability to share technical and business matters with confidence is a skill that is as rare as it is sought after.

A Word on Ethics

SAP customers spend millions of dollars on SAP systems, which can run literally every aspect of their business. Themes such as system availability and data integrity are paramount in these organizations. For this reason, most companies are looking for responsible individuals with the utmost integrity. In fact, many of the elite corporations today maintain that they are looking for the right kind of people to hire more than specific talents. They realize that they can train people to learn skill sets but finding quality people who are loyal, reliable, and yes, ethical, is more important. So, in whatever you pursue, strive for integrity in all that you do. Someone will notice, and one day it will pay off with just the career change you want.

No Substitute for a Little Hustle

Though it may seem a little cliché, there is a lot of truth to the statement "There is no substitute for a little hustle." Often, the only distinction between those who achieve their goals and those who complain about how they cannot get out of their current situation is simply a little hard work. Many SAP professionals have done just that—*worked* their way into a position. There is nothing in this hour that says you are guaranteed an SAP position if you follow these directions. However, there are some great tips, and if you take advantage of what you have learned and apply a little hustle, you will be well positioned to work your way into an SAP career sooner than you think.

Summary

Now that we have looked at the what, the where, and the how of discovering a career in SAP, the rest is up to you. The authors of this book can attest to the fact that there's a slew of challenging and rewarding opportunities available to the willing and able. If you are serious about making a career change to SAP, follow the simple advice in this hour and get to work. Make every effort to achieve your goal by managing your own career rather than letting others drive for you. Markets change and companies rise and fall, but SAP professionals are generally in high demand regardless of the economy. Work on your skills—business, technical, and soft skills—while you continue to pursue the avenues outlined this hour. We wish you all the best in your endeavors, and hope to call you an esteemed colleague and peer someday soon. May your efforts be blessed!

Case Study: Hour 23

Consider the following SAP careers case study and the questions that follow, the answers to which may be found in Appendix A, "Case Study Answers."

Situation

After 10 years in various business and IT roles, you are ready for a change. You heard about the new SAP ERP implementation down the road at MNC Global's banking affiliate, and through several job boards are aware that the firm is actively hiring. Answer the following questions as you research what opportunities are available and how you might work your way into a new SAP career at MNC Global.

Questions

1. You have heard that MNC Global is relying on a number of consulting firms to assist with its implementation. Where might you be able to find information on these SAP partners?

2. As a banking conglomerate, which one of the three major industry categories might MNC Global fall into, and why might that prove insightful in your job search?

3. With a background in accounting and your ability to pick up technology quickly, what might be a good fit for you in the business/functional arena?

4. In your time at your current employer, you led a number of high-profile projects. What certification might you pursue to enhance your education and improve your chances of obtaining an SAP project management position?

5. You have shown a strong ability to act as a liaison between the business teams and the IT folks at your current employer. What intangible soft skill do you think you might possess that you could highlight in your interview at MNC Global?

SAP Resources

What You'll Learn in This Hour:

▶ An overview of several professional resources, including SAP-focused books, magazines, user groups, and other materials

▶ A review of helpful SAP-oriented websites

▶ An introduction to select SAP career resources

▶ A review of additional SAP resources, including SAP-sponsored and other SAP-focused conferences and events

Although SAP is one of the largest software vendors in the world, there is not an over-abundance of freely available support and similar resources. True, a couple hundred books are available, but at any point in time perhaps only 20 to 30 of these are current enough to be useful. In the same way, there are a number of magazines dedicated to SAP, a number of websites outside of SAP's own web-based resources, and certainly hordes of consulting companies teeming with billable resources. But if you simply have a few questions and very little money to spend, where should you go? To answer this question, this hour outlines additional SAP resources available to users, developers, and other SAP professionals, complementing the material covered in Hour 23, "Where Do I Start?"

Professional Resources

Professional resources for SAP span the gamut from inexpensive books to magazine sub-scriptions, membership in professional user-based organizations, and more. Part of the reason for this diversity is SAP's size—beyond its installed base and the hundreds of thousands of users who depend on SAP day in and day out, there's a supporting cast of another hundred thousand consultants, contractors, developers, engineers, and other support personnel. Some of the more prominent and useful professional resources are outlined in the following sections.

Americas' SAP Users' Group (ASUG)

In almost every facet of business, it is helpful to network with people who are using similar products in the pursuit of similar goals. SAP is no exception. Americas' SAP Users' Group (known as ASUG) is an independent, not-for-profit organization composed of SAP customer companies and eligible third-party vendors, consulting houses, hardware vendors, and others. Visit ASUG's website at http://www.asug.com (see Figure 24.1).

FIGURE 24.1
ASUG is an independent, not-for-profit organization of SAP customer companies and eligible third parties.

ASUG's goals of educating members, facilitating networking among colleagues and SAP representatives, and influencing SAP's global product and service direction forms the foundation of all that ASUG does. ASUG provides a forum for members to communicate mutual concerns to SAP, influence software development, exchange ideas and best practices, and establish future priorities. ASUG is dedicated to the advancement, understanding, and productive use of SAP products.

Brief History of ASUG

Founded in 1990, ASUG began immediately following the SAPPHIRE conference that year in Orlando, Florida. One year later, ASUG was officially incorporated. Starting with a group of 15 participants, by the end of 1996 the organization had grown to more than 450 member companies, representing both R/2 and R/3 installations in North, Central, and South America. In the same year, ASUG expanded its customer-only membership to include third parties (vendors and consultants) under a new Associate Membership category. By the close of 1998, the organization was 950 corporate memberships strong, with more than 12,000 participants. ASUG now boasts an installation base of over 1,750 companies and more than 50,000 members. In 2008, it plans to release a new design for its members on ASUG.com.

The two types of ASUG membership are Installation Member and Associate Member. The former reflects membership at a corporate level of those companies that have installed and run SAP. Fees range from $500 for SAP Business One customers up to $5,000 for large customers with more than $5 billion in revenues. This membership gives all employees of the company benefits from ASUG. Each company designates a "champion" (the single point of contact for the company), along with a primary contact, executive contact, and up to six secondary contacts.

Associate Members include licensed vendors (that is, entities that are licensed Logo, Platform, Alliance, or Implementation Partners) along with certified Complementary Software Program (CSP) participants. Noncertified partners such as small consulting firms can qualify for Associate Member privileges, too.

With ASUG membership comes access to the members-only site within the parent ASUG website. This provides access to a discussion forum, the Member Network, various ASUG-sponsored webcasts, and past presentations and other materials. ASUG members also enjoy discounted rates to attend the annual ASUG conference, access to local and regional chapter meetings, webinars, teleconferences, group meetings, symposiums, and more. Joining ASUG enables a member company to learn from the shared experiences of other users, forging solutions to common user challenges and influencing and shaping SAP's product development over the next few years. And with Installation Membership, the special opportunity to influence SAP AG makes for probably the most compelling reason to "join the club."

For more information about ASUG, use the following contact information:

> Americas' SAP Users' Group
> 401 North Michigan Avenue
> Chicago, IL 60611-4267
> Phone: (312) 321-5142
> FAX: (312) 245-1081
> Email: memberservices@ASUG.com
> www.asug.com

SAP Professional Journal

A bimonthly publication, the *SAP Professional Journal* targets a wide cross-section of SAP professionals, from developers to systems administrators to infrastructure/basis support personnel and more. But the journal also targets the business professionals who rely on SAP to keep their respective companies running. Within the pages of the *SAP Professional Journal*, you'll find technology tutorials, reviews of new products and options, coding and other technical tips, case studies, integration and systems management advice, migration and upgrade guidance, and a wealth of installation and support best practices. And these are not cursory articles or short abstracts— we're talking detailed materials here, the kind that are at once useful.

Perhaps even better than the printed journal is access to the online version. Take a look at www.sappro.com for a list of articles in the latest issue (plus abstracts). Even better, use this resource as a search engine, helping you to find some of the best technical materials and SAP best practices available anywhere. With more than 5,000 pages worth of published articles and other documents, this investment will pay big dividends for the entire SAP support department.

SAPinsider

SAPinsider is published by the same organization that publishes the *SAP Professional Journal*—Wellesley Information Services (WIS). Its format is decidedly different, though, in that it's a quarterly publication, it's free to qualified subscribers (typically anyone supporting or using SAP), and it's sponsored directly by SAP AG. In fact, *SAPinsider* is a joint venture between WIS and SAP. To this last point, the Editorial Board of Directors responsible for publishing valuable real-world *SAPinsider* content reflects a cross-section of some of SAP's most well-known executive and technical names. This helps ensure leading-edge insight. Important lessons learned are imparted every quarter, making *SAPinsider* an excellent addition to any SAP professional's reading.

In addition to solid technical advice, *SAPinsider* provides product walkthroughs and reviews, up-to-date news from SAP developers, and a number of useful regular columns—NetWeaver, Under Development, Recommended Reading (book reviews, slanted naturally toward SAP Press), and a New and Noteworthy section used by partners and SAP product organizations alike to share important findings. This variety of resources and information can help you stay well rounded and abreast of the most current developments in the SAP community. It's no wonder that more than 125,000 professionals who develop, implement, support, and use SAP applications depend on *SAPinsider*. For information, visit www.sapinsideronline.com.

SAPNetWeaver Magazine

The newest addition to the small circle of SAP-focused magazines on the market today is *SAPNetWeaver Magazine*. Founded in 2005, it is the self-described independent authority on SAP NetWeaver. The purpose of this magazine is to share insight and findings that reflect the real world of SAP NetWeaver implementations. Thus, you will find that this is one of those magazines that seeks to align the business and IT sides of SAP, such that its articles appeal to a broad readership. It succeeds in doing just that.

Although the magazine is young, it has proven itself an excellent read thus far. And why not?—it fills an important void. Managers will find the analysts' coverage, thoughts from industry experts, and real-world anecdotes and high-level case studies just what they need to build a business case for moving in a particular direction. Technologists and architects will find the best practices, detailed case studies, and independent insight proffered by SAP experts indispensable as well, enabling them to make better and bolder decisions while mitigating the risk of deploying products without the benefit of long histories (a nicer way of saying "new products are necessarily immature products"). *SAPNetWeaver Magazine* is offered quarterly. Go to www.sapnetweavermagazine.com to learn more about why this might be the magazine you've been waiting for.

Books

More than 400 books are available on the market today for SAP. Using online bookstores such as barnesandnoble.com (www.bn.com) and www.amazon.com, you can easily search for and uncover the latest SAP-related books. It's also worth your time looking at www.SAP-press.com, which, unsurprisingly, offers a wealth of SAP books covering topics as diverse as SAP Solution Manager, SOA, performance optimization, ABAP and Java programming, Workflow, SAP Service and Support, and nearly every SAP product sold by SAP.

Additional sites include www.SAP-Resources.com/saprbooks1.htm, useful simply because it's both up to date and fairly comprehensive. This site mentions nearly 100 of the bestselling SAP books on the market. And because each book is hyperlinked to Amazon, it's a simple matter of quickly reading over reviews, examining pricing and shipping options, looking for used-book deals, and ultimately placing an order for a copy.

Technical Newsletters

WIS Publications, the same entity that publishes the *SAP Professional Journal*, offers a number of technical newsletters as well. Each newsletter is laser-focused on a particular topic, such as the following:

▶ *SAP Financials Expert*—Geared toward finance and IT teams that use or support FI, CO, or SAP ERP Financials. It covers quite a bit of reporting options, ranging from R/3 and BW Reporting, to SEM, Financial Accounting (FA), Profitability Analysis (PA), G/L, Treasury, A/P, A/R, Controlling, and more. See www.ficoexpertonline.com for details.

▶ *BW/BI Expert*—If you are tasked with deploying, upgrading, optimizing, or supporting SAP BW (or in a broader sense, business intelligence), this newsletter focused on deploying and tuning BW for use as the central hub in a sea of transactional systems is what you are looking for. Look to www.bwexpertonline.com for more information.

▶ *SCM Expert*—If your SAP team is tasked with optimizing your company's supply chain, this is your newsletter. All the usual supply chain functions are covered, including procurement, warehousing, manufacturing schedules, sales, and distribution. But more than SAP APO is targeted; *SCM Expert* targets core R/3 and SAP ERP modules as well, including SD, PP, MM, QM, and PS. Refer to www.scmexpertonline.com for details.

▶ *CRM Expert*—If your team is responsible for unlocking critical CRM functionality, such as marketing, sales, service, and analytics, including the various CRM user interfaces (three different ones exist), *CRM Expert* is just the ticket for you. Check out www.crmexpertonline.com as well.

Internet Resources

Many SAP Internet resources are available for you to communicate, learn, and share your own ideas and findings about your SAP system with SAP professionals, vendors, and the entire virtual user community. Always on and always available, the Internet is an ideal source for obtaining troubleshooting information in a pinch. It is always a good idea to search the Net every now and then for new SAP resources—you'll be amazed at the wealth of new material made available practically every day. The best of these resources is covered next.

SAP Fans

SAP Fans, located on the Internet at www.sapfans.com, continues to be an excellent source of unbiased SAP information (the site is not affiliated with SAP AG). SAP Fans is designed as a forum to exchange ideas with other SAP customers working with SAP R/3, R/2, and other SAP systems. This website includes user-based, technical, and other "discussion" forums that provide you with the opportunity to post questions, comments, and experiences about your SAP system, and retrieve responses from other SAP professionals. These forums are grouped into a number of areas. Arguably the most useful is the Technical area, which includes

Logistics	Financials
Human Resources	Basis
SAP Security	SAPscript/Smart Forms
ABAP	SAP CRM
Business Workflow	Business Warehouse
SEM	APO and SCM
Implementation Issues	Industry Solutions
SAP Portals/Internet	Interfaces
Third-Party Products	"Other"

There's also a Non-Technical forum area, intended to host general discussions, share job postings and resumes, and focus on educational services, list training courses, and address certification questions. Finally, the Knowledge Corner, which is moderated in real time, lets you pose functional, technical, and ABAP-related questions. Using these discussion forums, you can easily post a question or problem that you are having with your SAP system (see Figure 24.2). Other SAP Fans users will see your posting and (hopefully!) respond with possible solutions (as in Figure 24.3).

The network of contacts you gain as you discuss and share similar experiences can prove invaluable. As of this writing, SAP Fans boasts more than 76,000 registered users and more than half a million posted articles. And because it's an ideal source for SAP news, events, products, books, and employment opportunities, you should bookmark SAP Fans as one of your favorites. Yes, some of the material is outdated. But much of it is extremely current, making it a very useful (not to mention very free!) resource.

FIGURE 24.2
In the SAP Fans user forums, you can post comments or questions or respond to other users' comments or questions.

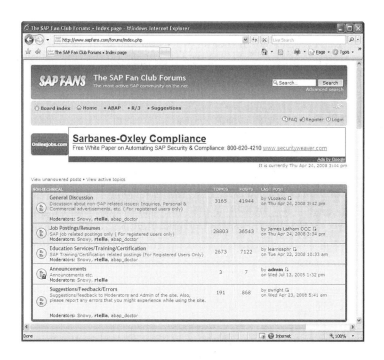

FIGURE 24.3
The SAP Fans discussion forum can prove an ideal source for answers to your SAP questions.

The Wayback Machine

Although there are plenty of recently constructed and oft-updated SAP-related web-sites at your disposal, you might find yourself looking for something that is no longer available on the Web. Most sites change significantly every few months or years. And some very useful sites have completely faded away with the times, such as the SAP Technical Journal (www.saptechjournal.com) and ERPcentral (www.erpcentral.com), the latter of which was a nice portal site featuring information on the ERP leaders in 2003 and earlier: SAP, Oracle, PeopleSoft, JD Edwards, Baan, and more. ERPcentral was a good source for installation and support best practices, for example.

But with ERPcentral "gone," how do you access the content on its site? For example, if you're still running an old version of R/3 and have misplaced your CDs and guides, but remember similar read-me information once available at ERPcentral, what can you do? The folks at SAP might be able to send you updated media, and your SAP Competency Center might have filed away some of its legacy documenta-tion, too. But trying to dig up data using this hit-and-miss approach can become a very big problem when time is of the essence.

The answer might be as simple as navigating to the Wayback Machine at www.waybackmachine.org (note the ".org" extension). As you can see in Figure 24.4, the site provides a search box where you can enter the URL of any site that has existed in the last 20-odd years. Simply enter the site name (such as http://www.saptechjournal.com) and click the Take Me Back button.

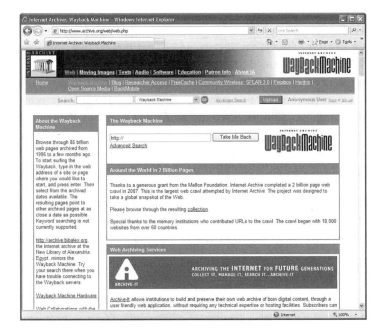

FIGURE 24.4
With the Wayback Machine, it's a breeze to pull up materials from websites that have been changed or decommis-sioned.

A list of search results spanning perhaps a great number of years appears. Click any of the hyperlinked dates to navigate to the version of the site as it looked on that particular day. Not all dates are available; settle on something close. Keep in mind that restricted sites, password-protected sites, and some materials on other sites are unavailable. But you'll be amazed at the wealth of newfound "old" data suddenly at your disposal. Old sites can be helpful when you're looking for a particularly difficult-to-find document, too.

SAP FAQ

The SAP FAQ originated in 1994 as a web-based adjunct to the de.alt.sap-r3 Usenet discussion forum from Germany's University of Oldenburg, a pioneering SAP academic installation site. As a longstanding, not-for-profit, technology-specific resource, the SAP FAQ has earned and maintained a position of global credibility and respect. Its objective is to serve as a comprehensive point of information about SAP for those who work with SAP, companies that are implementing SAP, students, and those who are looking into SAP as a potential ERP solution or career option.

TechTarget and SearchSAP.com

What used to be termed the SAP FAQ's "by-subscription" discussion forum, ask-the-experts forum, and other similar resources are now accessed through TechTarget, the parent to SearchSAP.com. In fact, when you type **www.sapfaq.com**, you are rerouted to http://itknowledgeexchange.techtarget.com/itanswers, a wonderful portal into a wealth of materials, moderated discussions, salary surveys, events and conferences, great tips, useful newsletters, and so much more. It's a great way to exchange ideas while staying on top of new trends and products. An awesome SAP product directory covers much more than the usual ERP, CRM, and Supply Chain topics. You can access hard-to-find information pertaining to disaster recovery and capacity planning, for example. You'll also find much to review if you're interested in trying to understand what kind of products are available in the hot areas of Business Process Management (BPM) or Reporting. From general, core FI and HR module–related discussions, to industry-specific dialogue, subscribers can select a customized combination of discussions that fit very specifically into their areas of interest and expertise. And given the no-cost approach to subscription, SearchSAP.com and TechTarget in general are no-brainers for SAP professionals on a budget. For more information or to subscribe, visit http://searchsap.techtarget.com.

The SAP ITtoolbox

With more than 700 discussion groups, and a history of serving those users with integrity, the ITtoolbox portal is a must-have subscription for nearly everyone.

ITtoolbox takes care to not inundate you with weekly trash; instead, you choose cafeteria-style your interests, and ITtoolbox works to provide you with updated interest-specific content as it becomes available. Interested in SAP careers, training, or certification? Want to review knowledge bases focused on PeopleSoft, SCM, ERP project management, or hardware platforms for SAP? ITtoolbox has it all. Register at the main site at www.ITtoolbox.com.

For its SAP community members, the SAP Knowledgebase link at the bottom of the main site takes you directly to the SAP ITtoolbox site, an online service providing wonderful tools and information geared toward assisting SAP practitioners in making informed decisions and completing their daily activities. Like its sister sites, the SAP ITtoolbox combines a functionally organized database of information with the benefits of global communication capabilities to quickly bring useful information to your fingertips. Just check out the weekly SAP decision makers and SAP-doers newsletters (delivered through email), and the SAP ITtoolbox will soon become one of your essential resources if not a favorite site.

SAP Conferences

In addition to the ASUG conference and regular ASUG-sponsored events, a growing number of other SAP conferences is available to SAP professionals, users, and others. Some of these, such as SAP TechEd, are geared toward technologists and developers, whereas others, such as SAPPHIRE, are geared toward executives and other decision makers. There's also a wealth of product-specific conferences and events hosted throughout the year by the same folks who publish the *SAP Professional Journal* and *SAPinsider*—WIS Publications.

SAPPHIRE

If you are seeking a high-level or executive-level perspective on where SAP is heading, consider attending the annual SAPPHIRE conference. One is held every year in the United States, Europe, and most recently Asia. A certain amount of technical sessions are offered, but SAPPHIRE is better known for touting a who's who of keynotes, customer case studies and success stories, and a great number of business-oriented presentation sessions. For example, SAPPHIRE '08 boasted 18 conference tracks ranging from core Financial Services and Discrete/Process Industries (SAP's bread and butter in many ways) to SAP NetWeaver/ESA, SAP xApps and Business Process Innovation, and others—reflecting 22 SAP solutions and 24 industry verticals. Review www.sapsapphire.com for information about the most recent or upcoming SAPPHIRE event.

SAP TechEd

There is no better way to get the inside SAP scoop on everything out there and everything coming around the corner than SAP TechEd. Because this event is not interested in hosting marketing sessions, you actually learn things that are immediately useful in your day-to-day life, whether optimizing your current system or planning for your next functional upgrade. Finally, only SAP TechEd consistently provides you the opportunity to easily, quickly, and cheaply take certification exams—this alone can save your travel and expense budget thousands, because you can combine multiple training and certification trips into one 4- or 5-day jaunt to great destinations such as San Diego, Boston, New Orleans, Las Vegas, and Orlando. Celebrate afterward with a family vacation!

Managing Your SAP Projects

If you're on a team tasked with planning and deploying SAP, consider attending one of the newer SAP conferences out there, WIS's Managing Your SAP Projects. By offering real-world advice focused on resolving issues and duplicating successes, Managing Your SAP Projects gives you the chance to drill down into what makes or breaks a successful implementation or upgrade, to walk through customer case studies, and to hear about high-level strategies and leadership tactics used by SAP project leaders and their teams. Such practical guidance learned in the trenches is worth the fee of $1695.

Because of the decidedly project management focus of this annual conference, certified Project Management Professionals (via the Project Management Institute, or PMI) will be glad to know that they can also earn PDU credits by attending many of the more than 90 sessions. This is helpful in maintaining PMP certification. And because this is very much a vendor-neutral conference—SAP AG does not sponsor it, although many of the speakers hail from various SAP organizations—those interested in perhaps a less-biased view of SAP will find the sessions refreshingly straightforward. Check out www.sapprojects2008.com for more information on the 2008 conference and links to other conference opportunities.

Other WIS-Sponsored Seminars and Conferences

Wellesley Information Services offers a host of other content-specific and product-specific conference venues. In 2008, WIS brought over 20 conferences and seminars to a variety of North American and European cities. Topics ranged from SAP ERP for Managers and Managing Your SAP Projects to technology-focused SCM, PLM, HR, BW, CRM, and other conferences. And the new SAP Solution Manager conference has received high marks from many SAP professionals. Like all of WIS's conferences, the SAP-neutral stance makes an excellent platform for knocking back a whole lot of great real-world information in just a few days. See http://www.wispubs.com/eventCalendar_SAP.cfm for a list of upcoming SAP-focused conferences near you.

Employment and Career Opportunities

Even today, one of the first things you will notice when you begin an SAP project is that you're suddenly in demand from others. Your email inbox and voicemail box will be bombarded with messages from recruiters offering to out-do your present salary, reduce your travel, increase your opportunities for advancement, and so on. It's not a bad deal, actually, but it can catch you off guard. Therefore, you need to be prepared.

SAP knowledge is a hot commodity today; a wealth of positions is available and growing for people with the right skills. This includes functional as well as technical skills, development as well as configuration expertise. Possessing in-depth knowledge on how to configure and set up a module in SAP ERP 6.0 is just as valuable as being able to write ABAP or Java code for SAP, or navigate an SAP system through a complex functional upgrade or OS/DB migration. And people with program management and project management skills gleaned through an SAP project are in great demand as well. Unsurprisingly, a great number of websites are devoted to making their employment opportunities available to you. A sample of these websites is provided next.

SAP-Resources.com

Touting itself as the "independent home of SAP-only jobs since 1998," SAP-Resources still provides sound value 10 years later. It provides a web-based recruitment service focused solely on the SAP marketplace. SAP-Resources enables you to approach the task of finding an SAP career opportunity in a couple of ways through the following services:

- ▶ The Jobs Database, which is constantly being added to, includes details of some of the hottest SAP positions currently available. Just enter some relevant keywords to perform a search.

- ▶ The Skills Profile Service is aimed at professionals who know that some of the best opportunities are never advertised and want to make their skill details available to the widest audience possible. It's simple to create and activate your skills profile and to be contacted by recruiters handling the hottest SAP opportunities. All levels of experience are always in demand. Check out the full details at the Professionals Information page.

▶ The Jobs-by-Email service provides subscribers with a daily email message listing the latest jobs posted to SAP-Resources (see Figure 24.5). For more information and to review employment opportunities, visit www.sap-resources.com.

One of the most exciting things about the site is the Top Recruiters box located off the main page. Navigate here to find who's placing the most people (based on job posting popularity). And click the Company Names link to review the actual postings in real time.

FIGURE 24.5
All services offered on SAP-Resources.com are free.

Softwarejobs.com

Another great venue for posting and reviewing SAP employment opportunities is www.softwarejobs.com. Its online career resources are free and useful, including consultation and resume-writing help, links to free industry-related magazines and similar materials, access to career events and continuing education, and even access to a free personality test, a free career test, and a cadre of career-boosting-related articles.

The site also offers free email, inexpensive background checks (to make the decision to hire you over 500 other candidates weigh in your favor), and a full-blown

Resource Center portal site to provide access to all this and more. Finally, softwarejobs.com's Job Seeker Tools section makes it easy to build a portfolio, manage and post your resume, conduct advanced job searches, and distribute your resume through a number of venues.

ITtoolbox for Careers

As discussed previously, the ITtoolbox website provides outstanding career and job assistance. From the home page you can launch the Career Center, giving you rapid access to recently posted jobs, the capability to sign up for "job alerts," the capability to introduce yourself to the IT industry's top recruiters, and access to the career-specific ITtoolbox knowledge bases.

Need to hire a couple of contractors for one of your own projects? ITtoolbox also features a section for employers. Use it to post a job opening, review the site's online Resume Database (access costs you $495; use your credit card), and you'll be knee-deep in thousands of resumes in no time. Be sure to bookmark this site as one of your favorites—one day, you'll use it.

Up and Coming

As SAP opportunities continue to grow, a number of other sites have popped up offering job databases worth checking out. A few popular sites are www.simplysap.com, www.justsapjobs.com, and www.sapcareers.com. In addition to these, it is always wise to take a look at SAP job offerings on mainstream sites such as www.monster.com and www.careerbuilder.com as well as IT job sites such as www.dice.com. These latter sites can be particularly helpful when looking for specific opportunities at firms in your region. With the wealth of jobs available, you are sure to find an opportunity worth pursuing (be sure to again review Hour 23 prior to pursuing or changing jobs in the world of SAP).

Summary

In this hour, we looked at several of the resources available to you, many of which are free, and all which are intended to help you get the most out of your SAP system and livelihood. As time goes on, these resources will only continue to grow and diversify—especially the Internet-based resources, SAP conferences, and career resources.

Through your personal exposure to SAP ERP, NetWeaver, and so on, coupled with the resources highlighted here and the skills you have learned, you will find yourself quickly moving from "sapling" status to a hardcore "sapper" (or "sapman," or "sap-ster," or whatever—insert your favorite title here!). So once again, welcome to the world of SAP. We hope you have enjoyed the past 24 hours—it has been our pleasure. We look forward to seeing or hearing from you soon!

Case Study: Hour 24

Consider this SAP resource-oriented case study and the questions that follow, the answers to which may be found in Appendix A, "Case Study Answers."

Situation

As a financial analyst at MNC Global Inc., you have been invited to join the SAP project team as it prepares for the new SAP ERP 6.0 implementation. Your input will be valuable to the success of the project. Your supervisor has asked you to do whatever it takes to get up to speed on SAP ERP, and SAP Financials in particular, as quickly as possible.

Questions

1. With what group could you get involved to find out what other SAP customers are doing in the SAP Financials arena?

2. What points should you keep in mind when shopping for SAP books?

3. How can you quickly find the top 100 or so books on SAP?

4. How can you keep up to date with the latest SAP information available on the Internet?

5. What SAP conference might make the most sense for you to attend?

APPENDIX

APPENDIX A

Case Study Answers

Hour 1: Answers

1. Although there are many smaller niche players in the business application market, three companies own the bulk of market share and mindshare in this space: SAP, Oracle, and Microsoft. Given SAP's dominance and MNC's size, scope, and global reach, the board should probably take an attitude of, Why not SAP?

2. MNC needs to investigate SAP ERP first and foremost to tie its end users to a single financial system of record. At the same time, though, the company also needs to look at SAP Supply Chain Management (SCM) to address its supply chain issues and SAP Customer Relationship Management to address lost sales and other market opportunities. Finally, the board might be interested in investigating SAP NetWeaver Portal as perhaps a first step toward unifying how its end users "go to work" and the SAP NetWeaver Process Integration product to integrate the company's diverse present-day solutions into a more cohesive albeit probably short-term system.

3. SAP offers a Mining industry solution that should be of great interest to MNC. By implementing the Mining industry solution atop SAP ERP, MNC could immediately leverage mining-specific industry and business best practices.

4. With 100,000 employees, MNC faces several infrastructure challenges. Questions related to the mix of front-end client devices need to be posed, along with details regarding network links between the 500 different sites and the company's primary data center that would eventually house SAP. Fortunately for MNC, the company's adoption of Microsoft Windows on its desktops and laptops will allow for several graphical user interfaces (that is, both Internet Explorer and SAP's own SAPGUI may be used).

   Language and currency issues will likely be no problem for MNC, though the board needs to investigate the specific languages and dialects it must support to be sure.

Hour 2: Answers

1. Running SAP implies running a business application developed by SAP, a large software company. Years ago, this was synonymous with running SAP R/3, the company's flagship online transaction processing system. Today, it could mean any number of products (and in all likelihood, several products tied together to create a robust foundation for enterprisewide cross-application business processes).

2. SAP R/3 was SAP's first client/server system. It evolved over many years alongside new SAP product offerings, and was eventually renamed R/3 Enterprise. Shortly afterward, SAP re-architected its suite of products and introduced a newer successor to R/3 Enterprise called ECC or ERP Central Component. Today, this core SAP application is simply named SAP ERP.

3. With regard to what is the most important and most immediate matter on the horizon relative to introducing SAP, four things should come to mind: aligning the business, application functionality, underlying technologies, and the core project management and oversight necessary to bring an SAP implementation to a successful conclusion.

4. SAP provides several "graphical user interfaces" for accessing and using its business software. The most popular user interface for SAP is the WinGUI, also called the Windows SAP GUI or "fat client."

   The concept of an SAP "client" can be confusing. It is not the same thing as an SAP "front-end client" (which is a desktop or laptop hosting the SAP GUI). Rather, an SAP client is essentially a self-contained business entity within each SAP system (R/3, ERP, SCM, and so on). By using a front-end client running one of SAP's user interfaces, an end user may log in to a client and then actually run business transactions. At a company like MNC, end users will access a specific (and different) client in each production SAP system deployed. And in some cases, a large geographically distributed company like MNC might host multiple SAP production clients in its ERP systems—some users might log in to the North America client, for example, whereas others might log in to the Asia client. Or the company might structure its clients around discrete businesses or functions.

Hour 3: Answers

1. SAP is but one of several ERP solution vendors on the market today; it is premature to decide upon SAP at this point, let alone specific SAP products and applications. Rather than focusing on vendors, solutions, or technologies, at this stage it's much more important to simply develop the business roadmap.

2. MNC's lack of repeat customers speaks to a problem with how to increase revenue. Interestingly, the company might decide to fix this problem (a prudent move) or simply refocus its efforts on a new revenue opportunity (commodity goods direct sales).

3. The task force needs to look at MNC's situation from four perspectives or views—business, functional, technical, and project implementation.

4. The functional view addresses the "what" of a business solution. It answers the question: What will a particular business process do?

5. The technical view addresses the "how" part of a business solution. It makes the business and functional views possible through the deployment of specific applications and technologies.

Hour 4: Answers

1. Pros of each platform choice are plentiful. The IBM/Oracle platform allows the Basis and DBA teams to easily continue to support the SAP systems without any retraining. The database migration to new hardware will require minimal effort too, because the underlying platform is not changing. On the other hand, the Intel/Windows/SQL Server platform is generally much less expensive than its counterparts simply from a hardware, OS licensing, and Oracle licensing perspective. This platform is common throughout the industry and is often lower in cost to support from a people and process perspective as well. An ROI or TCO study that is MNC Global-specific should be conducted to really capture the differences though.

2. Disadvantages of the IBM/Oracle solution for MNC hinge primarily on cost. Since the MNC acquisition has outsourced this support, they don't have any internal platform expertise to speak of, either. On the other hand, the Windows/SQL environment might run into more scalability issues (depending solely on the hardware platform selected). And the time and expense necessary for managing security, patching, and general change control is typically greater than its UNIX counterparts.

3. MNC Global has a difficult choice to make. Choosing an Intel-based Windows/SQL Server platform would accomplish the goals of lowering cost while enabling SAP R/3 4.6C to be upgraded soon. Deploying new and powerful server and disk subsystem hardware will not only speed up the migration process but provide a platform with longevity as well.

4. There are some potentially good alternatives that MNC should explore. First, migrating to Windows/Oracle might be beneficial (assuming the SQL-vs-Oracle licensing cost is less of an issue), particularly given MNC's existing expertise in Oracle. In this way, MNC could benefit from low-cost hardware while running an easily supported OS. MNC might also explore MaxDB running atop Linux.

    Performance-enhancing technologies include deployment of 64-bit hardware and software, as well as the ability to deploy Windows on both commodity x64 and highly available and tremendously scalable IA64 platforms.

Hour 5: Answers

1. MNC's current IT teams will all need to be staffed and trained specifically for SAP. However, the data center team probably has the necessary knowledge to require only basic staff augmentation.

2. Point the technical teams to SAP's Master Guides for detailed planning and preparation advice (see http://service.sap.com/instguides).

3. Though MNC Global's current use of a four-system landscape (development, test, pre-production staging, and, of course, production) is admirable, given the technical gaps, training gaps, and likely need for a business/functional sandbox as well as a DR solution, it would be preferable in the short run to recommend a six- or seven-system landscape (staging might double as a DR environment, in this case).

4. The SAP Employee Self Service functionality requires Java; however, depending on the installation scenario, you might recommend an ABAP+Java installation as well.

5. Two additional DR solutions outside of basic tape backup/restore capabilities include using database log shipping and implementing a DR solution involving hardware-based storage replication technologies.

Hour 6: Answers

1. SAP Business All-in-One is the best solution if the business processes are very complex.

2. SAP Business One is the ideal solution for a small company with straight-forward business processes.

3. SAP Business ByDesign would be a good fit for a company without an IT staff or no plans to develop such an organization, as it is hosted by SAP and can be configured directly by the package's business users.

Hour 7: Answers

1. Strategic benefits that MNC may realize by implementing new NetWeaver functionality include reduced TCO and greater potential for innovation. The end users that need the BI reports may then receive their reports via push technology (information broadcasting) rather than by logging in to the SAP GUI and manually searching for them. This reduces time spent on this task as well as allows the users to focus on other business challenges, which ultimately creates cost savings and a more efficient workforce for MNC.

2. SAP provides several resources useful for planning and implementing information broadcasting on its BI 7.0 system. These include the SAP NetWeaver 7.0 Master Guide as well the installations guides for NW 7.0 systems, standalone engines, and clients, which are broken out by OS and DB platform combinations (all available at http://service.sap.com/instguidesNW70; keep in mind you must have a valid SAP Service Marketplace user ID to access these resources).

3. By looking in the SAP NW 7.0 Master Guide, you can see that the IT Scenario category associated with information broadcasting is "Enterprise Reporting, Query, and Analysis."

4. The following are the installable software units:

   a. **Systems with usage types**—AS ABAP, BI, AS Java, EPC, EP, and BI Java

   b. **Standalone engines**—TREX

   c. **Clients**—Web Browser, SAP GUI, BI Business Explorer, and Adobe Reader

Hour 8: Answers

1. SAP ERP Human Capital Management (HCM) comprises a number of hot solutions in great demand today. It is a compelling solution for many reasons, including its integration with SAP ERP Financials, Manufacturing, and other SAP solutions, its world-class talent management functionality, its ability to enable and empower global teams and ability to connect a firm's workforce to a single system of record and accountability, its built-in business intelligence capabilities, its ability to be run as an outsourced business process, SAP's extensive SAP ERP HCM partner network, the solution's open and extensible technology platform, and generally its reputation as a "safe choice" for HR organizations.

2. The components of Plant Maintenance include Preventative Maintenance, Service Management, Maintenance Order Management, Maintenance Projects, Equipment and Technical Objects, and Plant Maintenance Information System.

3. SAP ERP Operations is an aging label for the umbrella comprising SAP's logistics offerings, which itself is composed of Procurement and Logistics Execution, Product Development and Manufacturing, and Sales and Service. Within these offerings are found business processes related to purchasing, plant maintenance, sales and distribution, manufacturing, materials management, warehousing, engineering, and construction. The umbrella solution SAP Manufacturing comprises SAP ERP Operations.

4. SAP purposely engineers overlap between particular solutions and modules to give a company the ability to customize a business solution reflecting the specific business modules and processes necessary to meet its needs.

5. An important component of SAP ERP is the Analytics solution offering, a targeted solution consisting of financials, operations, and workforce analytics.

Hour 9: Answers

1. Three support-oriented features of SAP CRM include marketing support, sales support, and service support.

2. SAP Manufacturing is an amalgamation of other SAP Business Suite components, products, and underlying technologies; it is assembled in the same way business scenarios are assembled, rather than purchased outright.

3. SRM's benefits are derived on four fronts—improved design collaboration (and therefore time-to-market); streamlined access to engineering documentation and other materials useful in optimizing product quality, manufacturing processes, and more; improved visibility into ERP back-end data; and the capability to mark up and "redline" computer-aided drawings.

4. In terms of maturity and years of availability, SAP SCM leads the pack ahead of the other Business Suite components.

5. The three general areas of a supply chain include supply, manufacturing, and distribution.

Hour 10: Answers

1. Given the timeframe, SAP's ASAP methodology might indeed be a good starting point. Go-Live is less than a year away, and Human Resources (more precisely, Human Capital Management) is a common module of SAP. However, given ASAP's age, it will probably provide little value beyond simply organizing the initial project around a standard methodology.

2. MNC's lack of SAP technical skills and leadership mandates that a Senior Solution Architect or Chief Technologist familiar with the SAP solution being deployed (and preferably MNC's industry) be brought in from SAP, the prime integrator or another systems integrator, or another third party.

3. Given that MNC has a mature Project Management Office (PMO), it should be assumed that the PMO will be adept at creating project plans, contingency plans, communications plans, and escalation processes, and managing quality and risk.

4. The VP of HR's past history with SAP is a major warning sign. Without the VP's buy-in, leadership, and activities aimed at promoting the new solution, the project will almost certainly fail, particularly given that the VP would naturally be one of the key stakeholders if not the project sponsor.

5. Considering the whole situation, you should tell the steering committee that the project needs to be put on hold until the issues outlined in this case study are addressed.

Hour 11: Answers

1. The technical team needs power user input in defining and reviewing how and to what extent SAP technologies and business applications will actually solve the firm's business problems. Without the perspective of its power users, MNC risks "solving" the wrong problems—or worse, inventing new ones.

2. The prime integrator knows SAP and knows specific functional or business areas, but is missing the first-hand knowledge held by MNC's power users. The power users working in the various accounting teams will serve as internal consultants to the prime integrator's consultants, coaching the implementation team in terms of how business is currently conducted and therefore how the work flows today.

3. The four types of testing supported by power users include unit or functional testing, systems integration testing, user acceptance testing, and load or stress testing.

4. With all the power users' knowledge of MNC's business processes and SAP's functional configuration, the biggest challenge faced by MNC after Go-Live might simply be retaining them (power users have been known to leave at the conclusion of a project only to return as SAP functional consultants or business process specialists with a prime integrator or other consulting organization).

5. The job of converting a firm's business requirements to functional specifications that may in turn be used to configure SAP appropriately is the responsibility of a special collection or matrix of people and teams—the functional business area or "row" leaders.

Hour 12: Answers

1. It is very likely that SAP Consulting might be engaged in the project, because it is often subcontracted on new SAP implementations. By the same token, someone from Novell or RedHat might be involved (your SAP/Linux partner) as well as Oracle. And given that MNC Global has standardized on HP ProLiants for SAP and non-SAP server infrastructure, you assume HP is likely playing a support role in the project as well.

2. Technical specialists generally hold knowledge in a particular technical tool or technology discipline; they might be called to design and customize interfaces between SAP and legacy systems, or help design the Go-Live plan, or migrate

data from the old system into the new SAP system, or provide guidance on a tool or bolt-on application. They might simply be asked to ready their particular technical piece of the project as well.

3. Several common pre-installation planning tasks include developing hostname naming conventions, developing operating system installation details or processes, determining whether to install SAP as a Unicode or non-Unicode system, and installing SAP Solution Manager to generate installation keys.

4. Technical implementation lessons learned include developing Service Level Agreements between IT and the business (as well as between various IT teams), ensuring technical buy-in on behalf of the project team, taking the approach of starting small but think big relative to taking on technical tasks, working out whether an implementation is to go live in a big-bang or phased approach, learning from mistakes, taking care not to allow expensive consultants and contractors to overstay their welcome, and carefully and proactively managing scope creep.

5. System characteristics that should be reflected in a well-thought-out SAP server hostname include geographic location, SAP software component, whether the server supports development, quality assurance, or production, whether the server is physical or has been virtualized, the host's function (database, message server, or application server), and the number of the SAP instance.

Hour 13: Answers

1. The transaction code to launch the ABAP Development Workbench is /nSE80.

2. The name of the development environment for creating SAP Java applications is the SAP NetWeaver Developer Studio (NWDS).

3. The four consecutive phases of the SAP Solution Manager Implementation Tool are Project Preparation, Business Blueprint, Configuration, and Testing.

4. In addition to ASAP, the Run SAP Roadmap as well as specific roadmaps for SAP Enterprise Portal and SAP Exchange Infrastructure are available.

5. The SAP Project Implementation Guide contains only the customizing steps necessary for the application components your company is implementing.

6. The Reference, Enterprise, and Project IMGs are the three project views available for the IMG.

7. You use the transaction code /nSPRO to launch the initial screen of the IMG.

Hour 14: Answers

1. SOA is the generic form of SAP's business-focused Enterprise SOA offering. SOA's foundation can be found in modular programming and design techniques from as early as the 1970s, whereas SAP's version of SOA came from its early work with Enterprise Services Architecture (ESA).

2. Web Services enable SOA; they are the vehicle by which a service-oriented architecture is brought to fruition. Web Services give legs to SOA in the same way enterprise services enable Enterprise SOA.

3. Although there are many challenges to adopting SOA, three core challenges have been identified: working around IT's organizational silos and therefore a lack of SOA ownership, encouraging investment in developing a true enterprise architecture upon which SOA can build, and helping organizations transition away from their comfortable if inflexible client/server architectures.

4. Advantages of Enterprise SOA as implemented by SAP include reusability and modular design, which together enable lean low-maintenance business processes to be built and deployed. This in turn will presumably make Enterprise SOA more cost-effective than its predecessors over the lifecycle of new SAP implementations.

Hour 15: Answers

1. Download the installation guides, starting with the master guide. Following the installation guides and related notes is probably the most critical step toward a successful installation.

2. Installations are always started from the installation master DVD. From there, you will select the software components and system variant.

3. SQL Server is only supported on the Windows operating system.

4. The SAP Software Distribution Center houses all SAP media in downloadable format (http://service.sap.com/swdc).

Hour 16: Answers

1. Leverage the OLE connectivity offered by the Microsoft desktop and use the %pc command to easily and quickly download reports directly into Word and Excel.

2. Once the Duet product has been purchased, the infrastructure implementation can be kept to a minimum by leveraging the existing infrastructure, including Microsoft Exchange and Microsoft SQL Server. Duet can be loaded on a single server and can be connected to an existing SAP Web Application Server Java, if one exists. Although this may not be the optimum solution, it's viable. Smaller IT shops that need to quickly add this can do so cheaply and then later grow into fully blown distributed and highly available solutions down the road.

3. In a pure Microsoft environment, Single Sign-On can be implemented with no infrastructure costs. This technology can virtually eliminate the need for users to call the IT help desk to simply change their user ID password.

Hour 17: Answers

1. The acronym CCMS stands for Computing Center Management System, SAP's built-in tool for systems monitoring and management.

2. The Alert Monitor provides access to SAP's monitoring architecture, which allows you to monitor not only your local SAP instance but also your entire SAP environment.

3. The Alert Monitor allows you to monitor SAP and non-SAP components, starting from ABAP stack instances to Internet Transaction Servers, and more.

4. SAP's central monitoring system makes all alerts available in a central CCMS (Computing Center Management System) environment called CEN. The CEN runs on every SAP NetWeaver Application Server and is capable of monitoring SAP ABAP, Java, dual-stack, standalone components, and non-SAP components.

5. Other CCMS monitoring tools can be accessed by following the menu path Tools, CCMS.

Hour 18: Answers

1. No, this advertisement is not accurate. The ad should read, "Project Manager with SAP upgrade skills, requires experience upgrading from R/3 4.6C to SAP ERP2005." Version of release changes are functional upgrades, whereas operating system or database changes constitute OS/DB migrations.

2. MNC Global can employ an SAP OS/DB migration along with the upgrade specialists necessary to move SAP to a platform that offers a lower TCO on greater IT innovation.

3. MNC Global should consider a Unicode conversion along with its upgrade. Unicode is the direction recommended by SAP for all customers.

Hour 19: Answers

1. You will need the hostname or IP address, the system ID, and the system number.

2. Drill down into the SAP menu path until you reach sales order entry (Logistics, Sales and Distribution, Sales, Order, Create)

3. Click "Status" from the System menu and look for the program entry.

4. The display transaction is VA03. Display transactions normally end in 3, whereas create and modify transactions end in 1 and 2, respectively.

Hour 20: Answers

1. SAP menus are good examples of the SAP tree structure.

2. The easiest way to save this data to an Excel spreadsheet is to type **%pc** in the command field and save the output in spreadsheet format.

3. The buffer statistics are displayed in an SAP Table control.

4. Highlight the text and press Ctrl+C. It is also possible to highlight the text, right-click, and then choose Copy Text.

Hour 21: Answers

1. To determine the instance to which your SAP GUI session is connected, view the status field and click the instance icon. You may determine the client to which you are connected here as well.

2. The color setting for the WinGUI session can be changed under Customize Local Layout (or Alt+F12), New Visual Design, Color Settings. The changes can be saved under Save As... .

3. Changes made through the Customizing button apply to any SAP system that you log in to via the front-end machine you customized, independent of the SAP server or SAP client in which you are processing. However, to make the colors settings SAP systems specific, you choose Customize Local Layout (or Alt+F12) and Set Color To System... . The changes will apply to all WinGUI sessions of the SAP system you selected (old and new WinGUI sessions).

4. The status bar at the bottom of the SAP GUI for Windows provides general information of the SAP system. Select the field System, and the WinGUI will let you know in which SAP system and in which SAP client you are currently processing.

Hour 22: Answers

1. The Ad Hoc Query reporting mechanism is used to pose ad hoc queries to the database.

2. To take a look at the attributes of a particular report in the General Report Selection Tree, select the report and then follow the menu path Edit, Node Attributes.

3. The menu path used to search for reports in the General Report Selection is Edit, Find, Node.

4. A *variant* is a group of selection criteria values (used to create a report) that has been saved and can then be used as a "shortcut" in the future. Instead of entering all the data fields again, simply enter the variant name.

5. The transaction code to access the Create InfoSets screen is /nSQ02.

6. The transaction code to access the Create SAP Queries screen is /nSQ01.

7. A query area includes SAP Query elements, queries, InfoSets, and query groups.

8. The two query areas in SAP ERP are standard and global.

9. After creating or modifying an InfoSet, you must save and generate it.

10. The transaction code to access the QuickViewer is /nSQVI.

Hour 23: Answers

1. Try SAP's partner search index at http://www.sap.com/ecosystem/customers/directories/SearchPartner.epx.

2. The banking industry falls under the category Financial and Public Services. With this knowledge, you can conduct your own research into the various business processes and functionality that will be required by MNC, and therefore gain an advantage on several fronts—developing your resume, honing your experience, and ultimately interviewing for a position.

3. With a background in accounting and the ability to pick up technology quickly, you might be a fit for an SAP super user role at MNC Global's banking affiliate.

4. You may wish to pursue PMI Project Management Professional (PMP) certification from the Project Management Institute.

5. With success as a liaison between the business and IT, you likely have strong communication skills in addition to solid business and technical skills, the combination of which will certainly prove to be a valuable asset in your interview with MNC Global.

Hour 24: Answers

1. It probably makes sense to join ASUG to find out what other SAP customers are doing in the SAP Financials arena.

2. One of the most important points to keep in mind when looking for SAP books is the SAP release or version number covered by the book. For example, nearly anything written prior to 1999 covers SAP R/3 exclusively. And anything written before 2003 doesn't even mention NetWeaver or SAP ERP.

3. You can find the top 100 or so books covering SAP by searching through Amazon, Barnes and Noble, and a host of other such online sites. Sort by date to find current titles, or by best-selling status to find titles that other people are actually buying. Look to www.sap-resources.com as well for a link to the most popular SAP books. Also, frequently visit websites such as www.softwarejobs.com and www.ITtoolbox.com.

4. It is a good idea to use an Internet search engine such as www.yahoo.com, www.google.com, or www.hotbot.com to search for new SAP sites on a periodic basis to keep up to date with the latest SAP information available. And be sure to visit SAP's primary website frequently as well!

5. As a financial analyst, you stand to get the most out of the SAPPHIRE event to learn about the latest SAP products in the financials area. You will also want to attend the Financials Conference hosted by WIS.

Index

EnjoySAP, 326-329

enterprise architecture (EA), 207

Enterprise Compensation
Management, 109

Enterprise Controlling module,
SAP ERP Financials, 103-104

Enterprise Services, SAP
NetWeaver 7.1, 94

Enterprise Services Inventory
(ESI), 200

Enterprise SOA, 203

benefits of, 203-204

cost effectiveness, 205

modular design,
204-205

reusability, 204

principles of, 201-202

versus SOA, 200-201

Environment, Health and Safety
(EH&S), 116

ERP, extending through
CRM, 125

ERPcentral, 401

ESI (Enterprise Services
Inventory), 200

executing reports, General
Report Selection, 346-347

Executive Information System
(EIS), 344-345

executive steering
committee, 145

crucial tasks performed
by, 146

members, 145

cross-bundle project
leader, 147-148

PMO, 148-150

project sponsor,
146-147

Exit Current Screen box, 307

exporting, 275

lists

to Microsoft Access, 246

to Microsoft Excel, 244

SAP data

to Microsoft Access,
237-238

to Microsoft Excel,
233-234

SAP query reports

to Microsoft Access,
246-247

to Microsoft Excel, 245

extended business
processes, 12

extending ERP through
CRM, 125

F

fat clients, 24

features

All-in-One, 81

adapting to
changing needs/
SAP NetWeaver, 82

cost of ownership/
Best Practices, 82

intuitive user
experience/SAP
NetWeaver Business
Client, 83

Business ByDesign, 78

Business One, 75-76

selecting the best
solution for SMEs, 73

features of SAP CRM, 125-126

field entry validation, input
fields, 307

fields, 301-302

display fields, 310

input fields, 302-303

canceling all data entered
on screen, 307

entries for, 304-306

field entry validation, 307

Insert mode, 303, 306

Overwrite mode, 304

required fields, 306-307

saving data, 308

project preparation, phased approach of implementation tools, 185

project preparation phase of ASAP project management roadmap, 141-143

project sponsor, 145-147

Project System Module, 117

project team

company-internal functional specialists, 162

power users, 162-163

row leaders, 161-162

prototyping, 165

public sector, CRM-specific processes, 127

Purchase Planning application (APO), 124

Q

QAdb (Question and Answer database), 158

quality assurance, 149

quality control, 149

Quality Management module, 117

quality planning, 149

queries, 362. See also SAP queries

query areas, 354-355

query groups, 352-353

assigning InfoSets to, 361

query reporting tools, structure of, 351-352

administrative decisions, 354-355

InfoSets, 353

query groups, 352-353

Quick Info option, Customizing of Local Layout button, 332

QuickView, creating, 372-374

R

radio buttons, screen objects, 312-313

RAID, disk subsystems, 45

RDBMS (relational database management system), 52

Real Estate Management module, 116-117

real-time offer management feature (CRM), 126

realization phase of ASAP project management roadmap, 158-159

records, 301

master records, 260

reducing costs, 31

relational database management system (RDBMS), 52

Release Notes, IMG (Implementation Guide), 196

Remaining Work Days field, 195

replatforming, 274

replicating data, 308

deleting data that is on a screen, 310

Hold Data function, 308

Set Data function, 308-309

report attributes, General Report Selection, 347

report trees, 345

reporting tools, 343

ABAP List Processing (ABAP programming), 344

ABAP Query, 344

Ad Hoc Query, 344

Executive Information System, 344-345

SAP Information System (report trees), 345

Structural Graphics, 344

reports

executing General Report Selection, 346-347

searching for, in General Report Selection, 347-348

Sams **Teach Yourself**

When you only have time
for the answers™

Whatever your need and whatever your time frame, there's a Sams **Teach Yourself** book for you. With a Sams **Teach Yourself** book as your guide, you can quickly get up to speed on just about any new product or technology—in the absolute shortest period of time possible. Guaranteed.

Learning how to do new things with your computer shouldn't be tedious or time-consuming. Sams **Teach Yourself** makes learning anything quick, easy, and even a little bit fun.

SQL in 24 Hours, Fourth Edition

Ryan Stephens, Ron Plew, Arie Jones
ISBN-13: 978-0-672-33018-6

C++ in One Hour a Day

Jesse Liberty
Bradley Jones
Siddhartha Rao
ISBN-13: 978-0-672-32941-8

SQL in 10 Minutes

Ben Forta
ISBN-13: 978-0-672-32567-0

PHP, MySQL, and Apache All in One

Julie C. Meloni
ISBN-13: 978-0-672-32976-0

Windows Server 2008 in 24 Hours

Joe Habraken
ISBN-13: 978-0-672-33012-4

Sams Teach Yourself books are available at most retail and online bookstores, in both print and e-book versions. For more information or to order direct visit our online bookstore at **informit.com/sams**

Online editions of all Sams Teach Yourself titles are available by subscription from Safari Books Online at **safari.samspublishing.com**

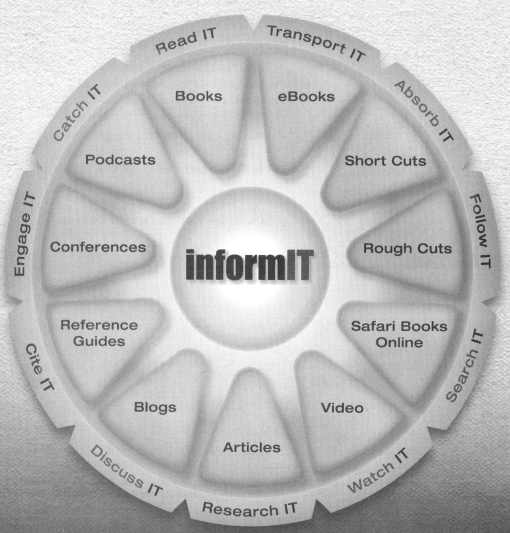

FREE Online Edition

Your purchase of **Sams Teach Yourself SAP in 24 Hours, 3rd Edition** includes access to a free online edition for 120 days through the Safari Books Online subscription service. Nearly every Sams book is available online through Safari Books Online, along with over 5,000 other technical books and videos from publishers such as Addison-Wesley Professional, Cisco Press, Exam Cram, IBM Press, O'Reilly, Prentice Hall, Que, and Sams.

SAFARI BOOKS ONLINE allows you to search for a specific answer, cut and paste code, download chapters, and stay current with emerging technologies.

Activate your FREE Online Edition at www.informit.com/safarifree

> **STEP 1:** Enter the coupon code: D8J9-51QK-5FU6-JDKW-LGQ7.

> **STEP 2:** New Safari users, complete the brief registration form.
> Safari subscribers, just login.

If you have difficulty registering on Safari or accessing the online edition, please e-mail customer-service@safaribooksonline.com